SOURCES of the WESTERN TRADITION

BRIEF EDITION

VOLUME II: FROM THE RENAISSANCE TO THE PRESENT

Marvin Perry

Baruch College, City University of New York

HOUGHTON MIFFLIN COMPANY   BOSTON   NEW YORK

Senior Sponsoring Editor: Nancy Blaine
Senior Development Editor: Julie Dunn
Senior Project Editor: Jane Lee
Editorial Assistant: Kristen Truncellito
Senior Art and Design Coordinator: Jill Haber
Senior Photo Editor: Jennifer Meyer Dare
Senior Composition Buyer: Chuck Dutton
Senior Manufacturing Coordinator: Marie Barnes
Marketing Manager: Sandra McGuire
Marketing Assistant: Molly Parke

Cover image: *Vaudeville, Man and Woman on Stage, 1917* by Charles Demuth (1883–1935), American. Credit: Barnes Foundation, Merion, PA/Superstock

Text Credits:

Chapter 1
Section 1 p. 5: From J. H. Robinson and H. W. Rolfe, *Petrarch, the First Modern Scholar and Man of Letters* (New York: G. P. Putnam's Sons, 1909), pp. 208, 210, 213. p. 6: From "Love for Greek Literature," from Henry Osborn Taylor, *Thought and Expression in the Sixteenth Century,* 2nd rev. ed. (New York: Frederick Ungar, 1930; repub. 1959), I, pp. 36–37. *Section 2* p. 9: From *The Prince,* by Niccolò Machiavelli, translated by Luigi, revised by E. R. P. Vincent, 1935, pp. 92–93, 97, 98–99, 101–103. Reprinted by permission of Oxford University Press. *Section 3* p. 14: Reprinted from *Luther's Works,* Volume 44, edited by James Atkinson, copyright © 1966 Fortress Press and Volume 31, edited by Harold Grimm, copyright © 1957 Muhlenberg Press. Used by permission of Augsburg Fortress. *Section 4* p. 17: From *The English Works of Thomas Hobbes of Malmesbury: Leviathan, or the Matter, Form and Power of a Commonwealth Ecclesiastical and Civil,* collected and edited by Sir William Molesworth (London: John Bohn, 1839), II, 110–113, 116–117, 154, 157–158, 160–161. *Section 5* p. 20: From *Select Documents of English Constitutional History,* ed. George Burton Adams and M. Morse Stephens (New York: Macmillan Company, 1902), pp. 464–465.

Credits are continued on page 303.

Printed in the U.S.A.

Library of Congress Control Number: 2005924530

ISBN: 0-618-53903-4

123456789-MP-09 08 07 06 05

Contents

Thematic Contents

SCIENCE

SOCIAL AND ECONOMIC CONDITIONS

GOVERNMENT AND IDEOLOGIES

WAR AND REVOLUTION

NATIONALISM AND RACISM

WOMEN

Preface

Teachers of the Western Civilization survey have long recognized the pedagogical value of primary sources, which are the raw materials of history. *Sources of the Western Tradition: Brief Edition* is an abridged version of the best-selling *Sources of the Western Tradition,* now in its sixth edition. This abridgment is intended for instructors who find traditional readers contain more selections than they can profitably utilize in a crowded curriculum or are discouraged by their cost. Although many selections have been dropped, this brief edition continues to contain a wide assortment of carefully selected and edited documents, principally primary sources, that fit the need of the survey and supplement standard texts.

I have based my choice of documents for the two volumes on several criteria. In order to introduce students to those ideas and values that characterize the Western tradition, *Sources of the Western Tradition* emphasizes primarily the works of the great thinkers. While focusing on the great ideas that have shaped the Western heritage, however, the reader also provides a balanced treatment of political, economic, and social history. I have tried to select documents that capture the characteristic outlook of an age and that provide a sense of the movement and development of Western history. The readings are of sufficient length to convey their essential meaning, and I have carefully extracted those passages that focus on the documents' main ideas.

An important feature of the reader is the grouping of several documents that illuminate a single theme; such a constellation of related readings reinforces understanding of important themes and invites comparison, analysis, and interpretation. For example, in Volume I, Chapter 7, The Renaissance and Reformation, Section 1, "The Humanists' Fascination with Antiquity," contains two interrelated readings: "The Father of Humanism," by Petrarch, and "Study of Greek Literature and a Humanist Educational Program," by Leonardo Bruni. In Volume II, Chapter 3, Era of the French Revolution, Section 3, "Expansion of Human Rights," contains three readings: *Vindication of the Rights of Woman,* by Mary Wollstonecraft; "Address to the National Assembly in Favor of the Abolition of the Slave Trade," by the Society of the Friends of Blacks; and "Petition of the Jews of Paris, Alsace, and Lorraine to the "National Assembly, January 28, 1790."

The brief edition retains the overriding concern of the complete edition: making the documents accessible so that students can comprehend and interpret them on their own. To facilitate this aim, I have preserved the pedagogical features of the complete edition that have been successful in its six editions. Introductions of three types explain the historical setting, the authors' intent, and the meaning and significance of the readings. First, introductions to each chapter—nine in Volume I and eleven in Volume II—provide comprehensive overviews to periods. Second, introductions to each numbered section or grouping treat the historical background for the reading(s) that follow(s). Third, each reading has a brief headnote that provides specific details about that reading.

Within some readings, interlinear notes, clearly set off from the text of the document, serve as transitions and suggest the main themes of the passages that follow. Used primarily in longer extracts of the great thinkers, these interlinear notes help to guide students through the readings.

To aid students' comprehension, brief, bracketed editorial definitions or notes that explain unfamiliar or foreign terms are inserted into the running text. When terms or concepts in the documents require fuller explanations, these appear at the bottom of pages as editor's footnotes. Where helpful, I have retained the notes of authors, translators, or editors from whose works the documents were acquired. (The latter have asterisks, daggers, et cetera, to distinguish them from my numbered explanatory notes.) The review questions that appear at the ends of sections enable students to check their understanding of the documents; sometimes the questions ask for comparisons with other readings, linking or contrasting key concepts.

For ancient sources, I have generally selected recent translations that are both faithful to the text and readable. For some seventeenth- and eighteenth-century English documents, the archaic spelling has been retained, when this does not preclude comprehension, in order to show students how the English language has evolved over time.

The brief edition retains a new feature of the sixth edition of the complete edition—a thematic table of contents for each volume. All of the documents in the book have been grouped together under broad, thematic categories to assist instructors in selecting sources that best fit the needs of their course. The thematic listing also provides students with potential research and essay topics. Many of the documents will be cross-listed under two or more categories—for instance, in Volume I, Saint Augustine's *The City of God* appears under "Religion," "Philosophy," "Social and Economic Conditions," and "Government and Politics." Chapter numbers appear to the left of the documents so that they can be easily referenced in class.

I am grateful to the staff of Houghton Mifflin Company who lent their talents to the project. I would like to thank Nancy Blaine, Senior Sponsoring Editor, for suggesting a brief edition of *Sources of the Western Tradition* and Julie Swasey, Senior Development Editor, for guiding the brief edition from its inception; Jane Lee, Senior Project Editor, for her careful attention to detail; and Ellen Whalen for her superb copyediting skills. Although George W. Bock and Angela Von Laue did not work on this brief edition, their excellent contribution to the larger edition has, no doubt, contributed to the quality of this new format.

Prologue
Examining Primary Sources

When historians try to reconstruct and apprehend past events, they rely on primary or original sources—official documents prepared by institutions and eyewitness reports. Similarly, when they attempt to describe the essential outlook or world-view of a given era, people, or movement, historians examine other types of primary sources—the literature, art, philosophy, and religious expressions of the time. These original sources differ from secondary or derivative sources—accounts of events and times written at a later date by people who may or may not have had access to primary sources. *Sources of the Western Tradition* consists principally of primary sources, which are the raw materials of history; they provide historians with the basic facts, details, and thinking needed for an accurate reconstruction of the past.

Historians have to examine a document with a critical spirit. The first question asked is: Is the document authentic and reliable? An early illustration of critical historical awareness was demonstrated by the Renaissance thinker Lorenzo Valla (c. 1407–1457) in *Declamation Concerning the False Decretals of Constantine.* The so-called Donation of Constantine, which was used by popes to support their claim to temporal authority, stated that the fourth-century Roman emperor Constantine had given the papacy dominion over the western Empire. By showing that some of the words in the document were unknown in Constantine's time and therefore could not have been used by the emperor, Valla proved that the document was forged by church officials several hundred years after Constantine's death. A more recent example of the need for caution is shown by the discovery of the "Hitler Diaries" in the mid-1980s. Several prominent historians "authenticated" the manuscript before it was exposed as a forgery—the paper dated from the 1950s and Hitler died in 1945. Nor can all eyewitness accounts be trusted, something Thucydides, the great Greek historian, noted 2,400 years ago.

[E]ither I was present myself at the events which I have described or else I heard of them from eye-witnesses whose reports I have checked with as much thoroughness as possible. Not that even so the truth was easy to discover: different eye-witnesses give different accounts of the same events, speaking out of partiality for one side or the other or else from imperfect memories.

An eyewitness's personal bias can render a document worthless. For example, in *The Auschwitz Lie* (1973), Thies Christophersen, a former SS guard at Auschwitz-Birkenau, denied the existence of gas chambers and mass killings in the notorious Nazi death camp, which he described as a sort of resort where prisoners, after work, could swim, listen to music in their rooms, or visit a brothel. Years later he was captured on videotape—he mistakenly thought the interviewers were fellow neo-Nazis—confessing that he had lied about the gas chambers because of loyalty to the SS and his desire to protect Germany's honor.

After examining the relevant primary sources and deciding on their usefulness, historians have to construct a consistent narrative and provide a plausible interpretation. Ideally, this requires that they examine documentary evidence in a wholly neutral, detached, and objective way. But is it possible to write history without being influenced by one's own particular viewpoint and personal biases?

No doubt several historians examining the same material might draw differing conclusions and each could argue his or her position persuasively. This is not surprising, for history is not an exact science and historians, like all individuals, are influenced by their upbringing and education, by their thoughts and feelings. Conflicting interpretations of historical events and periods are expected and acceptable features of historiography. But what is not acceptable is the deliberate distortion and suppression of evidence in order to substantiate one's own prejudices.

A flagrant example of writers of history misusing sources and distorting evidence in order to fortify their own prejudices is the recent case of British historian David Irving, author of numerous books on World War II, several of them well reviewed. Increasingly Irving revealed an undisguised admiration for Hitler and an antipathy toward Jews, which led him to minimize and disguise atrocities committed by the Third Reich. Addressing neo-Nazi audiences in several lands, he asserted that the Holocaust is "a major fraud. . . . There were no gas chambers. They were fakes and frauds." In *Lying About Hitler: History, Holocaust and the David Irving Trial* (2001), Richard J. Evans, a specialist in modern German history with a broad background in archival research, exposed instance after instance of how Irving, in his attempt to whitewash Hitler, misquoted sources, "misrepresented data, . . . skewed documents [and] ignored or deliberately suppressed material when it ran counter to his arguments. . . . [W]hen I followed Irving's claims and statements back to the original documents on which they purported to rest . . . Irving's work in this respect was revealed as a house of cards, a vast apparatus of deception and deceit."

The sources in this anthology can be read on several levels. First, they enhance understanding of the historical period in which they were written, shedding light on how people lived and thought and the chief concerns of the time. Several of the sources, written by some of humanity's greatest minds, have broader implications. They are founts of wisdom, providing insights of enduring value into human nature and the human condition. The documents also reveal the evolution of those core ideas and values—reason, freedom, and respect for human dignity—that constitute the Western heritage. Equally important, several documents reveal the precariousness of these values and the threats to them. It is the hope of the editor that an understanding of the evolution of the Western tradition will foster a renewed commitment to its essential ideals.

The documents in these volumes often represent human beings struggling with the vital questions of their day. As such they invite the reader to react actively and imaginatively to the times in which they were produced and to the individuals who produced them. The documents should also be approached with a critical eye. The reader has always to raise several pointed questions regarding the author's motivation, objectivity, logic, and accuracy. In addition, depending on the content of a particular document, the reader should consider the following questions: What does the document reveal about the times in which it was written? About the author? About the nature, evolution, and meaning of the Western tradition? About human nature and human relations? About good and evil? About progress? About war and peace? About gender relations? About life and death? Doubtless other questions will come to mind. In many instances, no doubt, the documents will impel readers to reflect on current issues and their own lives.

Introduction
The Middle Ages and the Modern World

Historians have traditionally divided Western history into three broad periods: ancient, medieval, and modern. What is meant by modernity? What has the modern world inherited from the Middle Ages? How does the modern West differ fundamentally from the Middle Ages?[1]

Medieval civilization began to decline in the fourteenth century, but no dark age comparable to the three centuries following Rome's fall descended on Europe; its economic and political institutions and technological skills had grown too strong. Instead, the waning of the Middle Ages opened up possibilities for another stage in Western civilization: the modern age.

The modern world is linked to the Middle Ages in innumerable ways. European cities, the middle class, the state system, English common law, universities—all had their origins in the Middle Ages. During medieval times, important advances were made in business practices, including partnerships, systematic bookkeeping, and the bill of exchange. By translating and commenting on the writings of Greek and Arabic thinkers, medieval scholars preserved a priceless intellectual heritage, without which the modern mind could never have evolved. In addition, numerous strands connect the thought of the scholastics and that of early modern philosophers.

Feudal traditions lasted long after the Middle Ages. Up to the French Revolution, for instance, French aristocrats enjoyed special privileges and exercised power over local government. In England, the aristocracy controlled local government until the Industrial Revolution transformed English society in the nineteenth century. Retaining the medieval ideal of the noble warrior, aristocrats continued to dominate the officer corps of European armies through the nineteenth century and even into the twentieth. Aristocratic notions of duty, honor, loyalty, and courtly love had endured into the twentieth century.

During the Middle Ages, Europeans began to take the lead over the Muslims, the Byzantines, the Chinese, and all the other peoples in the use of technology. Medieval technology and inventiveness stemmed in part from Christianity, which taught that God had created the world specifically for human beings to subdue and exploit. Consequently, medieval people employed animal power and labor-saving machinery to relieve human drudgery. Moreover, Christianity taught that God was above nature, not within it, so the Christian had no spiritual obstacle to exploiting nature—unlike, for instance, the Hindu. In contrast to classical humanism, the Christian outlook did not consider manual work degrading; even monks combined it with study.

The Christian stress on the sacred worth of the individual and on the higher law of God has never ceased to influence Western civilization. Even though in modern times the various Christian churches have not often taken the lead in political and social reform, the ideals identified with the Judeo-Christian tradition have become part of the Western heritage. As such, they have inspired social reformers who may no longer identify with their ancestral religion.

Believing that God's law was superior to state or national decrees, medieval philosophers provided a theoretical basis for opposing tyrannical kings who violated Christian prin-

[1]Material for this introduction is taken from Marvin Perry, et al., *Western Civilization,* 7th ed. (Boston: Houghton Mifflin, 2004), pp. 290–295.

ciples. The idea that both the ruler and the ruled are bound by a higher law would, in a secularized form, become a principal element of modern liberal thought.

Feudalism also contributed to the history of liberty. According to feudal theory, the king, as a member of the feudal community, was duty-bound to honor agreements made with his vassals. Lords possessed personal rights, which the king was obliged to respect. Resentful of a king who ran roughshod over customary feudal rights, lords also negotiated contracts with the crown, such as the famous Magna Carta (1215), to define and guard their customary liberties. To protect themselves from the arbitrary behavior of a king, feudal lords initiated what came to be called *government by consent* and the *rule of law.*

During the Middle Ages, then, there gradually emerged the idea that law was not imposed on inferiors by an absolute monarch but required the collaboration of the king and his subjects; that the king, too, was bound by the law; and that lords had the right to resist a monarch who violated agreements. A related phenomenon was the rise of representative institutions, with which the king was expected to consult on the realm's affairs. The most notable such institution was the British Parliament; although subordinate to the king, it became a permanent part of the state. Later, in the seventeenth century, Parliament would successfully challenge royal authority. Thus, continuity exists between the feudal tradition of a king bound by law and the modern practice of limiting the authority of the head of state.

Although the elements of continuity are clear, the characteristic outlook of the Middle Ages is as different from that of the modern age as it was from the outlook of the ancient world. Religion was the integrating feature of the Middle Ages, whereas science and secularism—a preoccupation with worldly life—determine the modern outlook. The period from the Italian Renaissance of the fifteenth century

through the eighteenth-century Age of Enlightenment constituted a gradual breaking away from the medieval world-view—a rejection of the medieval conception of nature, the individual, and the purpose of life. The transition from medieval to modern was neither sudden nor complete, for there are no sharp demarcation lines separating historical periods. While many distinctively medieval ways endured in the sixteenth, seventeenth, and even eighteenth centuries, these centuries saw as well the rise of new intellectual, political, and economic forms, which marked the emergence of modernity.

Medieval thought began with the existence of God and the truth of his revelation as interpreted by the church, which set the standards and defined the purposes for human endeavor. The medieval mind rejected the fundamental principle of Greek philosophy: the autonomy of reason. Without the guidance of revealed truth, reason was seen as feeble.

Scholastics engaged in genuine philosophical speculation, but they did not allow philosophy to challenge the basic premises of their faith. Unlike either ancient or modern thinkers, medieval schoolmen ultimately believed that reason alone could not provide a unified view of nature or society. A rational soul had to be guided by a divine light. For all medieval philosophers, the natural order depended on a supernatural order for its origin and purpose. To understand the natural world properly, it was necessary to know its relationship to the higher world. The discoveries of reason had to accord with Scripture as interpreted by the church. In medieval thought, says historian-philosopher Ernst Cassirer,

[N]either science nor morality, neither law nor state, can be erected on its own foundations. Supernatural assistance is always needed to bring them to true perfection. . . . Reason is and remains the servant of revelation; within the sphere of natural intellectual and psychological forces, reason leads toward, and prepares the ground for, revelation.[2]

In the modern view, both nature and the human intellect are self-sufficient. Nature is a mathematical system that operates without miracles or any other form of divine intervention. To comprehend nature and society, the mind needs no divine assistance; it accepts no authority above reason. The modern mentality finds it unacceptable to reject the conclusions of science on the basis of clerical authority and revelation or to ground politics, law, or economics on religious dogma. It refuses to settle public issues by appeals to religious belief.

The medieval philosopher understood both nature and society to be a hierarchical order. God was the source of moral values, and the church was responsible for teaching and upholding these ethical norms. Kings acquired their right to rule from God. The entire social structure constituted a hierarchy: the clergy guided society according to Christian standards; lords defended Christian society from its enemies; and serfs, lowest in the social order, toiled for the good of all. In the hierarchy of knowledge, a lower form of knowledge derived from the senses, and the highest type of knowledge, theology, dealt with God's revelation. To the medieval mind, this hierarchical ordering of nature, society, and knowledge had a divine sanction.

Rejecting the medieval division of the universe into higher and lower realms and superior and inferior substances, the modern view postulated the uniformity of nature and nature's laws: the cosmos knows no privilege of rank; heavenly bodies follow the same laws of nature as earthly objects. Space is geometric and homogeneous, not hierarchical, heterogeneous, and qualitative. The universe was no longer conceived as finite and closed but as infinite, and the operations of nature were explained mathematically. The modern thinker studies mathematical law and chemical composition, not grades of perfection. Spiritual meaning is not sought in an examination of the material world. Roger Bacon, for example, described seven coverings of the eye and then concluded that God had fashioned the eye in this manner in order to express the seven gifts of the Spirit. This way of thinking is alien to the modern outlook. So, too, is the medieval belief that natural disasters, such as plagues and famines, are God's punishments for people's sins.

The outlook of the modern West also broke with the rigid division of medieval society into three orders: clergy, nobles, and commoners. The intellectual justification for this arrangement, as expressed by the English prelate John of Salisbury (c. 1115–1180), has been rejected by modern Westerners: "For inferiors owe it to their superiors to provide them with service, just as the superiors in their turn owe it to their inferiors to provide them with all things needful for their protection and succor."[3] Opposing the feudal principle that an individual's obligations and rights are a function of his or her rank in society, the modern view stressed equality of opportunity and equal treatment under the law. It rejected the idea that society should be guided by clergy, who were deemed to possess a special wisdom; by nobles, who were entitled to special privileges; and by monarchs, who were thought to receive their power from God.

The modern West also rejected the personal and customary character of feudal law. As the modern state developed, law assumed an impersonal and objective character. For example, if the lord demanded more than the customary forty days of military service, the vassal might refuse to comply, because he would see the lord's request as an unpardonable violation of custom and agreement, as well as an infringement on his liberties. In the modern state, with a constitution and a representative assembly, if a new law

---

[2]Ernst Cassirer, *The Philosophy of the Enlightenment* (Boston: Beacon, 1955), p. 40.

[3]John of Salisbury, *Policraticus,* trans. John Dickinson (New York: Russell & Russell, 1963), pp. 243–244.

increasing the length of military service is passed, it merely replaces the old law. People do not refuse to obey it because the government has broken faith or violated custom.

In the modern world, the individual's relationship to the universe has been radically transformed. Medieval people lived in a geocentric universe that was finite in space and time. The universe was small, enclosed by a sphere of stars, beyond which were the heavens. The universe, it was believed, was some four thousand years old, and, in the not-too-distant future, Christ would return and human history would end. People in the Middle Ages knew why they were on earth and what was expected of them; they never doubted that heaven would be their reward for living a Christian life. Preparation for heaven was the ultimate aim of life. J. H. Randall, Jr., a historian of ideas, eloquently sums up the medieval view of a purposeful universe, in which the human being's position was clearly defined:

> The world was governed throughout by the omnipotent will and omniscient mind of God, whose sole interests were centered in man, his trial, his fall, his suffering and his glory. Worm of the dust as he was, man was yet the central object in the whole universe. . . . And when his destiny was completed, the heavens would be rolled up as a scroll and he would dwell with the Lord forever. Only those who rejected God's freely offered grace and with hardened hearts refused repentance would be cut off from this eternal life.[4]

This comforting medieval vision is alien to the modern outlook. Today, in a universe some 12 billion years old, in which the earth is a tiny speck floating in an endless cosmic ocean, where life evolved over tens of millions of years, many Westerners no longer believe that human beings are special children of God; that heaven is their ultimate goal; that under their feet is hell, where grotesque demons torment sinners; and that God is an active agent in human history. To many intellectuals, the universe seems unresponsive to the religious supplications of people, and life's purpose is sought within the limits of earthly existence. Science and secularism have driven Christianity and faith from their central position to the periphery of human concerns.

The modern outlook developed gradually from the Renaissance to the eighteenth-century Age of Enlightenment. Mathematics rendered the universe comprehensible. Economic and political thought broke free of the religious frame of reference. Science became the great hope of the future. The thinkers of the Enlightenment wanted to liberate humanity from superstition, ignorance, and traditions that could not pass the test of reason. They saw themselves as emancipating culture from theological dogma and clerical authority. Rejecting the Christian idea of a person's inherent sinfulness, they held that the individual was basically good and that evil resulted from faulty institutions, poor education, and bad leadership. Thus, the concept of a rational and free society in which individuals could realize their potential slowly emerged.

---

[4]J. H. Randall, Jr., *The Making of the Modern Mind* (Boston: Houghton Mifflin, 1940), p. 34.

CHAPTER 1

The Rise of Modernity

THE TRIUMPH OF GALATEA, Raphael, 1513. This fresco from the Palazzo della Farnesina in Rome exemplifies the Renaissance artist's elevation of the human form. The mythological subject is also humanistic in its evocation of the ancient Greek tradition. *(Giraudon/Art Resource, N.Y.)*

From the fifteenth through the seventeenth centuries, medieval attitudes and institutions broke down, and distinctly modern cultural, economic, and political forms emerged. For many historians, the Renaissance, which originated in the city-states of Italy, marks the starting point of the modern era. The Renaissance was characterized by a rebirth of interest in the humanist culture and outlook of ancient Greece and Rome. Although Renaissance individuals did not repudiate Christianity, they valued worldly activities and interests to a much greater degree than did the people of the Middle Ages, whose outlook was dominated by Christian otherworldliness. Renaissance individuals were fascinated by *this* world and by life's possibilities; they aspired to live a rich and creative life on earth and to fulfill themselves through artistic and literary activity.

During the High Middle Ages there had been a revival of Greek and Roman learning. Yet there were two important differences between the period called the Twelfth-Century Awakening and the Renaissance. First, many more ancient works were restored to circulation during the Renaissance than during the cultural revival of the Middle Ages. Second, medieval scholastics had tried to fit the ideas of the ancients into a Christian framework; they used Greek philosophy to explain Christian teachings. Renaissance scholars, on the other hand, valued ancient works for their own sake, believing that Greek and Roman authors could teach much about the art of living.

A distinguishing feature of the Renaissance period was the humanist movement, an educational and cultural program based on the study of ancient Greek and Latin literature. By studying the humanities—history, literature, rhetoric, moral and political philosophy—humanists aimed to revive the worldly spirit of the ancient Greeks and Romans, which they believed had been lost in the Middle Ages.

Humanists were thus fascinated by the writings of the ancients. From the works of Thucydides, Plato, Cicero, Seneca, and other ancient authors, humanists sought guidelines for living life well in this world and looked for stylistic models for their own literary efforts. To the humanists, the ancients had written brilliantly, in an incomparable literary style, on friendship, citizenship, love, bravery, statesmanship, beauty, excellence, and every other topic devoted to the enrichment of human life.

Like the humanist movement, Renaissance art also marked a break with medieval culture. The art of the Middle Ages had served a religious function; its purpose was to lift the mind to God. It depicted a spiritual universe in which the supernatural was the supreme reality. The Renaissance shattered the dominance of religion over art, shifting attention from heaven to the natural world and to the human being; Renaissance artists often dealt with religious themes, but they placed their subjects in a naturalistic setting.

The Renaissance began in the late fourteenth century in the northern Italian city-states, which had grown prosperous from the revival of trade in the Middle Ages. Italian merchants and bankers had the wealth to acquire libraries and fine works of art and to support art, literature, and scholarship. Surrounded by reminders of ancient Rome—amphitheaters, monuments, and sculpture—the well-to-do took an interest in classical culture and thought. In the late fifteenth and the sixteenth centuries, Renaissance ideas spread to Germany, France, Spain, and England through books available in great numbers due to the invention of the printing press.

The reformation of the church in the sixteenth century was rooted in demands for spiritual renewal. The principal source of the reform spirit was a widespread popular yearning for a more genuine spirituality. It took many forms: the rise of new pious practices; greater interest in mystical experiences and in the study of the Bible; the development of communal ways for lay people to live and work following the apostles' example; and a heightened search for ways within secular society to imitate more perfectly the life of Christ—called the New Devotion movement. This deepening spirituality led many people to criticize the church for its worldliness and materialism—its involvement in European power politics and its pursuit of wealth and luxury.

In Germany, a spirit of discontent with social and economic conditions coincided with the demand for reform of the church and religious life. For several decades before Martin Luther's revolt against the papacy, the economic conditions of the knights, the peasants, and the lower-class urban workers had deteriorated. The knights' grievances included loss of their political power to the centralizing governments of the German princes and increasing restrictions on their customary feudal privileges. Peasants protested that lords had steadily withdrawn certain of their customary rights and had added burdens, increasing the lords' income and control over their estates. The knights and peasants were squeezed into an ever-worsening social and economic niche. In the cities, the lower-class artisans and laborers were similarly oppressed. Those in the urban upper classes, who controlled town governments, enhanced their own economic privileges at the expense of lower-class citizens. The church, which was a major landowner and active in commercial enterprises in the towns, played an important role in these conflicts. All these grievances formed the explosive background to Martin Luther's challenge to the authority of the church and the imperial government.

These divisions in the Christian church marked a turning point in European history and culture, ending forever the coherent world-view of medieval Christendom. The Reformation split the peoples of Europe into two broad political, intellectual, and spiritual camps: Protestant and Catholic. With the moral, political, and ideological power of the church significantly diminished, post-Reformation society was open to increasing secularization on all fronts. By ending the religious unity of the Middle Ages and weakening the Catholic Church, the Reformation contributed significantly to the rise of modernity.

The period from the Renaissance through the Scientific Revolution saw the breakdown of distinctively medieval cultural, political, and economic forms. The Renaissance produced a more secular attitude and expressed confidence in human capacities. Shortly afterward, the

Protestant Reformation ended the religious unity of medieval Latin Christendom and weakened the political power of the church. At the same time the discovery of new trade routes to East Asia and of new lands across the Atlantic widened the imagination and ambitions of Christian Europeans and precipitated a commercial revolution. This great expansion of economic activity furthered capitalism and initiated a global economy—two developments associated with the modern world. The European economy was tied to Asian spices, African slaves, and American silver. A wide variety of goods circulated all over the globe. From the West Indies and East Asia, sugar, rice, tea, cacao, and tobacco flowed into Europe. From the Americas, potatoes, corn, sweet potatoes, and manioc (from which tapioca is made) spread to the rest of the world. Europeans paid for Asian silks and spices with American silver.

The increasing demand for goods and a rise in prices produced more opportunities for the accumulation and investment of capital by private individuals, which is the essence of capitalism. State policies designed to increase national wealth and power also stimulated the growth of capitalism. Governments subsidized new industries, chartered joint-stock companies to engage in overseas trade, and struck at internal tariffs and guild regulations that hampered domestic economic growth. Improvements in banking, shipbuilding, mining, and manufacturing further stimulated economic growth.

In the sixteenth and seventeenth centuries the old medieval political order dissolved, and the modern state began to emerge. The modern state has a strong central government that issues laws that apply throughout the land and a permanent army of professional soldiers paid by the state. Trained bureaucrats, responsible to the central government, collect taxes, enforce laws, and administer justice. The modern state has a secular character; promotion of religion is not the state's concern, and churches do not determine state policy. These features of the modern state were generally not prevalent in the Middle Ages, when the nobles, church, and towns possessed powers and privileges that impeded central authority, and kings were expected to rule in accordance with Christian principles. In the sixteenth and seventeenth centuries, monarchs were exercising central authority with ever-greater effectiveness at the expense of nobles and clergy. The secularization of the state became firmly established after the Thirty Years' War (1618–1648); with their states worn out by Catholic–Protestant conflicts, kings came to act less for religious motives than for reasons of national security and power.

1   The Humanists' Fascination with Antiquity

Humanists believed that a refined person must know the literature of Greece and Rome. They strove to imitate the style of the ancients, to speak and write as eloquently as the Greeks and Romans. Toward these ends, they sought to read, print, and restore to circulation every scrap of ancient literature that could still be found.

Petrarch
THE FATHER OF HUMANISM

During his lifetime, Francesco Petrarca, or Petrarch (1304–1374), had an astounding reputation as a poet and scholar. Often called the "father of humanism," he inspired other humanists through his love for classical learning; his criticism of medieval Latin as barbaric in contrast to the style of Cicero, Seneca, and other Romans; and his literary works based on classical models. Petrarch saw his own age as a restoration of classical brilliance after an interval of medieval darkness.

A distinctly modern element in Petrarch's thought is the subjective and individualistic character of his writing. In talking about himself and probing his own feelings, Petrarch demonstrates a self-consciousness characteristic of the modern outlook.

Like many other humanists, Petrarch remained devoted to Christianity: "When it comes to thinking or speaking of religion, that is, of the highest truth, of true happiness and eternal salvation," he declared, "I certainly am not a Ciceronian or a Platonist but a Christian." Petrarch was a forerunner of the Christian humanism best represented by Erasmus. Christian humanists combined an intense devotion to Christianity with a great love for classical literature, which they much preferred to the dull and turgid treatises written by scholastic philosopher-theologians. In the following passage, Petrarch criticizes his contemporaries for their ignorance of ancient writers and shows his commitment to classical learning.

. . . O inglorious age! that scorns antiquity, its mother, to whom it owes every noble art—that dares to declare itself not only equal but superior to the glorious past. I say nothing of the vulgar, the dregs of mankind, whose sayings and opinions may raise a laugh but hardly merit serious censure. . . .

. . . But what can be said in defense of men of education who ought not to be ignorant of antiquity and yet are plunged in this same darkness and delusion?

You see that I cannot speak of these matters without the greatest irritation and indignation. There has arisen of late a set of dialecticians [experts in logical argument],[1] who are not only ignorant but demented. Like a black army of ants from some old rotten oak, they swarm forth from their hiding places and devastate the fields of sound learning. They condemn Plato and Aristotle, and laugh at Socrates and Pythagoras.[2] And, good God! under what silly and incompetent leaders these opinions are put forth. . . . What shall we say

Throughout the text, the editors' notes carry numbers, whereas notes from the original sources are indicated by asterisks, daggers, et cetera.

[2] The work of Aristotle (384–322 B.C.), a leading Greek philosopher, had an enormous influence among medieval and Renaissance scholars. A student of the philosopher Socrates, Plato (c. 427–347 B.C.) was one of the greatest philosophers of ancient Greece. His work grew to be extremely influential in the West during the Renaissance period, as new texts of his writings were discovered and translated into Latin and more Westerners could read the originals in Greek. Pythagoras (c. 582–c. 507 B.C.) was a Greek philosopher whose work influenced both Socrates and Plato.

[3] Cicero (106–43 B.C.) was a Roman statesman and rhetorician. His Latin style was especially admired and emulated during the Renaissance.

[1] Throughout the text, words in brackets have been added as glosses by the editors. Brackets around glosses from the original sources have been changed to parentheses to distinguish them.

of men who scorn Marcus Tullius Cicero,[3] the bright sun of eloquence? Of those who scoff at Varro and Seneca,[4] and are scandalized at what they choose to call the crude, unfinished style of Livy and Sallust [Roman historians]? . . .

Such are the times, my friend, upon which we have fallen; such is the period in which we live

and are growing old. Such are the critics of today, as I so often have occasion to lament and complain—men who are innocent of knowledge and virtue, and yet harbour the most exalted opinion of themselves. Not content with losing the words of the ancients, they must attack their genius and their ashes. They rejoice in their ignorance, as if what they did not know were not worth knowing. They give full rein to their license and conceit, and freely introduce among us new authors and outlandish teachings.

---

[4]Varro (116–27 B.C.) was a Roman scholar and historian. Seneca (4 B.C.–A.D. 65) was a Roman statesman, dramatist, and Stoic philosopher whose literary style was greatly admired during the Renaissance.

Leonardo Bruni
STUDY OF GREEK LITERATURE AND A HUMANIST EDUCATIONAL PROGRAM

Leonardo Bruni (1374–1444) was a Florentine humanist who extolled both intellectual study and active involvement in public affairs, an outlook called civic humanism. In the first reading from his *History of His Own Times in Italy,* Bruni expresses the humanist's love for ancient Greek literature and language.

In a treatise, *De Studiis et Literis* (On Learning and Literature), written around 1405 and addressed to the noble lady Baptista di Montefeltro (1383–1450), daughter of the Count of Urbino, Bruni outlines the basic course of studies that the humanists recommended as the best preparation for a life of wisdom and virtue. In addition to the study of Christian literature, Bruni encourages a wide familiarity with the best minds and stylists of ancient Greek and Latin cultures.

LOVE FOR GREEK LITERATURE

Then first came a knowledge of Greek, which had not been in use among us for seven hundred years. Chrysoloras the Byzantine,[1] a man of noble birth and well versed in Greek letters, brought Greek learning to us. When his country was invaded by the Turks, he came by sea, first to Venice. The report of him soon spread, and he was cordially invited and besought and promised a public stipend, to come to Florence and open his store of riches to the youth. I was then studying Civil Law,[2] but . . . I burned

---

[1]Chrysoloras (c. 1355–1415), a Byzantine writer and teacher, introduced the study of Greek literature to the Italians, helping to open a new age of Western humanistic learning.

[2]Civil Law refers to the Roman law as codified by Emperor Justinian in the early sixth century A.D. and later studied in medieval law schools.

with love of academic studies, and had spent no little pains on dialectic and rhetoric. At the coming of Chrysoloras I was torn in mind, deeming it shameful to desert the law, and yet a crime to lose such a chance of studying Greek literature; and often with youthful impulse I would say to myself: "Thou, when it is permitted thee to gaze on Homer, Plato and Demosthenes,[3] and the other [Greek] poets, philosophers, orators, of whom such glorious things are spread abroad, and speak with them and be instructed in their admirable teaching, wilt thou desert and rob thyself? Wilt thou neglect this opportunity so divinely offered? For seven hundred years, no one in Italy has possessed Greek letters; and yet we confess that all knowledge is derived from them. How great advantage to your knowledge, enhancement of your fame, increase of your pleasure, will come from an understanding of this tongue? There are doctors of civil law everywhere; and the chance of learning will not fail thee. But if this one and only doctor of Greek letters disappears, no one can be found to teach thee." Overcome at length by these reasons, I gave myself to Chrysoloras, with such zeal to learn, that what through the wakeful day I gathered, I followed after in the night, even when asleep.

ON LEARNING AND LITERATURE

. . . The foundations of all true learning must be laid in the sound and thorough knowledge of Latin: which implies study marked by a broad spirit, accurate scholarship, and careful attention to details. Unless this solid basis be secured it is useless to attempt to rear an enduring edifice. Without it the great monuments of literature are unintelligible, and the art of composition impossible. To attain this essential knowledge we must never relax our careful attention to the grammar of the language, but perpetually confirm and extend our acquain-

tance with it until it is thoroughly our own. . . . To this end we must be supremely careful in our choice of authors, lest an inartistic and debased style infect our own writing and degrade our taste; which danger is best avoided by bringing a keen, critical sense to bear upon select works, observing the sense of each passage, the structure of the sentence, the force of every word down to the least important particle. In this way our reading reacts directly upon our style. . . .

But we must not forget that true distinction is to be gained by a wide and varied range of such studies as conduce to the profitable enjoyment of life, in which, however, we must observe due proportion in the attention and time we devote to them.

First amongst such studies I place History: a subject which must not on any account be neglected by one who aspires to true cultivation. For it is our duty to understand the origins of our own history and its development; and the achievements of Peoples and of Kings.

For the careful study of the past enlarges our foresight in contemporary affairs and affords to citizens and to monarchs lessons of incitement or warning in the ordering of public policy. From History, also, we draw our store of examples of moral precepts.

In the monuments of ancient literature which have come down to us History holds a position of great distinction. We specially prize such [Roman] authors as Livy, Sallust and Curtius;[4] and, perhaps even above these, Julius Caesar; the style of whose Commentaries, so elegant and so limpid, entitles them to our warm admiration. . . .

The great Orators of antiquity must by all means be included. Nowhere do we find the virtues more warmly extolled, the vices so fiercely decried. From them we may learn, also, how to express consolation, encouragement, dissuasion or advice. If the principles which orators set forth are portrayed for us by philosophers, it

---

[3]Demosthenes (384–322 B.C.) was an Athenian statesman and orator whose oratorical style was much admired by Renaissance humanists.

[4]Q. Curtius Rufus, a Roman historian and rhetorician of the mid-first century A.D., composed a biography of Alexander the Great.

is from the former that we learn how to employ the emotions—such as indignation, or pity—in driving home their application in individual cases. Further, from oratory we derive our store of those elegant or striking turns of expression which are used with so much effect in literary compositions. Lastly, in oratory we find that wealth of vocabulary, that clear easy-flowing style, that verve and force, which are invaluable to us both in writing and in conversation.

I come now to Poetry and the Poets. . . . For we cannot point to any great mind of the past for whom the Poets had not a powerful attraction. Aristotle, in constantly quoting Homer, Hesiod, Pindar, Euripides and other [Greek] poets, proves that he knew their works hardly less intimately than those of the philosophers. Plato, also, frequently appeals to them, and in this way covers them with his approval. If we turn to Cicero, we find him not content with quoting Ennius, Accius,[5] and others of the Latins, but rendering poems from the Greek and employing them habitually. . . . Hence my view that familiarity with the great poets of antiquity is essential to any claim to true education. For in their writings we find deep speculations upon Nature, and upon the Causes and Origins of things, which must carry weight with us both from their antiquity and from their authorship. Besides these, many im-

portant truths upon matters of daily life are suggested or illustrated. All this is expressed with such grace and dignity as demands our admiration. . . . To sum up what I have endeavoured to set forth. That high standard of education to which I referred at the outset is only to be reached by one who has seen many things and read much. Poet, Orator, Historian, and the rest, all must be studied, each must contribute a share. Our learning thus becomes full, ready, varied and elegant, available for action or for discourse in all subjects. But to enable us to make effectual use of what we know we must add to our knowledge the power of expression. These two sides of learning, indeed, should not be separated: they afford mutual aid and distinction. Proficiency in literary form, not accompanied by broad acquaintance with facts and truths, is a barren attainment; whilst information, however vast, which lacks all grace of expression, would seem to be put under a bushel or partly thrown away. Indeed, one may fairly ask what advantage it is to possess profound and varied learning if one cannot convey it in language worthy of the subject. Where, however, this double capacity exists— breadth of learning and grace of style—we allow the highest title to distinction and to abiding fame. If we review the great names of ancient [Greek and Roman] literature, Plato, Democritus, Aristotle, Theophrastus, Varro, Cicero, Seneca, Augustine, Jerome, Lactantius, we shall find it hard to say whether we admire more their attainments or their literary power.

---

[5]Ennius (239–169 B.C.) wrote the first great Latin epic poem, which was based on the legends of Rome's founding and its early history. Accius (c. 170–c. 90 B.C.), also a Roman, authored a history of Greek and Latin literature.

REVIEW QUESTIONS

1. What do historians mean by the term "Renaissance humanism"?
2. What made Petrarch aware that a renaissance, or rebirth, of classical learning was necessary in his time?
3. Why did Leonardo Bruni abandon his earlier course of studies to pursue the study of Greek literature?
4. What subjects made up the basic course of studies advocated by Bruni?

2 Break with Medieval Political Theory

Turning away from the religious orientation of the Middle Ages, Renaissance thinkers discussed the human condition in secular terms and opened up possibilities for thinking about moral and political problems in new ways. Thus, Niccolò Machiavelli (1469–1527), a Florentine statesman and political theorist, broke with medieval political theory. Medieval political thinkers held that the ruler derived power from God and had a religious obligation to rule in accordance with God's precepts. Machiavelli, though, ascribed no divine origin to kingship, nor did he attribute events to the mysterious will of God; and he explicitly rejected the principle that kings should adhere to Christian moral teachings. For Machiavelli, the state was a purely human creation. Successful kings or princes, he asserted, should be concerned only with preserving and strengthening the state's power and must ignore questions of good and evil, morality and immorality. Machiavelli did not assert that religion was supernatural in origin and rejected prevailing belief that Christian morality should guide political life. For him, religion's value derived from other factors: a ruler could utilize religion to unite his subjects and to foster obedience to law.

Niccolò Machiavelli
THE PRINCE

In contrast to medieval thinkers, Machiavelli did not seek to construct an ideal Christian community but to discover how politics was *really* conducted. In *The Prince,* written in 1513 and published posthumously in 1532, he studied politics in the cold light of reason, as the following passage illustrates.

It now remains to be seen what are the methods and rules for a prince as regards his subjects and friends. And as I know that many have written of this, I fear that my writing about it may be deemed presumptuous, differing as I do, especially in this matter, from the opinions of others. But my intention being to write something of use to those who understand, it appears to me more proper to go to the real truth of the matter than to its imagination; and many have imagined republics and principalities which have never been seen or known to exist in reality; for how we live is so far removed from how we ought to live, that he who abandons what is done for what ought to

be done, will rather learn to bring about his own ruin than his preservation.

Machiavelli removed ethics from political thinking. A successful ruler, he contended, is indifferent to moral and religious considerations. But will not the prince be punished on the Day of Judgment for violating Christian teachings? In startling contrast to medieval theorists, Machiavelli simply ignored the question. The action of a prince, he said, should be governed solely by necessity.

A man who wishes to make a profession of goodness in everything must necessarily come to grief among so many who are not good. Therefore it is necessary for a prince, who wishes to maintain himself, to learn how not to be good, and to use this knowledge and not use it, according to the necessity of the case.

Leaving on one side, then, those things which concern only an imaginary prince, and speaking of those that are real, I state that all men, and especially princes, who are placed at a greater height, are reputed for certain qualities which bring them either praise or blame. Thus one is considered liberal, another . . . miserly; . . . one a free giver, another rapacious; one cruel, another merciful; one a breaker of his word, another trustworthy; one effeminate and pusillanimous, another fierce and high-spirited; one humane, another haughty; one lascivious, another chaste; one frank, another astute; one hard, another easy; one serious, another frivolous; one religious, another an unbeliever, and so on. I know that every one will admit that it would be highly praiseworthy in a prince to possess all the above-named qualities that are reputed good, but as they cannot all be possessed or observed, human conditions not permitting of it, it is necessary that he should be prudent enough to avoid the scandal of those vices which would lose him the state, and guard himself if possible against those which will not lose it [for] him, but if not able to, he can indulge them with less scruple. And yet he must not mind incurring the scandal of those vices, without which it would be difficult to save the state, for if one considers well, it will be found that some things which seem virtues would, if followed, lead to one's ruin, and some others which appear vices result in one's greater security and wellbeing. . . .

. . . I say that every prince must desire to be considered merciful and not cruel. He must, however, take care not to misuse this mercifulness. Cesare Borgia was considered cruel, but his cruelty had brought order to the Romagna,[1] united it, and reduced it to peace and fealty. If this is considered well, it will be seen that he was really much more merciful than the Florentine people, who, to avoid the name of cruelty, allowed Pistoia[2] to be destroyed. A prince, therefore, must not mind incurring the charge of cruelty for the purpose of keeping his subjects united and faithful; for, with a very few examples, he will be more merciful than those who, from excess of tenderness, allow disorders to arise, from whence spring bloodshed and rapine; for these as a rule injure the whole community, while the executions carried out by the prince injure only individuals. . . .

Machiavelli's rigorous investigation of politics led him to view human nature from the standpoint of its limitations and imperfections. The astute prince, he said, recognizes that human beings are by nature selfish, cowardly, and dishonest, and regulates his political strategy accordingly.

From this arises the question whether it is better to be loved more than feared, or feared more than loved. The reply is, that one ought to be both feared and loved, but as it is difficult for the two to go together, it is much safer to be feared than loved, if one of the two has to be wanting. For it may be said of men in general that they are ungrateful, voluble, dissemblers, anxious to avoid danger, and covetous of gain; as long as you benefit them, they are entirely yours; they offer you their blood, their goods, their life, and their children, as I have before said, when the necessity is remote; but when it approaches, they revolt. And the prince who has relied solely on their words, without making other preparations, is ruined; for the friendship which is gained by purchase and not through grandeur and nobility of spirit is bought but not secured, and at a pinch is not to be expended in your service. And men have less

---

[1]Cesare Borgia (c. 1476–1507) was the bastard son of Rodrigo Borgia, then a Spanish cardinal, and later Pope Alexander VI (1492–1503). With his father's aid he attempted to carve out for himself an independent duchy in north-central Italy, with Romagna as its heart. Through cruelty, violence, and treachery, he succeeded at first in his ambition, but ultimately his principality collapsed. Romagna was eventually incorporated into the Papal State under Pope Julius II (1503–1513).
[2]Pistoia, a small Italian city in Tuscany, came under the control of Florence in the fourteenth century.

scruple in offending one who makes himself loved than one who makes himself feared; for love is held by a chain of obligation which, men being selfish, is broken whenever it serves their purpose; but fear is maintained by a dread of punishment which never fails.

Still, a prince should make himself feared in such a way that if he does not gain love, he at any rate avoids hatred; for fear and the absence of hatred may well go together, and will be always attained by one who abstains from interfering with the property of his citizens and subjects or with their women. And when he is obliged to take the life of any one, let him do so when there is a proper justification and manifest reason for it; but above all he must abstain from taking the property of others, for men forget more easily the death of their father than the loss of their patrimony [inheritance]. Then also pretexts for seizing property are never wanting, and one who begins to live by rapine will always find some reason for taking the goods of others, whereas causes for taking life are rarer and more fleeting.

But when the prince is with his army and has a large number of soldiers under his control, then it is extremely necessary that he should not mind being thought cruel; for without this reputation he could not keep an army united or disposed to any duty. Among the noteworthy actions of Hannibal[3] is numbered this, that although he had an enormous army, composed of men of all nations and fighting in foreign countries, there never arose any dissension either among them or against the prince, either in good fortune or in bad. This could not be due to anything but his inhuman cruelty, which together with his infinite other virtues, made him always venerated and terrible in the sight of his soldiers, and without it his other virtues would not have sufficed to produce that effect. Thoughtless writers admire on the one hand his actions, and on the other blame the principal cause of them. . . .

Again in marked contrast to the teachings of Christian (and ancient) moralists, Machiavelli said that the successful prince will use any means to achieve and sustain political power. If the end is desirable, all means are justified.

How laudable it is for a prince to keep good faith and live with integrity, and not with astuteness, every one knows. Still the experience of our times shows those princes to have done great things who have had little regard for good faith, and have been able by astuteness to confuse men's brains, and who have ultimately overcome those who have made loyalty their foundation.

You must know, then, that there are two methods of fighting, the one by law, the other by force: the first method is that of men, the second of beasts; but as the first method is often insufficient, one must have recourse to the second. It is therefore necessary for a prince to know well how to use both the beast and the man. . . .

A prince being thus obliged to know well how to act as a beast must imitate the fox and the lion, for the lion cannot protect himself from traps, and the fox cannot defend himself from wolves. One must therefore be a fox to recognise traps, and a lion to frighten wolves. Those that wish to be only lions do not understand this. Therefore, a prudent ruler ought not to keep faith when by so doing it would be against his interest, and when the reasons which made him bind himself no longer exist. If men were all good, this precept would not be a good one; but as they are bad, and would not observe their faith with you, so you are not bound to keep faith with them. Nor have legitimate grounds ever failed a prince who wished to show [plausible] excuse for the non-fulfilment of his promise. Of this one could furnish an infinite number of modern examples, and show how many times peace has been broken, and how many promises rendered worthless, by the faithlessness of princes, and those that have been best able to imitate the fox have succeeded best. But it is necessary to be able to disguise this character well, and to be a great feigner and

---

[3]Hannibal (247–182 B.C.) was a brilliant Carthaginian general whose military victories almost destroyed Roman power. He was finally defeated at the battle of Zama in 202 B.C. by the Roman general Scipio Africanus.

dissembler; and men are so simple and so ready to obey present necessities, that one who deceives will always find those who allow themselves to be deceived. . . .

. . . Thus it is well to seem merciful, faithful, humane, sincere, religious, and also to be so; but you must have the mind so disposed that when it is needful to be otherwise you may be able to change to the opposite qualities. And it must be understood that a prince, and especially a new prince, cannot observe all those things which are considered good in men, being often obliged, in order to maintain the state, to act against faith, against charity, against humanity, and against religion. And, therefore, he must have a mind disposed to adapt itself according to the wind, and as the variations of fortune dictate, and, as I said before, not deviate from what is good, if possible, but be able to do evil if constrained.

A prince must take great care that nothing goes out of his mouth which is not full of the above-named five qualities, and, to see and hear him, he should seem to be all mercy, faith, in-

tegrity, humanity, and religion. And nothing is more necessary than to seem to have this last quality, for men in general judge more by the eyes than by the hands, for every one can see, but very few have to feel. Everybody sees what you appear to be, few feel what you are, and those few will not dare to oppose themselves to the many, who have the majesty of the state to defend them; and in the actions of men, and especially of princes, from which there is no appeal, the end justifies the means. Let a prince therefore aim at conquering and maintaining the state, and the means will always be judged honourable and praised by every one, for the vulgar is always taken by appearances and the issue of the event; and the world consists only of the vulgar, and the few who are not vulgar are isolated when the many have a rallying point in the prince. A certain prince of the present time, whom it is well not to name, never does anything but preach peace and good faith, but he is really a great enemy to both, and either of them, had he observed them, would have lost him state or reputation on many occasions.

REVIEW QUESTIONS

1. In what ways was Niccolò Machiavelli's advice to princes a break from the teachings of medieval political and moral philosophers?
2. What was Machiavelli's view of human nature? How did it influence his political thought?
3. Would Machiavelli's political advice help or hurt a politician in a modern democratic society?

3 The Lutheran Reformation

The reformation of the Western Christian church in the sixteenth century was precipitated by Martin Luther (1483–1546). A pious German Augustinian monk and theologian, Luther had no intention of founding a new church or overthrowing the political and ecclesiastical order of late medieval Europe. He was educated in the tradition of the New Devotion, which called for spiritual renewal, and as a theology professor at the university in Wittenberg, Germany, he opposed rationalistic, scholastic theology. Sympathetic at first to the ideas of Christian humanists like Erasmus, Luther too sought a reform of morals and an end to abusive practices within the church. But a visit to the papal court in Rome in 1510 left him profoundly shocked at its worldliness and disillusioned with the papacy's role in the church's governance.

Martin Luther
ON PAPAL POWER, JUSTIFICATION BY FAITH, THE INTERPRETATION OF THE BIBLE, AND THE NATURE OF THE CLERGY

To finance the rebuilding of St. Peter's church in Rome, the papacy in 1515 offered indulgences to those who gave alms for this pious work. An indulgence was a mitigation or remission of the austere penance imposed by a priest in absolving a penitent who confessed a sin and indicated remorse. Indulgences were granted by papal decrees for those who agreed to perform some act of charity, almsgiving, prayer, pilgrimage, or other pious work. Some preachers of this particular papal indulgence deceived people into believing that a "purchase" of this indulgence would win them, or even the dead, a secure place in heaven.

In 1517, Luther denounced the abuses connected with the preaching of papal indulgences. The quarrel led quickly to other and more profound theological issues. His opponents defended the use of indulgences on the basis of papal authority, shifting the debate to questions about the nature of papal power within the church. Luther responded with a vigorous attack on the whole system of papal governance. The principal points of his criticism were set out in his *Address to the Christian Nobility of the German Nation Concerning the Reform of the Christian Estate,* published in August 1520. In the first excerpt that follows, Luther argued that the papacy was blocking any reform of the church and appealed to the nobility of Germany to intervene by summoning a "free council" to reform the church.

A central point of contention between Luther and Catholic critics was his theological teaching on justification (salvation) by faith and on the role of good works in the scheme of salvation. Luther had suffered anguish about his unworthiness before God. Then, during a mystical experience, Luther suddenly perceived that his salvation came not because of his good works but as a free gift from God due to Luther's faith in Jesus Christ. Thus, while never denying that a Christian was obliged to perform good works, Luther argued that such pious acts were not helpful in achieving salvation. His claim that salvation or justification was attained through faith in Jesus Christ as Lord and Savior, and through that act of faith alone, became the rallying point of the Protestant reformers.

The Catholic position, not authoritatively clarified until the Council of Trent (1545–1563), argued that justification came not only through faith, but through hope and love as well, obeying God's commandments and doing good works. In *The Freedom of a Christian,* published in 1520, Luther outlined his teaching on justification by faith and on the inefficacy of good works; the second excerpt is from this work.

Another dispute between Luther and papal theologians was the question of interpretation of the Bible. In the medieval church, the final authority in any dispute over the meaning of Scriptural texts or church doctrine was ordinarily the pope alone, speaking as supreme head of the church or in concert with the bishops in an ecumenical council. The doctrine of papal infallibility (that the pope could not err in teaching matters of faith and morals) was already well known, but belief in this doctrine had not been formally required. Luther argued that the literal text of Scripture was alone the foundation of Christian truth, not the teaching of popes or councils. Moreover, Luther denied any special ordination of the clergy to power or authority in the church. He said that all believers were priests, and the clergy did not hold any power beyond that of the laity; therefore the special privileges of the clergy were unjustified. The third excerpt contains Luther's views on the interpretation of Scripture and the nature of priestly offices.

ON PAPAL POWER

The Romanists [traditional Catholics loyal to the papacy] have very cleverly built three walls around themselves. Hitherto they have protected themselves by these walls in such a way that no one has been able to reform them. As a result, the whole of Christendom has fallen abominably.

In the first place, when pressed by the temporal power they have made decrees and declared that the temporal power had no jurisdiction over them, but that, on the contrary, the spiritual power is above the temporal. In the second place, when the attempt is made to reprove them with the Scriptures, they raise the objection that only the pope may interpret the Scriptures. In the third place, if threatened with a council, their story is that no one may summon a council but the pope.

In this way they have cunningly stolen our three rods from us, that they may go unpunished. They have [settled] themselves within the safe stronghold of these three walls so that they can practice all the knavery and wickedness which we see today. Even when they have been compelled to hold a council they have weakened its power in advance by putting the princes under oath to let them remain as they were. In addition, they have given the pope full authority over all decisions of a council, so that it is all the same whether there are many councils or no councils. They only deceive us with puppet shows and sham fights. They fear terribly for their skin in a really free council! They have so intimidated kings and princes with this technique that they believe it would be an offense against God not to be obedient to the Romanists in all their knavish and ghoulish deceits. . . .

The Romanists have no basis in Scripture for their claim that the pope alone has the right to call or confirm a council. This is just their own ruling, and it is only valid as long as it is not harmful to Christendom or contrary to the laws of God. Now when the pope deserves punishment, this ruling no longer obtains, for not to punish him by authority of a council is harmful to Christendom. . . .

Therefore, when necessity demands it, and the pope is an offense to Christendom, the first man who is able should, as a true member of the whole body, do what he can to bring about a truly free council. No one can do this so well as the temporal authorities, especially since they are also fellow-Christians, fellow-priests, fellow-members of the spiritual estate, fellow-lords over all things. Whenever it is necessary or profitable they ought to exercise the office and work which they have received from God over everyone.

JUSTIFICATION BY FAITH

You may ask, "What then is the Word of God, and how shall it be used, since there are so many words of God?" I answer: The Apostle explains this in Romans 1. The Word is the gospel of God concerning his Son, who was made flesh, suffered, rose from the dead, and was glorified through the Spirit who sanctifies. To preach Christ means to feed the soul, make it righteous, set it free, and save it, provided it believes the preaching. Faith alone is the saving and efficacious use of the Word of God, according to Rom. 10 (:9): "If you confess with your lips that Jesus is Lord and believe in your heart that God raised him from the dead, you will be saved." Furthermore, "Christ is the end of the law, that every one who has faith may be justified" (Rom. 10:4). Again, in Rom. 1 (:17), "He who through faith is righteous shall live." The Word of God cannot be received and cherished by any works whatever but only by faith. Therefore it is clear that, as the soul needs only the Word of God for its life and righteousness, so it is justified by faith alone and not any works; for if it could be justified by anything else, it would not need the Word, and consequently it would not need faith.

This faith cannot exist in connection with works—that is to say, if you at the same time claim to be justified by works, whatever their character—for that would be the same as "limping with two different opinions" (I Kings 18:21), as worshipping Baal and kissing one's own hand (Job 31:27–28), which, as Job says, is a very great iniquity. Therefore the moment you begin to have faith you learn that all things in you are altogether blameworthy, sinful, and damnable, as the Apostle says in Rom. 3 (:23), "Since all have sinned and fall short of the glory of God," and, "None is righteous, no, not one; . . . all have turned aside, together they have gone wrong" (Rom. 3:10–12). When you have learned this you will know that you need Christ, who suffered and rose again for you so that, if you believe in him, you may through this faith become a new man in so far as your sins are forgiven and you are justified by the merits of another, namely, of Christ alone.

Since, therefore, this faith can rule only in the inner man, as Rom. 10 (:10) says, "For man believes with his heart and so is justified," and since faith alone justifies, it is clear that the inner man cannot be justified, freed, or saved by any outer work or action at all, and that these works, whatever their character, have nothing to do with this inner man. On the other hand, only ungodliness and unbelief of heart, and no outer work, make him guilty and a damnable servant of sin. Wherefore it ought to be the first concern of every Christian to lay aside all confidence in works and increasingly to strengthen faith alone and through faith to grow in the knowledge, not of works, but of Christ Jesus, who suffered and rose for him, as Peter teaches in the last chapter of his first Epistle (I Pet. 5:10). No other work makes a Christian. . . .

Our faith in Christ does not free us from works

but from false opinions concerning works, that is, from the foolish presumption that justification is acquired by works. Faith redeems, corrects, and preserves our consciences so that we know that righteousness does not consist in works, although works neither can nor ought to be wanting; just as we cannot be without food and drink and all the works of this mortal body, yet our righteousness is not in them, but in faith; and yet those works of the body are not to be despised or neglected on that account. In this world we are bound by the needs of our bodily life, but we are not righteous because of them. "My kingship is not of this world" (John 18:36), says Christ. He does not, however, say, "My kingship is not here, that is, in this world." And Paul says, "Though we live in the world we are not carrying on a worldly war" (II Cor. 10:3), and in Gal. 2 (:20), "The life I now live in the flesh I live by faith in the Son of God." Thus what we do, live, and are in works and ceremonies, we do because of the necessities of this life and of the effort to rule our body. Nevertheless we are righteous, not in these, but in the faith of the Son of God.

THE INTERPRETATION OF THE BIBLE AND THE NATURE OF THE CLERGY

They (the Roman Catholic Popes) want to be the only masters of Scriptures. . . . They assume sole authority for themselves and would persuade us with insolent juggling of words that the Pope, whether he be bad or good, cannot err in matters of faith. . . .

. . . They cannot produce a letter to prove that the interpretation of Scripture . . . belongs to the Pope alone. They themselves have usurped this power . . . and though they allege that this power was conferred on Peter when the keys were given to him, it is plain enough that the keys were not given to Peter alone but to the entire body of Christians (Matt. 16:19; 18:18). . . .

. . . Every baptized Christian is a priest already, not by appointment or ordination from the Pope or any other man, but because Christ Himself has begotten him as a priest . . . in baptism. . . .

The Pope has usurped the term "priest" for his anointed and tonsured hordes [clergy and monks]. By this means they have separated themselves from the ordinary Christians and have called themselves uniquely the "clergy of God," God's heritage and chosen people who must help other Christians by their sacrifice and worship. . . . Therefore the Pope argues that he alone has the right and power to ordain and do what he will. . . .

[But] the preaching office is no more than a public service which happens to be conferred on someone by the entire congregation all the members of which are priests. . . .

. . . The fact that a pope or bishop anoints, makes tonsures, ordains, consecrates [makes holy], and prescribes garb different from those of the laity . . . nevermore makes a Christian and a spiritual man. Accordingly, through baptism all of us are consecrated to the priesthood, as St. Peter says. . . . (I Peter 2:9).

To make it still clearer, if a small group of pious Christian laymen were taken captive and settled in a wilderness and had among them no priest consecrated by a bishop, if they were to agree to choose one from their midst, married or unmarried, and were to charge him with the office of baptizing, saying Mass, absolving [forgiving of sins], and preaching, such a man would be as truly a priest as he would if all bishops and popes had consecrated him.

REVIEW QUESTIONS

1. Why did Martin Luther see the papacy as the crucial block to any meaningful reform of the church?
2. How did Luther's teaching undermine the power of the clergy and traditional forms of piety?

---

4   Justification of Absolute Monarchy

Effectively blocking royal absolutism in the Middle Ages were the dispersion of power between kings and feudal lords, the vigorous sense of personal freedom and urban autonomy of the townspeople, and the limitations on royal power imposed by the church. However, by the late sixteenth century, monarchs were asserting their authority over competing groups with ever-greater effectiveness. In this new balance of political forces, European kings acted out their claim to absolute power as monarchs chosen by and responsible to God alone. This theory, called the divine right of kings, became the dominant political ideology of seventeenth- and eighteenth-century Europe.

Thomas Hobbes
LEVIATHAN

Thomas Hobbes (1588–1679), a British philosopher and political theorist, witnessed the agonies of the English civil war, including the execution of Charles I in 1649. These developments fortified Hobbes's conviction that absolutism was the most desirable and logical form of government. Only the unlimited power of a sovereign, said Hobbes, could contain human passions that disrupt the social order and threaten civilized life; only absolute rule could provide an environment secure enough for people to pursue their individual interests.

Leviathan (1651), Hobbes's principal work of political thought, broke with medieval political theory. Medieval thinkers assigned each group of people—clergy, lords, serfs, guildsmen—a place in a fixed social order; an individual's social duties were set by ancient traditions believed to have been ordained by God. During early modern times, the great expansion of commerce and capitalism spurred the new individualism already pronounced in Renaissance culture; group ties were shattered by competition and accelerating social mobility. Hobbes gave expression to a society where people confronted each other as competing individuals.

Hobbes was influenced by the new scientific thought that saw mathematical knowledge as the avenue to truth. Using geometry as a model, Hobbes began with what he believed were self-evident axioms regarding human nature, from which he deduced other truths. He aimed at constructing political philosophy on a scientific foundation and rejected the authority of tradition and religion as inconsistent with a science of politics. Thus, although Hobbes supported absolutism, he dismissed the idea advanced by other theorists of absolutism that the monarch's power derived from God. He also rejected the idea that the state should not be obeyed when it violated God's law. *Leviathan* is a rational and secular political statement. In this modern approach, rather than in Hobbes's justification of absolutism, lies the work's significance.

Hobbes had a pessimistic view of human nature. Believing that people are innately selfish and grasping, he maintained that competition and dissension, rather than cooperation, characterize human relations. Even when reason teaches that cooperation is more advantageous than competition, Hobbes observed that people are reluctant to alter their ways, because passion, not reason, governs their behavior. In the following passages from *Leviathan,* Hobbes describes the causes of human conflicts.

Nature hath made men so equall, in the faculties of body, and mind; as that though there bee found one man sometimes manifestly stronger in body, or of quicker mind than another; yet when all is reckoned together, the difference between man, and man, is not so considerable, as that one man can thereupon claim to himselfe any benefit, to which another may not pretend, as well as he. For as to the strength of body, the weakest has strength enough to kill the strongest, either by secret machination, or by confederacy with others, that are in the same danger with himselfe. . . .

And so as to the faculties of the mind . . . men are . . . [more] equall than unequall. . . .

From this equality of ability, ariseth equality of hope in the attaining of our Ends. And therefore if any two men desire the same thing, which neverthelesse they cannot both enjoy,

they become enemies; and in the way to their End, . . . endeavour to destroy, or subdue one another. . . . If one plant, sow, build, or possesse a convenient Seat, others may probably be expected to come prepared with forces united, to dispossesse, and deprive him, not only of the fruit of his labour, but also of his life, or liberty. . . .

So that in the nature of man, we find three principall causes of quarrell. First, Competition; Secondly, Diffidence [unsureness]; Thirdly, Glory.

The first, maketh men invade for Gain; the second, for Safety; and the third, for Reputation. The first use Violence, to make themselves Masters of other men's persons, wives, children, and cattell; the second, to defend them; the third, for trifles, as a word, a smile, a different opinion, and any other signe of undervalue, either direct in their Persons, or by reflexion in their Kindred, their Friends, their Nation, their Profession, or their Name.

Hereby it is manifest, that during the time men live without a common Power to keep them all in awe, they are in that condition which is called Warre; and such a warre, as is of every man, against every man. . . .

Hobbes then describes a state of nature—the hypothetical condition of humanity prior to the formation of the state—as a war of all against all. For Hobbes, the state of nature is a logical abstraction, a device employed to make his point. Only a strong ruling entity—the state—will end the perpetual strife and provide security. For Hobbes, the state is merely a useful arrangement that permits individuals to exchange goods and services in a secure environment. The ruling authority in the state, the sovereign, must have supreme power, or society will collapse and the anarchy of the state of nature will return.

Whatsoever therefore is consequent to a time of Warre, where every man is Enemy to every man; the same is consequent to the time, wherein men live without other security, than what their own strength, and their own invention shall furnish them withall. In such condition, there is no place for Industry; because the fruit thereof is uncertain: and consequently no Culture of the Earth; no Navigation, nor use of the commodities that may be imported by Sea; no commodious Building; no Instruments of moving, and removing such things as require much force; no Knowledge of the face of the Earth; no account of Time; no Arts; no Letters; no Society; and which is worst of all, continuall feare, and danger of violent death; And the life of man, solitary, poore, nasty, brutish, and short. . . .

The Passions that encline men to Peace, are Feare of Death; Desire of such things as are necessary to commodious living; and a Hope by their Industry to obtain them. And Reason suggesteth convenient Articles of Peace, upon which men may be drawn to agreement. . . .

And because the condition of Man, (as hath been declared in the precedent Chapter) is a condition of Warre of every one against every one; in which case every one is governed by his own Reason; and there is nothing he can make use of, that may not be a help unto him, in preserving his life against his enemyes; It followeth, that in such a condition, every man has a Right to every thing; even to one another's body. And therefore, as long as this naturall Right of every man to every thing endureth, there can be no security to any man, (how strong or wise soever he be,) of living out the time, which Nature ordinarily alloweth men to live. . . .

. . . If there be no Power erected, or not great enough for our security; every man will and may lawfully rely on his own strength and art, for caution against all other men. . . .

The only way to erect . . . a Common Power, as may be able to defend them from the invasion of [foreigners] and the injuries of one another, and thereby to secure them in such sort, as that by their owne industrie, and by the fruites of the Earth, they may nourish themselves and live contentedly; is, to conferre all their power and strength upon one Man, or upon one Assembly of men, that may reduce all their Wills, by plurality of voices, unto one Will . . . and therein to submit their Wills, every one to his Will, and their Judgements, to his Judgement. This is more than Consent, or Concord; it is a reall Unitie of them all, in one and the same Person, made by Covenant of every man with every man, in such manner, as if every man should say to every man, *I Authorise and give up my Right of Governing my selfe, to this Man, or to this Assembly of men, on this condition, that thou give up thy Right to him, and Authorise all his Actions in like manner.* This done, the Multitude so united in one Person, is called a COMMON-WEALTH. . . . For by this Authoritie, given him by every particular man in the Common-wealth, he hath the use of so much Power and Strength . . . conferred on him, that by terror thereof, he is inabled to forme the wills of them all, to Peace at home, and mutuall [aid] against their enemies abroad. And in him consisteth the Essence of the Common-wealth; which (to define it), is *One*

Person, of whose Acts a great Multitude, by mutuall Covenants one with another, have made themselves every one the Author, to the end he may use the strength and means of them all, as he shall think expedient, for their Peace and Common Defence.

And he that carryeth this Person, is called SOVERAIGNE, and said to have *Soveraigne Power;* and every one besides, his SUBJECT. . . .

. . . They that have already Instituted a Common-wealth, being thereby bound by Covenant . . . cannot lawfully make a new Covenant, amongst themselves, to be obedient to any other, in any thing whatsoever, without his permission. And therefore, they that are subjects to a Monarch, cannot without his leave cast off Monarchy, and return to the confusion of a disunited Multitude; nor transferre their Person from him that beareth it, to another Man, or other Assembly of men: for they . . . are bound, every man to every man, to [acknowledge] . . . that he that already is their Soveraigne, shall

do, and judge fit to be done; so that [those who do not obey] break their Covenant made to that man, which is injustice: and they have also every man given the Soveraignty to him that beareth their Person; and therefore if they depose him, they take from him that which is his own, and so again it is injustice. . . . And whereas some men have pretended for their disobedience to their Soveraigne, a new Covenant, made, not with men, but with God; this also is unjust: for there is no Covenant with God, but by mediation of some body that representeth God's Person; which none doth but God's Lieutenant, who hath the Soveraignty under God. But this pretence of Covenant with God, is so evident a [lie], even in the pretender's own consciences, that it is not onely an act of an unjust, but also of a vile, and unmanly disposition. . . .

. . . Consequently none of [the sovereign's] Subjects, by any pretence of forfeiture, can be freed from his Subjection.

REVIEW QUESTIONS

1. What was Thomas Hobbes's view of human nature and what conclusions did he draw from it about the best form of government?
2. What has been the political legacy of Hobbes's notion of the state?

---

5 The Triumph of Constitutional Monarchy in England: The Glorious Revolution

The struggle against absolute monarchy in England during the early seventeenth century reached a climax during the reign of Charles I (1625–1649). The king's failure to support the Protestant cause during the Thirty Years' War (1618–1648) on the Continent and his fervent support of the Anglican Episcopal Church earned him many enemies. Among them were the Puritans, Presbyterians, and Independents (Congregationalists), who composed an influential minority in his early Parliaments. Faced with rising costs of government, the king tried to obtain more revenues by vote of Parliament, but the parliamentarians refused to consent to new taxes unless the king followed policies they supported. After four bitter years of controversy, the king dismissed Parliament in 1629. He ruled in an increasingly absolutist manner without calling a new Parliament for the next eleven years and levied many taxes without the consent of the people's representatives.

Charles's policies collapsed in 1640 when he was compelled to summon Parliament to raise money for an army to put down a rebellion of Scottish Presbyterians. The new Parliament set forth demands for reforms of church and state, which the king refused. He claimed monarchical power and policies to be un-limited by parliamentary controls or consent.

Parliament raised its own army as civil war broke out between its supporters and those of the king. The parties were divided not only on constitutional issues but also by religious differences. Most of the Puritans, Presbyterians, and Independents supported the parliamentary cause; Anglicans and Catholics were overwhelmingly royalist. Captured by the Scottish Presbyterian rebels in 1646 and turned over to the English parliamentary army in 1647, Charles was held prisoner for two years until the Puritan parliamentary general Oliver Cromwell (1599–1658) decided to put him on trial for treason. The king was found guilty and executed in 1649.

The revolutionary parliamentary regime evolved into a military dictatorship headed by Cromwell. After Cromwell's death, Parliament restored the monarchy in 1660 and invited the late king's heir to end his exile and take the throne. Charles II (1660–1685), by discretion and skilled statesmanship, managed to avoid a major confrontation with Parliament. When his brother James II (1685–1688), a staunch Catholic, succeeded to the throne, the hostility between Parliament and monarchy mounted. Parliament feared that James II aimed to impose Catholicism and absolutism on England.

When the king's wife gave birth to a son, making the heir to the throne another Catholic, almost all factions (except the Catholics) abandoned James II and invited the Dutch Protestant Prince William of Orange and his wife Mary, James II's Protestant daughter, to come to England. James and his Catholic family and friends fled to France. Parliament declared the throne vacant and offered it to William and Mary as joint sovereigns. As a result of the bloodless "Glorious Revolution," the English monarchy became clearly limited by the will of Parliament.

THE ENGLISH DECLARATION OF RIGHTS

In depriving James II of the throne, Parliament had destroyed forever in Britain the theory of divine right as an operating principle of government and had firmly established a limited constitutional monarchy. The appointment of William and Mary was accompanied by a declaration of rights (later enacted as the Bill of Rights), which enumerated and declared illegal James II's arbitrary acts. The Declaration of Rights, excerpted below, compelled William and Mary and future monarchs to recognize the right of the people's representatives to dispose of the royal office and to set limits on its powers. These rights were subsequently formulated into laws passed by Parliament. Prior to the American Revolution, colonists protested that British actions in the American colonies violated certain rights guaranteed in the English Bill of Rights. Several of these rights were later included in the Constitution of the United States.

And whereas the said late king James the Second having abdicated the government and the throne being thereby vacant, His Highness the prince of Orange (whom it hath pleased Almighty God to make the glorious instrument of delivering this kingdom from popery and arbitrary power) did (by the advice of the lords spiritual and temporal and divers principal persons of the commons)[1] cause letters to be written to the lords spiritual and temporal, being Protestants; and other letters to the several counties, cities, universities, boroughs and Cinque ports[2] for the choosing of such persons to represent them, as were of right to be sent to parliament, to meet and sit at Westminster upon the two and twentieth day of January in this year one thousand six hundred eighty and eight,[3] in order to [guarantee] . . . that their religion, laws and liberties might not again be in danger of being subverted; upon which letters elections having been accordingly made.

And thereupon the said lords spiritual and temporal and commons pursuant to their respective letters and elections being now assembled in a full and free representative of this nation, taking into their most serious consideration the best means for attaining the ends aforesaid, do in the first place (as their ancestors in like case have usually done) for the vindicating and asserting their ancient rights and liberties, declare:

That the pretended power of suspending of laws or the execution of laws by regal authority without consent of parliament is illegal.

That the pretended power of dispensing with laws or the execution of laws by regal authority as it hath been assumed and exercised of late is illegal.

That the commission for erecting the late court of commissioners for ecclesiastical causes and all other commissions and courts of like nature are illegal and pernicious.

That the levying money for or to the use of the crown by pretence of prerogative without grant of parliament for a longer time or in other manner than the same is or shall be granted is illegal.

That it is the right of the subjects to petition the king and all commitments and prosecutions for such petitioning are illegal.

That the raising or keeping a standing army within the kingdom in time of peace unless it be with consent of parliament is against law.

That the subjects which are Protestants may have arms for their defence suitable to their conditions and as allowed by law.

That election of members of parliament ought to be free.

That the freedom of speech and debates or proceedings in parliament ought not to be impeached or questioned in any court or place out of parliament.

That excessive bail ought not to be required nor excessive fines imposed nor cruel and unusual punishments inflicted.

That jurors ought to be duly impanelled and returned and jurors which pass upon men in trials for high treason ought to be freeholders [landholders].

That all grants and promises of fines and forfeitures of particular persons before conviction are illegal and void.

And that for redress of all grievances and for the amending, strengthening and preserving of the laws parliaments ought to be held frequently.

And they do claim, demand and insist upon all and singular the premises as their undoubted rights and liberties and that no declarations, judgments, doings or proceedings to the prejudice of the people in any of the said premises ought in any wise to be drawn hereafter into consequence or example.

---

[1]"The lords spiritual" refers to the bishops of the Church of England who sat in the House of Lords, and "the lords temporal" refers to the nobility entitled to sit in the House of Lords. "The commons" refers to the elected representatives in the House of Commons.

[2]The Cinque ports along England's southeastern coast (originally five in number) enjoyed special privileges because of their military duties in providing for coastal defense.

[3]The year was in fact 1689 because until 1752, the English used March 25 as the beginning of the new year.

REVIEW QUESTIONS

1. How did the Declaration of Rights limit royal authority? With what result?
2. In what ways did the Glorious Revolution influence the American rebellion in the 1770s?

Intellectual Revolutions

GALILEO GALILEI'S (1564–1642) support of Copernicanism and rejection of the medieval division of the universe into higher and lower realms make him a principal shaper of modern science. *(The Granger Collection, New York.)*

The Scientific Revolution of the sixteenth and seventeenth centuries replaced the medieval view of the universe with a new cosmology and produced a new way of investigating nature. It overthrew the medieval conception of nature as a hierarchical order ascending toward a realm of perfection. Rejecting reliance on authority, the thinkers of the Scientific Revolution affirmed the individual's ability to know the natural world through the method of mathematical reasoning, the direct observation of nature, and carefully controlled experiments.

The medieval view of the universe had blended the theories of Aristotle and Ptolemy, two ancient Greek thinkers, with Christian teachings. In that view, a stationary earth stood in the center of the universe just above hell. Revolving around the earth were seven planets: the moon, Mercury, Venus, the sun, Mars, Jupiter, and Saturn. Because people believed that earth did not move, it was not considered a planet. Each planet was attached to a transparent sphere that turned around the earth. Encompassing the universe was a sphere of fixed stars; beyond the stars lay three heavenly spheres, the outermost of which was the abode of God. An earth-centered universe accorded with the Christian idea that God had created the universe for men and women and that salvation was the aim of life.

Also agreeable to the medieval Christian view was Aristotle's division of the universe into a lower, earthly realm and a higher realm beyond the moon. Two sets of laws operated in the universe, one on earth and the other in the celestial realm. Earthly objects were composed of four elements: earth, water, fire, and air; celestial objects were composed of the divine ether—a substance too pure, too clear, too fine, too spiritual to be found on earth. Celestial objects naturally moved in perfectly circular orbits around the earth; earthly objects, composed mainly of the heavy elements of earth and water, naturally fell downward, whereas objects made of the lighter elements of air and fire naturally flew upward toward the sky.

The destruction of the medieval world picture began with the publication in 1543 of *On the Revolutions of the Heavenly Spheres,* by Nicolaus Copernicus, a Polish mathematician, astronomer, and clergyman. In Copernicus's system, the sun was in the center of the universe, and the earth was another planet that moved around the sun. Most thinkers of the time, committed to the Aristotelian–Ptolemaic system and to the biblical statements that seemed to support it, rejected Copernicus's conclusions.

The work of Galileo Galilei, an Italian mathematician, astronomer, and physicist, was decisive in the shattering of the medieval cosmos and the shaping of the modern scientific outlook. Galileo advanced the modern view that knowledge of nature derives from direct observation and from mathematics. For Galileo, the universe was a "grand book which . . . is written in the language of mathematics, and its characters are triangles, circles, and other geometric figures without which it is humanly impossible to understand a single word of it." Galileo also pioneered experimental physics, advanced the modern idea that nature is uniform throughout the universe, and attacked reliance on scholastic authority rather than on experimentation in resolving scientific controversies.

Johannes Kepler (1571–1630), a contemporary of Galileo, discovered three laws of planetary motion that greatly advanced astronomical knowledge. Kepler showed that the path of a planet was an ellipse, not a circle as Ptolemy (and Copernicus) had believed, and that planets do not move at uniform speed but accelerate as they near the sun. He devised formulas to calculate accurately both a planet's speed at each point in its orbit around the sun and a planet's location at a particular time. Kepler's laws provided further evidence that Copernicus had been right, for they made sense only in a sun-centered universe, but Kepler could not explain why planets stayed in their orbits rather than flying off into space or crashing into the sun. The resolution of that question was left to Sir Isaac Newton.

Newton's great achievement was integrating the findings of Copernicus, Galileo, and Kepler into a single theoretical system. In *Principia Mathematica* (1687), he formulated the mechanical laws of motion and attraction that govern celestial and terrestrial objects.

The Scientific Revolution was instrumental in shaping the modern outlook. It destroyed the medieval conception of the universe and established the scientific method as the means for investigating nature and acquiring knowledge, even in areas having little to do with the study of the physical world. By demonstrating the powers of the human mind, the Scientific Revolution gave thinkers great confidence in reason and led eventually to a rejection of traditional beliefs in magic, astrology, and witches. In the eighteenth century, this growing skepticism led thinkers to question miracles and other Christian beliefs that seemed contrary to reason.

The Enlightenment of the eighteenth century culminated the movement toward modernity that started in the Renaissance era. The thinkers of the Enlightenment, called *philosophes,* attacked medieval otherworldliness, dethroned theology from its once-proud position as queen of the sciences, and based their understanding of nature and society on reason alone, unaided by revelation or priestly authority.

From the broad spectrum of Western history, several traditions flowed into the Enlightenment: the rational spirit born in classical Greece, the Stoic emphasis on natural law that applies to all human beings, and the Christian belief that all individuals are equal in God's eyes. A more immediate influence on the Enlightenment was Renaissance humanism, which focused on the individual and worldly human accomplishments and which criticized medieval theology-philosophy for its preoccupation with questions that seemed unrelated to the human condition. In many ways, the Enlightenment grew directly out of the Scientific Revolution. The philosophes praised both Newton's discovery of the mechanical laws that govern the universe and the scientific method that made this discovery possible. They wanted to transfer the scientific method—the reliance on experience and the critical use of the intellect—to the realm of society. They maintained that independent of clerical authority, human beings through reason could grasp the natural laws that govern the social world, just as Newton had uncovered the laws of nature that operate in the physical world. The philosophes said that those institutions and traditions that could not meet the test of reason, because they were based on authority, ignorance, or superstition, had to be reformed or dispensed with.

For medieval philosophers, reason had been subordinate to revelation; the Christian outlook determined the medieval concept of nature, morality, government, law, and life's purpose. During the Renaissance and Scientific Revolution, reason increasingly asserted its autonomy. For example, Machiavelli rejected the principle that politics should be based on Christian teachings; he recognized no higher world as the source of a higher truth. Galileo held that on questions regarding nature, one should trust to observation, experimentation, and mathematical reasoning and should not rely on Scripture. Descartes rejected reliance on past authority and maintained that through thought alone one could attain knowledge that has absolute certainty. Agreeing with Descartes that the mind is self-sufficient, the philosophes rejected the guidance of revelation and its priestly interpreters. They believed that through the use of reason, individuals could comprehend and reform society.

The Enlightenment philosophes articulated basic principles of the modern outlook: confidence in the self-sufficiency of the human mind, belief that individuals possess natural rights that governments should not violate, and the desire to reform society in accordance with rational principles. Their views influenced the reformers of the French Revolution and the founding fathers of the United States.

1 Expanding the New Astronomy

The brilliant Italian scientist Galileo Galilei (1564–1642) rejected the medieval division of the universe into higher and lower realms and proclaimed the modern idea of nature's uniformity. Learning that a telescope had been invented in Holland, Galileo built one for himself and used it to investigate the heavens. Through his telescope, Galileo saw craters and mountains on the moon; he concluded that celestial bodies were not pure, perfect, and immutable, as had been believed. There was no difference in quality between heavenly and earthly bodies; nature was the same throughout.

Galileo Galilei
THE STARRY MESSENGER

In the following reading from *The Starry Messenger* (1610), Galileo reported the findings observed through his telescope, which led him to proclaim the uniformity of nature, a key principle of modern science.

About ten months ago a report reached my ears that a certain Fleming [a native of Flanders]* had constructed a spyglass by means of which visible objects, though very distant from the eye of the observer, were distinctly seen as if nearby. Of this truly remarkable effect several experiences were related, to which some persons gave credence while others denied them. A few days later the report was confirmed to me in a letter from a noble Frenchman at Paris, Jacques Badovere,† which caused me to apply myself wholeheartedly to inquire into the means by which I might arrive at the invention of a similar instrument. This I did shortly afterwards, my basis being the theory of refraction. First I prepared a tube of lead, at the ends of which I fitted two glass lenses, both plane on one side while on the other side one was spherically convex and the other concave. Then placing my eye near the concave lens I perceived objects satisfactorily large and near, for they appeared three times closer and nine times larger than when seen with the naked eye alone. Next I constructed another one, more accurate, which represented objects as enlarged more than sixty times. Finally, sparing neither labor nor expense, I succeeded in constructing for myself so excellent an instrument that objects seen by means of it appeared nearly one thousand times larger and over thirty times closer than when regarded with our natural vision.

It would be superfluous to enumerate the number and importance of the advantages of such an instrument at sea as well as on land. But forsaking terrestrial observations, I turned to celestial ones, and first I saw the moon from as near at hand as if it were scarcely two terrestrial radii [a measure of distance, obscure today] away. After that I observed often with wondering delight both the planets and the fixed stars, and since I saw these latter to be very crowded, I began to seek (and eventually found) a method by which I might measure their distances apart. . . .

Now let us review the observations made during the past two months, once more inviting the attention of all who are eager for true philosophy to the first steps of such important contemplations. Let us speak first of that surface of the moon which faces us. For greater clarity I distinguish two parts of this surface, a lighter and a darker; the lighter part seems to surround and to pervade the whole hemisphere, while the darker part discolors the moon's surface like a kind of cloud, and makes it appear covered with spots. Now those spots which are fairly dark and rather large are plain to everyone and have been seen throughout the ages; these I shall call the "large" or "ancient" spots, distinguishing them from others that are smaller in size but so numerous as to occur all over the lunar surface, and especially the lighter part. The latter spots had never been seen by anyone before me. From observations of these spots repeated many times I have been led to the opinion and conviction that the surface of the moon is not smooth, uniform, and precisely spherical as a great number of

---

*Credit for the original invention is generally assigned to Hans Lipperhey, a lens grinder in Holland who chanced upon this property of combined lenses and applied for a patent on it in 1608.

†Badovere studied in Italy toward the close of the sixteenth century and is said to have been a pupil of Galileo's in about 1598. When he wrote concerning the new instrument in 1609, he was in the French diplomatic service at Paris, where he died in 1620.

philosophers believe it (and the other heavenly bodies) to be, but is uneven, rough, and full of cavities and prominences, being not unlike the face of the earth, relieved by chains of mountains and deep valleys. . . .

With his telescope, Galileo discovered four moons orbiting Jupiter, an observation that overcame a principal objection to the Copernican system. Galileo showed that a celestial body could indeed move around a center other than the earth; that earth was not the common center for all celestial bodies; that a celestial body (earth's moon or Jupiter's moons) could orbit a planet at the same time that the planet revolved around another body (namely, the sun).

On the seventh day of January in this present year 1610, at the first hour of night, when I was viewing the heavenly bodies with a telescope, Jupiter presented itself to me; and because I had prepared a very excellent instrument for myself, I perceived (as I had not before, on account of the weakness of my previous instrument) that beside the planet there were three starlets, small indeed, but very bright. Though I believed them to be among the host of fixed stars, they aroused my curiosity somewhat by appearing to lie in an exact straight line parallel to the ecliptic, and by their being more splendid than others of their size. Their arrangement with respect to Jupiter and each other was the following:

East   **✳   ✳   O   ✳**   *West*

that is, there were two stars on the eastern side and one to the west. The most easterly star and the western one appeared larger than the other. I paid no attention to the distances between them and Jupiter, for at the outset I thought them to be fixed stars, as I have said.[‡] But re-

turning to the same investigation on January eighth—led by what, I do not know—I found a very different arrangement. The three starlets were now all to the west of Jupiter, closer together, and at equal intervals from one another as shown in the following sketch:

East   **O   ✳   ✳   ✳**   *West*

On the tenth of January, however, the stars appeared in this position with respect to Jupiter:

East   **✳   ✳   O**   *West*

that is, there were but two of them, both easterly, the third (as I supposed) being hidden behind Jupiter. . . . There was no way in which such alterations could be attributed to Jupiter's motion, yet being certain that these were still the same stars I had observed . . . my perplexity was now transformed into amazement. I was sure that the apparent changes belonged not to Jupiter but to the observed stars, and I resolved to pursue this investigation with greater care and attention. . . .

I had now decided beyond all question that there existed in the heavens three stars wandering about Jupiter as do Venus and Mercury about the sun, and this became plainer than daylight from observations on similar occasions which followed. Nor were there just three such stars; four wanderers complete their revolutions about Jupiter. . . .

Here we have a fine and elegant argument for quieting the doubts of those who, while accepting with tranquil mind the revolutions of the planets about the sun in the Copernican system, are mightily disturbed to have the moon

---

[‡]The reader should remember that the telescope was nightly revealing to Galileo hundreds of fixed stars never previously observed. His unusual gifts for astronomical observation are illustrated by his having noticed and remembered these three merely by reason of their alignment, and recalling them so well that when by chance he happened to see them the following night he was certain that they had changed their positions.

alone revolve about the earth and accompany it in an annual rotation about the sun. Some have believed that this structure of the universe should be rejected as impossible. But now we have not just one planet rotating about another while both run through a great orbit around the sun; our own eyes show us four stars which wander around Jupiter as does the moon around the earth, while all together trace out a grand revolution about the sun in the space of twelve years.

Galileo Galilei
LETTER TO THE GRAND DUCHESS CHRISTINA AND *DIALOGUE CONCERNING THE TWO CHIEF WORLD SYSTEMS— PTOLEMAIC AND COPERNICAN*

The first reading illustrates Galileo's active involvement in a struggle for freedom of inquiry many years before the *Dialogue* was published. In 1615, in a letter addressed to Grand Duchess Christina of Tuscany, Galileo argued that passages from the Bible had no authority in scientific disputes.

The second reading (from the *Dialogue*) reveals Galileo's views on Aristotle. Medieval scholastics regarded Aristotle as the supreme authority on questions concerning nature, an attitude that was perpetuated by early modern scholastics. Galileo insisted that such reliance on authority was a hindrance to scientific investigation, that it is through observation, experiment, and reason that one arrives at physical truth.

BIBLICAL AUTHORITY

Some years ago, as Your Serene Highness well knows, I discovered in the heavens many things that had not been seen before our own age. The novelty of these things, as well as some consequences which followed from them in contradiction to the physical notions commonly held among academic philosophers, stirred up against me no small number of professors—as if I had placed these things in the sky with my own hands in order to upset nature and overturn the sciences. They seemed to forget that the increase of known truths stimulates the investigation, establishment, and growth of the arts; not their diminution or destruction.

Showing a greater fondness for their own opinions than for truth, they sought to deny and disprove the new things which, if they had cared to look for themselves, their own senses would have demonstrated to them. To this end they hurled various charges and published numerous writings filled with vain arguments, and they made the grave mistake of sprinkling these with passages taken from places in the Bible which they had failed to understand properly, and which were ill suited to their purposes. . . .

. . . Men who were well grounded in astronomical and physical science were persuaded as soon as they received my first message. There were others who denied them or remained in doubt only because of their novel and unexpected character, and because they had not yet had the opportunity to see for themselves. These men have by degrees come to be satisfied. But some, besides allegiance to their original error, possess I know not what fanciful interest in remaining hostile not so much toward the things in question as toward their discoverer. No longer being able to deny them, these men now take refuge in obstinate silence, but being more than ever exasperated by that which has pacified and quieted other men, they divert their thoughts to other fancies and seek new ways to damage me. . . .

. . . Possibly because they are disturbed by the known truth of other propositions of mine which differ from those commonly held, and therefore mistrusting their defense so long as they confine themselves to the field of philosophy, these men have resolved to fabricate a shield for their fallacies out of the mantle of pretended religion and the authority of the Bible. These they apply, with little judgment, to the refutation of arguments that they do not understand and have not even listened to.

First they have endeavored to spread the opinion that such propositions in general are contrary to the Bible and are consequently damnable and heretical. . . . Hence they have had no trouble in finding men who would preach the damnability and heresy of the new doctrine from their very pulpits with unwonted confidence, thus doing impious and inconsiderate injury not only to that doctrine and its followers but to all mathematics and mathematicians in general. . . .

. . . They go about invoking the Bible, which they would have minister to their deceitful purposes. Contrary to the sense of the Bible and the intention of the holy [Church] Fathers, if I am not mistaken, they would extend such authorities until even in purely physical matters—where faith is not involved—they would have us altogether abandon reason and the evidence of our senses in favor of some biblical passage, though under the surface meaning of its words this passage may contain a different sense.

I hope to show that I proceed with much greater piety than they do, when I argue not against condemning [Copernicus's] book, but against condemning it in the way they suggest—that is, without understanding it, weighing it, or so much as reading it. For Copernicus never discusses matters of religion or faith, nor does he use arguments that depend in any way upon the authority of sacred writings which he might have interpreted erroneously. He stands always upon physical conclusions pertaining to the celestial motions, and deals with them by astronomical and geometrical demonstrations, founded primarily upon sense experiences and very exact observations. He did not ignore the Bible, but he knew very well that if his doctrine were proved, then it could not contradict the Scriptures when they were rightly understood. . . .

The reason produced for condemning the opinion that the earth moves and the sun stands still is that in many places in the Bible one may read that the sun moves and the earth stands still. Since the Bible cannot err, it follows as a necessary consequence that anyone takes an erroneous and heretical position who maintains that the sun is inherently motionless and the earth movable.

With regard to this argument, I think in the first place that it is very pious to say and prudent to affirm that the holy Bible can never speak untruth—whenever its true meaning is understood. But I believe nobody will deny that it is often very abstruse, and may say things which are quite different from what its bare words signify. Hence in expounding the Bible if one were always to confine oneself to the unadorned grammatical meaning, one might fall into error. . . .

. . . Now the Bible, merely to condescend to popular capacity, has not hesitated to obscure some very important pronouncements, attributing to God himself some qualities extremely remote from (and even contrary to) His essence. Who, then, would positively declare that this principle has been set aside, and the

Bible has confined itself rigorously to the bare and restricted sense of its words, when speaking but casually of the earth, of water, of the sun, or of any other created thing? Especially in view of the fact that these things in no way concern the primary purpose of the sacred writings, which is the service of God and the salvation of souls—matters infinitely beyond the comprehension of the common people.

This being granted, I think that in discussions of physical problems we ought to begin not from the authority of scriptural passages, but from sense-experiences and necessary demonstrations. . . . Nothing physical which sense-experience sets before our eyes, or which necessary demonstrations prove to us, ought to be called in question (much less condemned) upon the testimony of biblical passages which may have some different meaning beneath their words. . . .

. . . I do not feel obliged to believe that that same God who has endowed us with senses, reason, and intellect has intended to forgo their use and by some other means to give us knowledge which we can attain by them. He would not require us to deny sense and reason in physical matters which are set before our eyes and minds by direct experience or necessary demonstrations. . . .

It is obvious that such [anti-Copernican] authors, not having penetrated the true senses of Scripture, would impose upon others an obligation to subscribe to conclusions that are repugnant to manifest reason and sense, if they had any authority to do so. God forbid that this sort of abuse should gain countenance and authority, for then in a short time it would be necessary to proscribe [banish] all the contemplative sciences. People who are unable to understand perfectly both the Bible and the sciences far outnumber those who do understand. The former, glancing superficially through the Bible, would arrogate to themselves the authority to decree upon every question of physics on the strength of some word which they have misunderstood, and which was employed by the sacred authors for some

different purpose. And the smaller number of understanding men could not dam up the furious torrent of such people, who would gain the majority of followers simply because it is much more pleasant to gain a reputation for wisdom without effort or study than to consume oneself tirelessly in the most laborious disciplines.

Galileo attacked the unquestioning acceptance of Aristotle's teachings in his *Dialogue Concerning the Two Chief World Systems—Ptolemaic and Copernican.* In the *Dialogue*, Simplicio is an Aristotelian and Salviati is a spokesman for Galileo; Sagredo, a third participant, introduces the problem of relying on the authority of Aristotle.

ARISTOTELIAN AUTHORITY

SAGREDO One day I was at the home of a very famous doctor in Venice, where many persons came on account of their studies, and others occasionally came out of curiosity to see some anatomical dissection performed by a man who was truly no less learned than he was a careful and expert anatomist. It happened on this day that he was investigating the source and origin of the nerves, about which there exists a notorious controversy between the Galenist and Peripatetic doctors.[1] The anatomist showed that the great trunk of nerves, leaving the brain and passing through the nape, extended on down the spine and then branched out through the whole body, and that only a single strand as fine as a thread arrived at the heart. Turning to a gentleman whom we knew to be a Peripa-

---

[1]Galenist doctors followed the medical theories of Galen (A.D. 130–c. 200), a Greek anatomist and physician whose writings had great authority among medieval and early modern physicians. Peripatetic doctors followed Aristotle's teachings.

tetic philosopher, and on whose account he had been exhibiting and demonstrating everything with unusual care, he asked this man whether he was at last satisfied and convinced that the nerves originated in the brain and not in the heart. The philosopher, after considering for awhile, answered: "You have made me see this matter so plainly and palpably that if Aristotle's text were not contrary to it, stating clearly that the nerves originate in the heart, I should be forced to admit it to be true." . . .

SIMPLICIO But if Aristotle is to be abandoned, whom shall we have for a guide in philosophy? Suppose you name some author.

SALVIATI We need guides in forests and in unknown lands, but on plains and in open places only the blind need guides. It is better for such people to stay at home, but anyone with eyes in his head and his wits about him could serve as a guide for them. In saying this, I do not mean that a person should not listen to Aristotle; indeed, I applaud the reading and careful study of his works, and I reproach only those who give themselves up as slaves to him in such a way as to subscribe blindly to everything he says and take it as an inviolable decree without looking for any other reasons. This abuse carries with it another profound disorder, that other people do not try harder to comprehend the strength of his demonstrations. And what is more revolting in a public dispute, when someone is dealing with demonstrable conclusions, than to hear him interrupted by a text (often written to some quite different purpose) thrown into his teeth by an opponent? If, indeed, you wish to continue in this method of studying, then put aside the name of philosophers and call yourselves historians, or memory experts; for it is not proper that those who never philosophize should usurp the honorable title of philosopher.

REVIEW QUESTIONS

1. What methods did Galileo Galilei use in his scientific investigations?
2. What was the implication for modern astronomy of Galileo's observation of the surface of the moon? Of the moons of Jupiter?
3. What was Galileo Galilei's objection to using the Bible as a source of knowledge of physical things? According to him, how did one acquire knowledge of nature?
4. What point was Galileo making in telling the story of the anatomical dissection?
5. What was Galileo's view on the use of Aristotle's works as a basis for scientific endeavors?

2 The Autonomy of the Mind

René Descartes (1596–1650), a French mathematician and philosopher, united the new currents of thought initiated during the Renaissance and the Scientific Revolution. Descartes said that the universe was a mechanical system whose inner laws could be discovered through mathematical thinking and formulated in mathematical terms. With Descartes' assertions on the power of thought, human beings became fully aware of their capacity to comprehend the world through their mental powers. For this reason he is regarded as the founder of modern philosophy.

The deductive approach stressed by Descartes presumes that inherent in the mind are mathematical principles, logical relationships, the principle of cause and effect, concepts of size and motion, and so on—ideas that exist independently of human experience with the external world. Descartes, for example, would say that the properties of a right-angle triangle ($a^2 + b^2 = c^2$) are implicit in human consciousness prior to any experience one might have with a triangle. These innate ideas, said Descartes, permit the mind to give order and coherence to the physical world. Descartes held that the mind arrives at truth when it "intuits" or comprehends the logical necessity of its own ideas and expresses these ideas with clarity, certainty, and precision.

René Descartes
DISCOURSE ON METHOD

In the *Discourse on Method* (1637), Descartes proclaimed the mind's autonomy and importance, and its ability and right to comprehend truth. In this work he offered a method whereby one could achieve certainty and thereby produce a comprehensive understanding of nature and human culture. In the following passage from the *Discourse on Method,* he explained the purpose of his inquiry. How he did so is almost as revolutionary as the ideas he wished to express. He spoke in the first person, autobiographically, as an individual employing his own reason, and he addressed himself to other individuals, inviting them to use their reason. He brought to his narrative an unprecedented confidence in the power of his own judgment and a deep disenchantment with the learning of his times.

PART ONE

From my childhood I lived in a world of books, and since I was taught that by their help I could gain a clear and assured knowledge of everything useful in life, I was eager to learn from them. But as soon as I had finished the course of studies which usually admits one to the ranks of the learned, I changed my opinion completely. For I found myself saddled with so many doubts and errors that I seemed to have gained nothing in trying to educate myself unless it was to discover more and more fully how ignorant I was.

Nevertheless I had been in one of the most celebrated schools in Europe, where I thought there should be wise men if wise men existed anywhere on earth. I had learned there everything that others learned, and, not satisfied with merely the knowledge that was taught, I had perused as many books as I could find which contained more unusual and recondite [obscure] knowledge. . . . And finally, it did not seem to

me that our times were less flourishing and fertile than were any of the earlier periods. All this led me to conclude that I could judge others by myself, and to decide that there was no such wisdom in the world as I had previously hoped to find. . . .

I revered our theology, and hoped as much as anyone else to get to heaven, but having learned on great authority that the road was just as open to the most ignorant as to the most learned, and that the truths of revelation which lead thereto are beyond our understanding, I would not have dared to submit them to the weakness of my reasonings. I thought that to succeed in their examination it would be necessary to have some extraordinary assistance from heaven, and to be more than a man.

I will say nothing of philosophy except that it has been studied for many centuries by the most outstanding minds without having produced anything which is not in dispute and consequently doubtful. I did not have enough presumption to hope to succeed better than the others; and when I noticed how many different opinions learned men may hold on the same subject, despite the fact that no more than one of them can ever be right, I resolved to consider almost as false any opinion which was merely plausible. . . .

This is why I gave up my studies entirely as soon as I reached the age when I was no longer under the control of my teachers. I resolved to seek no other knowledge than that which I might find within myself, or perhaps in the great book of nature. I spent a few years of my adolescence traveling, seeing courts and armies, living with people of diverse types and stations of life, acquiring varied experience, testing myself in the episodes which fortune sent me, and, above all, thinking about the things around me so that I could derive some profit from them. For it seemed to me that I might find much more of the truth in the cogitations [reflections] which each man made on things which were important to him, and where he would be the loser if he judged badly, than in the cogitations of a man of letters in his study, concerned with speculations which produce no effect, and which have no consequences to him. . . .

. . . After spending several years in thus studying the book of nature and acquiring experience, I eventually reached the decision to study my own self, and to employ all my abilities to try to choose the right path. This produced much better results in my case, I think, than would have been produced if I had never left my books and my country. . . .

PART TWO

. . . As far as the opinions which I had been receiving since my birth were concerned, I could not do better than to reject them completely for once in my lifetime, and to resume them afterwards, or perhaps accept better ones in their place, when I had determined how they fitted into a rational scheme. And I firmly believed that by this means I would succeed in conducting my life much better than if I built only upon the old foundations and gave credence to

the principles which I had acquired in my childhood without ever having examined them to see whether they were true or not. . . .

. . . Never has my intention been more than to try to reform my own ideas, and rebuild them on foundations that would be wholly mine. . . . The decision to abandon all one's preconceived notions is not an example for all to follow. . . .

As for myself, I should no doubt have . . . [never attempted it] if I had had but a single teacher or if I had not known the differences which have always existed among the most learned. I had discovered in college that one cannot imagine anything so strange and unbelievable but that it has been upheld by some philosopher; and in my travels I had found that those who held opinions contrary to ours were neither barbarians nor savages, but that many of them were at least as reasonable as ourselves. I had considered how the same man, with the same capacity for reason, becomes different as a result of being brought up among Frenchmen or Germans than he would be if he had been brought up among Chinese or cannibals; and how, in our fashions, the thing which pleased us ten years ago and perhaps will please us again ten years in the future, now seems extravagant and ridiculous; and I felt that in all these ways we are much more greatly influenced by custom and example than by any certain knowledge. Faced with this divergence of opinion, I could not accept the testimony of the majority, for I thought it worthless as a proof of anything somewhat difficult to discover, since it is much more likely that a single man will have discovered it than a whole people. Nor, on the other hand, could I select anyone whose opinions seemed to me to be preferable to those of others, and I was thus constrained to embark on the investigation for myself.

Nevertheless, like a man who walks alone in the darkness, I resolved to go so slowly and circumspectly that if I did not get ahead very rapidly I was at least safe from falling. Also, I did not want to reject all the opinions which had slipped irrationally into my consciousness since birth, until I had first spent enough time planning how to accomplish the task which I was then undertaking, and seeking the true method of obtaining knowledge of everything which my mind was capable of understanding. . . .

Descartes' method consists of four principles that place the capacity to arrive at truth entirely within the province of the human mind. First one finds a self-evident principle, such as a geometric axiom. From this general principle, other truths are deduced through logical reasoning. This is accomplished by breaking a problem down into its elementary components and then, step by step, moving toward more complex knowledge.

. . . I thought that some other method [besides that of logic, algebra, and geometry] must be found to combine the advantages of these three and to escape their faults. Finally, just as the multitude of laws frequently furnishes an excuse for vice, and a state is much better governed with a few laws which are strictly adhered to, so I thought that instead of the great number of precepts of which logic is composed, I would have enough with the four following ones, provided that I made a firm and unalterable resolution not to violate them even in a single instance.

The first rule was never to accept anything as true unless I recognized it to be evidently such: that is, carefully to avoid precipitation and prejudgment, and to include nothing in my conclusions unless it presented itself so clearly and distinctly to my mind that there was no occasion to doubt it.

The second was to divide each of the difficulties which I encountered into as many parts as possible, and as might be required for an easier solution.

The third was to think in an orderly fashion, beginning with the things which were simplest and easiest to understand, and gradually and by degrees reaching toward more complex knowledge, even treating as though ordered materials which were not necessarily so.

The last was always to make enumerations so complete, and reviews so general, that I would be certain that nothing was omitted. . . .

What pleased me most about this method was that it enabled me to reason in all things, if not perfectly, at least as well as was in my power. In addition, I felt that in practicing it my mind was gradually becoming accustomed to conceive its objects more clearly and distinctly. . . .

Descartes was searching for an incontrovertible truth that could serve as the first principle of philosophy. His arrival at the famous dictum "I think, therefore I am" marks the beginning of modern philosophy.

PART FOUR

. . . As I desired to devote myself wholly to the search for truth, I thought that I should . . . reject as absolutely false anything of which I could have the least doubt, in order to see whether anything would be left after this procedure which could be called wholly certain. Thus, as our senses deceive us at times, I was ready to suppose that nothing was at all the way our senses represented them to be. As there are men who make mistakes in reasoning even on the simplest topics in geometry, I judged that I was as liable to error as any other, and rejected as false all the reasoning which I had previously accepted as valid demonstration. Finally, as the same precepts which we have when awake may come to us when asleep without their being true, I decided to suppose that nothing that had ever entered my mind was more real than the illusions of my dreams. But I soon noticed that while I thus wished to think everything false, it was necessarily true that I who thought so was something. Since this truth, *I think, therefore I am,* was so firm and assured that all the most extravagant suppositions of the sceptics[1] were unable to shake it, I judged that I could safely accept it as the first principle of the philosophy I was seeking.

---

[1]The skeptics belonged to the ancient Greek philosophic school that held true knowledge to be beyond human grasp and treated all knowledge as uncertain.

1. Why was René Descartes critical of the learning of his day?
2. What are the implications of Descartes' famous words: "I think, therefore I am"?

---

3 The Mechanical Universe

By demonstrating that all bodies in the universe—earthly objects as well as moons, planets, and stars—obey the same laws of motion and gravitation, Sir Isaac Newton (1646–1723) completed the destruction of the medieval view of the universe. The idea that the same laws governed the movement of earthly and heavenly bodies was completely foreign to medieval thinkers, who drew a sharp division between a higher celestial world and a lower terrestrial one. In the *Principia Mathematica* (1687), Newton showed that the same forces that hold celestial bodies in their orbits around the sun make apples fall to the ground. For Newton, the universe was like a giant clock, all of whose parts obeyed strict mechanical principles and worked together in perfect precision. To Newton's contemporaries, it seemed as if mystery had been banished from the universe.

Isaac Newton
PRINCIPIA MATHEMATICA

In the first of the following passages from *Principia Mathematica,* Newton stated the principle of universal law and lauded the experimental method as the means of acquiring knowledge.

RULES OF REASONING
IN PHILOSOPHY

Rule I.   We are to admit no more causes of natural things than such as are both true and sufficient to explain their appearances.

To this purpose the philosophers say that Nature does nothing in vain, and more is in vain when less will serve; for Nature is pleased with simplicity, and affects not the pomp of superfluous causes.

Rule II.   Therefore to the same natural effects we must, as far as possible, assign the same causes.

As to respiration in a man and in a beast; the descent of stones [meteorites] in *Europe* and in *America;* the light of our culinary fire and of the sun; the reflection of light in the earth, and in the planets.

Rule III.   The qualities of bodies, which admit neither [intensification] nor remission of degrees, and which are found to belong to all bodies within the reach of our experiments, are to be esteemed the universal qualities of all bodies whatsoever.

For since the qualities of bodies are only known to us by experiments, we are to hold for universal all such as universally agree with experiments; and such as are not liable to diminution can never be quite taken away. We are certainly not to relinquish the evidence of experiments for the sake of dreams and vain fictions of our own devising; nor are we to recede from the analogy of Nature, which [is] . . . simple, and always consonant to itself. We no other way know the extension of bodies than by our senses, nor do these reach it in all bodies; but because we perceive extension in all that are sensible, therefore, we ascribe it universally to all others also. That abundance of bodies are hard, we learn by experience; and because the hardness of the whole arises from the hardness of the parts, we, therefore, justly infer the hardness of the undivided particles not only of the bodies we feel but of all others. That all bodies are impenetrable, we gather not from reason, but from sensation. The bodies which we handle we find impenetrable, and thence, conclude impenetrability to be an universal property of all bodies whatsoever. That all bodies are moveable, and endowed with certain powers (which we call . . . {*inertia*}) of persevering in their motion, or in their rest, we only infer from the like properties observed in the bodies which we have seen. The extension, hardness, impenetrability, mobility, . . . of the whole, result from the extension, hardness, impenetrability, mobility, . . . of the parts; and thence we conclude the least particles of all bodies to be also all extended, and hard and impenetrable, and moveable. . . . And this is the foundation of all philosophy. . . .

Lastly, if it universally appears, by experiments and astronomical observations, that all bodies about the earth gravitate towards the earth, and that in proportion to the quantity of matter which they severally contain; that the moon likewise, according to the quantity of its matter, gravitates towards the earth; that, on the other hand, our sea gravitates towards the moon; and all the planets mutually one towards another; and the comets in like manner towards the sun; we must, in consequence of this rule, universally allow that all bodies whatsoever are endowed with a principle of mutual gravitation. . . .

Rule IV.   In experimental philosophy we are to look upon propositions collected by general induction from phenomena as accurately or very nearly true, notwithstanding any contrary hypotheses that may be imagined, till such time as other phenomena occur, by which they may either be made more accurate, or liable to exceptions.

This rule we must follow, that the argument of induction may not be evaded by hypotheses.

Newton describes further his concepts of gravity and scientific methodology.

GRAVITY

Hitherto, we have explained the phenomena of the heavens and of our sea by the power of gravity, but have not yet assigned the cause of this power. This is certain, that it must proceed from a cause that penetrates to the very centres of the sun and planets, without suffering the least diminution of its force; that operates not according to the quantity of the surfaces of the particles upon which it acts (as mechanical causes used to do) but according to the quantity of the solid matter which they contain, and propagates its virtue on all sides to immense distances, decreasing always in the duplicate portion of the distances. . . .

Hitherto I have not been able to discover the cause of those properties of gravity from the phenomena, and I frame no hypothesis; for whatever is not deduced from the phenomena is to be called an hypothesis; and hypotheses, whether metaphysical or physical, whether of occult qualities or mechanical, have no place in experimental philosophy. In this philosophy particular propositions are inferred from the phenomena, and afterward rendered general by induction. Thus it was the impenetrability, the mobility, and the impulsive forces of bodies, and the laws of motion and of gravitation were discovered. And to us it is enough that gravity does really exist, and acts according to the laws which we have explained, and abundantly serves to account for all the motions of the celestial bodies, and of our sea.

A devout Anglican, Newton believed that God had created this superbly organized universe. The following selection is also from the *Principia*.

GOD AND THE UNIVERSE

This most beautiful system of the sun, planets, and comets could only proceed from the counsel and dominion of an intelligent and powerful Being. And if the fixed stars are the centers of other like systems, these, being formed by the like wise counsel, must be all subject to the dominion of One, especially since the light of the fixed stars is of the same nature with the light of the sun and from every system light passes into all the other systems; and lest the systems of the fixed stars should, by their gravity, fall on each other mutually, he hath placed those systems at immense distances from one another.

This Being governs all things not as the soul of the world, but as Lord over all; and on account of his dominion he is wont to be called "Lord God" . . . or "Universal Ruler." . . . It is the dominion of a spiritual being which constitutes a God. . . . And from his true dominion it

follows that the true God is a living, intelligent and powerful Being. . . . [H]e governs all things, and knows all things that are or can be done. . . . He endures for ever, and is every where present; and by existing always and every where, he constitutes duration and space. . . . In him are all things contained and moved; yet neither affects the other: God suffers nothing from the motion of bodies; bodies find no resistance from the omnipresence of God. . . . As a blind man has no idea of colors so we have no idea of the manner by which the all-wise God preserves and understands all things. He is utterly void of all body and bodily figure, and can therefore neither be seen, nor heard, nor touched; nor ought to be worshipped under the representation of any corporeal thing. We have ideas of his attributes, but what the real substance of any thing is we know not. . . . Much less, then, have we any idea of the substance of God. We know him only by his most wise and excellent contrivances of things. . . . [W]e reverence and adore him as his servants; and a god without dominion, providence, and final causes, is nothing else but Fate and Nature. Blind metaphysical necessity, which is certainly the same always and everywhere, could produce no variety of things. All that diversity of natural things which we find suited to different times and places could arise from nothing but the ideas and will of a Being necessarily existing. . . . And thus much concerning God; to discourse of whom from the appearances of things does certainly belong to Natural Philosophy.

REVIEW QUESTIONS

1. What did Isaac Newton mean by universal law? What examples of universal law did he provide?
2. What method for investigating nature did Newton advocate?
3. Summarize Newton's arguments for God's existence.
4. For Newton, what is God's relationship to the universe?

4   Political Liberty

John Locke (1632–1704), a British statesman, philosopher, and political theorist, was a principal source of the Enlightenment. Eighteenth-century thinkers were particularly influenced by Locke's advocacy of religious toleration, his reliance on experience as the source of knowledge, and his concern for liberty. In his first *Letter Concerning Toleration* (1689), Locke declared that Christians who persecute others in the name of religion vitiate Christ's teachings. Locke's political philosophy as formulated in the *Two Treatises on Government* (1690) was a rational and secular attempt to understand and improve the human condition. The Lockean spirit pervades the American Declaration of Independence, the Constitution, and the Bill of Rights and is the basis of the liberal tradition that aims to protect individual liberty from despotic state authority.

Viewing human beings as brutish and selfish, Thomas Hobbes (see page 16) had prescribed a state with unlimited power; only in this way, he said, could people be protected from each other and civilized life preserved. Locke, regarding people as essentially good and humane, developed a conception of the state differing fundamentally from Hobbes's. Locke held that human beings are born with natural rights of life, liberty, and property; they establish the state to protect these rights. Consequently, neither executive nor legislature, neither king nor assembly has the authority to deprive individuals of their natural rights. Whereas Hobbes justified absolute monarchy, Locke explicitly endorsed constitutional government in which the power to govern derives from the consent of the governed and the state's authority is limited by agreement.

John Locke
SECOND TREATISE ON GOVERNMENT

Locke said that originally, in establishing a government, human beings had never agreed to surrender their natural rights to any state authority. The state's founders intended the new polity to preserve these natural rights and to implement the people's will. Therefore, as the following passage from Locke's *Second Treatise on Government* illustrates, the power exercised by magistrates cannot be absolute or arbitrary.

. . . *Political power* is that power, which every man having in the state of nature, has given up into the hands of the society, and therein to the governors, whom the society hath set over itself, with this express or tacit trust, that it shall be employed for their good, and the preservation of their property: now this *power*, which every man has *in the state of nature*, and which he parts with to the society in all such cases where the society can secure him, is to use such means, for the preserving of his own property, as he thinks good, and nature allows him; and to punish the breach of the law of nature in others, so as (according to the best of his reason) may most conduce to the preservation of himself, and the rest of mankind. So that the *end and measure of this power,* when in every man's hands in the state of nature, being the preservation of all of his society, that is, all mankind in general, it can have no other *end or measure,* when in the hands of the magistrate, but to preserve the members of that society in their lives, liberties, and possessions; and so cannot be an absolute, arbitrary power over their lives and fortunes, which are as much as possible to be preserved; but a *power to make laws,* and annex such *penalties* to them, as may tend to the preservation of the whole, by cutting off those parts, and those only, which are so corrupt, that they threaten the sound and healthy, without which no severity is lawful. And this *power has its original only from compact,* and agreement, and the mutual consent of those who make up the community. . . .

These are the *bounds,* which the trust, that is put in them by the society, and the law of God and nature, have *set to the legislative* power of every common-wealth, in all forms of government.

First, They are to govern by *promulgated established laws,* not to be varied in particular cases, but to have one rule for rich and poor, for the favourite at court, and the country man at plough.

Secondly, These *laws* also ought to be designed *for* no other end ultimately, but *the good of the people.*

Thirdly, They must *not raise taxes* on the *property of the people, without the consent of the people,* given by themselves, or their deputies. And this properly concerns only such governments, where the *legislative* is always in being, or at least where the people have not reserved any part of the legislative to deputies, to be from time to time chosen by themselves.

Fourthly, The *legislative* neither must *nor can transfer the power of making laws* to any body else, or place it any where, but where the people have. . . .

If government fails to fulfill the end for which it was established—the preservation of the individual's right to life, liberty, and property—the people have a right to dissolve that government.

. . . The *legislative acts against the trust* reposed in them, when they endeavour to invade the property of the subject, and to make themselves, or any part of the community, masters, or arbitrary disposers of the lives, liberties, or fortunes of the people.

The reason why men enter into society, is the preservation of their property; and the end why they chuse and authorize a legislative, is, that there may be laws made, and rules set, as guards and fences to the properties of all the members of the society, to limit the power, and moderate the dominion of every part and member of the society: for since it can never be supposed to be the will of the society, that the legislative should have a power to destroy that which every one designs to secure, by entering into society, and for which the people submitted themselves to legislators of their own making; whenever the *legislators endeavour to take away, and destroy the property of the people,* or to reduce them to slavery under arbitrary power, they put themselves into a state of war with the people, who are thereupon absolved from any farther obedience, and are left to the common refuge, which God hath provided for all men, against force and violence. Whensoever therefore the *legislative* shall transgress this fundamental rule of society; and either by ambition, fear, folly or corruption, *endeavour to grasp* themselves, *or put into the hands of any other, an absolute power* over the lives, liberties, and estates of the people; by this breach of trust they *forfeit the power* the people had put into their hands for quite contrary ends, and it devolves to the people, who have a right to resume their original liberty, and, by the establishment of a new legislative, (such as they shall think fit) provide for their own safety and security, which is the end for which they are in society. What I have said here, concerning the legislative in general, holds true also concerning the supreme executor, who having a double trust put in him, both to have a part in the legislative, and the supreme execution of the law, acts against both, when he goes about to set up his own arbitrary will as the law of the society. He *acts* also *contrary to his trust,* when he either employs the force, treasure, and offices of the society, to corrupt the *representatives,* and gain them to his purposes; or openly pre-engages the *electors,* and prescribes to their choice, such, whom he has, by sollicitations, threats, promises, or otherwise, won to his designs; and employs them to bring in such, who have promised beforehand what to vote, and what to enact. . . .

Locke responds to the charge that his theory will produce "frequent rebellion." Indeed, says Locke, the true rebels are the magistrates who, acting contrary to the trust granted them, violate the people's rights.

. . . Such *revolutions happen* not upon every little mismanagement in public affairs. *Great mistakes* in the ruling part, many wrong and inconvenient laws, and all the *slips* of human frailty, will be *borne by the people* without mutiny or murmur. But if a long train of abuses, prevarications [lies] and artifices [tricks], all tending the same way, make the design visible to the people, and they cannot but feel what they lie under, and see whither they are going; it is not to be wondered at, that they should then rouze themselves, and endeavour to put the rule into such hands which may secure to them the ends for which government was at first erected. . . .

. . . I answer, that *this doctrine* of a power in the people of providing for their safety a-new, by a new legislative, when their legislators have acted contrary to their trust, by invading their property, is the *best defence against rebellion,* and the probablest means to hinder it: for *rebellion* being an opposition, not to persons, but authority, which is founded only in the constitutions and laws of the government; those, whoever they be, who by force break through, and by force justify their violation of them, are truly and properly *rebels:* for when men, by entering into society and civil government, have excluded force, and introduced laws for the preservation of property, peace, and unity amongst themselves, those who set up force again in opposition to the laws, do [rebel], that is, bring back again the state of war, and are properly rebels: which they who are in power, (by the pretence they have to authority, the temptation of force they have in their hands, and the flattery of those about them) being likeliest to do; the properest way to prevent the evil, is to shew them the danger and injustice of it, who are under the greatest temptation to run into it.

The end of government is the good of mankind; and which is *best for mankind,* that the people should always be exposed to the boundless will of tyranny, or that the rulers should be sometimes liable to be opposed, when they grow exorbitant in the use of their power, and employ it for the destruction, and not the preservation of the properties of their people?

Thomas Jefferson
DECLARATION OF INDEPENDENCE

Written in 1776 by Thomas Jefferson (1743–1826) to justify the American colonists' break with Britain, the Declaration of Independence enumerated principles quite familiar to English statesmen and intellectuals. The preamble to the Declaration, excerpted below, articulated clearly Locke's philosophy of natural rights. Locke had viewed life, liberty, and property as the individual's essential natural rights; Jefferson substituted the "pursuit of happiness" for property.

A DECLARATION BY THE REPRESENTATIVES OF THE UNITED STATES OF AMERICA, IN GENERAL CONGRESS ASSEMBLED.

When in the Course of human Events, it becomes necessary for one People to dissolve the Political Bands which have connected them with another, and to assume among the Powers of the Earth, the separate and equal Station to which the Laws of Nature and of Nature's God entitle them, a decent Respect to the Opinions of Mankind requires that they should declare the causes which impel them to the Separation.

We hold these Truths to be self-evident, that all Men are created equal, that they are endowed by their Creator with certain unalienable Rights, that among these are Life, Liberty, and the Pursuit of Happiness—That to secure these Rights, Governments are instituted among Men, deriving their just Powers from the Consent of the Governed, That whenever any Form of Government becomes destructive of these Ends, it is the Right of the People to alter or to abolish it, and to institute new Gov-ernment, laying its Foundation on such Principles, and organizing its Powers in such Form, as to them shall seem most likely to effect their Safety and Happiness. Prudence, indeed, will dictate that Governments long established should not be changed for light and transient Causes; and accordingly all Experience hath shewn, that Mankind are more disposed to suffer, while Evils are sufferable, than to right themselves by abolishing the Forms to which they are accustomed. But when a long Train of Abuses and Usurpations, pursuing invariably the same Object, evinces a Design to reduce them under absolute Despotism, it is their right, it is their duty, to throw off such Government, and to provide new Guards for their future Security. Such has been the patient Sufferance of these Colonies; and such is now the Necessity which constrains them to alter their former Systems of Government. The History of the present King of Great-Britain is a History of repeated Injuries and Usurpations, all having in direct Object the Establishment of an absolute Tyranny over these States. . . .

REVIEW QUESTIONS

1. What is Locke's view of human nature, the origin and purpose of political authority, and the right of rebellion?
2. Compare Locke's theory of natural rights with the principles stated in the American Declaration of Independence. Compare with that of Thomas Hobbes (page 16).

---

5 Attack on Religion

Christianity came under severe attack during the eighteenth century. The philosophes rejected Christian doctrines that seemed contrary to reason. Deism, the dominant religious outlook of the philosophes, taught that religion should accord with reason and natural law. To deists, it seemed reasonable to believe in God, for this superbly constructed universe required a creator in the same manner that a watch required a watchmaker. But, said the deists, after God had constructed the universe, he did not interfere in its operations; the universe was governed by mechanical laws. Deists denied that the Bible was God's work, rejected clerical authority, and dismissed miracles—like Jesus walking on water—as incompatible with natural law. To them, Jesus was not divine but an inspired teacher of morality. Many deists still considered themselves Christians; the clergy, however, viewed the deists' religious views with horror.

Voltaire
A PLEA FOR TOLERANCE AND REASON

François Marie Arouet (1694–1778), known to the world as Voltaire, was the recognized leader of the French Enlightenment. Few of the philosophes had a better mind, and none had a sharper wit. A relentless critic of the Old Regime (the social structure in prerevolutionary France), Voltaire attacked superstition, religious fanaticism and persecution, censorship, and other abuses of eighteenth-century French society. Spending more than two years in Great Britain, Voltaire acquired a great admiration for English liberty, toleration, commerce, and science. In *Letters Concerning the English Nation* (1733), he drew unfavorable comparisons between a progressive Britain and a reactionary France.

Voltaire's angriest words were directed against established Christianity, to which he attributed many of the ills of modern society. Voltaire regarded Christianity as "the Christ-worshiping superstition" that someday would be destroyed "by the weapons of reason." He rejected revelation and the church hierarchy and was repulsed by Christian intolerance, but he accepted Christian morality and believed in God as the prime mover who set the universe in motion.

The following passages compiled from Voltaire's works—grouped according to topic—provide insight into the outlook of the philosophes. The excerpts come from sources that include his *Treatise on Tolerance* (1763), *The Philosophical Dictionary* (1764), and *Commentary on the Book of Crime and Punishments* (1766).

TOLERANCE

It does not require any great art or studied elocution to prove that Christians ought to tolerate one another. I will go even further and say that we ought to look upon all men as our brothers. What! call a Turk, a Jew, and a Siamese, my brother? Yes, of course; for are we not all children of the same father, and the creatures of the same God?

What is tolerance? . . . We are all full of weakness and errors; let us mutually pardon our follies. This is the last law of nature. . . .

It is clear that every private individual who persecutes a man, his brother, because he is not of the same opinion, is a monster. . . .

Of all religions, the Christian ought doubtless to inspire the most tolerance, although hitherto the Christians have been the most intolerant of all men.

. . . Tolerance has never brought civil war; intolerance has covered the earth with carnage. . . .

What! Is each citizen to be permitted to believe and to think that which his reason rightly or wrongly dictates? He should indeed, provided that he does not disturb the public order; for it is not contingent on man to believe or not to believe; but it is contingent on him to respect the [practices] of his country; and if you say that it is a crime not to believe in the dominant religion, you accuse then yourself the first Christians, your ancestors, and you justify those whom you accuse of having martyred them.

You reply that there is a great difference, that all religions are the work of men, and that the Apostolic Roman Catholic Church is alone the work of God. But in good faith, ought our religion because it is divine reign through hate, violence, exiles, usurpation of property, prisons, tortures, murders, and thanksgivings to God for these murders? The more the Christian religion is divine, the less it pertains to man to require it; if God made it, God will sustain it without you. You know that intolerance produces only hypocrites or rebels; what distressing alternatives! In short, do you want to sustain through executioners the religion of a God whom executioners have put to death and who taught only gentleness and patience?

———

I shall never cease, my dear sir, to preach tolerance from the housetops, despite the complaints of your priests and the outcries of ours, until persecution is no more. The progress of reason is slow, the roots of prejudice lie deep. Doubtless, I shall never see the fruits of my efforts, but they are seeds which may one day germinate.

DOGMA

. . . Is Jesus the Word? If He be the Word, did He emanate from God in time or before time? If He emanated from God, is He co-eternal and consubstantial with Him, or is He of a similar substance? Is He distinct from Him, or is He not? Is He made or begotten? Can He beget in

His turn? Has He paternity? or productive virtue without paternity? Is the Holy Ghost made? or begotten? or produced? or proceeding from the Father? or proceeding from the Son? or proceeding from both? Can He beget? can He produce? is His hypostasis consubstantial with the hypostasis of the Father and the Son? and how is it that, having the same nature—the same essence as the Father and the Son, He cannot do the same things done by these persons who are Himself?

Assuredly, I understand nothing of this; no one has ever understood any of it, and that is why we have slaughtered one another.

The Christians tricked, cavilled [faulted frivolously], hated, and excommunicated one another, for some of these dogmas inaccessible to human intellect.

FANATICISM

Fanaticism is to superstition what delirium is to fever, what rage is to anger. He who has ecstasies and visions, who takes dreams for realities, and his own imaginations for prophecies is an enthusiast; he who reinforces his madness by murder is a fanatic. . . .

The most detestable example of fanaticism is that exhibited on the night of St. Bartholomew,[1] when the people of Paris rushed from house to house to stab, slaughter, throw out of the window, and tear in pieces their fellow citizens who did not go to mass.

There are some cold-blooded fanatics; such as those judges who sentence men to death for no other crime than that of thinking differently from themselves. . . .

Once fanaticism has infected a brain, the disease is almost incurable. I have seen convulsionaries who, while speaking of the miracles of Saint Paris [a fourth-century Italian bishop], gradually grew heated in spite of themselves.

———

[1]"St. Bartholomew" refers to the day of August 24, 1572, when the populace of Paris, instigated by King Charles IX at his mother's urging, began a week-long slaughter of Protestants.

Their eyes became inflamed, their limbs shook, fury disfigured their face, and they would have killed anyone who contradicted them.

There is no other remedy for this epidemic malady than that philosophical spirit which, extending itself from one to another, at length softens the manners of men and prevents the access of the disease. For when the disorder has made any progress, we should, without loss of time, flee from it, and wait till the air has become purified.

PERSECUTION

What is a persecutor? He whose wounded pride and furious fanaticism arouse princes and magistrates against innocent men, whose only crime is that of being of a different opinion. "Impudent man! you have worshipped God; you have preached and practiced virtue; you have served man; you have protected the orphan, have helped the poor; you have changed deserts, in which slaves dragged on a miserable existence, into fertile lands peopled by happy families; but I have discovered that you despise me, and have never read my controversial work. You know that I am a rogue; that I have forged G[od]'s signature, that I have stolen. You might tell these things; I must anticipate you. I will, therefore, go to the confessor [spiritual counselor] of the prime minister, or the magistrate; I will show them, with outstretched neck and twisted mouth, that you hold an erroneous opinion in relation to the cells in which the Septuagint was studied; that you have even spoken disrespectfully ten years ago of Tobit's dog,[2] which you asserted to have been a spaniel, while I proved that it was a greyhound. I will denounce you as the enemy of God and man!" Such is the language of the persecutor; and if precisely these words do not

issue from his lips, they are engraven on his heart with the pointed steel of fanaticism steeped in the bitterness of envy. . . .

O God of mercy! If any man can resemble that evil being who is described as ceaselessly employed in the destruction of your works, is it not the persecutor?

SUPERSTITION

In 1749 a woman was burned in the Bishopric of Würzburg [a city in central Germany], convicted of being a witch. This is an extraordinary phenomenon in the age in which we live. Is it possible that people who boast of their reformation and of trampling superstition under foot, who indeed supposed that they had reached the perfection of reason, could nevertheless believe in witchcraft, and this more than a hundred years after the so-called reformation of their reason?

In 1652 a peasant woman named Michelle Chaudron, living in the little territory of Geneva [a major city in Switzerland], met the devil going out of the city. The devil gave her a kiss, received her homage, and imprinted on her upper lip and right breast the mark that he customarily bestows on all whom he recognizes as his favorites. This seal of the devil is a little mark which makes the skin insensitive, as all the demonographical jurists of those times affirm.

The devil ordered Michelle Chaudron to bewitch two girls. She obeyed her master punctually. The girls' parents accused her of witchcraft before the law. The girls were questioned and confronted with the accused. They declared that they felt a continual pricking in certain parts of their bodies and that they were possessed. Doctors were called, or at least, those who passed for doctors at that time. They examined the girls. They looked for the devil's seal on Michelle's body—what the statement of the case called *satanic marks*. Into them they drove a long needle, already a painful torture. Blood flowed out, and Michelle made it known, by her cries, that satanic marks certainly do not make one insensitive. The judges, seeing no definite proof that

---

[2]The Septuagint, the version of the Hebrew Scriptures used by Saint Paul and other early Christians, was a Greek translation done by Hellenized Jews in Alexandria sometime in the late third or the second century B.C. Tobit's dog appears in the Book of Tobit, a Hebrew book contained in the Catholic version of the Bible.

Michelle Chaudron was a witch, proceeded to torture her, a method that infallibly produces the necessary proofs: this wretched woman, yielding to the violence of torture, at last confessed every thing they desired.

The doctors again looked for the satanic mark. They found a little black spot on one of her thighs. They drove in the needle. The torment of the torture had been so horrible that the poor creature hardly felt the needle; thus the crime was established. But as customs were becoming somewhat mild at that time, she was burned only after being hanged and strangled.

In those days every tribunal of Christian Europe resounded with similar arrests. The [twigs] were lit everywhere for witches, as for heretics. People reproached the Turks most for having neither witches nor demons among them. This absence of demons was considered an infallible proof of the falseness of a religion.

A zealous friend of public welfare, of humanity, of true religion, has stated in one of his writings on behalf of innocence, that Christian tribunals have condemned to death over a hundred thousand accused witches. If to these judicial murders are added the infinitely superior number of massacred heretics, that part of the world will seem to be nothing but a vast scaffold covered with torturers and victims, surrounded by judges, guards and spectators.

Thomas Paine
THE AGE OF REASON

Exemplifying the deist outlook was Thomas Paine (1737–1809), an Englishman who moved to America in 1774. Paine's *Common Sense* (1776) was an eloquent appeal for American independence. Paine is also famous for *The Rights of Man* (1791–1792), in which he defended the French Revolution. In *The Age of Reason* (1794–1796), he denounced Christian mysteries, miracles, and prophecies as superstition and called for a natural religion that accorded with reason and science.

I believe in one God, and no more; and I hope for happiness beyond this life.

I believe in the equality of man; and I believe that religious duties consist in doing justice, loving mercy, and endeavoring to make our fellow-creatures happy.

But, lest it should be supposed that I believe many other things in addition to these, I shall, in the progress of this work, declare the things I do not believe, and my reasons for not believing them.

I do not believe in the creed professed by the Jewish church, by the Roman church, by the Greek church, by the Turkish church, by the Protestant church, nor by any church that I know of. My own mind is my own church. . . .

When Moses told the children of Israel that he received the two tablets of the [Ten] commandments from the hands of God, they were not obliged to believe him, because they had no other authority for it than his telling them so; and I have no other authority for it than some historian telling me so. The commandments carry no internal evidence of divinity with them; they contain some good moral precepts, such as any man qualified to be a lawgiver, or a legislator, could produce himself, without having recourse to supernatural intervention. . . .

When also I am told that a woman called the Virgin Mary, said, or gave out, that she was with child without any cohabitation with a man, and that her betrothed husband, Joseph, said that an angel told him so, I have a right to believe them or not; such a circumstance required a much stronger evidence than their bare word for it; but we have not even this—for neither Joseph nor Mary wrote any such matter themselves; it is only reported by others that *they said so*—it is hearsay upon hearsay, and I do not choose to rest my belief upon such evidence.

It is, however, not difficult to account for the credit that was given to the story of Jesus Christ being the son of God. He was born when the heathen mythology had still some fashion and repute in the world, and that mythology had prepared the people for the belief of such a story. Almost all the extraordinary men that lived under the heathen mythology were reputed to be the sons of some of their gods. It was not a new thing, at that time, to believe a man to have been celestially begotten; the intercourse of gods with women was then a matter of familiar opinion. Their Jupiter [chief Roman god], according to their accounts, had cohabited with hundreds: the story, therefore, had nothing in it either new, wonderful, or obscene; it was conformable to the opinions that then prevailed among the people called Gentiles, or Mythologists, and it was those people only that believed it. The Jews who had kept strictly to the belief of one God, and no more, and who had always rejected the heathen mythology, never credited the story. . . .

Nothing that is here said can apply, even with the most distant disrespect, to the real character of Jesus Christ. He was a virtuous and an amiable man. The morality that he preached and practised was of the most benevolent kind; and though similar systems of morality had been preached by Confucius [Chinese philosopher], and by some of the Greek philosophers, many years before; by the Quakers [members of the Society of Friends] since; and by many good men in all ages, it has not been exceeded by any. . . .

. . . The resurrection and ascension [of Jesus Christ], supposing them to have taken place, admitted of public and ocular demonstration, like that of the ascension of a balloon, or the sun at noon-day, to all Jerusalem at least. A thing which everybody is required to believe, requires that the proof and evidence of it should be equal to all, and universal; and as the public visibility of this last related act was the only evidence that could give sanction to the former part, the whole of it falls to the ground, because that evidence never was given. Instead of this, a small number of persons, not more than eight or nine, are introduced as proxies for the whole world, to say they saw it, and all the rest of the world are called upon to believe it. But it appears that Thomas [one of Jesus' disciples] did not believe the resurrection, and, as they say, would not believe without having ocular and manual demonstration himself. *So neither will I,* and the reason is equally as good for me, and for every other person, as for Thomas.

It is in vain to attempt to palliate [conceal] or disguise this matter. The story, so far as relates to the supernatural part, has every mark of fraud and imposition stamped upon the face of it. Who were the authors of it is as impossible for us now to know, as it is for us to be assured that the books in which the account is related were written by the persons whose names they bear; the best surviving evidence we now have respecting this affair is the Jews. They are regularly descended from the people who lived in the times this resurrection and ascension is said to have happened, and they say, *it is not true.*

REVIEW QUESTIONS

1. What arguments did Voltaire offer in favor of religious toleration?
2. Why did Voltaire ridicule Christian theological disputation?
3. What did Voltaire mean by *fanaticism*? What examples of fanaticism did he provide? How was it to be cured?
4. What Christian beliefs did Thomas Paine reject? Why?

6 Compendium of Knowledge

A 38-volume *Encyclopedia,* whose 150 or more contributors included leading Enlightenment thinkers, was undertaken in Paris during the 1740s as a monumental effort to bring together all human knowledge and to propagate Enlightenment ideas. The *Encyclopedia*'s numerous articles on science and technology and its limited coverage of theological questions attest to the new interests of eighteenth-century intellectuals. Serving as principal editor, Denis Diderot (1713–1784) steered the project through difficult periods, including the suspension of publication by French authorities. After the first two volumes were published, the authorities denounced the work for containing "maxims that would tend to destroy royal authority, foment a spirit of independence and revolt, . . . and lay the foundations for the corruption of morals and religion." In 1759, Pope Clement XIII condemned the *Encyclopedia* for having "scandalous doctrines [and] inducing scorn for religion." It required careful diplomacy and clever ruses to finish the project and still incorporate ideas considered dangerous by religious and governmental authorities. With the project's completion in 1772, Diderot and Enlightenment opinion triumphed over clerical censors and powerful elements at the French court.

Denis Diderot
ENCYCLOPEDIA

The *Encyclopedia* was a monument to the Enlightenment, as Diderot himself recognized. "This work will surely produce in time a revolution in the minds of man, and I hope that tyrants, oppressors, fanatics, and the intolerant will not gain thereby. We shall have served humanity." Some articles from the *Encyclopedia* follow.

Encyclopedia . . . In truth, the aim of an *encyclopedia* is to collect all the knowledge scattered over the face of the earth, to present its general outlines and structure to the men with whom we live, and to transmit this to those who will come after us, so that the work of past centuries may be useful to the following centuries, that our children, by becoming more educated, may at the same time become more virtuous and happier, and that we may not die without having deserved well of the human race. . . .

. . . We have seen that our *Encyclopedia* could only have been the endeavor of a philosophical century. . . .

I have said that it could only belong to a philosophical age to attempt an *encyclopedia;* and I have said this because such a work constantly demands more intellectual daring than is commonly found in [less courageous periods]. All things must be examined, debated, investigated without exception and without regard for anyone's feelings. . . . We must ride roughshod over all these ancient puerilities [foolishnesses], overturn the barriers that reason never erected, give back to the arts and sciences the liberty that is so precious to them. . . . We have for quite some time needed a reasoning age when men would no longer seek the rules in classical authors but in nature. . . .

Fanaticism . . . is blind and passionate zeal born of superstitious opinions, causing people to commit ridiculous, unjust, and cruel actions, not only without any shame or remorse, but even with a kind of joy and comfort. *Fanaticism,* therefore, is only superstition put into practice. . . .

Fanaticism has done much more harm to the world than impiety. What do impious people claim? To free themselves of a yoke, while *fanatics* want to extend their chains over all the earth. Infernal zealomania! . . .

Government . . . The good of the people must be the great purpose of the *government.* The governors are appointed to fulfill it; and the civil constitution that invests them with this power is bound therein by the laws of nature and by the law of reason, which has determined that purpose in any form of *government* as the cause of its welfare. The greatest good of the people is its liberty. Liberty is to the body of the state what health is to each individual; without health man cannot enjoy pleasure; without liberty the state of welfare is excluded from nations. A patriotic governor will therefore see that the right to defend and to maintain liberty is the most sacred of his duties. . . .

If it happens that those who hold the reins of *government* find some resistance when they use their power for the destruction and not the conservation of things that rightfully belong to the people, they must blame themselves, because the public good and the advantage of society are the purposes of establishing a *government.* Hence it necessarily follows that power cannot be arbitrary and that it must be exercised according to the established laws so that the people may know its duty and be secure within the shelter of laws, and so that governors at the same time should be held within just limits and not be tempted to employ the power they have in hand to do harmful things to the body politic. . . .

History . . . *On the usefullness of history.* The advantage consists of the comparison that a statesman or a citizen can make of foreign laws, morals, and customs with those of his country. This is what stimulates modern nations to surpass one another in the arts, in commerce, and in agriculture. The great mistakes of the past are useful in all areas. We cannot describe too often the crimes and misfortunes caused by absurd quarrels. It is certain that by refreshing our memory of these quarrels, we prevent a repetition of them. . . .

Humanity . . . is a benevolent feeling for all men, which hardly inflames anyone without a great and sensitive soul. This sublime and noble enthusiasm is troubled by the pains of other people and by the necessity to alleviate them. With these sentiments an individual would wish to cover the entire universe in order to abolish slavery, superstition, vice, and misfortune. . . .

Intolerance . . . Any method that would tend to stir up men, to arm nations, and to soak the earth with blood is impious.

It is impious to want to impose laws upon man's conscience: this is a universal rule of conduct. People must be enlightened and not constrained. . . .

What did Christ recommend to his disciples when he sent them among the Gentiles? Was it to kill or to die? Was it to persecute or to suffer? . . .

Which is the true voice of humanity, the persecutor who strikes or the persecuted who moans?

Peace . . . War is the fruit of man's depravity; it is a convulsive and violent sickness of the body politic. . . .

If reason governed men and had the influence over the heads of nations that it deserves, we would never see them inconsiderately surrender themselves to the fury of war; they would not show that ferocity that characterizes wild beasts. . . .

Political Authority No man has received from nature the right to command others. Liberty is a gift from heaven, and each individual of the same species has the right to enjoy it as soon as he enjoys the use of reason. . . .

The prince owes to his very subjects the *authority* that he has over them; and this *authority* is limited by the laws of nature and the state. The laws of nature and the state are the conditions under which they have submitted or are supposed to have submitted to its government. . . .

Moreover the government, although hereditary in a family and placed in the hands of one person, is not private property, but public property that consequently can never be taken from the people, to whom it belongs exclusively, fundamentally, and as a freehold. Consequently it is always the people who make the lease or the agreement: they always intervene in the contract that adjudges its exercise. It is not the state that belongs to the prince, it is the prince who belongs to the state: but it does rest with the prince to govern in the state, because the state has chosen him for that purpose: he has bound himself to the people and the administration of affairs, and they in their turn are bound to obey him according to the laws. . . .

The Press [*press* includes newspapers, magazines, books, and so forth] . . . People ask if freedom of the *press* is advantageous or prejudicial to a state. The answer is not difficult. It is of the greatest importance to conserve this practice in all states founded on liberty. I would even say that the disadvantages of this liberty are so inconsiderable compared to its advantages that this ought to be the common right of the universe, and it is certainly advisable to authorize its practice in all governments. . . .

REVIEW QUESTIONS

1. Why was the publication of the *Encyclopedia* a vital step in the philosophes' hopes for reform?
2. To what extent were John Locke's political ideals reflected in the *Encyclopedia*?
3. Why was freedom of the press of such significance to the enlightened philosophes?

7 Humanitarianism

A humanitarian spirit pervaded the philosophes' outlook. Showing a warm concern for humanity, they attacked militarism, slavery, religious persecution, torture, and other violations of human dignity, as can be seen in passages from the *Encyclopedia* and Voltaire's works earlier in this chapter. Through reasoned arguments they sought to make humankind recognize and renounce its own barbarity. In the following selections, other eighteenth-century reformers denounce judicial torture and slavery.

Caesare Beccaria
ON CRIMES AND PUNISHMENTS

In *On Crimes and Punishments* (1764), Caesare Beccaria (1738–1794), an Italian economist and criminologist, condemned torture, commonly used to obtain confessions in many European countries, as irrational and inhuman.

The true relations between sovereigns and their subjects, and between nations, have been discovered. Commerce has been reanimated by the common knowledge of philosophical truths diffused by the art of printing, and there has sprung up among nations a tacit rivalry of industriousness that is most humane and truly worthy of rational beings. Such good things we owe to the productive enlightenment of this age. But very few persons have studied and fought against the cruelty of punishments and the irregularities of criminal procedures, a part of legislation that is as fundamental as it is widely neglected in almost all of Europe. Very few persons have undertaken to demolish the accumulated errors of centuries by rising to general principles, curbing, at least, with the sole force that acknowledged truths possess, the unbounded course of ill-directed power which has continually produced a long and authorized example of the most cold-blooded barbarity. And yet the groans of the weak, sacrificed to cruel ignorance and to opulent indolence; the barbarous torments, multiplied with lavish and useless severity, for crimes either not proved or wholly imaginary; the filth and horrors of a prison, intensified by that cruellest tormentor of the miserable, uncertainty—all these ought to have roused that breed of magistrates who direct the opinions of men. . . .

But what are to be the proper punishments for such crimes?

Is the death-penalty really *useful* and *necessary* for the security and good order of society? Are torture and torments *just,* and do they attain the *end* for which laws are instituted? What is the best way to prevent crimes? Are the same punishments equally effective for all times? What influence have they on customary behavior? These problems deserve to be analyzed with that geometric precision which the mist of sophisms [false arguments], seductive eloquence, and timorous doubt cannot withstand. If I could boast only of having been the first to present to Italy, with a little more clarity, what other nations have boldly written and are beginning to practice, I would account myself fortunate. But if, by defending the rights of man and of unconquerable truth, I should help to save from the spasm and agonies of death some wretched victim of tyranny or of no less fatal ignorance, the thanks and tears of one innocent mortal in his transports of joy would console me for the contempt of all mankind. . . .

A cruelty consecrated by the practice of most nations is torture of the accused during his trial, either to make him confess the crime or to clear up contradictory statements, or to discover accomplices, or to purge him of infamy in some metaphysical and incomprehensible way, or, finally, to discover other crimes of which he might be guilty but of which he is not accused.

No man can be called *guilty* before a judge has sentenced him, nor can society deprive him of public protection before it has been decided that he has in fact violated the conditions under which such protection was accorded him. What right is it, then, if not simply that of might, which empowers a judge to inflict punishment on a citizen while doubt still remains as to his guilt or innocence? Here is the dilemma, which is nothing new: the fact of the crime is either certain or uncertain; if certain, all that is due is the punishment established by the laws, and tortures are useless because the criminal's confession is useless; if uncertain, then one must not torture the innocent, for such, according to the laws, is a man whose crimes are not yet proved. . . .

. . . The impression of pain may become so great that, filling the entire sensory capacity of the tortured person, it leaves him free only to choose what for the moment is the shortest way of escape from pain. The response of the accused is then as inevitable as the impressions of fire and water. The sensitive innocent man will then confess himself guilty when he believes that, by so doing, he can put an end to his torment. Every difference between guilt and innocence disappears by virtue of the very means one pretends to be using to discover it. [Torture] is an infallible means indeed—for absolving robust scoundrels and for condemning innocent persons who happen to be weak. Such are the fatal defects of this so-called criterion of truth, a criterion fit for a cannibal. . . .

Of two men, equally innocent or equally guilty, the strong and courageous will be acquitted, the weak and timid condemned, by virtue of this rigorous rational argument: "I, the judge, was supposed to find you guilty of such and such a crime; you, the strong, have been able to resist the pain, and I therefore absolve you; you, the weak, have yielded, and I therefore condemn you. I am aware that a confession wrenched forth by torments ought to be of no weight whatsoever, but I'll torment you again if you don't confirm what you have confessed."

A strange consequence that necessarily follows from the use of torture is that the innocent person is placed in a condition worse than that of the guilty, for if both are tortured, the circumstances are all against the former. Either he confesses the crime and is condemned, or he is declared innocent and has suffered a punishment he did not deserve. The guilty man, on the contrary, finds himself in a favorable situation; that is, if, as a consequence of having firmly resisted the torture, he is absolved as innocent, he will have escaped a greater punishment by enduring a lesser one. Thus the innocent cannot but lose, whereas the guilty may gain. . . .

It would be superfluous to [cite] . . . the innumerable examples of innocent persons who have confessed themselves criminals because of the agonies of torture; there is no nation, there is no age that does not have its own to cite.

Denis Diderot
ENCYCLOPEDIA
"MEN AND THEIR LIBERTY ARE NOT OBJECTS OF COMMERCE. . . ."

Montesquieu, Voltaire, David Hume, Benjamin Franklin, Thomas Paine, and several other philosophes condemned slavery and the slave trade. In Book 15 of *The Spirit of the Laws* (1748), Montesquieu scornfully refuted all justifications for slavery. Ultimately, he said, slavery, which violates the fundamental principle of justice underlying the universe, derived from base human desires to dominate and exploit other human beings. In 1780, Paine helped draft the act abolishing slavery in Pennsylvania. Five years earlier, he wrote:

> Our Traders in Men . . . must know the wickedness of that SLAVE-TRADE, if they attend to reasoning, or the dictates of their own hearts, and [those who] shun and stifle all these willfully sacrifice Conscience, and the character of integrity to that Golden Idol. . . . Most shocking of all is alleging the sacred Scriptures to favour this wicked practice.

The *Encyclopedia* denounced slavery as a violation of the individual's natural rights.

[This trade] is the buying of unfortunate Negroes by Europeans on the coast of Africa to use as slaves in their colonies. This buying of Negroes, to reduce them to slavery, is one business that violates religion, morality, natural laws, and all the rights of human nature.

Negroes, says a modern Englishman full of enlightenment and humanity, have not become slaves by the right of war; neither do they deliver themselves voluntarily into bondage, and consequently their children are not born slaves. Nobody is unaware that they are bought from their own princes, who claim to have the right to dispose of their liberty, and that traders have them transported in the same way as their other goods, either in their colonies or in America, where they are displayed for sale.

If commerce of this kind can be justified by a moral principle, there is no crime, however atrocious it may be, that cannot be made legitimate. Kings, princes, and magistrates are not the proprietors of their subjects: they do not, therefore, have the right to dispose of their liberty and to sell them as slaves.

On the other hand, no man has the right to buy them or to make himself their master. Men and their liberty are not objects of commerce; they can be neither sold nor bought nor paid for at any price. We must conclude from this that a man whose slave has run away should only blame himself, since he had acquired for money illicit goods whose acquisition is prohibited by all the laws of humanity and equity.

There is not, therefore, a single one of these unfortunate people regarded only as slaves who does not have the right to be declared free, since he has never lost his freedom, which he could not lose and which his prince, his father, and any person whatsoever in the world had not the power to dispose of. Consequently the sale that has been completed is invalid in itself. This Negro does not divest himself and can never divest himself of his natural right; he carries it everywhere with him, and he can demand everywhere that he be allowed to enjoy it. It is, therefore, patent inhumanity on the part of judges in free countries where he is transported, not to emancipate him immediately by declaring him free, since he is their fellow man, having a soul like them.

REVIEW QUESTIONS

1. What were Caesare Beccaria's arguments against the use of torture in judicial proceedings? In your opinion, is torture ever justified?
2. What ideals of the Enlightenment philosophes are reflected in Beccaria's arguments?

---

8 Literature as Satire: Critiques of European Society

The French philosophes, particularly Voltaire, Diderot, and Montesquieu, often used the medium of literature to decry the ills of their society and advance Enlightenment values. In the process they wrote satires that are still read and admired for their literary merits and insights into human nature and society. The eighteenth century also saw the publication of Jonathan Swift's *Gulliver's Travels* (1726), one of the greatest satirical works written in English.

Voltaire
CANDIDE

Several eighteenth-century thinkers, including German philosopher Gottfried Wilhelm Leibnitz (1646–1716) and English poet Alexander Pope, subscribed to the view that God had created the best of all possible worlds, that whatever evil or misfortune existed served a purpose—it contributed to the general harmony of the universe. This is the meaning of Pope's famous lines in his *Essay on Man:* "One truth is clear, WHATEVER IS IS RIGHT." This view, known as philosophical optimism, implied that individuals must accept their destiny and make no attempt to change it. In *Candide* (1759), his most important work of fiction, Voltaire bitterly attacked and ridiculed philosophical optimism. In effect Voltaire asked: "In a world where we constantly experience cruelty, injustice, superstition, intolerance, and a host of other evils, how can it be said that this is the best of all possible worlds?" But Voltaire does not resign himself to despair, for he is an ardent reformer who believes that through reason human beings can improve society.

An immediate inspiration for Voltaire's response to philosophical optimism was the catastrophic earthquake that struck Lisbon, Portugal, on November 1, 1755, claiming sixty thousand victims. How does such a catastrophe fit into the general harmony of things in this best of all possible worlds? Like the biblical Book of Job, *Candide* explored the question: Why do the innocent suffer? And because Voltaire delved into this mystery with wit, irony, satire, and wisdom, the work continues to be hailed as a literary masterpiece.

The illegitimate Candide (son of the sister of the baron in whose castle he lives in Westphalia) is tutored by the philosopher Pangloss, a teacher of "metaphysicotheologo-cosmolonigology": that is, a person who speaks nonsense. The naive Pangloss clings steadfastly to the belief that all that happens, even the worst misfortunes, are for the best.

Candide falls in love with Cunegund, the beautiful daughter of the baron of the castle; but the baron forcibly removes Candide from the castle when he discovers their love. Candide subsequently suffers a series of disastrous misfortunes, but he continues to adhere to the belief firmly instilled in him by Pangloss, that everything happens for the best and that this is the best of all possible worlds. Later, he meets an old beggar, who turns out to be his former teacher, Pangloss, who tells Candide that the Bulgarians have destroyed the castle and killed Cunegund and her family. Candide and Pangloss then travel together to Lisbon, where they survive the terrible earthquake, only to have Pangloss hanged (but he escapes death) by the Inquisition. Soon thereafter, Candide is reunited with Cunegund, who despite having been raped and sold into prostitution, has not been killed. Following further adventures and misfortunes, the lovers are again separated when Cunegund is captured by pirates.

After experiencing more episodes of human wickedness and natural disasters, Candide abandons the philosophy of optimism, declaring "that we must cultivate our gardens." By this Voltaire meant that we can never achieve utopia, but neither should we descend to the level of brutes. Through purposeful and honest work, and the deliberate pursuit of virtue, we can improve, however modestly, the quality of human existence.

The following excerpt from *Candide* starts with Candide's first misfortune after being driven out of the castle at Westphalia. In addition to ridiculing philosophical optimism, Voltaire expresses his revulsion for militarism.

CHAPTER II

What Befell Candide Among the Bulgarians

Candide, thus driven out of this terrestrial paradise, wandered a long time, without knowing where he went; sometimes he raised his eyes, all bedewed with tears, toward Heaven, and sometimes he cast a melancholy look toward the magnificent castle where dwelt the fairest of young baronesses. He laid himself down to sleep in a furrow, heartbroken and supperless. The snow fell in great flakes, and, in the morning when he awoke, he was almost frozen to death; however, he made shift to crawl to the next town, which was called Waldberghoff-trarbk-dikdorff, without a penny in his pocket, and half dead with hunger and fatigue. He took up his stand at the door of an inn. He had not been long there before two men dressed in blue fixed their eyes steadfastly upon him.

"Faith, comrade," said one of them to the other, "yonder is a well-made young fellow, and of the right size."

Thereupon they went up to Candide, and with the greatest civility and politeness invited him to dine with them.

"Gentlemen," replied Candide, with a most engaging modesty, "you do me much honor, but, upon my word, I have no money."

"Money, sir!" said one of the men in blue to him. "Young persons of your appearance and merit never pay anything. Why, are not you five feet five inches high?"

"Yes, gentlemen, that is really my size," replied he with a low bow.

"Come then, sir, sit down along with us. We will not only pay your reckoning, but will never suffer such a clever young fellow as you to want money. Mankind were born to assist one another."

"You are perfectly right, gentlemen," said Candide; "that is precisely the doctrine of Master Pangloss; and I am convinced that everything is for the best."

His generous companions next entreated him to accept a few crowns, which he readily complied with, at the same time offering them his note for the payment, which they refused, and sat down to table.

"Have you not a great affection for—"

"Oh, yes!" he replied. "I have a great affection for the lovely Miss Cunegund."

"Maybe so," replied one of the men, "but that is not the question! We are asking you whether you have not a great affection for the King of the Bulgarians?"*

"For the King of the Bulgarians?" said Candide. "Not at all. Why, I never saw him in my life."

"Is it possible! Oh, he is a most charming king! Come, we must drink his health."

"With all my heart, gentlemen," Candide said, and he tossed off his glass.

"Bravo!" cried the blues. "You are now the support, the defender, the hero of the Bulgarians; your fortune is made; you are on the high road to glory."

So saying, they put him in irons and carried him away to the regiment. There he was made to wheel about to the right, to the left, to draw his ramrod, to return his ramrod, to present, to fire, to march, and they gave him thirty blows with a cane. The next day he performed his exercise a little better, and they gave him but twenty. The day following he came off with ten and was looked upon as a young fellow of surprising genius by all his comrades.

————

*I.e., Prussians.

Candide was struck with amazement and could not for the soul of him conceive how he came to be a hero. One fine spring morning, he took it into his head to take a walk, and he marched straight forward, conceiving it to be a privilege of the human species, as well as of the brute creation, to make use of their legs how and when they pleased. He had not gone above two leagues when he was overtaken by four other heroes, six feet high, who bound him neck and heels, and carried him to a dungeon. A court-martial sat upon him, and he was asked which he liked best, either to run the gauntlet six and thirty times through the whole regiment, or to have his brains blown out with a dozen musket balls. In vain did he remonstrate to them that the human will is free, and that he chose neither. They obliged him to make a choice, and he determined, in virtue of that divine gift called free will, to run the gauntlet six and thirty times. He had gone through his discipline twice, and the regiment being composed of two thousand men, they composed for him exactly four thousand strokes, which laid bare all his muscles and nerves, from the nape of his neck to his rump. As they were preparing to make him set out the third time, our young hero, unable to support it any longer, begged as a favor they would be so obliging as to shoot him through the head. The favor being granted, a bandage was tied over his eyes, and he was made to kneel down. At that very instant, his Bulgarian Majesty, happening to pass by, inquired into the delinquent's crime, and being a prince of great penetration, he found, from what he heard of Candide, that he was a young meta-physician, entirely ignorant of the world. And, therefore, out of his great clemency, he condescended to pardon him, for which his name will be celebrated in every journal, and in every age. A skillful surgeon made a cure of Candide in three weeks by means of emollient unguents prescribed by Dioscorides. His sores were now skinned over, and he was able to march when the King of

the Bulgarians gave battle to the King of the Abares.[†]

CHAPTER III

How Candide Escaped from the Bulgarians, and What Befell Him Afterwards

Never was anything so gallant, so well accoutered, so brilliant, and so finely disposed as the two armies. The trumpets, fifes, oboes, drums, and cannon, made such harmony as never was heard in hell itself. The entertainment began by a discharge of cannon, which, in the twinkling of an eye, laid flat about six thousand men on each side. The musket bullets swept away, out of the best of all possible worlds, nine or ten thousand scoundrels that infested its surface. The bayonet was next the sufficient reason for the deaths of several thousands. The whole might amount to thirty thousand souls. Candide trembled like a philosopher and concealed himself as well as he could during this heroic butchery.

At length, while the two kings were causing *Te Deum*[‡] to be sung in each of their camps, Candide took a resolution to go and reason somewhere else upon causes and effects. After passing over heaps of dead or dying men, the first place he came to was a neighboring village, in the Abarian territories, which had been burned to the ground by the Bulgarians in accordance with international law. Here lay a number of old men covered with wounds, who beheld their wives dying with their throats cut and hugging their children to their breast all stained with blood. There several young virgins, whose bellies had been ripped open after they had satisfied the natural necessities of the Bulgarian heroes, breathed their last; while others, half burned in the flames,

---

[†]I.e., French. The Seven Years' War had begun in 1756.
[‡]A Te Deum ("We praise thee, God") is a special liturgical hymn praising and thanking God for granting some special favor, like a military victory or the end of a war.

begged to be dispatched out of the world. The ground about them was covered with the brains, arms, and legs of dead men.

Candide made all the haste he could to another village, which belonged to the Bulgarians, and there he found that the heroic Abares had treated it in the same fashion. From thence continuing to walk over palpitating limbs or through ruined buildings, at length he arrived beyond the theater of war, with a little provision in his pouch, and Miss Cunegund's image in his heart.

Denis Diderot
SUPPLEMENT TO THE VOYAGE OF BOUGANVILLE

Enlightenment thinkers often used examples from the non-European world in order to attack European values that seemed contrary to nature and reason. Denis Diderot reviewed Louis Antoine de Bouganville's *Voyage Around the World* (1771) and in the next year wrote *Supplement to the Voyage of Bouganville* (published posthumously in 1796). In this work, Diderot explored some ideas, particularly the sex habits of Tahitians, treated by the French explorer. Diderot also denounced European imperialism and the exploitation of non-Europeans, and questioned traditional Christian sexual standards. In *Supplement*, Diderot constructed a dialogue between a Tahitian (Orou), who possesses the wisdom of a French *philosophe*, and a chaplain, whose defense of Christian sexual mores reveals Diderot's critique of the Christian view of human nature. Diderot thus used a representative of an alien culture to attack those European customs and beliefs that the *philosophes* detested. In the opening passage, before Orou's dialogue, a Tahitian elder rebukes Bouganville and his companions for bringing the evils of European civilization to his island.

"We [Tahitians] are free—but see where you [Europeans] have driven into our earth the symbol of our future servitude. You are neither a god nor a devil—by what right, then, do you enslave people? Orou! You who understand the speech of these men, tell every one of us, as you have told me, what they have written on that strip of metal—'This land belongs to us.' This land belongs to you! And why? Because you set foot in it? If some day a Tahitian should land on your shores, and if he should engrave on one of your stones or on the bark of one of your trees: 'This land belongs to the people of Tahiti,' what would you think? You are stronger than we are! And what does that signify? When one of our lads carried off some of the miserable trinkets with which your ship is loaded, what an uproar you made, and what revenge you took! And at that very moment you were plotting, in the depths of your hearts, to steal a whole country! You are not slaves; you would suffer death rather than be enslaved, yet you want to make slaves of us! Do you believe, then, that the Tahitian does not know how to die in defense of his liberty? This Tahitian, whom you want to treat as a chattel, as a dumb animal—this Tahitian is your brother. You are both children of Nature—what right do you have over him that he does not have over you?

"You came; did we attack you? Did we plunder your vessel? Did we seize you and expose you to the arrows of our enemies? Did we force you to work in the fields alongside our beasts of burden? We respected our own image in you.

Leave us our own customs, which are wiser and more decent than yours. We have no wish to barter what you call our ignorance for your useless knowledge. We possess already all that is good or necessary for our existence. Do we merit your scorn because we have not been able to create superfluous wants for ourselves? When we are hungry, we have something to eat; when we are cold, we have clothing to put on. You have been in our huts—what is lacking there, in your opinion? You are welcome to drive yourselves as hard as you please in pursuit of what you call the comforts of life, but allow sensible people to stop when they see they have nothing to gain but imaginary benefits from the continuation of their painful labors. If you persuade us to go beyond the bounds of strict necessity, when shall we come to the end of our labor? When shall we have time for enjoyment? We have reduced our daily and yearly labors to the least possible amount, because to us nothing seemed more desirable than leisure. Go and bestir yourselves in your own country; there you may torment yourselves as much as you like; but leave us in peace, and do not fill our heads with a hankering after your false needs and imaginary virtues. Look at these men—see how healthy, straight and strong they are. See these women—how straight, healthy, fresh and lovely they are. Take this bow in your hands—it is my own—and call one, two, three, four of your comrades to help you try to bend it. I can bend it myself. I work the soil, I climb mountains, I make my way through the dense forest, and I can run four leagues [about 12 miles] on the plain in less than an hour. Your young comrades have been hard put to it to keep up with me, and yet I have passed my ninetieth year. . . .

"Woe to this island! Woe to all the Tahitians now living, and to all those yet to be born, woe from the day of your arrival! We used to know but one disease—the one to which all men, all animals and all plants are subject—old age. But you have brought us a new one [venereal disease]: you have infected our blood. We shall perhaps be compelled to exterminate with our own hands some of our young girls, some of our women, some of our children, those who have lain with your women, those who have lain with your men. Our fields will be spattered with the foul blood that has passed from your veins into ours. Or else our children, condemned to die, will nourish and perpetuate the evil disease that you have given their fathers and mothers, transmitting it forever to their descendants.". . .

Before the arrival of Christian Europeans, lovemaking was natural and enjoyable. Europeans introduced an alien element, guilt.

But a while ago, the young Tahitian girl blissfully abandoned herself to the embraces of a Tahitian youth and awaited impatiently the day when her mother, authorized to do so by her having reached the age of puberty, would remove her veil and uncover her breasts. She was proud of her ability to excite men's desires, to attract the amorous looks of strangers, of her own relatives, of her own brothers. In our presence, without shame, in the center of a throng of innocent Tahitians who danced and played the flute, she accepted the caresses of the young man whom her young heart and the secret promptings of her senses had marked out for her. The notion of crime and the fear of disease have come among us only with your coming. Now our enjoyments, formerly so sweet, are attended with guilt and terror. That man in black [a priest], who stands near to you and listens to me, has spoken to our young men, and I know not what he has said to our young girls, but our youths are hesitant and our girls blush. Creep away into the dark forest, if you wish, with the perverse companion of your pleasures, but allow the good, simple Tahitians to reproduce themselves without shame under the open sky and in broad daylight.

In the following conversation between Orou and the chaplain, Christian sexual mores and the concept of God are questioned. Orou addresses the chaplain.

[OROU] "You are young and healthy and you have just had a good supper. He who sleeps alone, sleeps badly; at night a man needs a woman at his side. Here is my wife and here are my daughters. Choose whichever one pleases you most, but if you would like to do me a favor, you will give your preference to my youngest girl, who has not yet had any children."

The mother said: "Poor girl! I don't hold it against her. It's no fault of hers."

The chaplain replied that his religion, his holy orders, his moral standards and his sense of decency all prevented him from accepting Orou's invitation.

Orou answered: "I don't know what this thing is that you call 'religion,' but I can only have a low opinion of it because it forbids you to partake of an innocent pleasure to which Nature, the sovereign mistress of us all, invites everybody. It seems to prevent you from bringing one of your fellow creatures into the world, from doing a favor asked of you by a father, a mother and their children, from repaying the kindness of a host, and from enriching a nation by giving it an additional citizen. I don't know what it is that you call 'holy orders,' but your chief duty is to be a man and to show gratitude. . . . I hope that you will not persist in disappointing us. Look at the distress you have caused to appear on the faces of these four women—they are afraid you have noticed some defect in them that arouses your distaste. But even if that were so, would it not be possible for you to do a good deed and have the pleasure of honoring one of my daughters in the sight of her sisters and friends? Come, be generous!"

THE CHAPLAIN "You don't understand—it's not that. They are all four of them equally beautiful. But there is my religion! My holy orders! . . .

. . . [God] spoke to our ancestors and gave them laws; he prescribed to them the way in which he wishes to be honored; he ordained that certain actions are good and others he forbade them to do as being evil."

OROU "I see. And one of these evil actions which he has forbidden is that of a man who goes to bed with a woman or girl. But in that case, why did he make two sexes?"

THE CHAPLAIN "In order that they might come together—but only when certain conditions are satisfied and only after certain initial ceremonies have been performed. By virtue of these ceremonies one man belongs to one woman and only to her; one woman belongs to one man and only to him."

OROU "For their whole lives?"

THE CHAPLAIN "For their whole lives."

OROU "So that if it should happen that a woman should go to bed with some man who was not her husband, or some man should go to bed with a woman that was not his wife . . . but that could never happen because the workman [God] would know what was going on, and since he doesn't like that sort of thing, he wouldn't let it occur."

THE CHAPLAIN "No. He lets them do as they will, and they sin against the law of God (for that is the name by which we call the great workman) and against the law of the country; they commit a crime."

OROU "I should be sorry to give offense by anything I might say, but if you don't mind, I'll tell you what I think."

THE CHAPLAIN "Go ahead."

OROU "I find these strange precepts contrary to nature, and contrary to reason. . . . Furthermore, your laws seem to me to be contrary to the general order of things. For in truth is there anything so senseless as a precept that forbids us to heed the changing impulses that are inherent in our being, or commands that require a degree of [steadfastness] which is not possible, that violate the liberty of both male and female by chaining them perpetually to one another? Is there anything more unreasonable than this perfect fidelity that would restrict us, for the enjoyment of pleasures so capricious, to a single partner—than an oath of immutability taken by two individuals made of flesh and blood under a sky that is not the same for a moment, in a cavern that threatens to collapse upon them, at the foot of a cliff that is crumbling into dust, under a tree that is withering, on a bench of stone that is being worn away? Take my word for it, you have reduced human beings to a worse condition than that of the animals. I don't know what your great workman is, but I am very happy that he never spoke to our forefathers, and I hope that he never speaks to our children, for if he does, he may tell them the same foolishness, and they may be foolish enough to believe it." . .

OROU "Are monks faithful to their vows of sterility?"

THE CHAPLAIN "No."

OROU "I was sure of it. Do you also have female monks?"

THE CHAPLAIN "Yes."

OROU "As well behaved as the male monks?"

THE CHAPLAIN "They are kept more strictly in seclusion, they dry up from unhappiness and die of boredom."

OROU "So nature is avenged for the injury done to her! Ugh! What a country! If everything is managed the way you say, you are more barbarous than we are."

REVIEW QUESTION

1. Draw up a list showing which element(s) of eighteenth-century society each of these satirical selections was ridiculing.

CHAPTER 3

Era of the French Revolution

WOMEN'S MARCH TO VERSAILLES. High prices and food shortages led thousands of women (and men) to march on Versailles in protest in October 1789. The king was compelled to return to Paris, a sign of his weakening power, and many aristocrats fled the country. *(Bibliothèque Nationale, Paris)*

In 1789, many participants and observers viewed the revolutionary developments in France as the fulfillment of the Enlightenment's promise—the triumph of reason over tradition and ignorance, of liberty over despotism. It seemed that the French reformers were eliminating the abuses of an unjust system and creating a new society founded on the ideals of the philosophes.

Eighteenth-century French society, the Old Regime, was divided into three orders, or estates. The First Estate (the clergy) and the Second Estate (the nobility) enjoyed special privileges sanctioned by law and custom. The church collected tithes (taxes on the land), censored books regarded as a threat to religion and morality, and paid no taxes to the state (although the church did make a "free gift" to the royal treasury). Nobles were exempt from most taxes, collected manorial dues from peasants (even from free peasants), and held the highest positions in the church, the army, and the government.

Opinion among the aristocrats was divided. Some nobles, influenced by the liberal ideals of the philosophes, sought to reform France; they wanted to end royal despotism and establish a constitutional government. To this extent, the liberal nobility had a great deal in common with the bourgeoisie. These liberal nobles saw the king's financial difficulties in 1788 as an opportunity to regenerate the nation under enlightened leadership. When they resisted the king's policies, they claimed that they were opposing royal despotism. But at the same time, many nobles remained hostile to liberal ideals and opposed reforms that threatened their privileges and honorific status.

Peasants, urban workers, and members of the bourgeoisie belonged to the Third Estate, which comprised about 96 percent of the population. The bourgeoisie—which included merchants, bankers, professionals, and government officials below the top ranks—provided the leadership and ideology for the French Revolution. For most of the eighteenth century, the bourgeoisie did not challenge the existing social structure, including the special privileges of the nobility. But by 1789 the bourgeoisie wanted to abolish those privileges and to open prestigious positions to men of talent regardless of their birth; it wanted to give France a constitution that limited the monarch's power, established a parliament, and protected the rights of the individual.

The immediate cause of the French Revolution was a financial crisis. The wars of Louis XIV and subsequent foreign adventures, including French aid to the American colonists during their revolution, had emptied the royal treasury. The refusal of the clergy and the nobles to surrender their tax exemptions compelled Louis XVI to call a meeting of the Estates General—a medieval assembly that had last met in 1614—to deal with impending bankruptcy. Many nobles intended to use the Estates General to weaken the French throne and regain powers lost a century earlier under the absolute rule of Louis XIV.

But the nobility's plans were unrealized; their revolt against the crown paved the way for the Third Estate's eventual destruction of the Old Regime.

Between June and November 1789 the bourgeoisie, aided by uprisings of the common people of Paris and the peasants in the countryside, gained control over the state and instituted reforms. During this opening and moderate phase of the Revolution (1789–1791), the bourgeoisie abolished the special privileges of the aristocracy and clergy, formulated a declaration of human rights, subordinated the church to the state, reformed the country's administrative and judicial systems, and drew up a constitution creating a parliament and limiting the king's power.

Between 1792 and 1794 came a radical stage. Three principal factors propelled the Revolution in a radical direction: pressure from the urban poor, the *sans-culottes,* who wanted the government to do something about their poverty; a counterrevolution led by clergy and aristocrats who wanted to undo the reforms of the Revolution; and war with the European powers that sought to check French expansion and to stifle the revolutionary ideals of liberty and equality.

The dethronement of Louis XVI, the establishment of a republic in September 1792, and the king's execution in January 1793 were all signs of growing radicalism. As the new Republic tottered under the twin blows of internal insurrection and foreign invasion, the revolutionary leadership grew more extreme. In June 1793 the Jacobins took power. Tightly organized, disciplined, and fiercely devoted to the Republic, the Jacobins mobilized the nation's material and human resources to defend it against the invading foreign armies. To deal with counterrevolutionaries, the Jacobins unleashed the Reign of Terror. Of the 500,000 people imprisoned for crimes against the Republic, some 16,000 were sentenced to death by guillotine and another 20,000 perished in prison before they could be tried. More than 200,000 died in the civil war in the provinces, and 40,000 were summarily executed by firing squad, guillotine, and mass drownings ordered by military courts authorized by the Convention. Although the Jacobins succeeded in saving the Revolution, their extreme measures aroused opposition. In the last part of 1794, power again passed into the hands of the moderate bourgeoisie, who wanted no part of Jacobin radicalism.

In 1799, Napoleon Bonaparte, a popular general with an inexhaustible yearning for power, overthrew the government and pushed the Revolution in still another direction, toward military dictatorship. Although Napoleon subverted the revolutionary ideal of liberty, he preserved the social gains of the Revolution—the abolition of the special privileges of the nobility and the clergy.

The era of the French Revolution was a decisive period in the shaping of the modern West. By destroying aristocratic privileges and opening careers to talent, it advanced the cause of equality under the law. By weakening the power of the clergy, it promoted the secularization of society. By abolishing the divine right of monarchy, drafting a constitution, and establishing a parliament, it accelerated the growth of the liberal-democratic state. By eliminating serfdom and the sale of government offices and by reforming the tax system, it fostered a rational approach to administration. In the nineteenth century, the ideals and reforms of the French Revolution spread in shock waves across Europe; in country after country, the old order was challenged by the ideals of liberty and equality.

1   Abuses of the Old Regime

The roots of the French Revolution lay in the aristocratic structure of French society. The Third Estate came to resent the special privileges of the aristocracy, a legacy of the Middle Ages, and the inefficient and corrupt methods of government. To many French people influenced by the ideas of the philosophes, French society seemed an affront to reason. By 1789, reformers sought a new social order based on rationality and equality.

GRIEVANCES OF THE THIRD ESTATE

At the same time that elections were held for the Estates General, the three estates drafted *cahiers de doléances,* the lists of grievances that deputies would take with them when the Estates General convened. The cahiers from all three estates expressed loyalty to the monarchy and the church and called for a written constitution and an elected assembly. The cahiers of the clergy and the nobility insisted on the preservation of traditional rights and privileges. The Cahier of the Third Estate of Dourdan, in the *généralité* of Orléans (one of the thirty-four administrative units into which prerevolutionary France was divided), expressed the reformist hopes of the Third Estate. Some of the grievances in the cahier follow.

29 March, 1789

The order of the third estate of the City, *Bailliage* [judicial district], and County of Dourdan, imbued with gratitude prompted by the paternal kindness of the King, who deigns to restore its former rights and its former constitution, forgets at this moment its misfortunes and impotence, to harken only to its foremost sentiment and its foremost duty, that of sacrificing everything to the glory of the *Patrie* [nation] and the service of His Majesty. It supplicates him to accept the grievances, complaints, and remonstrances which it is permitted to bring to the foot of the throne, and to see therein only the expression of its zeal and the homage of its obedience.

It wishes:

A Documentary Survey of the French Revolution by Stewart, © 1951. Adapted by permission of Prentice-Hall, Inc., Upper Saddle River, NJ.

1. That his subjects of the third estate, equal by such status to all other citizens, present themselves before the common father without other distinction which might degrade them.

2. That all the orders [the three estates], already united by duty and a common desire to contribute equally to the needs of the State, also deliberate in common concerning its needs.

3. That no citizen lose his liberty except according to law; that, consequently, no one be arrested by virtue of special orders, or, if imperative circumstances necessitate such orders, that the prisoner be handed over to the regular courts of justice within forty-eight hours at the latest.

4. That no letters or writings intercepted in the post [mails] be the cause of the detention of any citizen, or be produced in court against him, except in case of conspiracy or undertaking against the State.

5. That the property of all citizens be inviolable, and that no one be required to make sacrifice thereof for the public welfare, except upon assurance of indemnification based upon the statement of freely selected appraisers. . . .

15. That every personal tax be abolished; that thus the *capitation* and the *taille* and its accessories be merged with the *vingtièmes*[1] in a tax on land and real or nominal property.

16. That such tax be borne equally, without distinction, by all classes of citizens and by all kinds of property, even feudal and contingent rights.

17. That the tax substituted for the *corvée* [taxes paid in labor, often road building] be borne by all classes of citizens equally and without distinction. That said tax, at present beyond the capacity of those who pay it and the needs to which it is destined, be reduced by at least one-half. . . .

---

[1] A *taille* was a tax levied on the value of a peasant's land or wealth. A capitation was a head or poll tax paid for each person. A *vingtième* was a tax on income and was paid chiefly by peasants.

JUSTICE

1. That the administration of justice be reformed, either by restoring strict execution of ordinances, or by reforming the sections thereof that are contrary to the dispatch and welfare of justice. . . .

7. That venality [sale] of offices be suppressed. . . .

8. That the excessive number of offices in the necessary courts be reduced in just measure, and that no one be given an office of magistracy if he is not at least twenty-five years of age, and until after a substantial public examination has verified his morality, integrity, and ability. . . .

10. That the study of law be reformed; that it be directed in a manner analogous to our legislation, and that candidates for degrees be subjected to rigorous tests which may not be evaded; that no dispensation of age or time be granted.

11. That a body of general customary law be drafted of all articles common to all the customs of the several provinces and *bailliages*. . . .

12. That deliberations of courts . . . which tend to prevent entry of the third estate thereto be rescinded and annulled as injurious to the citizens of that order, in contempt of the authority of the King, whose choice they limit, and contrary to the welfare of justice, the administration of which would become the patrimony of those of noble birth instead of being entrusted to merit, enlightenment, and virtue.

13. That military ordinances which restrict entrance to the service to those possessing nobility be reformed.

That naval ordinances establishing a degrading distinction between officers born into the order of nobility and those born into that of the third estate be revoked, as thoroughly injurious to an order of citizens and destructive of the competition so necessary to the glory and prosperity of the State.

FINANCES

1. That if the Estates General considers it necessary to preserve the fees of *aides* [tax on commodities], such fees be made uniform throughout the entire kingdom and reduced to a single denomination. . . .

2. That the tax of the *gabelle* [tax on salt] be eliminated if possible, or that it be regulated among the several provinces of the kingdom. . . .

3. That the taxes on hides, which have totally destroyed that branch of commerce and caused it to go abroad, be suppressed forever.

4. That . . . all useless offices, either in police or in the administration of justice, be abolished and suppressed.

AGRICULTURE

4. That the right to hunt may never affect the property of the citizen; that, accordingly, he may at all times travel over his lands, have injurious herbs uprooted, and cut *luzernes* [alfalfa], *sainfoins* [fodder], and other produce whenever it suits him; and that stubble may be freely raked immediately after the harvest. . . .

11. . . . That individuals as well as communities be permitted to free themselves from the rights of *banalité* [peasants were required to use the lord's mill, winepress, and oven], and *corvée,* by payments in money or in kind, at a rate likewise established by His Majesty on the basis of the deliberations of the Estates General. . . .

15. That the militia, which devastates the country, takes workers away from husbandry, produces premature and ill-matched marriages, and imposes secret and arbitrary taxes upon those who are subject thereto, be suppressed and replaced by voluntary enlistment at the expense of the provinces.

Emmanuel Sieyès
BOURGEOIS DISDAIN FOR SPECIAL PRIVILEGES OF THE ARISTOCRACY

In a series of pamphlets, including *The Essay on Privileges* (1788) and *What Is the Third Estate?* (1789), Abbé Emmanuel Sieyès (1748–1836) expressed the bourgeoisie's disdain for the nobility. Although educated at Jesuit schools to become a priest, Sieyès had come under the influence of Enlightenment ideas. In *What Is the Third Estate?* he denounced the special privileges of the nobility, asserted that the people are the source of political authority, and maintained that national unity stands above estate or local interests. The ideals of the Revolution—liberty, equality, and fraternity—are found in Sieyès's pamphlet, excerpts of which follow.

The plan of this book is fairly simple. We must ask ourselves three questions.

1. What is the Third Estate? *Everything.*
2. What has it been until now in the political order? *Nothing.*
3. What does it want to be? *Something.* . . .

. . . Only the well-paid and honorific posts are filled by members of the privileged order [nobles]. Are we to give them credit for this? We could do so only if the Third Estate was unable or unwilling to fill these posts. We know the answer. Nevertheless, the privileged have dared to preclude the Third Estate. "No matter how useful you are," they said, "no matter how able you are, you can go so far and no further. Honors are not for the like of you." . . .

. . . Has nobody observed that as soon as the government becomes the property of a separate class, it starts to grow out of all proportion and that posts are created not to meet the needs of the governed but of those who govern them? . . .

It suffices to have made the point that the so-called usefulness of a privileged order to the public service is a fallacy; that, without help from this order, all the arduous tasks in the service are performed by the Third Estate; that without this order the higher posts could be infinitely better filled; that they ought to be the natural prize and reward of recognised ability and service; and that if the privileged have succeeded in usurping all well-paid and honorific posts, this is both a hateful iniquity towards the generality of citizens and an act of treason to the commonwealth.

Who is bold enough to maintain that the Third Estate does not contain within itself everything needful to constitute a complete nation? It is like a strong and robust man with one arm still in chains. If the privileged order were removed, the nation would not be something less but something more. What then is the Third Estate? All; but an "all" that is fettered and oppressed. What would it be without the privileged order? It would be all; but free and flourishing. Nothing will go well without the Third Estate; everything would go considerably better without the two others. . . .

. . . The privileged, far from being useful to the nation, can only weaken and injure it; . . . the nobility may be a *burden* for the nation. . . .

The nobility, however, is . . . a foreigner in our midst because of its *civil and political* prerogatives.

What is a nation? A body of associates living under *common* laws and represented by the same *legislative assembly,* etc.

Is it not obvious that the nobility possesses privileges and exemptions which it brazenly calls its rights and which stand distinct from the rights of the great body of citizens? Because of these special rights, the nobility does not belong to the common order, nor is it subjected to the common laws. Thus its private rights make it a people apart in the great nation.

REVIEW QUESTIONS

1. The principle of equality pervaded the cahiers of the Third Estate. Discuss this statement.
2. How important did Emmanuel Sieyès say the nobility (the privileged order) was to the life of the nation?
3. What importance did Sieyès attach to the contribution of the Third Estate (the bourgeoisie) to the life of the nation?

---

2 Liberty, Equality, Fraternity

In August 1789 the newly created National Assembly adopted the Declaration of the Rights of Man and of Citizens, which expressed the liberal and universal ideals of the Enlightenment. The Declaration proclaimed that sovereignty derives from the people: that is, that the people are the source of political power; that men are born free and equal in rights; and that it is the purpose of government to protect the natural rights of the individual. Because these ideals contrasted markedly with the outlook of an absolute monarchy, a privileged aristocracy, and an intolerant clergy, some historians view the Declaration of

Rights as the death knell of the Old Regime. Its affirmation of liberty, reason, and natural rights inspired liberal reformers in other lands.

DECLARATION OF THE RIGHTS OF MAN AND OF CITIZENS

Together with John Locke's *Second Treatise on Government,* the American Declaration of Independence, and the Constitution of the United States, the Declaration of the Rights of Man and of Citizens, which follows, is a pivotal document in the development of modern liberalism.

The Representatives of the people of FRANCE, formed into a NATIONAL ASSEMBLY, considering that ignorance, neglect, or contempt of human rights, are the sole causes of public misfortunes and corruptions of Government, have resolved to set forth in a solemn declaration, these natural, imprescriptible, and unalienable rights: that this declaration, being constantly present to the minds of the members of the body social, they may be ever kept attentive to their rights and their duties: that the acts of the legislative and executive powers of Government, being capable of being every moment compared with the end of political institutions, may be more respected: and also, that the future claims of the citizens, being directed by simple and incontestible principles, may always tend to the maintenance of the Constitution, and the general happiness.

For these reasons the NATIONAL ASSEMBLY doth recognize and declare, in the presence of the Supreme Being, and with the hope of his blessing and favor, the following *sacred* rights of men and of citizens:

I. *Men are born, and always continue, free, and equal in respect of their rights. Civil distinctions, therefore, can be founded only on public utility.*

II. *The end of all political associations, is, the preservation of the natural and imprescriptible rights of man; and these rights are liberty, property, security, and resistance of oppression.*

III. *The nation is essentially the source of all sovereignty; nor can any* INDIVIDUAL *or* ANY BODY OF MEN*, be entitled to any authority which is not expressly derived from it.*

IV. Political Liberty consists in the power of doing whatever does not injure another. The exercise of the natural rights of every man, has no other limits than those which are necessary to secure to every *other* man the free exercise of the same rights; and these limits are determinable only by the law.

V. The law ought to prohibit only actions hurtful to society. What is not prohibited by the law, should not be hindered; nor should any one be compelled to that which the law does not require.

VI. The law is an expression of the will of the community. All citizens have a right to concur, either personally, or by their representatives, in its formation. It should be the same to all, whether it protects or punishes; and *all being equal in its sight, are equally eligible to all honors, places, and employments, according to their different abilities, without any other distinction than that created by their virtues and talents.*

VII. No man should be accused, arrested, or held in confinement, except in cases determined by the law, and according to the forms which it has prescribed. All who promote, solicit, execute, or cause to be executed, arbitrary orders, ought to be punished; and every citizen called upon or apprehended by virtue of the law, ought immediately to obey, and renders himself culpable by resistance.

VIII. The law ought to impose no other penalties but such as are absolutely and evidently necessary; and no one ought to be punished, but in virtue of a law promulgated before the offence, and legally applied.

IX. Every man being presumed innocent till he has been convicted, whenever his detention becomes indispensible, all rigor [harshness] to him, more than is necessary to secure his person, ought to be provided against by the law.

X. No man ought to be molested on account of his opinions, not even on account of his *religious* opinions, provided his avowal of them does not disturb the public order established by the law.

XI. The unrestrained communication of thoughts and opinions being one of the most precious rights of man, every citizen may speak, write, and publish freely, provided he is responsible for the abuse of this liberty in cases determined by the law.

XII. A public force being necessary to give security to the rights of men and of citizens, that force is instituted for the benefit of the community, and not for the particular benefit of the persons with whom it is entrusted.

XIII. A common contribution being necessary for the support of the public force, and for defraying the other expenses of government, it ought to be divided equally among the members of the community, according to their abilities.

XIV. Every citizen has a right, either by himself or his representative, to a free voice in determining the necessity of public contributions, the appropriation of them, and their amount, mode of assessment and duration.

XV. Every community has a right to demand of all its agents, an account of their conduct.

XVI. Every community in which a separation of powers and a security of rights is not provided for, wants a constitution.

XVII. The rights to property being inviolable and sacred, no one ought to be deprived of it, except in cases of evident public necessity, legally ascertained, and on condition of a previous just indemnity.

REVIEW QUESTIONS

1. What does the Declaration say about the nature of political liberty? What are its limits, and how are they determined?
2. How does the Declaration show the influence of John Locke (see page 38)?
3. The ideals of the Declaration have become deeply embedded in the Western outlook. Discuss this statement.

---

3 Expansion of Human Rights

The abolition of the special privileges of the aristocracy and the ideals proclaimed by the Declaration of the Rights of Man and of Citizens aroused the hopes of reformers in several areas: in what was considered radicalism, even by the framers of the Declaration of the Rights of Man, some women began to press for equal rights; humanitarians called for the abolition of the slave trade; and Jews, who for centuries had suffered disabilities and degradation, petitioned for full citizenship.

Mary Wollstonecraft
VINDICATION OF THE RIGHTS OF WOMAN

When in 1789 the French revolutionaries issued their "Declaration of the Rights of Man," it was only a matter of time before a woman published a "Declaration of the Rights of Woman." That feat was accomplished in 1791 in France by Olympe de Gouges. In England, Mary Wollstonecraft (1759–1797), strongly influenced by her, published her own statement, *Vindication of the Rights of Woman,* in 1792. Her protest against the prevailing submissiveness of women was reinforced by the philosophy of the Enlightenment and the ideals of the French Revolution, which she observed firsthand from 1792 to 1794. A career woman, she made her living as a prolific writer closely associated with the radicals of her time, one of whom, William Godwin, she married shortly before her death. Wollstonecraft became famous for her vigorous protests against the subjection of women. Children, husbands, and society generally, she pleaded in *Vindication of the Rights of Woman,* were best served by well-educated, self-reliant, and strong women capable of holding their own in the world.

. . . I have turned over various books written on the subject of education, and patiently observed the conduct of parents and the management of schools; but what has been the result?—a profound conviction that the neglected education of my fellow creatures is the grand source of the misery I deplore, and that women, in particular, are rendered weak and wretched. . . . The conduct and manners of women, in fact, evidently prove that their minds are not in a healthy state. . . . One cause of this . . . I attribute to a false system of education, gathered from the books written on this subject by men who, considering females rather as women than human creatures, have been more anxious to make them alluring mistresses than affectionate wives and rational mothers. . . .

. . . A degree of physical superiority of men cannot . . . be denied, and it is a noble prerogative! But not content with this natural pre-eminence, men endeavour to sink us still lower, merely to render us alluring objects for a moment. . . .

My own sex, I hope, will excuse me, if I treat them like rational creatures, instead of flattering their *fascinating* graces, and viewing them as if they were in a state of perpetual childhood, unable to stand alone. I earnestly wish to point out in what true dignity and human happiness consists. I wish to persuade women to endeavour to acquire strength, both of mind and body. . . .

Dismissing, then, those pretty feminine phrases, which the men condescendingly use to soften our slavish dependence, and despising that weak elegancy of mind, exquisite sensibility, and sweet docility of manners, supposed to be the sexual characteristics of the weaker vessel, I wish to show that elegance is inferior to virtue, that the first object of laudable ambition is to obtain a character as a human being, regardless of the distinction of sex. . . .

The education of women has of late been more attended to than formerly; yet they are still reckoned a frivolous sex, and ridiculed or pitied by the writers who endeavour by satire or instruction to improve them. It is acknowledged that they spend many of the first years of their lives in acquiring a smattering of accomplishments; meanwhile strength of body and mind are sacrificed to libertine notions of beauty, to the desire of establishing themselves—the only way women can rise in the world—by marriage. And this desire making mere animals of them, when they marry they act as such children may be expected to act,—they dress, they paint, and nickname God's creatures. Surely these weak beings are only fit for a seraglio [harem]! Can they be expected to govern a family with judgment, or take care of the poor babes whom they bring into the world? . . .

Contending for the rights of woman, my main argument is built on this simple principle, that if she be not prepared by education to become the companion of man, she will stop the progress of knowledge and virtue; for truth must be common to all, or it will be inefficacious with respect to its influence on general practice. And how can woman be expected to co-operate unless she knows why she ought to be virtuous? unless freedom strengthens her reason till she comprehends her duty, and sees in what manner it is connected with her real good. If children are to be educated to understand the true principle of patriotism, their mother must be a patriot; and the love of mankind, from which an orderly train of virtues spring, can only be produced by considering the moral and civil interest of mankind; but the education and situation of woman at present shuts her out from such investigations. . . .

Consider—I address you as a legislator—whether, when men contend for their freedom, and to be allowed to judge for themselves respecting their own happiness, it be not inconsistent and unjust to subjugate women, even though you firmly believe that you are acting in the manner best calculated to promote their happiness? Who made man the exclusive judge, if woman partake with him of the gift of reason?

In this style argue tyrants of every denomination, from the weak king to the weak father of a family; they are all eager to crush reason, yet always assert that they usurp its throne only to be useful. Do you not act a similar part when you *force* all women, by denying them civil and political rights, to remain immured [imprisoned] in their families groping in the dark? for surely, sir, you will not assert that a duty can be binding which is not founded on reason? If, indeed, this be their destination, arguments may be drawn from reason; and thus augustly supported, the more understanding women acquire, the more they will be attached to their duty—comprehending it—for unless they comprehend it, unless their morals be fixed on the same immutable principle as those of man, no authority can make them discharge it in a virtuous manner. They may be convenient slaves, but slavery will have its constant effect, degrading the master and the abject dependent.

But if women are to be excluded, without having a voice, from a participation of the natural rights of mankind, prove first, to ward off the charge of injustice and inconsistency, that they [lack] reason, else this flaw in your NEW CONSTITUTION will ever show that man must, in some shape, act like a tyrant, and tyranny, in whatever part of society it rears its brazen front, will ever undermine morality. . . .

In what does man's pre-eminence over the brute creation consist? The answer is as clear as that a half is less than the whole, in Reason. . . . Yet . . . deeply rooted processes have clouded reason. . . . Men, in general, seem to employ their reason to justify prejudices, which they have imbibed, they can scarcely trace how, rather than to root them out.

The power of generalising ideas, of drawing comprehensive conclusions from individual observations . . . has not only been denied to women; but writers have insisted that it is inconsistent, with a few exceptions, with their sexual character. Let men prove this, and I shall grant that woman only exists for man. I must, however, previously remark, that the power of generalising ideas, to any great extent, is not very common amongst men or women. But this exercise is the true cultivation of the understanding; and everything conspires to render the cultivation of the understanding more difficult in the female than the male world. . . .

I shall not go back to the remote annals of antiquity to trace the history of woman; it is sufficient to allow that she has always been either a slave or a despot, and to remark that each of these situations equally retards the progress of reason. The grand source of female folly and vice has ever appeared to me to arise from narrowness of mind; and the very constitution of civil governments has put almost insuperable obstacles in the way to prevent the cultivation of the female understanding; yet virtue can be built on no other foundation. . . .

When do we hear of women who, starting out of obscurity, boldly claim respect on account of their great abilities or daring virtues? Where are they to be found? . . .

With respect to women, when they receive a careful education, they are either made fine ladies, brimful of sensibility, and teeming with capricious fancies, or mere notable women. The latter are often friendly, honest creatures, and have a shrewd kind of good sense, joined with worldly prudence, that often render them more useful members of society than the fine sentimental lady, though they possess neither greatness of mind nor taste. The intellectual world is shut against them. Take them out of their family or neighbourhood, and they stand still; the mind finding no employment, for literature affords a fund of amusement which they have never sought to relish, but frequently to despise. The sentiments and taste of more cultivated minds appear ridiculous, even in those whom chance and family connections have led them to love; but in mere acquaintance they think it all affectation.

A man of sense can only love such a woman on account of her sex, and respect her because she is a trusty servant. He lets her, to preserve his own peace, scold the servants, and go to church in clothes made of the very best materials. . . . [W]omen, whose minds are not enlarged by cultivation, or . . . by reflection, are very unfit to manage a family, for, by an undue stretch of power, they are always tyrannising to

support a superiority that only rests on the arbitrary distinction of fortune.

Women have seldom sufficient serious employment to silence their feelings; a round of little cares, or vain pursuits frittering away all strength of mind and organs, they become naturally only objects of sense. In short, the whole tenor of female education (the education of society) tends to render the best disposed romantic and inconstant; and the remainder vain and [contemptible]. In the present state of society this evil can scarcely be remedied, I am afraid, in the slightest degree; should a more laudable ambition ever gain ground they may be brought nearer to nature and reason, and become more virtuous and useful as they grow more respectable. . . .

Women . . . all want to be ladies. Which is simply to have nothing to do, but listlessly to go they scarcely care where, for they cannot tell what.

But what have women to do in society? I may be asked, but to loiter with easy grace. . . . Women might certainly study the art of healing, and be physicians as well as nurses. . . . They might also study politics . . . for the reading of history will scarcely be more useful than the study of romances. . . . Business of various kinds, they might likewise pursue, if they were educated in a more orderly manner, which might save many from common and legal prostitution. . . . The few employments open to a woman, so far from being liberal, are menial. . . .

Some of these women might be restrained from marrying by a proper spirit of delicacy, and others may not have had it in their power to escape in this pitiful way from servitude; is not that Government then very defective, and very unmindful of the happiness of one-half of its members, that does not provide for honest, independent women, by encouraging them to fill respectable stations? . . .

It is a melancholy truth; yet such is the blessed effect of civilisation! the most respectable women are the most oppressed; and, unless they have understandings far superior to the common run of understandings, taking in both sexes, they must, from being treated like contemptible beings, become contemptible. How many women thus waste life away the prey of discontent, who might have practised as physicians, regulated a farm, managed a shop, and stood erect, supported by their own industry, instead of hanging their heads. . . .

Would men but generously snap our chains, and be content with rational fellowship instead of slavish obedience, they would find us more observant daughters, more affectionate sisters, more faithful wives, more reasonable mothers—in a word, better citizens. We should then love them with true affection, because we should learn to respect ourselves; and the peace of mind of a worthy man would not be inter-rupted by the idle vanity of his wife, nor the babes sent to nestle in a strange bosom, having never found a home in their mother's. . . .

. . . The sexual distinction which men have so warmly insisted upon, is arbitrary. . . . Asserting the rights which women in common with men ought to contend for, I have not attempted to [make light of] their faults; but to prove them to be the natural consequence of their education and station in society. If so, it is reasonable to suppose that they will change their character, and correct their vices and follies, when they are allowed to be free in a physical, moral, and civil sense.

Let woman share the rights, and she will emulate the virtues of man; for she must grow more perfect when emancipated. . . .

Society of the Friends of Blacks
ADDRESS TO THE NATIONAL ASSEMBLY IN FAVOR OF THE ABOLITION OF THE SLAVE TRADE

Planters in the French West Indies and shipbuilding and sugar refining interests opposed any attempts to eliminate slavery or the slave trade since they profited handsomely from these institutions. On February 5, 1790, the Society of the Friends of Blacks, using the language of the Declaration of the Rights of Man, called for the abolition of the slave trade. Recognizing the power of proslavery forces, the society made it clear that it was not proposing the abolition of slavery itself. In 1791, the slaves of Saint Domingue revolted, and in 1794, the Jacobins in the National Convention abolished slavery in the French colonies. The island's white planters resisted the decree, and in 1801 Napoleon sent twenty thousand troops to Saint Domingue in an unsuccessful attempt to restore slavery. In 1804, the black revolutionaries established the independent state of Haiti.

Following are excerpts from the Society of the Friends of Blacks' address to the National Assembly.

The humanity, justice, and magnanimity that have guided you in the reform of the most profoundly rooted abuses gives hope to the Society of the Friends of Blacks that you will receive with benevolence its demand in favor of that numerous portion of humankind, so cruelly oppressed for two centuries.

This Society, slandered in such cowardly and unjust fashion, only derives its mission from the humanity that induced it to defend the blacks even under the past despotism. Oh! Can there be a more respectable title in the eyes of this august Assembly which has so often avenged the rights of man in its decrees?

You have declared them, these rights; you have engraved on an immortal monument that all men are born and remain free and equal in rights; you have restored to the French people these rights that despotism had for so long despoiled; . . . you have broken the chains of feudalism that still degraded a good number of our fellow citizens; you have announced the destruction of all the stigmatizing distinctions that religious or political prejudices introduced into the great family of humankind. . . .

We are not asking you to restore to French blacks those political rights which alone, nevertheless, attest to and maintain the dignity of man; we are not even asking for their liberty. No; slander, bought no doubt with the greed of the shipowners, ascribes that scheme to us and spreads it everywhere; they want to stir up everyone against us, provoke the planters and their numerous creditors, who take alarm even at gradual emancipation. They want to alarm all the French, to whom they depict the prosperity of the colonies as inseparable from the slave trade and the perpetuity of slavery.

No, never has such an idea entered into our minds; we have said it, printed it since the beginning of our Society, and we repeat it in order to reduce to nothing this grounds of argument, blindly adopted by all the coastal cities, the grounds on which rest almost all their addresses [to the National Assembly]. The immediate emancipation of the blacks would not only be a fatal operation for the colonies; it would even be a deadly gift for the blacks, in the state of abjection and incompetence to which cupidity [greed] has reduced them. It would be to abandon to themselves and without assistance children in the cradle or mutilated and impotent beings.

It is therefore not yet time to demand that liberty; we ask only that one cease butchering thousands of blacks regularly every year in order to take hundreds of captives; we ask that one henceforth cease the prostitution, the profaning of the French name, used to authorize these thefts, these atrocious murders; we demand in a word the abolition of the slave trade. . . .

In regard to the colonists, we will demonstrate to you that if they need to recruit blacks in Africa to sustain the population of the colonies at the same level, it is because they wear out the blacks with work, whippings, and starvation; that, if they treated them with kindness and as good fathers of families, these blacks would multiply and that this population, always growing, would increase cultivation and prosperity. . . .

Have no doubt, the time when this commerce will be abolished, even in England, is not far off. It is condemned there in public opinion, even in the opinion of the ministers. . . .

If some motive might on the contrary push them [the blacks] to insurrection, might it not be the indifference of the National Assembly about their lot? Might it not be the insistence on weighing them down with chains, when one consecrates everywhere this eternal axiom: *that all men are born free and equal in rights.* So then therefore there would only be fetters and gallows for the blacks while good fortune glimmers only for the whites? Have no doubt, our happy revolution must re-electrify the blacks whom vengeance and resentment have electrified for so long, and it is not with punishments that the effect of this upheaval will be repressed. From one insurrection badly pacified will twenty others be born, of which one alone can ruin the colonists forever.

It is worthy of the first free Assembly of France to consecrate the principle of philanthropy which makes of humankind only one single family, to declare that it is horrified by this annual carnage which takes place on the coasts of Africa, that it has the intention of abolishing it one day, of mitigating the slavery that is the result, of looking for and preparing, from this moment, the means.

PETITION OF THE JEWS OF PARIS, ALSACE, AND LORRAINE TO THE NATIONAL ASSEMBLY, JANUARY 28, 1790

After several heated debates, the National Assembly granted full citizenship to the Jews on September 27, 1791. Influenced by the French example, almost all European states in the nineteenth century would also emancipate the Jews dwelling within their borders. In the following *Petition of the Jews of Paris, Alsace, and Lorraine to the National Assembly, January 28, 1790,* the Jews pointed to historic wrongs and invoked the ideals of the Revolution as they called for equal rights.

A great question is pending before the supreme tribunal of France. *Will the Jews be citizens or not?*

Already, this question has been debated in the National Assembly; and the orators, whose intentions were equally patriotic, did not agree at all on the result of their discussion. Some wanted Jews admitted to civil status. Others found this admission dangerous. A third opinion consisted of preparing the complete improvement of the lot of the Jews by gradual reforms.

In the midst of all these debates, the national assembly believed that it ought to adjourn the question. . . .

It was also said that the adjournment was based on the necessity of knowing with assurance what were the true desires of the Jews; given, it was added, the disadvantages of according to this class of men rights more extensive than those they want.

But it is impossible that such a motive could have determined the decree of the national assembly.

First, the wish of the Jews is perfectly well-known, and cannot be equivocal. They have presented it clearly in their addresses of 26 and 31 August, 1789. The Jews of Paris repeated it in a *new address* of 24 December. They ask that all the degrading distinctions that they have suffered to this day be abolished and that they be declared CITIZENS. . . .

Their desires, moreover, as we have just said, are well known; and we will repeat them here. They ask to be CITIZENS. . . .

In truth, [the Jews] are of a religion that is condemned by the one that predominates in France. But the time has passed when one could say that it was only the dominant religion that could grant access to advantages, to prerogatives, to the lucrative and honorable posts in society. For a long time they confronted the Protestants with this maxim, worthy of the Inquisition, and the Protestants had no civil standing in France. Today, they have just been reestablished in the possession of this status; they are assimilated to the Catholics in everything; the intolerant maxim that we have just recalled can no longer be used against them. Why would they continue to use it as an argument against the Jews?

In general, civil rights are entirely independent from religious principles. And all men of whatever religion, whatever sect they belong to, whatever creed they practice, provided that their creed, their sect, their religion does not offend the principles of a pure and severe morality, all these men, we say, equally able to serve the fatherland, defend its interests, contribute to its splendor, should all equally have the title and the rights of citizen. . . .

[The Jews] are reproached at the same time for the vices that make them unworthy of civil status and the principles which render them at once unworthy and incompetent. A rapid glance at the bizarre as well as cruel destiny of these unfortunate individuals will perhaps remove the disfavor with which some seek to cover them. . . .

Always persecuted since the destruction of Jerusalem, pursued at times by fanaticism and at others by superstition, by turn chased from the kingdoms that gave them an asylum and then called back to these same kingdoms, excluded from all the professions and arts and crafts, deprived even of the right to be heard as witnesses against a Christian, relegated to separate districts like another species of man with whom one fears having communication, pushed out of certain cities which have the privilege of not receiving them, obligated in others to pay for the air that they breathe as in Augsburg where they pay a *florin* an hour or in Bremen a *ducat* a day, subject in several places to shameful tolls. Here is the list of a part of the harassment still practiced today against the Jews.

And [critics of the Jews] would dare to complain of the state of degradation into which some of them can be plunged! They would dare to complain of their ignorance and their vices! Oh! Do not accuse the Jews, for that would only precipitate onto the Christians themselves all the weight of these accusations. . . .

Let us now enter into more details. The Jews have been accused of the crime of usury. But first of all, all of them are not usurers; and it would be as unjust to punish them all for the offense of some as to punish all the Christians for the usury committed by some of them and the speculation of many. . . .

Reflect, then, on the condition of the Jews. Excluded from all the professions, ineligible for all the positions, deprived even of the capacity to acquire property, not daring and not being able to sell openly the merchandise of their commerce, to what extremity are you reducing them? You do not want them to die, and yet you refuse them the means to live: you refuse them the means, and you crush them with taxes. You leave them therefore really no other resource than usury. . . .

Everything that one would not have dared to undertake, moreover, or what one would only have dared to undertake with an infinity of precautions a long time ago, can now be done and one must dare to undertake it in this moment of universal regeneration, when all ideas and all sentiments take a new direction; and we must hasten to do so. Could one still fear the influence of a prejudice against which reason has appealed for such a long time, when all the former abuses are destroyed and all the former prejudices overturned? Will not the numerous changes effected in the political machine uproot from the people's minds most of the ideas that dominated them? Everything is changing; the lot of the Jews must change at the same time; and the people will not be more surprised by this particular change than by all those which they see around them everyday. This is therefore the moment, the true moment to make justice triumph: attach the improvement of the lot of the Jews to the revolution; amalgamate, so to speak, this partial revolution to the general revolution. Your efforts will be crowned with success, and the people will not protest, and time will consolidate your work and render it unshakable.

REVIEW QUESTIONS

1. According to Mary Wollstonecraft, what benefits would society derive from giving equal rights to women?
2. Why did Wollstonecraft object to the traditional attitudes of men toward women?
3. How, in Wollstonecraft's opinion, should women change?

4. Why did the Society of the Friends of Blacks ask only for the abolition of the slave trade and not the abolition of slavery itself?
5. On what grounds did the Jews of Paris, Alsace, and Lorraine petition the National Assembly to grant the Jews citizenship? What historic wrongs did they decry? What views of religion and politics did they uphold?
6. What did the demands of Mary Wollstonecraft, the Society of the Friends of Blacks, and the Jews of Paris, Alsace, and Lorraine have to do with the French Revolution and the ideas of the Enlightenment, and how did they exemplify the expansion of human rights?

---

4 The Jacobin Regime

In the summer of 1793 the French Republic was threatened with internal insurrection and foreign invasion. During this period of acute crisis, the Jacobins provided strong leadership. They organized a large national army of citizen soldiers who, imbued with love for the nation, routed the invaders on the northern frontier. To deal with internal enemies, the Jacobins instituted the Reign of Terror, in which Maximilien Robespierre (1758–1794) played a pivotal role.

It was not because they were bloodthirsty or power mad that many Jacobins, including Robespierre, supported the use of terror. Rather, they were idealists who believed that terror was necessary to rescue the Republic and the Revolution from destruction. Deeply committed to republican democracy, Robespierre saw himself as the bearer of a higher faith, molding a new society founded on reason, good citizenship, patriotism, and virtue. Robespierre viewed those who prevented the implementation of this new society as traitors and sinners who had to be killed for the good of humanity.

Maximilien Robespierre
REPUBLIC OF VIRTUE

In his speech of February 5, 1794, Robespierre provided a comprehensive statement of his political theory, in which he equated democracy with virtue and justified the use of terror in defending democracy.

What is the objective toward which we are reaching? The peaceful enjoyment of liberty and equality; the reign of that eternal justice whose laws are engraved not on marble or stone but in the hearts of all men, even in the heart of the slave who has forgotten them or of the tyrant who disowns them.

We wish an order of things where all the low and cruel passions will be curbed, all the beneficent and generous passions awakened by the laws, where ambition will be a desire to deserve glory and serve the *patrie* [nation]; where distinctions grow only out of the very system of equality; where the citizen will be subject to the authority of the magistrate, the magistrate to that of the people, and the people to that of justice; where the *patrie* assures the well-being of each individual, and where each individual shares with pride the prosperity and glory of the *patrie;* where every soul expands by the continual communication of republican sentiments, and by the need to merit the esteem of a great people; where the arts will embellish the liberty that ennobles them, and commerce will be the source of public wealth and not merely of the monstrous riches of a few families.

We wish to substitute in our country . . . all the virtues and miracles of the republic for all the vices and absurdities of the monarchy.

We wish, in a word, to fulfill the intentions of nature and the destiny of humanity, realize the promises of philosophy, and acquit providence of the long reign of crime and tyranny. We wish that France, once illustrious among enslaved nations, may, while eclipsing the glory of all the free peoples that ever existed, become a model to nations, a terror to oppressors, a consolation to the oppressed, an ornament of the universe; and that, by sealing our work with our blood, we may witness at least the dawn of universal happiness—this is our ambition, this is our aim.

What kind of government can realize these prodigies [great deeds]? A democratic or republican government only. . . .

A democracy is a state where the sovereign people, guided by laws of their own making, do for themselves everything that they can do well, and by means of delegates everything that they cannot do for themselves.

It is therefore in the principles of democratic government that you must seek the rules of your political conduct.

But in order to found democracy and consolidate it among us, in order to attain the peaceful reign of constitutional laws, we must complete the war of liberty against tyranny. . . . [S]uch is the aim of the revolutionary government that you have organized. . . .

But the French are the first people in the world who have established true democracy by calling all men to equality and to full enjoyment of the rights of citizenship; and that is, in my opinion, the true reason why all the tyrants leagued against the republic will be vanquished.

There are from this moment great conclusions to be drawn from the principles that we have just laid down.

Since virtue [good citizenship] and equality are the soul of the republic, and your aim is to found and to consolidate the republic, it follows that the first rule of your political conduct must be to relate all of your measures to the maintenance of equality and to the development of virtue; for the first care of the legislator must be to strengthen the principles on which the government rests. Hence all that tends to excite a love of country, to purify moral standards, to exalt souls, to direct the passions of the human heart toward the public good must be adopted or established by you. All that tends to concentrate and debase them into selfish egotism, to awaken an infatuation for trivial things, and scorn for great ones, must be rejected or repressed by you. In the system of the French revolution, that which is immoral is impolitic, and that which tends to corrupt is counterrevolutionary. Weakness, vices, and prejudices are the road to monarchy. . . .

. . . Externally all the despots surround you; internally all the friends of tyranny conspire. . . . It is necessary to annihilate both the internal and external enemies of the republic or perish with its fall. Now, in this situation your first political maxim should be that one guides the people by reason, and the enemies of the people by terror.

If the driving force of popular government in peacetime is virtue, that of popular government during a revolution is both *virtue and terror:* virtue, without which terror is destructive; terror, without which virtue is impotent. Terror is only justice that is prompt, severe, and inflexible; it is thus an emanation of virtue; it is less a distinct principle than a consequence of the general principle of democracy applied to the most pressing needs of the *patrie.*

In a series of notes written in the summer of 1793, Robespierre expressed his policy toward counterrevolutionaries.

DESPOTISM IN DEFENSE OF LIBERTY

What is our goal? The enforcement of the constitution for the benefit of the people.

Who will our enemies be? The vicious and the rich.

What means will they employ? Slander and hypocrisy.

What things may be favorable for the employment of these? The ignorance of the *sans-culottes.*[1]

The people must therefore be enlightened. But what are the obstacles to the enlightenment of the people? Mercenary writers who daily mislead them with impudent falsehoods.

---

[1] *Sans-culottes* literally means without the fancy breeches worn by the aristocracy. The term refers generally to a poor city dweller (who wore simple trousers). Champions of equality, the sans-culottes hated the aristocracy and the rich bourgeoisie.

What conclusions may be drawn from this? 1. These writers must be proscribed [suppressed] as the most dangerous enemies of the people. 2. Right-minded literature must be scattered about in profusion.

What are the other obstacles to the establishment of liberty? Foreign war and civil war.

How can foreign war be ended? By putting republican generals in command of our armies and punishing those who have betrayed us.

How can civil war be ended? By punishing traitors and conspirators, particularly if they are deputies or administrators; by sending loyal troops under patriotic leaders to subdue the aristocrats of Lyon, Marseille, Toulon, the Vendée, the Jura, and all other regions in which the standards of rebellion and royalism have been raised; and by making frightful examples of all scoundrels who have outraged liberty and spilled the blood of patriots.

1. Proscription [suppressing] of perfidious and counterrevolutionary writers and propagation of proper literature.
2. Punishment of traitors and conspirators, particularly deputies and administrators.
3. Appointment of patriotic generals; dismissal and punishment of others.
4. Sustenance and laws for the people.

General Louis de Lignières Turreau
UPRISING IN THE VENDÉE

In the Vendée in western France, peasants loyal to the monarchy, to their priests, and to Catholic tradition (all of which the Revolution had attacked) and led by nobles waged war against the Republic. It was a merciless conflict. Republican authorities executed, generally without a trial, thousands of suspects by firing squad and mass drowning. Frenzied republican soldiers, under orders from their superiors, burned villages, slaughtered livestock, and indiscriminately killed tens of thousands of peasants. Following is a letter from General Turreau to the minister of war on January 19, 1794, in which he describes the brutal campaign his troops waged against the peasants in the Vendée.

My purpose is to burn everything, to leave nothing but what is essential to establish the necessary quarters for exterminating the rebels. This great measure is one which you should prescribe; you should also make an advance statement as to the fate of the women and children we will come across in this rebellious countryside. If they are all to be put to the sword, I cannot undertake such action without authorization.

All brigands caught bearing arms, or convicted of having taken up arms to revolt against their country, will be bayoneted. The same will apply to girls, women and children in the same circumstances. Those who are merely under suspicion will not be spared either, but no execution may be carried out except by previous order of the general.

All villages, farms, woods, heathlands, generally anything which will burn, will be set on fire, although not until any perishable supplies found there have been removed. But, it must be repeated, these executions must not take place until so ordered by the general.

I hasten to describe to you the measures which I have just put in hand for the extermination of all remaining rebels scattered about the interior of the Vendée. I was convinced that the only way to do this was by deploying a sufficient number of columns to spread right across the countryside and effect a general sweep, which would completely purge the cantons as they passed. Tomorrow, therefore, these twelve columns will set out simultaneously, moving from east to west. Each column commander has orders to search and burn forests, villages, market towns and farms, omitting, however, those places which I consider important posts and those which are essential for establishing communications.

In a letter dated December 26, 1793, a high government official describes mass drowning.

I am writing to you about the more than twelve hundred brigands shot at Savenay; but, according to the intelligence that I have since been given and that I do not doubt, it seems that more than two thousand were shot. They call that "sending to the hospital." Here, an entirely different method is used to get rid of this bad element. These criminals are put into boats which are then sunk. This is called "sending to the water tower." In truth, if the brigands have sometimes complained about dying of hunger, they cannot at least complain about dying of thirst. About twelve hundred were made to drink today. I do not know who thought up this kind of punishment, but it is much more speedy than the guillotine which henceforth seems destined to cut off the heads of nobles, priests and all those who, according to the rank which they formerly occupied, had a great influence over the common people.

REVIEW QUESTIONS

1. Compare and contrast Maximilien Robespierre's vision of the Republic of Virtue with the ideals of the Declaration of the Rights of Man and of Citizens in Section 2. What did Robespierre mean by virtue?
2. On what grounds did Robespierre justify terror?
3. Like medieval inquisitors, Robespierre regarded people with different views not as opponents but as sinners. Discuss this statement.
4. How did the Jacobins justify their ruthless policies in the Vendée?

5 Napoleon: Destroyer and Preserver of the Revolution

In 1799, a group of conspirators that included Napoleon Bonaparte (1769–1821), an ambitious and popular general, staged a successful coup d'état. Within a short time, Napoleon became a one-man ruler, and in 1804 he crowned himself emperor of the French. Under Napoleon's military dictatorship, political freedom (a principal goal of the French Revolution) was suppressed. Nevertheless, Napoleon preserved, strengthened, and spread to other lands many of the Revolution's reforms. He supported religious tolerance, secular education, and access to positions according to ability; he would not restore the privileges of the aristocracy and church.

Napoleon Bonaparte
LEADER, GENERAL, TYRANT, REFORMER

Napoleon was a brilliant military commander who carefully planned each campaign, using speed, deception, and surprise to confuse and demoralize his opponents. By rapid marches, Napoleon would concentrate a superior force against a segment of the enemy's strung-out forces. Recognizing the importance of good morale, he sought to inspire his troops by appealing to their honor, their vanity, and their love of France.

In 1796, Napoleon, then a young officer, was given command of the French army in Italy. In the Italian campaign, he demonstrated a genius for propaganda and psychological warfare, as the following proclamations to his troops indicate.

LEADER AND GENERAL

April 26, 1796

March 27, 1796

Soldiers:

Soldiers, you are naked, ill fed! The Government owes you much; it can give you nothing. Your patience, the courage you display in the midst of these rocks, are admirable; but they procure you no glory, no fame is reflected upon you. I seek to lead you into the most fertile plains in the world. Rich provinces, great cities will be in your power. There you will find honor, glory, and riches. Soldiers of Italy, would you be lacking in courage or constancy [steadfastness]?

In a fortnight you have won six victories, taken twenty-one standards, fifty-five pieces of artillery, several strong positions, and conquered the richest part of Piedmont [a region in northern Italy]; you have captured 15,000 prisoners and killed or wounded more than 10,000 men. . . .

. . . You have won battles without cannon, crossed rivers without bridges, made forced marches without shoes, camped without brandy and often without bread. Soldiers of liberty, only republican phalanxes [infantry troops] could have endured what you have endured. Soldiers, you have our thanks! The grateful *Patrie* [nation] will owe its prosperity to you. . . .

The two armies which but recently attacked you with audacity are fleeing before you in terror; the wicked men who laughed at your misery and rejoiced at the thought of the triumphs of your enemies are confounded and trembling.

But, soldiers, as yet you have done nothing compared with what remains to be done. . . .

. . . Undoubtedly the greatest obstacles have been overcome; but you still have battles to fight, cities to capture, rivers to cross. Is there one among you whose courage is abating? . . . No. . . . All of you are consumed with a desire to extend the glory of the French people; all of you long to humiliate those arrogant kings who dare to contemplate placing us in fetters; all of you desire to dictate a glorious peace, one which will indemnify the *Patrie* for the immense sacrifices it has made; all of you wish to be able to say with pride as you return to your villages, "I was with the victorious army of Italy!"

Friends, I promise you this conquest; but there is one condition you must swear to fulfill—to respect the people whom you liberate, to repress the horrible pillaging committed by scoundrels incited by our enemies. Otherwise you would not be the liberators of the people; you would be their scourge. . . . Plunderers will be shot without mercy; already, several have been. . . .

Peoples of Italy, the French army comes to break your chains; the French people is the friend of all peoples; approach it with confidence; your property, your religion, and your customs will be respected.

We are waging war as generous enemies, and we wish only to crush the tyrants who enslave you.

The following passages from Napoleon's diary shed light on his generalship, ambition, and leadership qualities.

1800

What a thing is imagination! Here are men who don't know me, who have never seen me, but who only knew of me, and they are moved by my presence, they would do anything for me! And this same incident arises in all centuries and in all countries! Such is fanaticism! Yes, imagination rules the world. The defect of our modern institutions is that they do not speak to the imagination. By that alone can man be governed; without it he is but a brute.

1800

The impact of an army, like the total of mechanical coefficients, is equal to the mass multiplied by the velocity.

A battle is a dramatic action which has its beginning, its middle, and its conclusion. The result of a battle depends on the instantaneous flash of an idea. When you are about to give battle concentrate all your strength, neglect nothing; a battalion often decides the day.

In warfare every opportunity must be seized; for fortune is a woman: if you miss her to-day, you need not expect to find her to-morrow.

There is nothing in the military profession I cannot do for myself. If there is no one to make gunpowder, I know how to make it; gun carriages, I know how to construct them; if it is founding a cannon, I know that; or if the details of tactics must be taught, I can teach them.

The presence of a general is necessary: he is the head, he is the all in all of an army. It was not the Roman army conquered Gaul, but Cæsar; it was not the Carthaginians made the armies of the Republic tremble at the very gates of Rome, but Hannibal; it was not the Macedonian army marched to the Indus [River], but Alexander; . . . it was not the Prussian army that defended Prussia during seven years against the three strongest Powers of Europe, but Frederick the Great.

Concentration of forces, activity, activity with the firm resolve to die gloriously: these are the three great principles of the military art that have always made fortune favourable in all my operations. Death is nothing; but to live defeated and ingloriously, is to die every day.

I am a soldier, because that is the special faculty I was born with; that is my life, my habit. I have commanded wherever I have been. I commanded, when twenty-three years old, at the siege of Toulon; . . . I carried the soldiers of the army of Italy with me as soon as I appeared among them; I was born that way. . . .

It was by becoming a Catholic that I pacified the Vendée [region in western France], and a [Muslim] that I established myself in Egypt; it was by becoming ultramontane[1] that I won over public opinion in Italy. If I ruled a people of Jews, I would rebuild the temple of Solomon! Paradise is a central spot whither the souls of men proceed along different roads; every sect has a road of its own. . . .

1802

My power proceeds from my reputation, and my reputation from the victories I have won. My power would fall if I were not to support it with more glory and more victories. Conquest has made me what I am; only conquest can maintain me. . . .

1804

My mistress is power; I have done too much to conquer her to let her be snatched away from me. Although it may be said that power came to me of its own accord, yet I know what labour, what sleepless nights, what scheming, it has involved. . . .

1809

Again I repeat that in war morale and opinion are half the battle. The art of the great captain has always been to make his troops appear very numerous to the enemy, and the enemy's very few to his own. So that to-day, in spite of the long time we have spent in Germany, the enemy

do not know my real strength. We are constantly striving to magnify our numbers. Far from confessing that I had only 100,000 men at Wagram [French victory over Austria in 1809] I am constantly suggesting that I had 220,000. In my Italian campaigns, in which I had only a handful of troops, I always exaggerated my numbers. It served my purpose, and has not lessened my glory. My generals and practised soldiers could always perceive, after the event, all the skilfulness of my operations, even that of having exaggerated the numbers of my troops.

In several ways, Napoleon anticipated the strategies of twentieth-century dictators. He concentrated power in his own hands, suppressed opposition, and sought to mold public opinion by controlling the press and education. The following Imperial Catechism of 1806, which schoolchildren were required to memorize and recite, is a pointed example of Napoleonic indoctrination.

TYRANT

Lesson VII. Continuation of the Fourth Commandment.

Q. What are the duties of Christians with respect to the princes who govern them, and what in particular are our duties towards Napoleon I, our Emperor?

A. Christians owe to the princes who govern them, and we owe in particular to Napoleon I, our Emperor, *love, respect, obedience, fidelity, military service* and the tributes laid for the preservation and defence of the Empire and of his throne; we also owe to him fervent prayers for his safety and the spiritual and temporal prosperity of the state.

Q. Why are we bound to all these duties towards our Emperor?

A. First of all, because God, who creates empires and distributes them according to His will, in loading our Emperor with gifts, both in peace and in war, has established him

---

[1]Favoring the pope over competing authorities.

as our sovereign and has made him the minister of His power and His image upon the earth. *To honor and to serve our Emperor is then to honor and to serve God himself.* Secondly, because our Lord Jesus Christ by His doctrine as well as by His example, has Himself taught us what we owe to our sovereign: He was born the subject of Caesar Augustus;[2] He paid the prescribed impost; and just as He ordered to render to God that which belongs to God, so He ordered to render to Caesar that which belongs to Caesar.

Q. Are there not particular reasons which ought to attach us more strongly to Napoleon I, our Emperor?

A. Yes; for it is he whom God has raised up under difficult circumstances to re-establish the public worship of the holy religion of our fathers and to be the protector of it. He has restored and preserved public order by his profound and active wisdom; he defends the state by his powerful arm; he has become the anointed of the Lord through the consecration which he received from the sovereign pontiff, head of the universal church.

Q. What ought to be thought of those who may be lacking in their duty towards our Emperor?

A. According to the apostle Saint Paul, they would be resisting the order established by God himself and would render themselves *worthy of eternal damnation.*

Q. Will the duties which are required of us towards our Emperor be equally binding with respect to his lawful successors in the order established by the constitutions of the Empire?

A. Yes, without doubt; for we read in the holy scriptures, that God, Lord of heaven and earth, by an order of His supreme will and through His providence, gives empires not only to one person in particular, but also to his family.

---

[2]Caesar Augustus (27 B.C.–A.D. 14) was the Roman emperor at the time that Jesus was born.

In the following letter (April 22, 1805) to Joseph Fouché, minister of police, Napoleon reveals his intention to regulate public opinion.

Repress the journals a little; make them produce wholesome articles. I want you to write to the editors of the . . . newspapers that are most widely read in order to let them know that the time is not far away when, seeing that they are no longer of service to me, I shall suppress them along with all the others. . . . Tell them that the . . . Revolution is over, and that there is now only one party in France; that I shall never allow the newspapers to say anything contrary to my interests; that they may publish a few little articles with just a bit of poison in them, but that one fine day somebody will shut their mouths.

With varying degrees of success, Napoleon's administrators in conquered lands provided positions based on talent, equalized taxes, and abolished serfdom and the courts of the nobility. They promoted freedom of religion, fought clerical interference with secular authority, and promoted secular education. By undermining the power of European clergy and aristocrats, Napoleon weakened the Old Regime irreparably in much of Europe. A letter from Napoleon to his brother Jérôme, King of Westphalia, illustrates Napoleon's desire for enlightened rule.

REFORMER

Fontainebleau, November 15, 1807
To Jérôme Napoléon, King of Westphalia

I enclose the Constitution for your Kingdom. It embodies the conditions on which I renounce all my rights of conquest, and all the claims I have acquired over your state. You must faithfully observe it. I am concerned for the happiness of your subjects, not only as it affects your reputation, and my own, but also for its influence on the whole European situation. Don't listen to those who say that your subjects are so accustomed to slavery that they will feel no gratitude for the benefits you give them. There is more intelligence in the Kingdom of Westphalia than they would have you believe; and your throne will never be firmly established except upon the trust and affection of the common people. What German opinion impatiently demands is that men of no rank, but of marked ability, shall have an equal claim upon your favour and your employment, and that every trace of serfdom, or of a feudal hierarchy between the sovereign and the lowest class of his subjects, shall be done away. The benefits of the Code Napoléon [legal code introduced by Napoleon], public trial, and the introduction of juries, will be the leading features of your government. And to tell you the truth, I count more upon their effects, for the extension and consolidation of your rule, than upon the most resounding victories. I want your subjects to enjoy a degree of liberty, equality, and prosperity hitherto unknown to the German people. I want this liberal regime to produce, one way or another, changes which will be of the utmost benefit to the system of the Confederation, and to the strength of your monarchy. Such a method of government will be a stronger barrier between you and Prussia than the Elbe [River], the fortresses, and the protection of France. What people will want to return under the arbitrary Prussian rule, once it has tasted the benefits of a wise and liberal administration? In Germany, as in France, Italy, and Spain, people long for equality and liberalism. I have been managing the affairs of Europe long enough now to know that the burden of the privileged classes was resented everywhere. Rule constitutionally. Even if reason, and the enlightenment of the age, were not sufficient cause, it would be good policy for one in your position; and you will find that the backing of public opinion gives you a great natural advantage over the absolute Kings who are your neighbours.

REVIEW QUESTIONS

1. In his proclamations how did Napoleon Bonaparte try to raise the morale of his troops?
2. How did Napoleon use propaganda to achieve his goals?
3. For what purpose was religious authority cited in the catechism of 1806? What would Machiavelli (see page 9) have thought of this device?
4. How did Napoleon both undermine and preserve the reforms of the Revolution?

CHAPTER 4
The Industrial Revolution

LAMBETH GASWORKS. Gustave Doré, 1872. This engraving shows the harsh conditions within industry during the latter half of the nineteenth century. At the time of this scene, most of the lighting in major cities like London was provided by gas. (*Engraving from Gustave Doré and Blanchard Jerold, London, A Pilgrimage [London, 1872]. Stock Montage.*)

In the last part of the eighteenth century, as a revolution for liberty and equality swept across France and sent shock waves across Europe, a different kind of revolution, a revolution in industry, was transforming life in Great Britain. In the nineteenth century the Industrial Revolution spread to the United States and to the European continent. Today, it encompasses virtually the entire world; everywhere the drive to substitute technology for human labor continues at a rapid pace.

After 1760, dramatic changes occurred in Britain in the way goods were produced and labor organized. New forms of power, particularly steam, replaced animal strength and human muscle. Better ways of obtaining and using raw materials were discovered, and a new form of organizing production and workers—the factory—came into common use. In the nineteenth century, technology moved from triumph to triumph with a momentum unprecedented in human history. The resulting explosion in economic production and productivity transformed society with breathtaking speed.

Rapid industrialization caused hardships for the new class of industrial workers, many of them recent arrivals from the countryside. Arduous and monotonous, factory labor was geared to the strict discipline of the clock, the machine, and the production schedule. Employment was never secure. Sick workers received no pay and were often fired; aged workers suffered pay cuts or lost their jobs. During business slumps, employers lowered wages with impunity, and laid-off workers had nowhere to turn for assistance. Because factory owners did not consider safety an important concern, accidents were frequent. Yet the Industrial Revolution was also a great force for human betterment. Ultimately it raised the standard of living, even for the lowest classes, lengthened life expectancy, and provided more leisure time and more possibilities for people to fulfill their potential.

The Industrial Revolution dramatically altered political and social life at all levels, but especially for the middle class, whose engagement in capitalist ventures brought greater political power and social recognition. During the course of the nineteenth century, the bourgeoisie came to hold many of the highest offices in western European states, completing a trend that had begun with the French Revolution.

Cities grew in size, number, and importance. Municipal authorities were unable to cope with the rapid pace of urbanization, and without adequate housing, sanitation, or recreational facilities, the exploding urban centers were another source of working-class misery. In pre-industrial Britain, most people had lived in small villages. They knew where their roots were; relatives, friends, and the village church gave them a sense of belonging. The industrial centers separated people from nature and from their places of origin, shattering traditional ways of life that had given men and women a sense of security.

The plight of the working class created a demand for reform, but the British government, committed to laissez-faire economic principles that militated against state involvement, was slow to act. In the last part of the nineteenth century, however, the development of labor unions, the rising political voice of the working class, and the growing recognition that the problems created by industrialization required government intervention speeded up the pace of reform. Rejecting the road of reform, Karl Marx called for a working-class revolution that would destroy the capitalist system.

1 Early Industrialization

Several factors help to explain why the Industrial Revolution began in Great Britain. That country had an abundant labor supply, large deposits of coal and iron ore, and capital available for investing in new industries. A large domestic middle class and overseas colonies provided markets for manufactured goods. Colonies were also a source for raw materials, particularly cotton for the textile industry. The Scientific Revolution and an enthusiasm for engineering fostered a spirit of curiosity and inventiveness. Britain had enterprising and daring entrepreneurs who organized new businesses and discovered new methods of production.

Edward Baines
BRITAIN'S INDUSTRIAL ADVANTAGES AND THE FACTORY SYSTEM

In 1835, Edward Baines (1800–1890), an early student of industrialization, wrote *The History of the Cotton Manufacture in Great Britain*—about one of the leading industries in the early days of the Industrial Revolution. In the passages that follow, Baines discusses the reasons for Britain's industrial transformation and the advantages of the factory system.

Three things may be regarded as of primary importance for the successful prosecution of manufactures, namely, water-power, fuel, and iron. Wherever these exist in combination, and where they are abundant and cheap, machinery may be manufactured and put in motion at small cost; and most of the processes of making and finishing cloth, whether chemical or mechanical, depending, as they do, mainly on the two great agents of water and heat, may likewise be performed with advantage. . . .

A great number of streams . . . furnish water-power adequate to turn many hundred mills: they afford the element of water, indispensable for scouring, bleaching, printing, dyeing, and other processes of manufacture: and when collected in their larger channels, or employed to feed canals, they supply a superior inland navigation, so important for the transit of raw materials and merchandise.

Not less important for manufactures than the copious supply of good water, is the great abundance of coal. . . . This mineral fuel animates the thousand arms of the steam-engine, and furnishes the most powerful agent in all chemical and mechanical operations.

In mentioning the advantages which Lancashire [the major cotton manufacturing area] possesses as a seat of manufactures, we must not omit its ready communication with the sea by means of its well-situated port, Liverpool, through the medium of which it receives, from Ireland, a large proportion of the food that supports its population, and whose commerce brings from distant shores the raw materials of its manufactures, and again distributes them, converted into useful and elegant clothing, amongst all the nations of the earth. Through the same means a plentiful supply of timber is obtained, so needful for building purposes.

To the above natural advantages, we must add, the acquired advantage of a canal communication, which ramifies itself through all the populous parts of this country, and connects it with the inland counties, the seats of other flourishing manufactures, and the sources whence iron, lime, salt, stone, and other articles in which Lancashire is deficient, are obtained. By this means Lancashire, being already possessed of the primary requisites for manufactures, is enabled, at a very small expense, to command things of secondary importance, and to appropriate to its use the natural advantages of the whole kingdom. The canals, having been accomplished by individual enterprise, not by national funds, were constructed to supply a want already existing: they were not, therefore, original sources of the manufactures, but have extended together with them, and are to be considered as having essentially aided and accelerated that prosperity from whose beginnings they themselves arose. The recent introduction of railways will have a great effect in making the operations of trade more intensely active, and perfecting the division of labour, already carried to so high a point. By the railway and the locomotive engine, the extremities of the land will, for every beneficial purpose, be united.

In comparing the advantages of England for manufactures with those of other countries, we can by no means overlook the excellent commercial position of the country—intermediate between the north and south of Europe; and its insular situation, which, combined with the command of the seas, secures our territory from invasion or annoyance. The German ocean, the Baltic, and the Mediterranean are the regular highways for our ships; and our western ports command an unobstructed passage to the Atlantic, and to every quarter of the world.

A temperate climate, and a hardy race of men, have also greatly contributed to promote the manufacturing industry of England.

The political and moral advantages of this country, as a seat of manufactures, are not less remarkable than its physical advantages. The arts are the daughters of peace and liberty. In no country have these blessings been enjoyed in so high a degree, or for so long a continuance, as in England. Under the reign of just laws, personal liberty and property have been secure; mercantile enterprise has been allowed to reap its reward; capital has accumulated in safety; the workman has "gone forth to his work and to his labour until the evening;" and, thus protected and favoured, the manufacturing prosperity of the country has struck its roots deep, and spread forth its branches to the ends of the earth.

England has also gained by the calamities of other countries, and the intolerance of other governments. At different periods, the Flemish and French protestants, expelled from their native lands, have taken refuge in England, and have repaid the protection given them by practising and teaching branches of industry, in which the English were then less expert than their neighbours. The wars which have at different times desolated the rest of Europe, and especially those which followed the French revolution, (when mechanical invention was producing the most wonderful effects in England,) checked the progress of manufacturing improvement on the continent, and left England for many years without a competitor. At the same time, the English navy held the sovereignty of the ocean, and under its protection the commerce of this country extended beyond all former bounds, and established a firm connexion between the manufacturers of Lancashire and their customers in the most distant lands.

When the natural, political, and adventitious causes, thus enumerated, are viewed together, it cannot be [a] matter of surprise that England has obtained a preeminence over the rest of the world in manufactures.

A crucial feature of the Industrial Revolution was a new production system—the making of goods in factories. By bringing all the operations of manufacturing under one roof, industrialists made the process of production more efficient. Baines describes the factory system's advantages over former methods.

. . . Hitherto the cotton manufacture had been carried on almost entirely in the houses of the workmen: the hand or stock cards,[1] the spinning wheel, and the loom, required no larger apartment than that of a cottage. A spinning jenny[2] of small size might also be used in a cottage, and in many instances was so used: when the number of spindles was considerably increased, adjacent work-shops were used. But the water-frame, the carding engine, and the other machines which [Richard] Arkwright brought out in a finished state, required both more space than could be found in a cottage, and more power than could be applied by the human arm. Their weight also rendered it necessary to place them in strongly-built mills,

---

[1]Prior to spinning, raw fibers had to be carded with a brushlike tool that cleaned and separated them.
[2]The spinning jenny, which was hand-powered, was the first machine that spun fiber onto multiple spindles at the same time; that is, it produced more thread or yarn in less time than the single-thread spinning wheel.

and they could not be advantageously turned by any power then known but that of water.

The use of machinery was accompanied by a greater division of labour than existed in the primitive state of the manufacture; the material went through many more processes; and of course the loss of time and the risk of waste would have been much increased, if its removal from house to house at every stage of the manufacture had been necessary. It became obvious that there were several important advantages in carrying on the numerous operations of an extensive manufacture in the same building. Where water power was required, it was economical to build one mill, and put up one waterwheel, rather than several. This arrangement also enabled the master spinner himself to superintend every stage of the manufacture: it gave him a greater security against the wasteful or fraudulent consumption of the material: it saved time in the transference of the work from hand to hand: and it prevented the extreme inconvenience which would have resulted from the failure of one class of workmen to perform their part, when several other classes of workmen were dependent upon them. Another circumstance which made it advantageous to have a large number of machines in one manufactory was, that mechanics must be employed on the spot, to construct and repair the machinery, and that their time could not be fully occupied with only a few machines.

All these considerations drove the cotton spinners to that important change in the economy of English manufactures, the introduction of the factory system; and when that system had once been adopted, such were its pecuniary [financial] advantages, that mercantile competition would have rendered it impossible, even had it been desirable, to abandon it.

REVIEW QUESTIONS

1. Apart from its natural resources, what other assets for industrial development did England possess?
2. What were the factory system's advantages over the domestic system of production?

2   The New Science of Political Economy

The new spirit of scientific inquiry manifest in the seventeenth and eighteenth centuries extended also into the economic field, creating the new science of political economy. Its pioneer was Adam Smith, author of the classic book *The Wealth of Nations* (1776). Smith was an optimist, in favor of leaving individuals' economic activities to their own devices. For that reason he condemned government interference in the economy—so common in his day under the protectionist government's mercantilism policy, which sought to increase the nation's wealth by expanding exports while minimizing imports. The "invisible hand"—essentially the free market—which according to Smith turned individual gain into social advantage, also favored free trade among nations, based on an international division of labor.

Adam Smith's optimistic assumptions were soon called into question by Thomas Robert Malthus (1766–1834). A Church of England clergyman and professor of history and political economy at a small college run by the East India Company, Malthus gave the study of political economy not only a moral but also a pessimistic twist, for he stressed the immutable poverty of nations. He contributed two books to the science of political economy. The first, *An Essay on the Principle of Population, as It Affects the Future Improvement of Society,* was published in 1798. It was followed in 1803 by a second and enlarged edition entitled *An Essay on the Principle of Population, or, a View of Its Past and Present Effects on Human Happiness.* In these works Malthus argued that population growth was the true reason for the misery of the poor.

ADAM SMITH
THE WEALTH OF NATIONS

The Wealth of Nations carries the important message of *laissez faire,* which means that the government should intervene as little as possible in economic affairs and leave the market to its own devices. It advocates the liberation of economic production from all limiting regulation in order to benefit "the people and the sovereign," not only in Great Britain but in the community of countries. Admittedly, in his advocacy of free trade Smith made allowance for the national interest, justifying "certain public works and certain public institutions," including the government and the state. He defended, for instance, the Navigation Acts, which stipulated that goods brought from its overseas colonies into England be carried in British ships. Neither did he want to ruin established industries by introducing free trade too suddenly. Adam Smith was an eighteenth-century cosmopolitan who viewed political economy as an international system. His preference was clearly for economic cooperation among nations as a source of peace. In the passage that follows, Smith argues that economic activity unrestricted by government best serves the individual and society.

Every individual is continually exerting himself to find out the most advantageous employment for whatever capital he can command. It is his own advantage, indeed, and not that of the society, which he has in view. But the study of his own advantage, naturally, or rather necessarily, leads him to prefer that employment which is most advantageous to the society. . . .

. . . As every individual, therefore, endeavours as much as he can both to employ his capital in the support of domestic industry, and so to direct that industry that its produce may be of the greatest value, every individual necessarily labours to render the annual revenue of the society as great as he can. He generally, indeed, neither intends to promote the public interest, nor knows how much he is promoting it. By preferring the support of domestic to that of foreign industry, he intends only his own security; and by directing that industry in such a manner as its produce may be of the greatest value, he intends only his own gain, and he is in this, as in many other cases, led by an invisible hand to promote an end which was no part of his intention. Nor is it always the worse for the society that it was no part of it. By pursuing his own interest he frequently promotes that of the society more effectually than when he really intends to promote it. I have never known much good done by those who affected to trade for the public good. . . .

. . . The statesman who should attempt to direct private people in what manner they ought to employ their capitals, would not only load himself with a most unnecessary attention, but assume an authority which could safely be trusted, not only to no single person, but to no council or senate whatever, and which would nowhere be so dangerous as in the hands of a man who had folly and presumption enough to fancy himself fit to exercise it. . . .

It is thus that every system which endeavours, either by extraordinary encouragements to draw towards a particular species of industry a greater share of the capital of the society than would naturally go to it, or, by extraordinary restraints, force from a particular species of industry some share of the capital which would otherwise be employed in it, is in reality subversive to the great purpose which it means to promote. It retards, instead of accelerating, the progress of the society towards real wealth and greatness; and diminishes, instead of increasing, the real value of the annual produce of its land and labour.

All systems either of preference or of restraint, therefore, being thus completely taken away, the obvious and simple system of natural liberty establishes itself of its own accord. Every man, as long as he does not violate the laws of justice, is left perfectly free to pursue his own interest his own way, and to bring both his industry and capital into competition with those of any other man, or order of men. The sovereign is completely discharged from a duty, in the attempting to perform which he must always be exposed to innumerable delusions, and for the proper performance of which no human wisdom or knowledge could ever be sufficient; the duty of superintending the industry of private people, and of directing it towards the employments most suitable to the interest of the society. According to the system of natural liberty, the sovereign has only three duties to attend to; three duties of great importance, indeed, but plain and intelligible to common understandings: first, the duty of protecting the society from the violence and invasion of other independent societies: secondly, the duty of protecting, as far as possible, every member of the society from the injustice or oppression of every other member of it, or the duty of establishing an exact administration of justice; and, thirdly, the duty of erecting and maintaining certain public works and certain public institutions which it can never be for the interest of any individual, or small number of individuals, to erect and maintain; because the profit could never repay the expense to any individual or small number of individuals, though it may frequently do much more than repay it to a great society.

Thomas R. Malthus
ON THE PRINCIPLE OF POPULATION

Malthus assumed that population tended forever to outgrow the resources needed to sustain it. The balance between population and its life-sustaining resources was elementally maintained, he gloomily argued, by famine, war, and other fatal calamities. As a clergyman, he believed in sexual abstinence as the means of limiting population growth. He also saw little need to better the condition of the poor, whom he considered the most licentious part of the population, because he believed that they would then breed faster and, by upsetting the population/resource balance, bring misery to all. This view—that poverty was an iron law of nature—buttressed supporters of strict laissez faire who opposed government action to aid the poor.

POPULATION'S EFFECTS ON SOCIETY

I have read some of the speculations on the perfectibility of man and of society with great pleasure. I have been warmed and delighted with the enchanting picture which they hold forth. I ardently wish for such happy improvements. But I see great and, to my understanding, unconquerable difficulties in the way to them. These difficulties it is my present purpose to state, declaring, at the same time, that so far from exulting in them, as a cause of triumphing over the friends of innovation, nothing would give me greater pleasure than to see them completely removed. . . .

[These difficulties are]

First, That food is necessary to the existence of man.

Secondly, That the passion between the sexes is necessary and will remain nearly in its present state.

These two laws, ever since we have had any knowledge of mankind, appear to have been fixed laws of our nature; and as we have not hitherto seen any alteration in them, we have no right to conclude that they will ever cease to be what they are now, without an immediate act of power in that Being who first arranged the system of the universe, and for the advantage of His creatures, still executes, according to fixed laws, all its various operations. . . .

Assuming, then, my postulata {assumptions} as granted, I say that the power of population is indefinitely greater than the power in the earth to produce subsistence for man.

Population, when unchecked, increases in a geometrical ratio. Subsistence only increases in an arithmetical ratio. A slight acquaintance with numbers will show the immensity of the first power in comparison of the second.

By that law of our nature which makes food necessary to the life of man, the effects of these two unequal powers must be kept equal.

This implies a strong and constantly operating check on population from the difficulty of subsistence. This difficulty must fall somewhere and must necessarily be severely felt by a large portion of mankind. . . .

This natural inequality of the two powers of population and of production in the earth, and that great law of our nature which must constantly keep their efforts equal, form the great difficulty that to me appears insurmountable in the way to perfectibility of society. . . .

Consequently, if the premises are just, the argument is conclusive against the perfectibility of the mass of mankind.

POPULATION'S EFFECTS ON HUMAN HAPPINESS

The ultimate check to population appears then to be a want of food, arising necessarily from the different ratios according to which population and food increase. But this ultimate check is never the immediate check, except in cases of actual famine.

The immediate check may be stated to consist in all those customs, and all those diseases, which seem to be generated by a scarcity of the means of subsistence; and all those causes, independent of this scarcity, which tend prematurely to weaken and destroy the human frame.

These checks to population, which are constantly operating with more or less force in every society, and keep down the number to the level of the means of subsistence, may be classed under two general heads—the preventive and the positive checks.

The preventive check, as far as it is voluntary, is peculiar to man, and arises from that distinctive superiority in his reasoning faculties which enables him to calculate distant consequences. Man cannot look around him and see the distress which frequently presses upon those who have large families; he cannot contemplate his present possessions or earnings which he now nearly consumes himself, and calculate the amount of each share, when with a little addition they must be divided, perhaps, among seven or eight, without feeling a doubt whether, if he follow the bent of his inclinations, he may be able to support the offspring which he will probably bring into the world. . . .

The conditions are calculated to prevent, and certainly do prevent, a great number of persons in all civilized nations from pursuing the dictate of nature in an early attachment to one woman. . . .

The positive checks to population are extremely various, and include every cause, whether arising from vice or misery, which in any degree contributes to shorten the natural duration of human life. Under this head, therefore, may be enumerated all unwholesome occupations, severe labor and exposure to the seasons, extreme poverty, bad nursing of children, great towns, excesses of all kinds, the whole train of common diseases and epidemics, wars, plague, and famine. . . .

POPULATION AND POVERTY

Almost everything that has been hitherto done for the poor, has tended, as if with solicitous care, to throw a veil of obscurity over this subject and to hide from them the true cause of their poverty. When the wages of labour are hardly sufficient to maintain two children, a man marries and has five or six. He of course finds himself miserably distressed. . . . He accuses his parish. . . . He accuses the avarice of the rich. . . . He accuses the partial and unjust institutions of society. . . . In searching for objects of accusation, he never [alludes] to the quarter from which all his misfortunes originate. The last person that he would think of accusing is himself. . . .

We cannot justly accuse them (the common people) of improvidence [thriftlessness] and want of industry, till . . . after it has been brought home to their comprehensions, that they are themselves the cause of their own poverty; that the means of redress are in their own hands, and in the hands of no other persons whatever; that the society in which they live and the government which presides over it, are totally without power in this respect; and however ardently they [government] may desire to relieve them, and whatever attempts they may make to do so, they are really and truly unable to execute what they benevolently wish, but unjustly promise.

REVIEW QUESTIONS

1. What did Adam Smith say were the results of a laissez-faire policy?
2. What, according to Smith, were the duties of the sovereign under the system of natural liberty? Do you think there are other duties that should be added?
3. What are the "fixed laws" of human nature according to Thomas Malthus? For Malthus, how did the power of population growth compare with that of the means to increase food?
4. What distinction did Malthus draw between preventive and positive checks to population growth?
5. Why is Malthus considered to have been a pessimist?
6. Do any of Malthus's arguments apply to our world today?

---

3   The Capitalist Ethic

The remarkable advance in industry and material prosperity in the nineteenth century has been hailed as the triumph of the middle class, or bourgeoisie, which included bankers, merchants, factory owners, professionals, and government officials. Unlike the upper classes, which lived on inherited wealth, middle-class people supported themselves by diligent, assiduous activity— what has been called "the capitalist (or bourgeois) ethic." A vigorous spirit of enterprise and the opportunity for men of ability to rise from common origins to riches and fame help explain the growth of industrialism in England. These industrial capitalists adopted the attitude of medieval monks that "idleness is the enemy of the soul," to which they added "time is money."

The ideal of dedicated and responsible hard work directed by an internal rather than an external discipline was seen as the ultimate source of human merit and was widely publicized in the nineteenth century. It encouraged upward mobility among the lower classes and sustained the morale of ambitious middle-class people immersed in the keen competition of private enterprise. By shaping highly motivated private citizens, the capitalist ethic also provided a vital source of national strength.

Samuel Smiles
SELF-HELP AND *THRIFT*

Samuel Smiles (1812–1904) was the most famous messenger of the capitalist ethic at its best. His father, a Scottish papermaker and general merchant, died early, leaving his eleven children to fend for themselves. Samuel was apprenticed to a medical office, in due time becoming a physician in general practice. Turned journalist, he edited the local newspaper in the English city of Leeds, hoping to cure the ills of society by promoting the social and intellectual development of the working classes. Leaving his editorial office, he stepped into railroad management as a friend of George Stephenson, the inventor of the locomotive and promoter of railroads, whose biography Smiles wrote in 1857. Two years later he published *Self-Help,* which had grown out of a lecture to a small mutual-improvement society in which people sought each other's help in bettering their condition. The book was an instant success and was translated into many languages, including Japanese. Having retired after twenty-one years as a railway administrator and prolific author, Smiles suffered a stroke. Recovered, he traveled widely, writing more books about deserving but often unknown achievers. All along, he practiced in his personal life the virtues that he preached. The following selections reveal not only Samuel Smiles's philosophy of life but also the values inspiring the achievements of capitalism.

SELF-HELP

"Heaven helps those who help themselves" is a well-tried maxim, embodying in a small compass the results of vast human experience. The spirit of self-help is the root of all genuine growth in the individual; and, exhibited in the lives of many, it constitutes the true source of national vigour and strength. Help from without is often enfeebling in its effects, but help from within invariably invigorates. Whatever is done *for* men or classes, to a certain extent takes away the stimulus and necessity of doing for themselves; and where men are subjected to over-guidance and over-government, the inevitable tendency is to render them comparatively helpless.

Even the best institutions can give a man no active help. Perhaps the most they can do is, to leave him free to develop himself and improve his individual condition. But in all times men have been prone to believe that their happiness and well-being were to be secured by means of institutions rather than by their own conduct. Hence the value of legislation as an agent in human advancement has usually been much over-estimated. . . . [N]o laws, however stringent, can make the idle industrious, the thriftless provident [financially prudent], or the drunken sober. Such reforms can only be effected by means of individual action, economy, and self-denial; by better habits, rather than by greater rights. . . .

National progress is the sum of individual industry, energy, and uprightness, as national decay is of individual idleness, selfishness, and vice. What we are accustomed to decry as great social evils, will, for the most part, be found to be but the outgrowth of man's own perverted life; and though we may endeavour to cut them down and extirpate them by means of Law, they will only spring up again with fresh luxuriance in some other form, unless the conditions of personal life and character are radically improved. If this view be correct, then it follows that the highest patriotism and philanthropy consist, not so much in altering laws and modifying institutions, as in helping and stimulating men to elevate and improve themselves by their own free and independent individual action.

It may be of comparatively little consequence how a man is governed from without, whilst everything depends upon how he governs himself from within. The greatest slave is not he who is ruled by a despot, great though that evil be, but he who is the thrall of his own moral ignorance, selfishness, and vice. . . .

Smiles's book *Thrift,* published in 1875, restates and expands on the themes stressed in *Self-Help.*

THRIFT

Every man is bound to do what he can to elevate his social state, and to secure his independence. For this purpose he must spare from his means in order to be independent in his condition. Industry enables men to earn their living; it should also enable them to learn to live. Independence can only be established by the exercise of forethought, prudence, frugality, and self-denial. To be just as well as generous, men must deny themselves. The essence of generosity is self-sacrifice.

The object of this book is to induce men to employ their means for worthy purposes, and not to waste them upon selfish indulgences. Many enemies have to be encountered in accomplishing this object. There are idleness, thoughtlessness, vanity, vice, intemperance. The last is the worst enemy of all. Numerous cases are cited in the course of the following book, which show that one of the best methods of abating the curse of Drink is to induce old and young to practice the virtue of Thrift. . . .

It is the savings of individuals which compose the wealth—in other words, the well-being—of every nation. On the other hand, it is the wastefulness of individuals which occasions the impoverishment of states. So that every thrifty person may be regarded as a public benefactor, and every thriftless person as a public enemy. . . .

. . . All that is great in man comes of labor—greatness in art, in literature, in science. Knowledge—"the wing wherewith we fly to heaven"—is only acquired through labor. Genius is but a capability of laboring intensely: it is the power of making great and sustained efforts. Labor may be a chastisement, but it is indeed a glorious one. It is worship, duty, praise, and immortality—for those who labor with the highest aims and for the purest purposes. . . .

. . . Of all wretched men, surely the idle are the most so—those whose life is barren of utility, who have nothing to do except to gratify their senses. Are not such men the most querulous [complaining], miserable, and dissatisfied of all, constantly in a state of *ennui* [boredom], alike useless to themselves and to others—mere cumberers [troublesome occu-

piers] of the earth, who, when removed, are missed by none, and whom none regret? Most wretched and ignoble lot, indeed, is the lot of the idlers.

Who have helped the world onward so much as the workers; men who have had to work from necessity or from choice? All that we call progress—civilization, well-being, and prosperity—depends upon industry, diligently applied—from the culture of a barley-stalk to the construction of a steamship; from the stitching of a collar to the sculpturing of "the statue that enchants the world."

All useful and beautiful thoughts, in like manner, are the issue of labor, of study, of observation, of research, of diligent elaboration. . . .

By the working-man we do not mean merely the man who labors with his muscles and sinews. A horse can do this. But *he* is preeminently the working-man who works with his brain also, and whose whole physical system is under the influence of his higher faculties. The man who paints a picture, who writes a book, who makes a law, who creates a poem, is a working-man of the highest order; not so necessary to the physical sustainment of the community as the plowman or the shepherd, but not less important as providing for society its highest intellectual nourishment. . . .

But a large proportion of men do not provide for the future. They do not remember the past. They think only of the present. They preserve nothing. They spend all that they earn. They do not provide for themselves; they do not provide for their families. They may make high wages, but eat and drink the whole of what they earn. Such people are constantly poor, and hanging on the verge of destitution. . . .

REVIEW QUESTIONS

1. What, according to Samuel Smiles, were the key values that should guide the individual?
2. How did Smiles define success in life?
3. What, in his opinion, were the enemies of individual and national achievement?
4. Do Smiles's writings offer good advice to the poor in the United States today? Explain why or why not.

4   The Dark Side of Industrialization

Among the numerous problems caused by rapid industrialization, none aroused greater concern among humanitarians than child labor in factories and mines. In preindustrial times, children had always been part of the labor force, indoors and out, a practice that was continued during the early days of the Industrial Revolution. In the cotton industry, for instance, the proportion of children and adolescents under eighteen was around 40–45 percent of the labor force; in some large firms the proportion was even greater. Employers discovered early that youngsters adapted more easily to machines and factory discipline than did adults, who were used to traditional handicraft routines. Child labor took children away from their parents, undermined family life, and deprived children of schooling. Factory routines dulled their minds, and the long hours spent in often unsanitary environments endangered their health.

Sadler Commission
REPORT ON CHILD LABOR

Due to concern about child labor, in 1832 a parliamentary committee chaired by Michael Thomas Sadler investigated the situation of children employed in British factories. The following testimony is drawn from the records of the Sadler Commission.

May 18, 1832

Michael Thomas Sadler, Esquire, in the chair.
Mr. Matthew Crabtree, called in; and Examined.

What age are you?—Twenty-two.[1]

What is your occupation?—A blanket manufacturer.

Have you ever been employed in a factory?—Yes.

At what age did you first go to work in one?—Eight.

How long did you continue in that occupation?—Four years.

Will you state the hours of labour at the period when you first went to the factory, in ordinary times?—From 6 in the morning to 8 at night.

Fourteen hours?—Yes.

With what intervals for refreshment and rest?—An hour at noon.

Then you had no resting time allowed in which to take your breakfast, or what is in Yorkshire called your "drinking"?—No.

When trade was brisk what were your hours?—From 5 in the morning to 9 in the evening.

Sixteen hours?—Yes.

With what intervals at dinner?—An hour.

How far did you live from the mill?—About two miles.

Was there any time allowed for you to get your breakfast in the mill?—No.

Did you take it before you left home?—Generally.

---

[1]In the original source, each paragraph was numbered; this reading includes paragraphs 2481–2519 and 2597–2604.

During those long hours of labour could you be punctual, how did you awake?—I seldom did awake spontaneously. I was most generally awoke or lifted out of bed, sometimes asleep, by my parents.

Were you always in time?—No.

What was the consequence if you had been too late?—I was most commonly beaten.

Severely?—Very severely, I thought.

In whose factory was this?—Messrs. Hague & Cook's, of Dewsbury.

Will you state the effect that those long hours had upon the state of your health and feelings?—I was, when working those long hours, commonly very much fatigued at night, when I left my work, so much so that I sometimes should have slept as I walked if I had not stumbled and started awake again, and so sick often that I could not eat, and what I did eat I vomited.

Did this labour destroy your appetite?—It did.

In what situation were you in that mill?—I was a piecener [see below].

Will you state to the Committee whether piecening is a very laborious employment for children, or not?—It is a very laborious employment. Pieceners are continually running to and fro, and on their feet the whole day.

The duty of the piecener is to take the cardings[2] from one part of the machinery, and to place them on another?—Yes.

So that the labour is not only continual, but it is unabated to the last?—It is unabated to the last.

Do you not think, from your own experience, that the speed of the machinery is so calculated as to demand the utmost exertions of a child, supposing the hours were moderate?—It is as much as they could do at the best; they are always upon the stretch, and it is commonly very difficult to keep up with their work.

State the condition of the children towards the latter part of the day, who have thus to keep up with the machinery?—It is as much as they can do when they are not very much fatigued to keep up with their work, and towards the close of the day, when they come to be more fatigued, they cannot keep up with it very well, and the consequence is that they are beaten to spur them on.

Were you beaten under those circumstances?—Yes.

Frequently?—Very frequently.

And principally at the latter end of the day?—Yes.

And is it your belief that if you had not been so beaten, you should not have got through the work?—I should not if I had not been kept up to it by some means.

Does beating then principally occur at the latter end of the day, when the children are exceedingly fatigued?—It does at the latter end of the day, and in the morning sometimes, when they are very drowsy, and have not got rid of the fatigue of the day before.

What were you beaten with principally?—A strap.

Any thing else?—Yes, a stick sometimes; and there is a kind of roller which runs on the top of the machine called a billy, perhaps two or three yards in length, and perhaps an inch and a half, or more, in diameter; the circumference would be four or five inches, I cannot speak exactly.

Were you beaten with that instrument?—Yes.

Have you yourself been beaten, and have you seen other children struck severely with that roller?—I have been struck very severely with it myself, so much so as to knock me down, and I have seen other children have their heads broken with it.

You think that it is a general practice to beat the children with the roller?—It is.

You do not think then that you were worse treated than other children in the mill?—No, I was not, perhaps not so bad as some were. . . .

Can you speak as to the effect of this labour in the mills and factories on the morals of the chil-

---

[2]*Cardings* were woolen fibers that had been combed in preparation for spinning and weaving.

dren, as far as you have observed?—As far as I have observed with regard to morals in the mills, there is every thing about them that is disgusting to every one conscious of correct morality.

Do you find that the children, the females especially, are very early demoralized in them?—They are.

Is their language indecent?—Very indecent; and both sexes take great familiarities with each other in the mills, without at all being ashamed of their conduct.

Do you connect their immorality of language and conduct with their excessive labour?—It may be somewhat connected with it, for it is to be observed that most of that goes on towards night, when they begin to be drowsy; it is a kind of stimulus which they use to keep them awake; they say some pert thing or other to keep themselves from drowsiness, and it generally happens to be some obscene language.

Have not a considerable number of the females employed in mills illegitimate children very early in life?—I believe there are; I have known some of them have illegitimate children when they were between 16 and 17 years of age.

How many grown up females had you in the mill?—I cannot speak to the exact number that were grown up; perhaps there might be thirty-four or so that worked in the mill at that time.

How many of those had illegitimate children?—A great many of them, eighteen or nineteen of them, I think.

Did they generally marry the men by whom they had the children?—No, it sometimes happens that young women have children by married men, and I have known an instance, a few weeks since, where one of the young women had a child by a married man.

REVIEW QUESTIONS

1. According to the testimony given the Sadler Commission, how young were the children employed in the factories? How many hours and at what times of day did they work?
2. What do you think were the reasons for the employment of children from the employers' point of view? From the parents' point of view?
3. What measures were employed in the factories to keep children alert at their tasks?

5 Factory Discipline

For the new industries to succeed, workers needed to adopt the rigorous discipline exercised by the new industrial capitalists themselves. But adapting to labor with machines in factories proved traumatic for the poor, uneducated, and often unruly folk, who previously had toiled on farms and in village workshops and were used to a less demanding pace.

FACTORY RULES

The problem of adapting a preindustrial labor force to the discipline needed for coordinating large numbers of workers in the factory was common to all industrializing countries. The Foundry and Engineering Works of the Royal Overseas Trading Company, in the Moabit section of Berlin, issued the following rules in 1844. The rules aimed at instilling obedience and honesty as well as "good order and harmony" among the factory's workers. The rules not only stressed timekeeping (with appropriate fines for latecomers), but also proper conduct in all aspects of life and work in the factory.

In every large works, and in the co-ordination of any large number of workmen, good order and harmony must be looked upon as the fundamentals of success, and therefore the following rules shall be strictly observed.

Every man employed in the concern . . . shall receive a copy of these rules, so that no one can plead ignorance. Its acceptance shall be deemed to mean consent to submit to its regulations.

(1) The normal working day begins at all seasons at 6 A.M. precisely and ends, after the usual break of half an hour for breakfast, an hour for dinner and half an hour for tea, at 7 P.M., and it shall be strictly observed.

Five minutes before the beginning of the stated hours of work until their actual commencement, a bell shall ring and indicate that every worker employed in the concern has to proceed to his place of work, in order to start as soon as the bell stops.

The doorkeeper shall lock the door punctually at 6 A.M., 8:30 A.M., 1 P.M. and 4:30 P.M.

Workers arriving 2 minutes late shall lose half an hour's wages; whoever is more than 2 minutes late may not start work until after the next break, or at least shall lose his wages until then. Any disputes about the correct time shall be settled by the clock mounted above the gatekeeper's lodge.

These rules are valid both for time- and for piece-workers, and in cases of breaches of these rules, workmen shall be fined in proportion to their earnings. The deductions from the wage shall be entered in the wage-book of the gatekeeper whose duty they are; they shall be unconditionally accepted as it will not be possible to enter into any discussions about them.

(2) When the bell is rung to denote the end of the working day, every workman, both on piece- and on day-wage, shall leave his workshop and the yard, but is not allowed to make preparations for his departure before the bell rings. Every breach of this rule shall lead to a fine of five silver groschen [pennies] to the sick fund. Only those who have obtained special permission by the overseer may stay on in the workshop in order to work.—If a workman has worked beyond the closing bell, he must give his name to the gatekeeper on leaving, on pain of losing his payment for the overtime.

(3) No workman, whether employed by time or piece, may leave before the end of the working day, without having first received permission from the overseer and having given his name to the gatekeeper. Omission of these two actions shall lead to a fine of ten silver groschen payable to the sick fund.

(4) Repeated irregular arrival at work shall lead to dismissal. This shall also apply to those who are found idling by an official or overseer, and refuse to obey their order to resume work.

(5) Entry to the firm's property by any but the designated gateway, and exit by any prohibited route, e.g. by climbing fences or walls, or by crossing the Spree [River], shall be punished by a fine of fifteen silver groschen to the sick fund for the first offences, and dismissal for the second.

(6) No worker may leave his place of work otherwise than for reasons connected with his work.

(7) All conversation with fellow-workers is prohibited; if any worker requires information about his work, he must turn to the overseer, or to the particular fellow-worker designated for the purpose.

(8) Smoking in the workshops or in the yard is prohibited during working hours; anyone caught smoking shall be fined five silver groschen for the sick fund for every such offence.

(9) Every worker is responsible for cleaning up his space in the workshop, and if in doubt,

he is to turn to his overseer.—All tools must always be kept in good condition, and must be cleaned after use. This applies particularly to the turner, regarding his lathe.

(10) Natural functions must be performed at the appropriate places, and whoever is found soiling walls, fences, squares, etc., and similarly, whoever is found washing his face and hands in the workshop and not in the places assigned for the purpose, shall be fined five silver groschen for the sick fund.

(11) On completion of his piece of work, every workman must hand it over at once to his foreman or superior, in order to receive a fresh piece of work. Pattern makers must on no account hand over their patterns to the foundry without express order of their supervisors. No workman may take over work from his fellow-workman without instruction to that effect by the foreman.

(12) It goes without saying that all overseers and officials of the firm shall be obeyed without question, and shall be treated with due deference. Disobedience will be punished by dismissal.

(13) Immediate dismissal shall also be the fate of anyone found drunk in any of the workshops.

(14) Untrue allegations against superiors or officials of the concern shall lead to stern reprimand, and may lead to dismissal. The same punishment shall be meted out to those who knowingly allow errors to slip through when supervising or stocktaking.

(15) Every workman is obliged to report to his superiors any acts of dishonesty or embezzlement on the part of his fellow workmen. If he omits to do so, and it is shown after subsequent discovery of a misdemeanour that he knew about it at the time, he shall be liable to be taken to court as an accessory after the fact and the wage due to him shall be retained as punishment. Conversely, anyone denouncing a theft in such a way as to allow conviction of the thief shall receive a reward of two Thaler [dollar equivalent], and, if necessary, his name shall be kept confidential.—Further, the gatekeeper and the watchman, as well as every official, are entitled to search the baskets, parcels, aprons etc. of the women and children who are taking the dinners into the works, on their departure, as well as search any worker suspected of stealing any article whatever. . . .

(18) Advances shall be granted only to the older workers, and even to them only in exceptional circumstances. As long as he is working by the piece, the workman is entitled merely to his fixed weekly wage as subsistence pay; the extra earnings shall be paid out only on completion of the whole piece contract. If a workman leaves before his piece contract is completed, either of his own free will, or on being dismissed as punishment, or because of illness, the partly completed work shall be valued by the general manager with the help of two overseers, and he will be paid accordingly. There is no appeal against the decision of these experts.

(19) A free copy of these rules is handed to every workman, but whoever loses it and requires a new one, or cannot produce it on leaving, shall be fined 2½ silver groschen, payable to the sick fund.

REVIEW QUESTIONS

1. Judging by the Berlin factory rules, what were the differences between preindustrial and industrial work routines?
2. How might these rules have affected the lives of families?

CHAPTER 5

Romanticism, Reaction, Revolution

WILLIAM BLAKE, "THE ANCIENT OF DAYS." Deeply religious feelings, marked by tormented inner visions, pervaded the works of English artist, poet, and mystic William Blake (1757–1827). *(The Pierpont Morgan Library/Art Resource, New York.)*

In 1815 the European scene had changed. Napoleon was exiled to the island of St. Helena, and a Bourbon king, in the person of Louis XVIII, again reigned in France. The Great Powers of Europe, meeting at Vienna, had drawn up a peace settlement that awarded territory to the states that had fought Napoleon and restored to power some rulers dethroned by the French emperor. The Congress of Vienna also organized the Concert of Europe to guard against a resurgence of the revolutionary spirit that had kept Europe in turmoil for some twenty-five years. The conservative leaders of Europe wanted no more Robespierres who resorted to terror and no more Napoleons who sought to dominate the continent.

However, reactionary rulers' efforts to turn the clock back to the Old Regime could not contain the forces unleashed by the French Revolution. Between 1820 and 1848 a series of revolts rocked Europe. The principal causes were liberalism (which demanded constitutional government and the protection of the freedom and rights of the individual citizen) and nationalism (which called for the reawakening and unification of the nation and its liberation from foreign domination).

In the 1820s, the Concert of Europe crushed a quasi-liberal revolution in Spain and liberal uprisings in Italy, and Tsar Nicholas I subdued liberal officers who challenged tsarist autocracy. The Greeks, however, successfully fought for independence from the Ottoman Turks.

Between 1830 and 1832, another wave of revolutions swept over Europe. Italian liberals and nationalists failed to free Italy from foreign rule or to wrest reforms from autocratic princes, and the tsar's troops crushed a Polish bid for independence from Russian rule. But in France, rebels overthrew the reactionary Bourbon Charles X in 1830 and replaced him with a more moderate ruler, Louis Philippe; a little later Belgium gained its independence from Holland.

The year 1848 was decisive in the struggle for liberty and nationhood. In France, democrats overthrew Louis Philippe and established a republic that gave all men the right to vote. However, in Italy and Germany, revolutions attempting to unify each land failed, as did a bid in Hungary for independence from the Hapsburg Empire. After enjoying initial successes, the revolutionaries were crushed by superior might, and their liberal and nationalist objectives remained largely unfulfilled. By 1870, however, many nationalist aspirations had been realized. The Hapsburg Empire granted Hungary autonomy in 1867, and by 1870–1871, the period of the Franco-Prussian War, Germany and Italy became unified states. That authoritarian and militaristic Prussia unified Germany, rather than liberals like those who had fought in the revolutions of 1848, affected the future of Europe.

In the early nineteenth century a new cultural orientation, romanticism, emphasized the liberation of human emotions and the free expression of personality in artistic creations. The romantics' attack on the rationalism of the Enlightenment and their veneration of the past influenced conservative thought, and their concern for a people's history and traditions contributed to the development of nationalism. By encouraging innovation in art, music, and literature, the romantics greatly enriched European cultural life.

1 Romanticism

Romantics attacked the outlook of the Enlightenment, protesting that the philosophes' excessive intellectualizing and their mechanistic view of the physical world and human nature distorted and fettered the human spirit and thwarted cultural creativity. The rationalism of the philosophes, said the romantics, had reduced human beings to soulless thinking machines, and vibrant nature to lifeless wheels, cogs, and pulleys. In contrast to the philosophes' scientific and analytic approach, the romantics asserted the intrinsic value of emotions and imagination and extolled the spontaneity, richness, and uniqueness of the human spirit. To the philosophes, the emotions obstructed clear thinking.

For romantics, feelings and imagination were the human essence, the source of cultural creativity, and the avenue to true understanding. Their beliefs led the romantics to rebel against strict standards of aesthetics that governed artistic creations. They held that artists, musicians, and writers must trust their own sensibilities and inventiveness and must not be bound by textbook rules; the romantics focused on the creative capacities inherent in the emotions and urged individuality and freedom of expression in the arts. In the Age of Romanticism, the artist and poet succeeded the scientist as the arbiters of Western civilization.

William Wordsworth
"TABLES TURNED"

The works of the great English poet William Wordsworth (1770–1850) exemplify many tendencies of the Romantic Movement. In the interval during which he tried to come to grips with his disenchantment with the French Revolution, Wordsworth's creativity reached its height. In the preface to *Lyrical Ballads* (1798), Wordsworth produced what has become known as the manifesto of romanticism. He wanted poetry to express powerful feelings and also contended that because it is a vehicle for the imagination, poetry is the source of truth. Wordsworth thus represented a shift in perspective comparable to the shift made by Descartes in philosophy, but for Wordsworth imagination and feeling, not mathematics and logic, yielded highest truth.

The philosophes had regarded nature as a giant machine, all of whose parts worked in perfect precision and whose laws could be uncovered through the scientific method. The romantics rejected this mechanical model. To them, nature was a living organism filled with beautiful forms whose inner meaning was grasped through the human imagination; they sought from nature a higher truth than mechanical law. In "Tables Turned" (1798), Wordsworth exalts nature as humanity's teacher.

Up! up! my Friend, and quit your books;
Or surely you'll grow double:
Up! up! my Friend, and clear your looks;
Why all this toil and trouble?

The sun, above the mountain's head,
A freshening lustre mellow
Through all the long green fields has spread,
His first sweet evening yellow.

Books! 'tis a dull and endless strife:
Come, hear the woodland linnet [Old World
    finch],
How sweet his music! on my life,
There's more of wisdom in it.

And hark! how blithe the throstle [thrush] sings!
He, too, is no mean preacher:
Come forth into the light of things,
Let Nature be your Teacher.

She has a world of ready wealth,
Our minds and hearts to bless—
Spontaneous wisdom breathed by health,
Truth breathed by cheerfulness.

One impulse from a vernal [springtime] wood
May teach you more of man,
Of moral evil and of good,
Than all the sages can.

Sweet is the lore which Nature brings;
Our meddling intellect
Mis-shapes the beauteous forms of things:—
We murder to dissect.

Enough of Science and of Art;
Close up those barren leaves [book pages];
Come forth, and bring with you a heart
That watches and receives.

William Blake
"MILTON"

William Blake (1757–1827) was a British engraver, poet, and religious mystic. He also affirmed the creative potential of the imagination and expressed distaste for the rationalist-scientific outlook of the Enlightenment, as is clear from these lines in his poem "Milton," written in 1804.

. . . the Reasoning Power in Man:
This is a false Body; an Incrustation [scab] over
    my Immortal
Spirit; a Selfhood, which must be put off &
    annihilated alway[s]
To cleanse the Face of my Spirit by Self-
    examination,
To bathe in the Waters of Life, to wash off the
    Not Human,
I come in Self-annihilation & the grandeur of
    Inspiration,

To cast off Rational Demonstration by Faith in
    the Saviour,
To cast off the rotten rags of Memory by
    Inspiration,
To cast off Bacon, Locke & Newton from
    Albion's covering,[1]
To take off his filthy garments & clothe him
    with Imagination,

---

[1]Bacon, Locke, and Newton were British thinkers who valued reason and science, and Albion is an ancient name for England.

To cast aside from Poetry all that is not
  Inspiration,
That it no longer shall dare to mock with the
  aspersion [defamation] of Madness

. . .

To cast off the idiot Questioner who is always
  questioning
But never capable of answering, who sits with a
  sly grin
Silent plotting when to question, like a thief
  in a cave,
Who publishes doubt & calls it knowledge,
  whose Science is Despair,
Whose pretence to knowledge is Envy, whose

whole Science is
To destroy the wisdom of ages to gratify
  ravenous Envy
That rages round him like a Wolf day & night
  without rest:
He smiles with condescension, he talks of
  Benevolence & Virtue,
And those who act with Benevolence & Virtue
  they murder time on time.
These are the destroyers of Jerusalem, these are
  the murderers
Of Jesus, who deny the Faith & mock at Eternal
  Life. . . .

REVIEW QUESTIONS

1. According to Wordsworth, how could the human being achieve goodness?
2. In "Tables Turned," what connection did Wordsworth see between nature and
   the human mind? How did his idea of nature differ from that of the scientist?
   According to Wordsworth, what effect did nature have on the imagination?
3. Why did William Blake attack reason?
4. The Romantic Movement was a reaction against the dominant ideas of the
   Enlightenment. Discuss this statement.

---

2 Conservatism

In the period after 1815, conservatism was the principal ideology of those who
repudiated the Enlightenment and the French Revolution. Conservatives valued tradition over reason, aristocratic and clerical authority over equality, and
the community over the individual. Edmund Burke (1729–1797), a leading
Anglo-Irish statesman and political thinker, was instrumental in shaping the
conservative outlook. His *Reflections on the Revolution in France* (1790) attacked
the violence and fundamental principles of the Revolution. Another leading
conservative was Joseph de Maistre (1753–1821), who fled his native Sardinia
in 1792 (and again in 1793) after it was invaded by the armies of the new French
Republic. De Maistre denounced the Enlightenment for spawning the French
Revolution, defended the church as a civilizing agent that made individuals
aware of their social obligations, and affirmed tradition as a model more valuable than instant reforms embodied in "paper constitutions."

The symbol of conservatism in the first half of the nineteenth century was Prince
Klemens von Metternich (1773–1859) of Austria. A bitter opponent of Jacobinism
and Napoleon, he became the pivotal figure at the Congress of Vienna (1814–1815),
where European powers met to redraw the map of Europe after their victory over
France. Metternich said that the Jacobins had subverted the pillars of civilization

and that Napoleon, by harnessing the forces of the Revolution, had destroyed the traditional European state system. No peace was possible with Napoleon, who championed revolutionary doctrines and dethroned kings, and whose rule rested not on legitimacy but on conquest and charisma. No balance of power could endure an adventurer who obliterated states and sought European domination.

Edmund Burke
REFLECTIONS ON THE REVOLUTION IN FRANCE

Burke regarded the revolutionaries as wild-eyed fanatics who had uprooted all established authority, tradition, and institutions, thereby plunging France into anarchy. Not sharing the faith of the philosophes in human goodness, Burke held that without the restraints of established authority, people revert to savagery. For Burke, monarchy, aristocracy, and Christianity represented civilizing forces that tamed the beast in human nature. By undermining venerable institutions, he said, the French revolutionaries had opened the door to anarchy and terror. Burke's *Reflections,* excerpts of which follow, was instrumental in the shaping of conservative thought.

. . . You [revolutionaries] chose to act as if you had never been moulded into civil society, and had every thing to begin anew. You began ill, because you began by despising every thing that belonged to you. . . . If the last generations of your country appeared without much lustre in your eyes, you might have passed them by, and derived your claims from a more early race of ancestors. Under a pious predilection for those ancestors, your imaginations would have realized in them a standard of virtue and wisdom, beyond the vulgar practice of the hour: and you would have risen with the example to whose imitation you aspired. Respecting your forefathers, you would have been taught to respect yourselves. You would not have chosen to consider the French as a people of yesterday, as a nation of low-born servile wretches, until the emancipating year of 1789. . . . By following wise examples you would have given new examples of wisdom to the world. You would have rendered the cause of liberty venerable in the eyes of every worthy mind in every nation. . . . You would have had

a free constitution; a potent monarchy; a disciplined army; a reformed and venerated clergy; a mitigated but spirited nobility, to lead your virtue. . . .

Compute your gains: see what is got by those extravagant and presumptuous speculations which have taught your leaders to despise all their predecessors, and all their contemporaries, and even to despise themselves, until the moment in which they became truly despicable. By following those false lights, France has bought undisguised calamities at a higher price than any nation has purchased the most unequivocal blessings! . . . France, when she let loose the reins of regal authority, doubled the licence, of a ferocious dissoluteness in manners, and of an insolent irreligion in opinions and practices; and has extended through all ranks of life . . . all the unhappy corruptions that usually were the disease of wealth and power. This is one of the new principles of equality in France. . . .

. . . The science of government being therefore so practical in itself, and intended for such practical purposes, a matter which requires experience, and even more experience than any person can gain in his whole life, however sagacious and observing he may be, it is with infinite caution that any man ought to venture upon pulling down an edifice which has answered in any tolerable degree for ages the common purposes of society, or on building it up again, without having models and patterns of approved utility before his eyes. . . .

. . . The nature of man is intricate; the objects of society are of the greatest possible complexity; and therefore no simple disposition or direction of power can be suitable either to man's nature, or to the quality of his affairs.

When ancient opinions of life are taken away, the loss cannot possibly be estimated. From that moment we have no compass to govern us; nor can we know distinctly to what port we steer. . . .

. . . Nothing is more certain than that our manners, our civilization, and all the good things which are connected with manners and with civilization have, in this European world of ours, depended for ages upon two principles and were, indeed, the result of both combined: I mean the spirit of a gentleman and the spirit of religion. . . .

Burke next compares the English people with the French revolutionaries.

. . . Thanks to our sullen resistance to innovation, thanks to the cold sluggishness of our national character, we still bear the stamp of our forefathers. . . . We are not the converts of Rousseau; we are not the disciples of Voltaire; Helvetius has made no progress amongst us.[1] Atheists are not our preachers; madmen are not our lawgivers. We know that *we* have made no discoveries, and we think that no discoveries are to be made, in morality, nor many in the great principles of government. . . . We fear God; we look up with awe to kings, with affection to parliaments, with duty to magistrates, with reverence to priests, and with respect to nobility. . . .

. . . We are afraid to put men to live and trade each on his own private stock of reason, because we suspect that this stock in each man is small, and that the individuals would do better to avail themselves of the general bank and capital of nations and of ages.

---

[1]Rousseau, Voltaire, and Helvétius were French philosophes of the eighteenth century noted, respectively, for advocating democracy, attacking the abuses of the Old Regime (see Chapter 2), and applying a scientific reason to moral principles.

Klemens von Metternich
THE ODIOUS IDEAS OF THE PHILOSOPHES

Two decades of revolutionary warfare had shaped Metternich's political thinking. After the fall of Napoleon, Metternich worked to restore the European balance and to suppress revolutionary movements. In the following memorandum to Tsar Alexander I, dated December 15, 1820, Metternich denounces the French philosophes for their "false systems" and "fatal errors" that weakened the social fabric and gave rise to the French Revolution. In their presumption, the philosophes forsook the experience and wisdom of the past, trusting only their own thoughts and inclinations.

The progress of the human mind has been extremely rapid in the course of the last three centuries. This progress having been accelerated more rapidly than the growth of wisdom (the only counterpoise to passions and to error); a revolution prepared by the false systems . . . has at last broken out. . . .

. . . There were . . . some men [the philosophes], unhappily endowed with great talents, who felt their own strength, and . . . who had the art to prepare and conduct men's minds to the triumph of their detestable enterprise—an enterprise all the more odious as it was pursued without regard to results, simply abandoning themselves to the one feeling of hatred of God and of His immutable moral laws.

France had the misfortune to produce the greatest number of these men. It is in her midst that religion and all that she holds sacred, that morality and authority, and all connected with them, have been attacked with a steady and systematic animosity, and it is there that the weapon of ridicule has been used with the most ease and success.

Drag through the mud the name of God and the powers instituted by His divine decrees, and the revolution will be prepared! Speak of a social contract,[1] and the revolution is accomplished! The revolution was already completed in the palaces of Kings, in the drawing-rooms and boudoirs of certain cities, while among the great mass of the people it was still only in a state of preparation. . . .

. . . The French Revolution broke out, and has gone through a complete revolutionary cycle in a very short period, which could only have appeared long to its victims and to its contemporaries. . . .

. . . The revolutionary seed had penetrated into every country. . . . It was greatly developed under the *régime* of the military despotism of Bonaparte. His conquests displaced a number of laws, institutions, and customs; broke through bonds sacred among all nations, strong enough to resist time itself; which is more than can be said of certain benefits conferred by these innovators.

---

[1]The social contract theory consisted essentially of the following principles: (1) people voluntarily enter into an agreement to establish a political community; (2) government rests on the consent of the governed; (3) people possess natural freedom and equality, which they do not surrender to the state. These principles were used to challenge the divine right of kings and absolute monarchy.

REVIEW QUESTIONS

1. Why was Edmund Burke opposed to the French Revolution?
2. What was Klemens von Metternich's opinion of "the progress of the human mind . . . in the . . . last three centuries" and its effect upon the society of his time?
3. What did Metternich mean by, "Drag through the mud the name of God and the powers instituted by His divine decrees, and the revolution will be prepared!"?

---

3 Liberalism

Conservatism was the ideology of the old order that was hostile to the Enlightenment and the French Revolution; in contrast, liberalism aspired to carry out the promise of the philosophes and the Revolution. Liberals called for a constitution that protected individual liberty and denounced censorship, arbitrary arrest, and other forms of repression. They believed that through reason and education, social evils could be remedied. Liberals rejected an essential feature of the Old Regime—the special privileges of the aristocracy and the clergy—

and held that the individual should be judged on the basis of achievement, not birth. At the core of the liberal outlook lay the conviction that the individual would develop into a good and productive human being and citizen if not co-erced by governments and churches.

John Stuart Mill
ON LIBERTY

Freedom of thought and expression were principal concerns of nineteenth-century liberals. The classic defense of intellectual freedom is *On Liberty* (1859), written by John Stuart Mill (1806–1873), a prominent British philosopher. Mill argued that no individual or government has a monopoly on truth, for all hu-man beings are fallible. Therefore, the government and the majority have no le-gitimate authority to suppress views, however unpopular; they have no right to interfere with a person's liberty so long as that person's actions do no injury to others. Nothing is more absolute, contended Mill, than the inviolable right of all adults to think and live as they please so long as they respect the rights of others. For Mill, toleration of opposing and unpopular viewpoints is a necessary trait in order for a person to become rational, moral, and civilized.

The object of this essay is to assert one very simple principle, as entitled to govern ab-solutely the dealings of society with the indi-vidual. . . . That principle is that the sole end for which mankind are warranted, individually or collectively, in interfering with the lib-erty of action of any of their number is self-protection. That the only purpose for which power can be rightfully exercised over any member of a civilized community, against his will, is to prevent harm to others. His own good, either physical or moral, is not a suffi-cient warrant. He cannot rightfully be com-pelled to do or forbear because it will be better for him to do so, because it will make him hap-pier, because, in the opinions of others, to do so would be wise or even right. These are good reasons for remonstrating with him, or reason-ing with him, or persuading him, or entreating him, but not for compelling him or visiting him with any evil in case he do otherwise. To justify that, the conduct from which it is de-sired to deter him must be calculated to pro-duce evil to someone else. The only part of the conduct of anyone for which he is amenable to

society is that which concerns others. In the part which merely concerns himself, his inde-pendence is, of right, absolute. Over himself, over his own body and mind, the individual is sovereign. . . .

. . . This, then, is the appropriate region of human liberty. It comprises, first, the inward domain of consciousness, demanding liberty of conscience in the most comprehensive sense, liberty of thought and feeling, absolute free-dom of opinion and sentiment on all subjects, practical or speculative, scientific, moral, or theological. The liberty of expressing and pub-lishing opinions may seem to fall under a dif-ferent principle, since it belongs to that part of the conduct of an individual which concerns other people, but, being almost of as much im-portance as the liberty of thought itself and resting in great part on the same reasons, is practically inseparable from it. Secondly, the principle requires liberty of tastes and pur-suits, of framing the plan of our life to suit our own character, of doing as we like, subject to such consequences as may follow, without im-pediment from our fellow creatures, so long as what we do does not harm them, even though they should think our conduct foolish, perverse, or wrong. Thirdly, from this liberty of each individual follows the liberty, within the same limits, of combination among individuals; freedom to unite for any purpose not involving harm to others: the persons combining being supposed to be of full age and not forced or deceived.

No society in which these liberties are not, on the whole, respected is free, whatever may be its form of government; and none is completely free in which they do not exist absolute and unqualified. The only freedom which deserves the name is that of pursuing our own good in our own way, so long as we do not attempt to deprive others of theirs or impede their efforts to obtain it. Each is the proper guardian of his own health, whether bodily *or* mental and spiritual. Mankind are greater gainers by suffering each other to live as seems good to themselves than by compelling each to live as seems good to the rest. . . .

. . . Let us suppose, therefore, that the government is entirely at one with the people, and never thinks of exerting any power of coercion unless in agreement with what it conceives to be their voice. But I deny the right of the people to exercise such coercion, either by themselves or by their government. The power itself is illegitimate. The best government has no more title to it than the worst. It is as noxious, or more noxious, when exerted in accordance with public opinion than when in opposition to it. If all mankind minus one were of one opinion, mankind would be no more justified in silencing that one person than he, if he had the power, would be justified in silencing mankind. Were an opinion a personal possession of no value except to the owner, if to be obstructed in the enjoyment of it were simply a private injury, it would make some difference whether the injury was inflicted only on a few persons or on many. But the peculiar evil of silencing the expression of an opinion is that it is robbing the human race, posterity as well as the existing generation—those who dissent from the opinion, still more than those who hold it. If the opinion is right, they are deprived of the opportunity of exchanging error for truth; if wrong, they lose, what is almost as great a benefit, the clearer perception and livelier impression of truth produced by its collision with error.

REVIEW QUESTIONS

1. What was the purpose of John Stuart Mill's essay?
2. For Mill, what is the "peculiar evil of silencing the expression of an opinion," however unpopular?
3. On what grounds would Mill permit society to restrict individual liberty? Do you think it is ever legitimate for the state to restrain an individual from harming himself?

4 The Rise of Modern Nationalism

Nationalism espoused the individual's allegiance to the national community and sought to unify divided nations and to liberate subject peoples. In the early nineteenth century, most nationalists were liberals who viewed the struggle for unification and freedom from foreign oppression as an extension of the struggle for individual rights. Few liberals recognized that nationalism was a potentially dangerous force that could threaten liberal ideals of freedom and equality.

Ernst Moritz Arndt
THE WAR OF LIBERATION

By glorifying a nation's language and ancient traditions and folkways, romanticism contributed to the evolution of modern nationalism, particularly in Germany. German romantics longed to create a true folk community in which the individual's soul would be immersed in the nation's soul. Through the national community, individuals could find the meaning in life for which they yearned. The romantic veneration of the past produced a mythical way of thinking about politics and history, one that subordinated reason to powerful emotions. In particular, some German romantics attacked the liberal–rational tradition of the Enlightenment and the French Revolution as hostile to the true German spirit.

The Napoleonic wars kindled nationalist sentiments in the German states. Hatred of the French occupier evoked a feeling of outrage and a desire for national unity among some Germans, who before the occupation had thought not of a German fatherland but of their own states and princes. These Germans called for a war of liberation against Napoleon. Attracting mostly intellectuals, the idea of political unification had limited impact on the rest of the people, who remained loyal to local princes and local territories. Nevertheless, the embryo of nationalism was conceived in the German uprising against Napoleon in 1813. The writings of Ernst Moritz Arndt (1769–1860), composed in the same year, vividly express the emerging nationalism. The following excerpts describe Arndt's view of the War of Liberation and present his appeal for German unity.

Fired with enthusiasm, the people rose, "with God for King and Fatherland." Among the Prussians there was only one voice, one feeling, one anger and one love, to save the Fatherland and to free Germany. The Prussians wanted war; war and death they wanted; peace they feared because they could hope for no honorable peace from Napoleon. War, war, sounded the cry from the Carpathians [mountains] to the Baltic [Sea], from the Niemen to the Elbe [rivers]. War! cried the nobleman and landed proprietor who had become impoverished. War! the peasant who was driving his last horse to death. . . . War! the citizen who was growing exhausted from quartering soldiers and paying taxes. War! the widow who was sending her only son to the front. War! the young girl who, with tears of pride and pain, was leaving her betrothed. Youths who were hardly able to bear arms, men with gray hair, officers who on account of wounds and mutilations had long ago been honorably discharged, rich landed proprietors and officials, fathers of large families and managers of extensive businesses—all were unwilling to remain behind. Even young women, under all sorts of disguises, rushed to arms; all wanted to drill, arm themselves and fight and die for the Fatherland. . . .

The most beautiful thing about all this holy zeal and happy confusion was that all differences of position, class, and age were forgotten . . . that the one great feeling for the Fatherland, its freedom and honor, swallowed all other feelings, caused all other considerations and relationships to be forgotten.

In another passage, Arndt appealed for German unity.

German man, feel again God, hear and fear the eternal, and you hear and fear also your *Volk* [folk, people, nation]; you feel again in

God the honor and dignity of your fathers, their glorious history rejuvenates itself again in you, their firm and gallant virtue reblossoms in you, the whole German Fatherland stands again before you in the august halo of past centuries! Then, when you feel and fear and honor all this, then you cry, then you lament, then you wrathfully reproach yourself that you have become so miserable and evil: then starts your new life and your new history. . . . From the North Sea to the Carpathians, from the Baltic to the Alps, from the Vistula to the Schelde [rivers], one faith, one love, one courage, and one enthusiasm must gather again the whole German folk in brotherly community; they must learn to feel how great, mighty, and happy their fathers were in obedience to one German emperor and one Reich, at a time when the many discords had not yet turned one against the other, when the many cowards and knaves had not yet betrayed them; . . . above the ruins and ashes of their destroyed Fatherland they must weepingly join hands and pray and swear all to stand like one man and to fight until the sacred land will be free. . . . Feel the infinite and sublime which slumbers hidden in the lap of the days, those light and mighty spirits which now glimmer in isolated meteors but which soon will shine in all suns and stars; feel the new birth of times, the higher, cleaner breath of spiritual life and do not longer be fooled and confused by the insignificant and small. No longer Catholics and Protestants, no longer Prussians and Austrians, Saxons and Bavarians, Silesians and Hanoverians, no longer of different faith, different mentality, and different will—be Germans, be one, will to be one by love and loyalty, and no devil will vanquish you.

Giuseppe Mazzini
YOUNG ITALY

In 1815, Italy was a fragmented nation. Hapsburg Austria ruled Lombardy and Venetia in the north and a Bourbon king sat on the throne of the Kingdom of the Two Sicilies in the south. The duchies of Tuscany, Parma, and Modena were ruled by Hapsburg princes subservient to Austria. The papal states in central Italy were ruled by the pope. The House of Savoy, an Italian dynasty, ruled the Kingdom of Piedmont, which became the cornerstone of Italian unification. Inspired by past Italian glories—the Roman Empire and the Renaissance—Italian nationalists demanded an end to foreign occupation and the unification of the Italian peninsula. As in other lands, national revival and unification appealed principally to intellectuals and the middle class.

A leading figure in the *Risorgimento*—the struggle for Italian nationhood—was Giuseppe Mazzini (1805–1872). Often called the "soul of the Risorgimento," Mazzini devoted his life to the creation of a unified and republican Italy; he believed that a free and democratic Italy would serve as a model to the other nations of Europe. In 1831, he founded Young Italy, a society dedicated to the cause of Italian unity. The following reading includes the oath taken by members of Young Italy.

Young Italy is a brotherhood of Italians who believe in a law of Progress and Duty, and are convinced that Italy is destined to become one nation,—convinced also that she possesses sufficient strength within herself to become one, and that the ill success of her former efforts is to be attributed not to the weakness, but to the misdirection of the revolutionary elements within her,—that the secret of force lies in constancy and unity of effort. They join this association in the firm intent of consecrating both thought and action to the great aim of reconstituting Italy as one independent sovereign nation of free men and equals. . . .

Young Italy is Republican. . . . Republican,— Because theoretically every nation is destined, by the law of God and humanity, to form a free and equal community of brothers; and the republican is the only form of government that insures this future. . . .

The means by which Young Italy proposes to reach its aim are—education and insurrection, to be adopted simultaneously, and made to harmonize with each other. Education must ever be directed to teach by example, word, and pen the necessity of insurrection. Insurrection, whenever it can be realized, must be so conducted as to render it a means of national education. . . .

Insurrection—by means of guerrilla bands— is the true method of warfare for all nations desirous of emancipating themselves from a foreign yoke. This method of warfare supplies the want—inevitable at the commencement of the insurrection—of a regular army; it calls the greatest number of elements into the field, and yet may be sustained by the smallest number. It forms the military education of the people, and consecrates every foot of the native soil by the memory of some warlike deed. . . .

Each member will, upon his initiation into the association of Young Italy, pronounce the following form of oath, in the presence of the initiator:

In the name of God and of Italy;

In the name of all the martyrs of the holy Italian cause who have fallen beneath foreign and domestic tyranny;

By the duties which bind me to the land wherein God has placed me, and to the brothers whom God has given me;

By the love—innate in all men—I bear to the country that gave my mother birth, and will be the home of my children;

By the hatred—innate in all men—I bear to evil, injustice, usurpation and arbitrary rule;

By the blush that rises to my brow when I stand before the citizens of other lands, to know that I have no rights of citizenship, no country, and no national flag;

By the aspiration that thrills my soul towards that liberty for which it was created, and is impotent to exert; towards the good it was created to strive after, and is impotent to achieve in the silence and isolation of slavery;

By the memory of our former greatness, and the sense of our present degradation;

By the tears of Italian mothers for their sons dead on the scaffold, in prison, or in exile;

By the sufferings of the millions,—

I, . . . believing in the mission intrusted by God to Italy, and the duty of every Italian to strive to attempt its fulfillment; convinced that where God has ordained that a nation shall be, He has given the requisite power to create it; that the people are the depositaries of that power, and that in its right direction for the people, and by the people, lies the secret of victory; convinced that virtue consists in action and sacrifice, and strength in union and constancy of purpose: I give my name to Young Italy, an association of men holding the same faith, and swear:

To dedicate myself wholly and forever to the endeavor with them to constitute Italy one free, independent, republican nation; to promote by every means in my power—whether by written or spoken word, or by action—the education of my Italian brothers towards the aim of Young Italy; towards association, the sole means of its accomplishment, and to virtue, which alone can render the conquest lasting; to abstain from enrolling myself in any other association from this time forth; to obey all the instructions, in conformity with the spirit of Young Italy, given me by those who represent with me the union of my Italian brothers; and to keep the secret of these instructions, even at the cost of my life; to assist my brothers of the association both by action and counsel—

NOW AND FOREVER.

This do I swear, invoking upon my head the wrath of God, the abhorrence of man, and the infamy of the perjurer, if I ever betray the whole or a part of this my oath.

REVIEW QUESTIONS

1. Ernst Moritz Arndt's writings show the interconnection between romanticism and nationalism. Discuss this statement.
2. Why do you suppose many students were attracted to Young Italy?
3. Giuseppe Mazzini was a democrat, a nationalist, and a romantic. Discuss this statement.

---

5 1848: The Year of Revolutions

In 1848, revolutions for political liberty and nationhood broke out in many parts of Europe. An uprising in Paris set this revolutionary tidal wave in motion. In February 1848, democrats seeking to create a French republic and to institute universal manhood suffrage precipitated a crisis; the pursuant uprising in Paris forced King Louis Philippe to abdicate. The leaders of the new French Republic championed political democracy but, with some notable exceptions like Louis Blanc (1811–1882), had little concern for the plight of the laboring poor.

The publication of the *Organization of Labor* (1839) had established Blanc as a leading French social reformer. Blanc urged the government to finance national workshops—industrial corporations, in which the directors would be elected by the workers—to provide employment for the urban poor. The government responded to Blanc's insistence that all workers have the "right to work" by indeed establishing national workshops, but these provided jobs for only a fraction of the unemployed, and many workers were given wages for doing nothing. Property owners regarded the workshops as a waste of government funds and as nests of working-class radicalism. When the government closed the workshops in June 1848, Parisian workers revolted.

Alexis de Tocqueville
THE JUNE DAYS

To the French workers the June 1848 revolt was against poverty and for a fairer distribution of property. Viewing this uprising as a threat to property and indeed to civilization, the rest of France rallied against the workers, who were crushed after several days of bitter street fighting. In his *Recollections* published posthumously in 1893, Alexis de Tocqueville (1805–1859), a leading statesman and political theorist, included a speech he made on January 29, 1848, before the French Chamber of Deputies, in which he warned the officials about the mood of the laboring poor.

. . . I am told that there is no danger because there are no riots; I am told that, because there is no visible disorder on the surface of society, there is no revolution at hand.

Gentlemen, permit me to say that I believe you are deceived. True, there is no actual disorder; but it has entered deeply into men's minds. See what is passing in the breasts of the working classes, who, I grant, are at present quiet. No doubt they are not disturbed by political passion, properly so-called, to the same extent that they have been; but can you not see that their passions, instead of political, have become social? Do you not see that there are gradually forming in their breasts opinions and ideas which are destined not only to upset this or that law, ministry, or even form of government, but society itself, until it totters upon the foundations on which it rests today? Do you not listen to what they say to themselves each day? Do you not hear them repeating unceasingly that all that is above them is incapable and unworthy of governing them; that the present distribution of goods throughout the world is unjust; that property rests on a foundation which is not an equitable foundation? And do you not realize that when such opinions take root, when they spread in an almost universal manner, when they sink deeply into the masses, they are bound to bring with them sooner or later, I know not when nor how, a most formidable revolution?

This, gentlemen, is my profound conviction: I believe that we are at this moment sleeping on a volcano. I am profoundly convinced of it. . . .

Later in his *Recollections,* de Tocqueville describes the second uprising in 1848, called the June Days.

I come at last to the insurrection of June, the most extensive and the most singular that has occurred in our history, and perhaps in any other: the most extensive, because, during four days, more than a hundred thousand men were engaged in it; the most singular, because the insurgents fought without a war-cry, without leaders, without flags, and yet with a marvellous harmony and an amount of military experience that astonished the oldest officers.

What distinguished it also, among all the events of this kind which have succeeded one another in France for sixty years, is that it did not aim at changing the form of government, but at altering the order of society. It was not, strictly speaking, a political struggle, in the sense which until then we had given to the word, but a combat of class against class, a sort of Servile War [slave uprising in ancient Rome]. It represented the facts of the Revolution of February in the same manner as the theories of Socialism represented its ideas; or rather it issued naturally from these ideas, as a son does from his mother. We behold in it nothing more than a blind and rude, but powerful, effort on the part of the workmen to escape from the necessities of their condition, which had been depicted to them as one of unlawful oppression, and to open up by main force a road towards that imaginary comfort with which they had been deluded. It was this mixture of greed and false theory which first gave birth to the insurrection and then made it so formidable. These poor people had been told that the wealth of the rich was in some way the produce of a theft practised upon themselves. They had been assured that the inequality of fortunes was as opposed to morality and the welfare of society as it was to nature. Prompted by their needs and their passions, many had believed this obscure and erroneous notion of right, which, mingled with brute force, imparted to the latter an energy, a tenacity and a power which it would never have possessed unaided.

It must also be observed that this formidable insurrection was not the enterprise of a certain number of conspirators, but the revolt of one whole section of the population against another. Women took part in it as well as men. While the latter fought, the former prepared and carried ammunition; and when at last the time had come to surrender, the women were the last to yield. These women went to battle with, as it were, a housewifely ardour: they looked to victory for the comfort of their husbands and the education of their children. . . .

As we know, it was the closing of the national workshops that occasioned the rising. Dreading to disband this formidable soldiery at one stroke, the Government had tried to disperse it by sending part of the workmen into the country. They refused to leave. On the 22nd of June, they marched through Paris in troops, singing in cadence, in a monotonous chant, "We won't be sent away, we won't be sent away. . . ."

. . . The spirit of insurrection circulated from one to the other of this immense class, and in each of its parts, as the blood does in the body; it filled the quarters where there was no fighting, as well as those which served as the scene of battle; it had penetrated into our houses, around, above, below us. The very places in which we thought ourselves the masters swarmed with domestic enemies; one might say that an atmosphere of civil war enveloped the whole of Paris, amid which, to whatever part we withdrew, we had to live. . . .

. . . It was easy to perceive through the multitude of contradictory reports that we had to do with the most universal, the best armed, and the most furious insurrection ever known in Paris. The national workshops and various revolutionary bands that had just been disbanded supplied it with trained and disciplined soldiers and with leaders. It was extending every moment, and it was difficult to believe that it would not end by being victorious, . . . all the great insurrections of the last sixty years had triumphed. . . .

Nevertheless, we succeeded in triumphing over this so formidable insurrection; nay more, it was just that which rendered it so terrible which saved us. . . . Had the revolt borne a less radical character and a less ferocious aspect, it is probable that the greater part of the middle class would have stayed at home; France would not have come to our aid; the National Assembly itself would perhaps have yielded, or at least a minority of its members would have advised it; and the energy of the whole body would have been greatly unnerved. But the insurrection was of such a nature that any understanding with it became at once impossible, and from the first it left us no alternative but to defeat it or to be destroyed ourselves.

REVIEW QUESTIONS

1. According to Alexis de Tocqueville, why did Parisian workers revolt in 1848?
2. How did the goals of Parisian workers who revolted in 1848 differ from those of members of Giuseppe Mazzini's Young Italy?
3. De Tocqueville observed that what distinguished this revolt was that it aimed to change the order of society, not the form of government. Explain.

CHAPTER 6

Culture, Society, and Politics, 1850–1914

EDVARD MUNCH (1863–1944), THE SCREAM, 1893. The dark forces of emotional torment and sexual aberration fill the canvases of Norwegian postimpressionist Edvard Munch. *(Lithograph, Digital Image © The Museum of Modern Art/Licensed by SCALA / Art Resource, New York.)*

In the last half of the nineteenth century, the people of Europe, more numerous than ever and concentrated in ever-growing cities, interacted with each other in a busy exchange of goods, ideas, and services, which led to remarkable creativity in industry, science, and the arts. The physical sciences flourished; medical science advanced; the psychoanalytic method developed under Sigmund Freud. New technologies speeded communication and transportation, which intensified human contact and competition. Industrialization, promoted by capitalist enterprise, spread throughout Europe and the United States, raising the standard of living and advancing expectations among the poor for a better life. The new mobility and social interdependence provided greater opportunity for individual gain, but they also increased social tensions.

One source of tension arose from the growing demands among the lower classes for social justice and a share of political power; the misery of the poor and disenfranchised masses became a hot political issue. Some reformers fought for legislation to improve the condition of the laboring poor. Rejecting this approach, Marxists called for revolution to overthrow the capitalist system. At the same time the agitation for women's rights mounted; women wanted to have rights equal to those of men in education and politics. Although women faced strenuous resistance with regard to suffrage, they continued to fight toward that goal. A third troublesome factor in European politics and society was anti-Semitism. Of long standing in European history, it became an active political force toward the end of the nineteenth century.

In the late nineteenth century, industrial growth and worldwide trade created among Europeans a new global competition for empire. Thus started a frantic race to occupy the last unclaimed parts of the world. The search for vital raw materials, markets, and investments intensified economic outreach, leading to ruthless exploitation and domination. The expenses of imperialism, usually greater than its economic benefits, were justified by rising nationalism, which fueled the quest for overseas possessions. What counted by the end of the century, as the traditional European rivalries expanded around the world, was global power; overseas possessions enhanced national prestige. Britain, thanks to its seapower, emerged as the colonial giant, claiming India as the core of the British Empire and provoking imitation by other ambitious European countries. Envious of the British Empire, other states did not want to be left behind.

The last half of the nineteenth century also experienced important intellectual and cultural developments. Romanticism dominated European art, literature, and music in the early nineteenth century. Stressing the feelings and the free expression of personality, the Romantic Movement was a reaction against the rationalism of the Enlightenment. In the middle decades of the century, realism and its close auxiliary naturalism supplanted romanticism as the chief norm of cultural expression. Rejecting religious, metaphysical, and romantic interpretations of reality, realists aspired to an exact and accurate portrayal of the external world and daily life. Realist and naturalist writers used the empirical approach: the careful collection, ordering, and interpretation of facts employed in science, which was advancing steadily in the nineteenth century. Among the most important scientific theories formulated was Charles Darwin's theory of evolution, which revolutionized conceptions of time and the origins of the human species.

The closing decades of the nineteenth century and the opening of the twentieth witnessed a crisis in Western thought. Rejecting the Enlightenment belief in the essential rationality of human beings, thinkers such as Friedrich Nietzsche and Sigmund Freud stressed the immense power of the nonrational in individual and social life. They held that subconscious drives, impulses, and instincts lay at the core of human nature, that people were moved more by religious-mythic images and symbols than by logical thought, that feelings determine human conduct more than reason does. This new image of the individual led to unsettling conclusions. If human beings are not fundamentally rational, then what are the prospects of resolving the immense problems of modern industrial civilization? Although most thinkers shared the Enlightenment's visions of humanity's future progress, doubters were also heard.

The crisis of thought also found expression in art and literature. Artists like Pablo Picasso and writers like James Joyce and Franz Kafka exhibited a growing fascination with the nonrational—with dreams, fantasies, sexual conflicts, and guilt, with tortured, fragmented, and dislocated inner lives. In the process, they rejected traditional aesthetic standards established during the Renaissance and the Enlightenment and experimented with new forms of artistic and literary representation.

These developments in thought produced insights into human nature and society, but they also contributed to the disorientation and insecurity that characterized the twentieth century.

---

1 Realism in Literature

The middle decades of the nineteenth century were characterized by the growing importance of science and industrialization in European life. A movement known as positivism sought to apply the scientific method to the study of society. Rejecting theological and metaphysical theories as unscientific, positivists sought to arrive at the general laws that underlie society by carefully assembling and classifying data.

This stress on a rigorous observation of reality also characterized realism and naturalism, the dominant movements in art and literature. In several ways, realism differed from romanticism, the dominant cultural movement in the first half of the century. Romantics were concerned with the inner life—with feelings, intuition, and imagination. They sought escape from the city into natural beauty, and they venerated the past, particularly the Middle Ages, which they viewed as noble, idyllic, and good in contrast to the spiritually impoverished present. Realists, on the other hand, shifted attention away from individual human feelings to the external world, which they investigated with the meticulous care of the scientist. Preoccupied with reality as it actually is, realist writers and artists depicted ordinary people, including the poor and humble, in ordinary circumstances. With a careful eye for detail and in a matter-of-fact way devoid of romantic exuberance and exaggeration, realists described peasants, factory workers, laundresses, beggars, criminals, and prostitutes.

Realism quickly evolved into naturalism. Naturalist writers held that human behavior was determined by the social environment. They argued that certain social and economic conditions produced predictable traits in men and women and that cause and effect operated in society as well as in physical nature.

Charles Dickens
HARD TIMES

In his numerous works, English writer Charles Dickens (1812–1870) depicted in detail the squalor of English industrial cities, the drudgery of factory labor, and the hypocrisy of a society that preached Christian morality but permitted these abuses to go on. Dickens recognized that the monotony and stupefying conditions of industrial life crushed the spirit of the workers, curtailing both their imagination and cultural development. Moreover, exploitation of the working class fostered class tensions, because the workers viewed governmental institutions as being impervious to their needs and intent solely on protecting the privileged status of entrepreneurs and business elites. Dickens blamed social institutions for the misery of the downtrodden and maintained that society must be fundamentally changed or it would implode. His works helped to awaken the moral conscience of his day. *Hard Times* (1854), excerpted below, is a harsh indictment of the industrial system and offers a good example of the Realist genre in literature.

It was a town of red brick, or of brick that would have been red if the smoke and ashes had allowed it; but as matters stood it was a town of unnatural red and black like the painted face of a savage. It was a town of machinery and tall chimneys, out of which interminable serpents of smoke trailed themselves for ever and ever, and never got uncoiled. It had a black canal in it, and a river that ran purple with ill-smelling dye, and vast piles of building full of windows where there was a rattling and a trembling all day long, and where the piston of the steam-engine worked monotonously up and down like the head of an elephant in a state of melancholy madness. It contained several large streets all very like one another, and many small streets still more like one another, inhabited by people equally like one another, who all went in and out at the same hours, with the same sound upon the same pavements, to do the same work, and to whom every day was the same as yesterday and tomorrow, and every year the counterpart of the last and the next. . . .

In the hardest working part of Coketown; in the innermost fortifications of that ugly citadel, where Nature was as strongly bricked out as killing airs and gases were bricked in; at the heart of the labyrinth of narrow courts upon courts, and close streets upon streets, which had come into existence piecemeal, every piece in a violent hurry for some one man's purpose, and the whole an unnatural family, shouldering, and trampling, and pressing one another to death; in the last close nook of this great exhausted receiver, where the chimneys, for want of air to make a draught, were built in an immense variety of stunted and crooked shapes, as though every house put out a sign of the kind of people who might be expected to be born in it; among the multitude of Coketown, generically called "the Hands,"— a race who would have found more favour with some people, if Providence had seen fit to make them only hands, or, like the lower creatures of the seashore, only hands and stomachs—lived a certain Stephen Blackpool, forty years of age. . . .

As Coketown cast ashes not only on its own head but on the neighbourhood's too—after the manner of those pious persons who do penance for their own sins by putting other people into sackcloth—it was customary for those who now and then thirsted for a draught of pure air, which is not absolutely the most wicked among the vanities of life, to get a few miles away by the railroad, and then begin their walk, or their lounge in the fields. . . .

Though the green landscape was blotted here and there with heaps of coal, it was green elsewhere, and there were trees to see, and there were larks singing (though it was Sunday), and there were pleasant scents in the air, and all was over-arched by a bright blue sky. In the distance one way, Coketown showed as a black mist; in another distance hills began to rise; in a third, there was a faint change in the light of the horizon where it shone upon the far-off sea. Under their feet, the grass was fresh; beautiful shadows of branches flickered upon it, and speckled it; hedgerows were luxuriant; everything was at peace. Engines at pits' mouths, and lean old horses that had worn the circle of their daily labour into the ground, were alike quiet; wheels had ceased for a short space to turn; and the great wheel of earth seemed to revolve without the shocks and noises of another time.

REVIEW QUESTION

1. Select one sentence that in your opinion best exemplifies Dickens's talent for realism. Explain why.

2 Theory of Evolution

In a century of outstanding scientific discoveries, none was more significant than the theory of evolution formulated by the English naturalist Charles Darwin (1809–1882). From December 1831 to 1836, Darwin had served as naturalist at sea on the *H.M.S. Beagle,* which surveyed parts of South America and some Pacific islands. He collected and classified many specimens of animal and plant life and from his investigations eventually drew several conclusions that startled the scientific community and enraged many members of the clergy.

Before Darwin's theory of evolution, most people adhered to the biblical account of creation found in Genesis, which said that God had created the universe, the various species of animal and plant life, and human beings, all in six days. The creation account also said that God had given each species of animal and plant a form that distinguished it from every other species. It was commonly held that the creation of the universe and of the first human beings had occurred some five or six thousand years ago.

On the basis of his study, Darwin held that all life on earth had descended from earlier living forms; that human beings had evolved from lower, nonhuman species; and that the process had taken millions of years. Adopting the Malthusian idea that population reproduces faster than the food supply increases, Darwin held that within nature there is a continual struggle for existence. He said that the advantage lies with those living things that are stronger, faster, better camouflaged from their enemies, or better fitted in some way—such as adaptability—for survival than are other members of their species; those more fit to survive pass along the advantageous trait to offspring. This principle of *natural selection* explains why some members of a species survive and reproduce and why those less fit perish.

Charles Darwin
NATURAL SELECTION

According to Darwin, members of a species inherit variations that distinguish them from others in the species, and over many generations these variations become more pronounced. In time, a new variety of life evolves that can no longer breed with the species from which it descended. In this way, new species emerge and older ones die out. Human beings were also a product of natural selection, evolving from earlier, lower, nonhuman forms of life. In this first passage, from his autobiography, Darwin described his empirical method and his discovery of a general theory that coordinated and illuminated the data he found. Succeeding excerpts are from his *The Origin of Species* (1859) and *The Descent of Man* (1871).

DARWIN'S DESCRIPTION OF HIS METHOD AND DISCOVERY

From September 1854 I devoted my whole time to arranging my huge pile of notes, to observing, and to experimenting in relation to the transmutation of species. During the voyage of the *Beagle* I had been deeply impressed by discovering in the Pampean formation[1] great fossil animals covered with armour like that on the existing armadillos; secondly, by the manner in which closely allied animals re-

---

[1]The Pampean formation refers to the vast plain that stretches across Argentina, from the Atlantic Ocean to the foothills of the Andes Mountains.

place one another in proceeding southwards over the Continent; and thirdly, by the South American character of most of the productions of the Galapagos archipelago,[2] and more especially by the manner in which they differ slightly on each island of the group; none of the islands appearing to be very ancient in a geological sense.

It was evident that such facts as these, as well as many others, could only be explained on the supposition that species gradually become modified; and the subject haunted me. But it was equally evident that neither the action of the surrounding conditions, nor the will of the organisms (especially in the case of plants) could account for the innumerable cases in which organisms of every kind are beautifully adapted to their habits of life—for instance, a woodpecker or a tree-frog to climb trees, or a seed for dispersal by hooks or plumes. I had always been much struck by such adaptations, and until these could be explained it seemed to me almost useless to endeavour to prove by indirect evidence that species have been modified.

After my return to England it appeared to me that by following the example of Lyell[3] in Geology, and by collecting all facts which bore in any way on the variation of animals and plants under domestication and nature, some light might perhaps be thrown on the whole subject. My first note-book was opened in July 1837. I worked on true Baconian principles,[4] and without any theory collected facts on a wholesale scale, more especially with respect to domesticated productions, by printed enquiries, by con-

versation with skilful breeders and gardeners, and by extensive reading. When I see the list of books of all kinds which I read and abstracted, including whole series of Journals and Transactions, I am surprised at my industry. I soon perceived that selection was the keystone of man's success in making useful races of animals and plants. But how selection could be applied to organisms living in a state of nature remained for some time a mystery to me.

In October 1838, that is, fifteen months after I had begun my systematic enquiry, I happened to read for amusement Malthus[5] on *Population,* and being well prepared to appreciate the struggle for existence which everywhere goes on from long-continued observation of the habits of animals and plants, it at once struck me that under these circumstances favourable variations would tend to be preserved and unfavourable ones to be destroyed. The result of this would be the formation of new species. Here, then, I had at last got a theory by which to work. . . .

It has sometimes been said that the success of *The Origin {of Species}* proved "that the subject was in the air," or "that men's minds were prepared for it." I do not think that this is strictly true, for I occasionally sounded not a few naturalists, and never happened to come across a single one who seemed to doubt about the permanence of species. Even Lyell and Hooker,[6] though they would listen with interest to me, never seemed to agree. I tried once or twice to explain to able men what I meant by Natural Selection, but signally failed. What I believe was strictly true is that innumerable well-observed facts were stored in the minds of naturalists ready to take their proper places as soon as any theory which would receive them was sufficiently explained. . . .

---

[2]The Galapagos Islands, a Pacific archipelago 650 miles west of Ecuador, are noted for their unusual wildlife, which Darwin observed.
[3]Sir Charles Lyell (1797–1875) was a Scottish geologist whose work showed that the planet had evolved slowly over many ages. Like Lyell, Darwin sought to interpret natural history by observing processes still going on.
[4]"Baconian principles" refers to Sir Francis Bacon (1561–1626), one of the first to insist that new knowledge should be acquired through experimentation and the accumulation of data.

[5]Thomas Malthus (1766–1834) was an English economist who maintained that population increases geometrically (2, 4, 8, 16, and so on) but the food supply increases arithmetically (1, 2, 3, 4, and so on). (See page 93.)
[6]Sir Joseph Dalton Hooker (1817–1911) was an English botanist who supported Darwin's ideas.

My *Descent of Man* was published in February 1871. As soon as I had become, in the year of 1837 or 1838, convinced that species were mutable productions, I could not avoid the belief that man must come under the same law.

In the following excerpt from *The Origin of Species* (1859), Darwin explained the struggle for existence and the principle of natural selection.

THE ORIGIN OF SPECIES

. . . Owing to this struggle [for existence], variations, however slight . . . , if they be in any degree profitable to the individuals of a species, in their infinitely complex relations to other organic beings and to their physical conditions of life, will tend to the preservation of such individuals, and will generally be inherited by the offspring. The offspring, also, will thus have a better chance of surviving, for, of the many individuals of any species which are periodically born, but a small number can survive. I have called this principle, by which each slight variation, if useful, is preserved, by the term Natural Selection, in order to mark its relation to man's power of selection. But the expression often used by Mr. Herbert Spencer[7] of the Survival of the Fittest is more accurate, and is sometimes equally convenient. . . .

A struggle for existence inevitably follows from the high rate at which all organic beings tend to increase. Every being, which during its natural lifetime produces several eggs or seeds, must suffer destruction during some period of its life, and during some season or occasional year, otherwise, on the principle of geometrical increase, its numbers would quickly become so inordinately great that no country could support the product. Hence, as more individuals are produced than can possibly survive, there must in every case be a struggle for existence, either one individual with another of the same species, or

with the individuals of distinct species, or with the physical conditions of life. It is the doctrine of Malthus applied with manifold force to the whole animal and vegetable kingdoms; for in this case there can be no artificial increase of food, and no prudential restraint from marriage. Although some species may be now increasing, more or less rapidly, in numbers, all cannot do so, for the world would not hold them.

There is no exception to the rule that every organic being naturally increases at so high a rate, that, if not destroyed, the earth would soon be covered by the progeny of a single pair. Even slow-breeding man has doubled in twenty-five years, and at this rate, in less than a thousand years, there would literally not be standing-room for his progeny. . . . The elephant is reckoned the slowest breeder of all known animals, and I have taken some pains to estimate its probable minimum rate of natural increase; it will be safest to assume that it begins breeding when thirty years old, and goes on breeding till ninety years old, bringing forth six young in the interval, and surviving till one hundred years old; if this be so, after a period of from 740 to 750 years there would be nearly nineteen million elephants alive, descended from the first pair. . . .

. . . Can we doubt (remembering that many more individuals are born than can possibly survive) that individuals having any advantage, however slight, over others, would have the best chance of surviving and of procreating their kind? On the other hand, we may feel sure that any variation in the least degree injurious would be rigidly destroyed. This preservation of favourable individual differences and variations, and the destruction of those which are injurious, I have called Natural Selection, or the Survival of the Fittest. . . .

. . . Natural Selection acts solely through the preservation of variations in some way advantageous, which consequently endure. Owing to the high geometrical rate of increase of all organic beings, each area is already fully stocked with inhabitants; and it follows from this, that as the favoured forms increase in

---

[7]The British philosopher Herbert Spencer (1820–1903) coined the term *survival of the fittest.*

number, so, generally, will the less favoured decrease and become rare. . . .

From these several considerations I think it inevitably follows, that as new species in the course of time are formed through natural selection, others will become rarer and rarer, and finally extinct. The forms which stand in closest competition with those undergoing modification and improvement will naturally suffer most. And we have seen in the chapter on the Struggle for Existence that it is the most closely-allied forms—varieties of the same species, and species of the same genus or of related genera—which, from having nearly the same structure, constitution, and habits, generally come into the severest competition with each other; consequently, each new variety or species, during the progress of its formation, will generally press hardest on its nearest kindred, and tend to exterminate them. We see the same process of extermination amongst our domesticated productions, through the selection of improved forms by man.

In *The Descent of Man* (1871), Darwin argued that human beings have evolved from lower forms of life.

THE DESCENT OF MAN

The main conclusion here arrived at, and now held by many naturalists who are well competent to form a sound judgment, is that man is descended from some less highly organised form. The grounds upon which this conclusion rests will never be shaken, for the close similarity between man and the lower animals in embryonic development, as well as in innumerable points of structure and constitution, both of high and of the most trifling importance,—the rudiments which he retains, and the abnormal reversions to which he is occasionally liable,—are facts which cannot be disputed. They have long been known, but until recently they told us nothing with respect to the origin of man. Now when viewed by the light of our knowledge of the whole organic world, their meaning is unmistakable. The great principle of

evolution stands up clear and firm, when these groups of facts are considered in connection with others, such as the mutual affinities of the members of the same group, their geographical distribution in past and present times, and their geological succession. It is incredible that all these facts should speak falsely. He who is not content to look, like a savage, at the phenomena of nature as disconnected, cannot any longer believe that man is the work of a separate act of creation. He will be forced to admit that the close resemblance of the embryo of man to that, for instance, of a dog—the construction of his skull, limbs and whole frame on the same plan with that of other mammals, independently of the uses to which the parts may be put—the occasional reappearance of various structures, for instance of several muscles, which man does not normally possess, but which are common to the Quadrumana[8]—and a crowd of analogous facts—all point in the plainest manner to the conclusion that man is the co-descendant with other mammals of a common progenitor.

We have seen that man incessantly presents individual differences in all parts of his body and in his mental faculties. These differences or variations seem to be induced by the same general causes, and to obey the same laws as with the lower animals. In both cases similar laws of inheritance prevail. Man tends to increase at a greater rate than his means of subsistence; consequently he is occasionally subjected to a severe struggle for existence, and natural selection will have effected whatever lies within its scope. A succession of strongly-marked variations of a similar nature is by no means requisite; slight fluctuating differences in the individual suffice for the work of natural selection. . . .

Man may be excused for feeling some pride at having risen, though not through his own exertions, to the very summit of the organic scale; and the fact of his having thus risen, in-

---

[8]An order of mammals, Quadrumana includes all primates (monkeys, apes, and baboons) except human beings; the primates' hind and forefeet can be used as hands as they have opposable first digits.

stead of having been [originally] placed there, may give him hope for a still higher destiny in the distant future. But we are not here concerned with hopes or fears, only with the truth as far as our reason permits us to discover it; and I have given the evidence to the best of my ability. We must, however, acknowledge, as it seems to me, that man with all his noble qualities, with sympathy which feels for the most debased, with benevolence which extends not only to other men but to the humblest living creature, with his god-like intellect which has penetrated into the movements and constitution of the solar system—with all these exalted powers—Man still bears in his bodily frame the indelible stamp of his lowly origin.

REVIEW QUESTIONS

1. How did Charles Darwin make use of Thomas Malthus's theory of population growth?
2. How did Darwin account for the extinction of old species and the emergence of new ones?
3. What did Darwin mean when he said that man "with his god-like intellect . . . still bears in his bodily frame the indelible stamp of his lowly origin"?

---

3   The Socialist Revolution

After completing a doctorate at the University of Jena in 1841, Karl Marx (1818–1883) edited a newspaper that was suppressed by the Prussian authorities for its radicalism and atheism. He left his native Rhineland for Paris, where he became friendly with Friedrich Engels. Expelled from France at the request of Prussia, Marx went to Brussels. In 1848, Marx and Engels produced for the Communist League the *Communist Manifesto,* advocating the violent overthrow of capitalism and the creation of a socialist society. Marx returned to Prussia and participated in a minor way in the Revolutions of 1848 in Germany. Expelled from Prussia in 1849, he went to England. He spent the rest of his life there, writing and agitating for the cause of socialism.

The *Communist Manifesto* presented a philosophy of history and a theory of society that Marx expanded upon in his later works, particularly *Capital* (1867). In the tradition of the Enlightenment, he maintained that history, like the operations of nature, was governed by scientific law. To understand the past and the present and to predict the essential outlines of the future, said Marx, one must concentrate on economic forces, on how goods are produced and how wealth is distributed. Marx's call for a working-class revolution against capitalism and for the making of a classless society established the ideology of twentieth-century communist revolutionaries.

Karl Marx and Friedrich Engels
COMMUNIST MANIFESTO

In the opening section of the *Manifesto,* the basic premise of the Marxian philosophy of history is advanced: class conflict—the idea that the social order is divided into classes based on conflicting economic interests.

BOURGEOIS AND PROLETARIANS

The history of all hitherto existing society is the history of class struggles.

Freeman and slave, patrician and plebeian [aristocrat and commoner, in the ancient world], lord and serf, guild-master [master craftsman] and journeyman [who worked for a guild-master], in a word, oppressor and oppressed, stood in constant opposition to one another, carried on an uninterrupted, now hidden, now open fight, that each time ended, either in a revolutionary reconstitution of society at large, or in the common ruin of the contending classes.

In the earlier epochs of history we find almost everywhere a complicated arrangement of society into various orders, a manifold gradation of social rank. In ancient Rome we have patricians, knights, plebeians, slaves; in the Middle Ages, feudal lords, vassals [landowners pledged to lords], guild-masters, journeymen, apprentices, serfs; in almost all of these classes, again, subordinate gradations.

The modern bourgeois society that has sprouted from the ruins of feudal society, has not done away with class antagonisms. It has but established new forms of struggle in place of the old ones.

Our epoch, the epoch of the bourgeoisie [capitalist class], possesses, however, this distinctive feature; it has simplified the class antagonisms. Society as a whole is more and more splitting up into two great hostile camps, into two great classes directly facing each other: Bourgeoisie and Proletariat [industrial workers].

From the serfs of the middle ages sprang the chartered burghers of the earliest towns. From these burgesses the first elements of the bourgeoisie were developed.

The discovery of America, the rounding of the Cape, opened up fresh ground for the rising bourgeoisie. The East-Indian and Chinese markets, the colonization of America, trade with the colonies, the increase in the means of exchange and in commodities generally, gave to commerce, to navigation, to industry, an impulse never before known, and thereby, to the revolutionary element in the tottering feudal society, a rapid development.

The feudal system of industry, under which industrial production was monopolized by closed guilds, now no longer sufficed for the growing wants of the new market. The manufacturing system took its place. The guild-masters were pushed on one side by the manufacturing middle class; division of labor between the different corporate guilds vanished in the face of division of labor in each single workshop.

Meantime the markets kept ever growing, the demand ever rising. . . . Thereupon steam and machinery revolutionized industrial production. The place of manufacture was taken by the giant, Modern Industry, the place of the industrial middle class, by industrial millionaires, the leaders of whole industrial armies, the modern bourgeois.

Modern Industry has established the world's market, for which the discovery of America paved the way. This market has given an immense development to commerce, to navigation, to communication by land. This development has, in its turn, reacted on the extension of industry; and in proportion, as industry, commerce, navigation, railways extended, in the same proportion, the bourgeoisie developed, increased its capital, and pushed into the background every class handed down from the Middle Ages.

We see, therefore, how the modern bourgeoisie is itself the product of a long course of development, of a series of revolutions in the modes of production and of exchange.

Each step in the development of the bourgeoisie was accompanied by a corresponding political advance of that class. An oppressed class under the sway of the feudal nobility, an armed and self-governing association in the mediaeval commune [town], . . . the bourgeoisie has at last, since the establishment of Modern Industry and of the world's market, conquered for itself, in the modern representative State, exclusive political sway. The executive of the modern State is but a committee for managing the common affairs of the whole bourgeoisie.

The bourgeoisie, historically, has played a most revolutionary part.

The bourgeoisie, wherever it has got the upper hand, has put an end to all feudal, patriarchal, idyllic relations. It has pitilessly torn asunder the motley feudal ties that bound man to his "natural superiors," and has left remaining no other nexus [link] between man and man than naked self-interest, than callous "cash payment." It has drowned the most heavenly ecstasies of religious fervor, of chivalrous enthusiasm, . . . in the icy water of egotistical calculation. It has resolved personal worth into exchange value, and in place of the numberless indefeasible chartered freedoms, has set up that single, unconscionable freedom—Free Trade. In one word, for exploitation, veiled by religious and political illusions, it has substituted naked, shameless, direct, brutal exploitation. . . .

The bourgeoisie, states the *Manifesto,* has subjected nature's forces to human control to an unprecedented degree and has replaced feudal organization of agriculture (serfdom) and manufacturing (guild system) with capitalist free competition. But the capitalists cannot control these "gigantic means of production and exchange." Periodically, capitalist society is burdened by severe economic crises; capitalism is afflicted with overproduction—more goods are produced than the market will absorb. In all earlier epochs, which were afflicted with scarcity, the *Manifesto* declares, such a condition "would have seemed an absurdity." To deal with the crisis, the capitalists curtail production, thereby intensifying the poverty of the proletariat, who are without work. In capitalist society, the exploited worker suffers from physical poverty—a result of low wages—and spiritual poverty—a result of the monotony, regimentation, and impersonal character of the capitalist factory system. For the proletariat, work is not the satisfaction of a need but a repulsive means for survival. The products they help make bring them no satisfaction; they are alienated from their labor.

In proportion as the bourgeoisie, *i.e.*, capital, is developed, in the same proportion is the proletariat, the modern working class, developed—a class of laborers, who live only so long as they find work, and who find work only so long as their labor increases capital. These laborers, who must sell themselves piecemeal, are a commodity, like every other article of commerce, and are consequently exposed to all the vicissitudes of competition, to all the fluctuations of the market.

Owing to the extensive use of machinery and to division of labor, the work of the proletarians has lost all individual character, and, consequently, all charm for the workman. He becomes an appendage of the machine, and it is only the most simple, most monotonous, and most easily acquired knack, that is required of him. Hence, the cost of production of a workman is restricted, almost entirely, to the means of subsistence that he requires for his maintenance, and for the propagation of his race. But the price of a commodity, and therefore also of labor, is equal to its cost of production. In proportion, therefore, as the repulsiveness of the work increases, the wage decreases. Nay more, in proportion as the use of machinery and division of labor increases, in the same proportion the burden of toil also increases, whether by prolongation of the working hours, by increase of the work exacted in a given time, or by increased speed of the machinery, etc.

Modern industry has converted the little workshop of the patriarchal master into the great factory of the industrial capitalist. Masses of laborers, crowded into the factory, are organized like soldiers. As privates of the industrial army they are placed under the command of a perfect hierarchy of officers and sergeants. Not only are they slaves of the bourgeois class, and of the bourgeois state; they are daily and hourly enslaved by the machine, by the overlooker, and, above all, by the individual bourgeois manufacturer himself. The more openly this despotism proclaims gain to be its end and aim, the more petty, the more hateful and the more embittering it is.

The less the skill and exertion of strength implied in manual labor, in other words, the more modern industry develops, the more is the labor of men superseded by that of women. Differences of age and sex have no longer any distinctive social validity for the working class. All are instruments of labor, more or less expensive to use, according to their age and sex.

No sooner has the laborer received his wages in cash, for the moment escaping exploitation by the manufacturer, than he is set upon by the other portions of the bourgeoisie, the landlord, the shop-keeper, the pawnbroker, etc. . . .

The exploited workers organize to defend their interests against the capitalist oppressors.

But with the development of industry the proletariat not only increases in number; it becomes concentrated in greater masses, its strength grows, and it feels that strength more. The various interests and conditions of life within the ranks of the proletariat are more and more equalized, in proportion as machinery obliterates all distinctions of labor and nearly everywhere reduces wages to the same low level. The growing competition among the bourgeois, and the resulting commercial crises, make the wages of the workers ever more fluctuating. The unceasing improvement of machinery, ever more rapidly developing, makes their livelihood more and more precarious: the collisions between individual workmen and individual bourgeois take more and more the character of collisions between two classes. Thereupon the workers begin to form combinations (trade unions) against the bourgeoisie; they club together in order to keep up the rate of wages; they found permanent associations in order to make provision beforehand for these occasional revolts. Here and there the contest breaks out into riots.

Now and then the workers are victorious, but only for a time. The real fruit of their battles lies, not in the immediate results, but in [their ever-expanding unity]. . . .

This organization of the proletarians into a class, and consequently into a political party, is continually being upset again by the competition between the workers themselves. But it ever rises up again, stronger, firmer, mightier. It compels legislative recognition of particular interests of the workers, by taking advantage of the divisions among the bourgeoisie itself. Thus the ten-hour bill[1] in England was carried. . . .

Increasingly, the proletariat, no longer feeling part of the old society, seeks to destroy it.

In the conditions of the proletariat, those of the old society at large are already virtually swamped. The proletarian is without property; his relation to his wife and children has no

---

[1]The Ten Hours Act (1847) provided a ten-and-a-half-hour day from 6 A.M. to 6 P.M., with an hour and a half for meals for women and children.

longer anything in common with the bourgeois family relations; modern industrial labor, modern subjection to capital, the same in England as in France, in America as in Germany, has stripped him of every trace of national character. Law, morality, religion, are to him so many bourgeois prejudices, behind which lurk in ambush just as many bourgeois interests.

All the preceding classes that got the upper hand sought to fortify their already acquired status by subjecting society at large to their conditions of appropriation. The proletarians cannot become masters of the productive forces of society, except by abolishing their own previous mode of appropriation, and thereby also every other previous mode of appropriation. They have nothing of their own to secure and to fortify; their mission is to destroy all previous securities for, and insurances of, individual property.

All previous historical movements were movements of minorities, or in the interest of minorities. The proletarian movement is the self-conscious, independent movement of the immense majority, in the interest of the immense majority. The proletariat, the lowest stratum of our present society, cannot stir, cannot raise itself up, without the whole superincumbent [overlying] strata of official society being [shattered].

Though not in substance, yet in form, the struggle of the proletariat with the bourgeoisie is at first a national struggle. The proletariat of each country must, of course, first of all settle matters with its own bourgeoisie.

In depicting the most general phases of the development of the proletariat, we traced the more or less veiled civil war, raging within existing society, up to the point where that war breaks out into open revolution, and where the violent overthrow of the bourgeoisie lays the foundation for the sway of the proletariat. . . .

The modern laborer . . . instead of rising with the progress of industry, sinks deeper and deeper below the conditions of existence of his own class. He becomes a pauper, and pauperism develops more rapidly than population

and wealth. And here it becomes evident that the bourgeoisie is unfit any longer to be the ruling class in society and to impose its conditions of existence upon society as an overriding law. It is unfit to rule because it is incompetent to assure an existence to its slave within his slavery, because it cannot help letting him sink into such a state that it has to feed him instead of being fed by him. Society can no longer live under this bourgeoisie, in other words its existence is no longer compatible with society.

The essential condition for the existence and for the sway of the bourgeois class, is the formation and augmentation of capital; the condition for capital is wage-labor. Wage-labor rests exclusively on competition between the laborers. The advance of industry, whose involuntary promoter is the bourgeoisie, replaces the isolation of the laborers, due to competition, by their revolutionary combination, due to association. The development of modern industry, therefore, cuts from under its feet the very foundation on which the bourgeoisie produces and appropriates products. What the bourgeoisie therefore produces above all, are its own gravediggers. Its fall and the victory of the proletariat are equally inevitable. . . .

Communists, says the *Manifesto,* are the most advanced and determined members of working-class parties. Among the aims of the communists are organization of the working class into a revolutionary party; overthrow of bourgeois power and the assumption of political power by the proletariat; and an end to exploitation of one individual by another and the creation of a classless society. These aims will be achieved by the abolition of bourgeois private property (private ownership of the means of production) and the abolition of the bourgeoisie as a class.

The Communists, therefore, are on the one hand, practically, the most advanced and resolute section of the working class parties of every country, that section which pushes forward all others; on the other hand, theoretically, they have over the great mass of the proletariat the advantage of clearly understanding the line of march, the conditions, and the ultimate general results of the proletarian movement.

The immediate aim of the Communists is the same as that of all the other proletarian parties: formation of the proletariat into a class, overthrow of the bourgeois supremacy, conquest of political power by the proletariat. . . .

The distinguishing feature of Communism is not the abolition of property generally, but the abolition of bourgeois property. But modern bourgeois private property is the final and most complete expression of the system of producing and appropriating products, that is based on class antagonisms, on the exploitation of the many by the few.

In this sense the theory of the Communists may be summed up in the single sentence: Abolition of private property. . . .

One argument leveled against communists by bourgeois critics, says the *Manifesto,* is that the destruction of the bourgeoisie would lead to the disappearance of bourgeois culture, which is "identical with the disappearance of all culture," and the loss of all moral and religious truths. Marx insists that these ethical and religious ideals lauded by the bourgeoisie are not universal truths at all but are common expressions of the ruling class at a particular stage in history.

That culture, the loss of which he [the bourgeois] laments, is for the enormous majority, a mere training to act as a machine.

But don't wrangle with us so long as you [the bourgeoisie] apply to our [the communists'] intended abolition of bourgeois property, the standard of your bourgeois notions of freedom, culture, law, etc. Your very ideas are but the outgrowth of the conditions of your bourgeois production and bourgeois property, just as your jurisprudence is but the will of your class made into a law for all, a will, whose essential character and direction are determined by the economical conditions of existence of your class.

The selfish misconception that induces you to transform into eternal laws of nature and of reason, the social forms springing from your present mode of production and form of property—historical relations that rise and disappear in the progress of production—this misconception you share with every ruling class that has preceded you. What you see clearly in the case of ancient property, what you admit in the case of feudal property, you are of course forbidden to admit in the case of your own bourgeois form of property. . . .

The charges against Communism made from a religious, a philosophical, and, generally, from an ideological standpoint, are not deserving of serious examination.

Does it require deep intuition to comprehend that man's ideas, views, and conceptions, in one word, man's consciousness changes with every change in the conditions of his material existence, in his social relations and in his social life?

What else does the history of ideas prove than that intellectual production changes its character in proportion as material production is changed? The ruling ideas of each age have ever been the ideas of its ruling class. . . .

. . . The ideas of religious liberty and freedom of conscience merely gave expression to the sway of free competition within the domain of knowledge.

"Undoubtedly," it will be said, "religious, moral, philosophical, and juridical ideas have been modified in the course of historic development. But religion, morality, philosophy, political science, and law, constantly survived this change.

"There are besides, eternal truths, such as Freedom, Justice, etc., that are common to all states of society. But Communism abolishes eternal truths, it abolishes all religion and all morality, instead of constituting them on a new basis; it therefore acts as a contradiction to all past historical experience."

What does this accusation reduce itself to? The history of all past society has consisted in the development of class antagonisms, antagonisms that assumed different forms at different epochs.

But whatever form they may have taken, one fact is common to all past ages, *viz.,* the exploitation of one part of society by the other. No wonder, then, that the social consciousness of past ages, despite all the multiplicity and variety it displays, moves within certain common forms, or general ideas, which cannot completely vanish except with the total disappearance of class antagonisms.

The Communist revolution is the most radical rupture with traditional property relations; no wonder that its development involves the most radical rupture with traditional ideas.

Aroused and united by communist intellectuals, says the *Manifesto,* the proletariat will wrest power from the bourgeoisie and overthrow the capitalist system that has oppressed them. In the new society, people will be fully free.

But let us have done with the bourgeois objections to Communism.

We have seen above that the first step in the revolution by the working class is to raise the proletariat to the position of the ruling class, to win the battle of democracy.

The proletariat will use its political supremacy to wrest, by degrees, all capital from the bourgeoisie; to centralize all instruments of production in the hands of the State, *i.e.,* of the proletariat organized as the ruling class; and to increase the total of productive forces as rapidly as possible. . . .

When, in the course of development, class distinctions have disappeared and all production has been concentrated in the hands of a vast association of the whole nation, the public power will lose its political character. Political power, properly so called, is merely the organized power of one class for oppressing another. If the proletariat during its contest with the bourgeoisie is compelled, by the force of circumstances, to organize itself as a class, if, by means of a revolution, it makes itself the ruling class, and, as such, sweeps away by force the old conditions of production, then it will, along with these conditions, have swept away the conditions for the existence of class antagonism, and of classes generally, and will thereby have abolished its own supremacy as a class.

In place of the old bourgeois society with its classes and class antagonisms we shall have an association in which the free development of each is the condition for the free development of all. . . .

The Communists disdain to conceal their views and aims. They openly declare that their ends can be attained only by the forcible overthrow of all existing social conditions. Let the ruling classes tremble at a communistic revolution. The proletarians have nothing to lose but their chains. They have a world to win.

Working men of all countries, unite!

REVIEW QUESTIONS

1. What do Karl Marx and Friedrich Engels mean by the term *class conflict*? What historical examples of class conflict are provided?
2. According to the *Manifesto,* what role has the state played in the class conflict?
3. How does the *Manifesto* describe the condition of the working class under capitalism?
4. According to the *Manifesto,* why is capitalism doomed? What conditions will bring about the end of capitalism?
5. "The ruling ideas of each age have ever been the ideas of its ruling class." What is meant by this statement? Do you agree or disagree? Explain.
6. Have Marx's predictions proven accurate? Explain your answer.

4 The Lower Classes

The members of the upper and middle classes in European society looked down
on "the lower classes"—industrial workers, domestic help, and peasants; and
still further down, the street people, the mentally disturbed, the homeless, the
unemployed, and vagrants; and at the bottom, the criminal underworld. These
"lower classes" were most vulnerable to the vicissitudes of the business cycle
and dependent on small and uncertain incomes; commonly they worked long
hours under dehumanizing strain and were housed in urban slums under unsanitary conditions; they were hungry, illiterate, often reduced to outright destitution, and desperate to earn some money. In the slums of London's East End,
one could see ragged men collect dog excrement for use in tanning leather;
prostitution thrived.

In the economic progress of the nineteenth century, the overall material
conditions of society improved remarkably, sharpening the social contrasts.
Concerned people spoke of "two nations," the rich and the poor. The poor,
however, were not entirely passive; workers began to rally, trying to improve
their condition by political action, thereby scaring the upper classes into social
awareness. At the same time, humanitarian concerns, often rising from religious inspiration, stirred some of the well-to-do. Toward the end of the nineteenth century, the misery of the poor caused lively public debate and heated
political agitation.

William Booth
IN DARKEST ENGLAND

The poor were not without compassionate friends. One of them was William
Booth (1829–1912), the founder of the Salvation Army. Growing up poor himself, he was apprenticed to a pawnbroker while still a boy. At fifteen, under
Methodist influence, he experienced a religious conversion, which eventually
turned him into a Methodist minister; his wife and helpmate was one of the first
Methodist woman preachers. Settled in London, he combined work at a pawn-
shop with ministering to the poor in the slums of London's East End. Booth and
his wife devoted themselves to rescuing and rehabilitating the homeless, the unemployed, and the sinners of the urban underworld. In 1879 the organization
that they had evolved officially became the Salvation Army. William Booth was
its general; ordained ministers were its officers; the soldiers were men and
women dedicated to saving others from the misery from which they themselves
had escaped. All wore the Salvation Army's special uniform. The Salvation
Army grew rapidly, spreading over the world. It now serves in seventy-seven
countries, with over 300,000 soldiers in the United States.

In 1890 General Booth published *In Darkest England and the Way Out,* de-
scribing the misery of the poor and outlining his methods of achieving spiritual
salvation through social service. In the opening two chapters, Booth outlined

the extent of poverty in England at the height of its imperial glory. He begins by comparing England with journalist-explorer Henry Stanley's description of the brutality, slavery, and disease in "Darkest Africa."

WHY "DARKEST ENGLAND"?

This summer the attention of the civilised world has been arrested by the story which Mr. Stanley has told of "Darkest Africa" and his journeyings across the heart of the Lost Continent. . . .

It is a terrible picture, and one that has engraved itself deep on the heart of civilisation. But while brooding over the awful presentation of life as it exists in the vast African forest, it seemed to me only too vivid a picture of many parts of our own land. As there is a darkest Africa is there not also a darkest England? Civilisation, which can breed its own barbarians, does it not also breed its own pygmies? May we not find a parallel at our own doors, and discover within a stone's throw of our cathedrals and palaces similar horrors to those which Stanley has found existing in the great Equatorial forest?

The more the mind dwells upon the subject, the closer the analogy appears. The [Arab] ivory raiders who brutally traffic in the unfortunate denizens of the forest glades, what are they but the [exploiters] who flourish on the weakness of our poor? . . . As in Africa, it is all trees, trees, trees with no other world conceivable; so is it here—it is all vice and poverty and crime. To many the world is all slum, with the Workhouse as an intermediate purgatory before the grave. . . . Who can battle against the ten thousand million trees? Who can hope to make headway against the innumerable adverse conditions which doom the dweller in Darkest England to eternal and immutable misery?

. . . Talk about Danté's Hell, and all the horrors and cruelties of the torture-chamber of the lost! The man who walks with open eyes and with bleeding heart through the shambles of our civilisation needs no such fantastic images of the poet to teach him horror. Often and often, when I have seen the young and the poor and the helpless go down before my eyes into the morass, trampled underfoot by beasts of prey in human shape that haunt these regions, it seemed as if God were no longer in His world, but that in His stead reigned a fiend, merciless as Hell, ruthless as the grave. Hard it is, no doubt, to read in Stanley's pages of the slave-traders coldly arranging for the surprise of a village, the capture of the inhabitants, the massacre of those who resist, and the violation of all the women; but the stony streets of London, if they could but speak, would tell of tragedies as awful, of ruin as complete, of ravishments as horrible, as if we were in Central Africa; only the ghastly devastation is covered, corpse-like, with the artificialities and hypocrisies of modern civilisation.

The lot of a negress in the Equatorial Forest is not, perhaps, a very happy one, but is it so very much worse than that of many a pretty orphan girl in our Christian capital? . . . A young penniless girl, if she be pretty, is often hunted from pillar to post by her employers, confronted always by the alternative—Starve or Sin. And when once the poor girl has consented to buy the right to earn her living by the sacrifice of her virtue, then she is treated as a slave and an outcast by the very men who have ruined her. . . . [A]nd she is swept downward. . . .

The blood boils with impotent rage at the sight of these enormities, callously inflicted, and silently borne by these miserable victims. Nor is it only women who are the victims, although their fate is the most tragic. Those firms which reduce sweating [hard labor at low wages] to a fine art, who systematically and deliberately defraud the workman of his pay, who grind the faces of the poor, and who rob the widow and the orphan, and who for a pretence make great professions of public-spirit and philanthropy, those men nowadays are sent to Parliament to make laws for the people. The old prophets sent them to Hell—but we have changed all that. They send their victims to Hell, and are rewarded by all that wealth can do to make their lives comfortable. Read the House of Lords' Report on the Sweating System, and ask if any African slave system, making due allowance for the superior civilisation, and therefore sensitiveness, of the victims, reveals more misery.

Darkest England, like Darkest Africa, reeks with malaria. The foul and fetid breath of our slums is almost as poisonous as that of the African swamp. Fever is almost as chronic there as on the Equator. Every year thousands of children are killed off by what is called defects of our sanitary system. They are in reality starved and poisoned, and all that can be said is that, in many cases, it is better for them that they were taken away from the trouble to come.

Just as in Darkest Africa it is only a part of the evil and misery that comes from the superior race who invade the forest to enslave and massacre its miserable inhabitants, so with us, much of the misery of those whose lot we are considering arises from their own habits. Drunkenness and all manner of uncleanness, moral and physical, abound. Have you ever watched by the bedside of a man in delirium tremens [trembling and delusions brought on by alcohol abuse]? Multiply the sufferings of that one drunkard by the hundred thousand, and you have some idea of what scenes are being witnessed in all our great cities at this moment. . . . A population sodden with drink, steeped in vice, eaten up by every social and physical malady, these are the denizens of Darkest England amidst whom my life has been spent, and to whose rescue I would now summon all that is best in the manhood and womanhood of our land. . . .

. . . [T]he grimmest social problems of our time should be sternly faced, not with a view to the generation of profitless emotion, but with a view to its solution. . . .

Relying on the statistics of Charles Booth (no relation), William Booth concluded that three million people, one-tenth of the population, were pauperized and degraded.

THE SUBMERGED TENTH

What, then, is Darkest England? For whom do we claim that "urgency" which gives their case priority over that of all other sections of their countrymen and countrywomen? . . .

. . . The [people] in Darkest England, for whom I appeal, are (1) those who, having no capital or income of their own, would in a month be dead from sheer starvation were they exclusively dependent upon the money earned by their own work; and (2) those who by their utmost exertions are unable to attain the regulation allowance of food which the law prescribes as indispensable even for the worst criminals in our gaols.

I sorrowfully admit that it would be Utopian in our present social arrangements to dream of attaining for every honest Englishman a gaol [jail] standard of all the necessaries of life. Some time, perhaps, we may venture to hope that every honest worker on English soil will always be as warmly clad, as healthily housed, and as regularly fed as our criminal convicts—but that is not yet.

Neither is it possible to hope for many years to come that human beings generally will be as well cared for as horses. Mr. Carlyle long ago remarked that the four-footed worker has already got all that this two-handed one is clamouring for. . . .

What, then, is the standard towards which we may venture to aim with some prospect of realisation in our time? It is a very humble one, but if realised it would solve the worst problems of modern Society.

It is the standard of the London Cab Horse. . . .

The first question, then, which confronts us is, what are the dimensions of the Evil? How many of our fellow-men dwell in this Darkest England? How can we take the census of those who have fallen below the Cab Horse standard to which it is our aim to elevate the most wretched of our countrymen? . . .

REVIEW QUESTIONS

1. What, according to William Booth, were the essential aspects of life in "Darkest England"? Why did he draw the comparison to darkest Africa?
2. Do any of Booth's scathing criticisms apply to contemporary America?

---

5 Feminism and Antifeminism

Inspired by the ideals of equality voiced in the Enlightenment and the French Revolution, women in nineteenth-century Europe and the United States began to demand equal rights, foremost the right to vote. In the United States, the women's suffrage movement held its first convention in 1848 in Seneca Falls, New York. The women adopted a Declaration of Principles that said in part: "We hold these truths to be self-evident: that all men and women are created equal." The struggle for equal rights and voting privileges continued, and by the end of the century, women were voting in a few state elections. Finally, in 1920, the Nineteenth Amendment gave women voting privileges throughout the United States.

In England, having failed to persuade Parliament in the mid-1860s to give them the vote, women organized reform societies, drew up petitions, and protested unfair treatment. The Women's Social and Political Union (WSPU), organized by Emmeline Pankhurst, employed militant tactics, which increased the hostility of their opponents.

During World War I, women worked in offices, factories, and service industries at jobs formerly held by men. Their wartime service made it clear that women played an essential role in the economic life of nations, and many political leaders argued for the extension of the vote to them. In 1918, British women over the age of thirty gained the vote, and in 1928, Parliament lowered the voting age for British women to twenty-one, the same as for men.

The first countries to permit women to vote were New Zealand in 1893 and Australia in 1902. In Europe, women were granted voting rights by stages, first for municipal elections, later for national ones. Finland extended voting rights to women in 1906; the other Scandinavian countries followed suit, but the majority of European countries did not allow women to vote until after World War I.

In their struggle for equal rights, women faced strong opposition. Opponents argued that feminist demands would threaten society by undermining marriage and the family. Thus in 1870, a member of the British House of Commons wondered "what would become, not merely of women's influence, but of her duties at home, her care of the household, her supervision of all those duties and surroundings which make a happy home . . . if we are to see women coming forward and taking part in the government of the country." This concern for the family was combined with a traditional biased view of woman's nature, as one writer for the *Saturday Review,* an English periodical, revealed:

The power of reasoning is so small in women that they need [outside] help, and if they have not the guidance and check of a religious conscience, it is useless to expect from them self-control on abstract principles. They do not calculate consequences, and they are reckless when they once give way, hence they are to be kept straight only through their affections, the religious sentiment and a well educated moral sense.

John Stuart Mill
THE SUBJECTION OF WOMEN

John Stuart Mill (see page 111), a British philosopher and a liberal, championed women's rights. His interest in the subject was awakened by Harriet Taylor, a longtime friend and an ardent feminist, whom he married in 1851. Mill and Taylor had an intense intellectual companionship both before and after their marriage, and Taylor helped shape his ideas on the position of women in society and the urgent need for reform. In 1867, Mill, as a member of Parliament, proposed that the suffrage be extended to women (the proposal was rejected by a vote of 194 to 74). In *The Subjection of Women* (1869), Mill argued that male dominance of women constituted a flagrant abuse of power. He maintained that female inequality, "a single relic of an old world of thought and practice exploded in everything else," violated the principle of individual rights and hindered the progress of humanity. Excerpts from Mill's classic in the history of feminism follow.

The object of this Essay is to explain, as clearly as I am able, the grounds of an opinion which I have held from the very earliest period when I had formed any opinions at all on social or political matters, and which, instead of being weakened or modified, has been constantly growing stronger by the progress of reflection and the experience of life: That the principle which regulates the existing social relations between the two sexes—the legal subordination of one sex to the other—is wrong in itself, and now one of the chief hindrances to human improvement; and that it ought to be replaced by a principle of perfect equality, admitting no power or privilege on the one side, nor disability [legal restriction] on the other. . . .

. . . The adoption of this system of inequality never was the result of deliberation, or forethought, or any social ideas, or any notion whatever of what [lead] to the benefit of hu-

manity or the good order of society. It arose simply from the fact that from the very earliest twilight of human society, every woman (owing to the value attached to her by men, combined with her inferiority in muscular strength) was found in a state of bondage to some man. . . .

But, it will be said, the rule of men over women differs from all these others in not being a rule of force: it is accepted voluntarily; women make no complaint, and are consenting parties to it. In the first place, a great number of women do not accept it. Ever since there have been women able to make their sentiments known by their writings (the only mode of publicity which society permits to them), an increasing number of them have recorded protests against their present social condition: and recently many thousands of them, headed by the most eminent women known to the public, have petitioned Parliament for their admission to the parliamentary suffrage. The claim of women to be educated as solidly, and in the same branches of knowledge, as men, is urged with growing intensity, and with a great prospect of success; while the demand for their admission into professions and occupations hitherto closed against them becomes every year more urgent. Though there are not in this country, as there are in the United States, periodical Conventions and an organized party to agitate for the Rights of Women, there is a numerous and active Society organized and managed by women, for the more limited object of obtaining the political franchise. Nor is it only in our own country and in America that women are beginning to protest, more or less collectively, against the disabilities under which they labour. France, and Italy, and Switzerland, and Russia now afford examples of the same thing. How many more women there are who silently cherish similar aspirations, no one can possibly know; but there are abundant tokens how many *would* cherish them, were they not so strenuously taught to repress them as contrary to the proprieties [proper behavior] of their sex. . . .

Men do not want solely the obedience of women, they want their sentiments. All men, except the most brutish, desire to have, in the woman most nearly connected with them, not a forced slave but a willing one; not a slave merely, but a favourite. They have therefore put everything in practice to enslave their minds. The masters of all other slaves rely, for maintaining obedience, on fear; either fear of themselves, or religious fears. The masters of women wanted more than simple obedience, and they turned the whole force of education to effect their purpose. All women are brought up from the very earliest years in the belief that their ideal of character is the very opposite to that of men; not self-will, and government by self-control, but submission, and yielding to the control of others. All the moralities tell them that it is the duty of women, and all the current sentimentalities that it is their nature, to live for others; to make complete abnegation of themselves, and to have no life but in their affections. And by their affections are meant the only ones they are allowed to have—those to the men with whom they are connected, or to the children who constitute an additional and indefeasible [permanent] tie between them and a man. When we put together three things—first, the natural attraction between opposite sexes; secondly, the wife's entire dependence on the husband, every privilege or pleasure she has being either his gift, or depending entirely on his will; and lastly, that the principal object of human pursuit, consideration, and all objects of social ambition, can in general be sought or obtained by her only through him—it would be a miracle if the object of being attractive to men had not become the polar star of feminine education and formation of character. And, this great means of influence over the minds of women having been acquired, an instinct of selfishness made men avail themselves of it to the utmost as a means of holding women in subjection, by representing to them meekness, submissiveness, and resignation of all individual will into the hands of a man, as an essential part of sexual attractiveness. Can it be doubted that any of the other yokes which mankind have succeeded in breaking would have subsisted till now if the same means had existed, and had been as sedulously [diligently] used to bow down their minds to it?

Mill argues that women should be able to participate in political life and should not be barred from entering the professions.

On the other point which is involved in the just equality of women, their admissibility to all the functions and occupations hitherto retained as the monopoly of the stronger sex. . . . I believe that their disabilities [in occupation and civil life] elsewhere are only clung to in order to maintain their subordination in domestic life; because the generality of the male sex cannot yet tolerate the idea of living with an equal. Were it not for that, I think that almost every one, in the existing state of opinion in politics and political economy, would admit the injustice of excluding half the human race from the greater number of lucrative occupations, and from almost all high social functions; ordaining from their birth either that they are not, and cannot by any possibility become, fit for employments which are legally open to the stupidest and basest of the other sex, or else that however fit they may be, those employments shall be interdicted [forbidden] to them, in order to be preserved for the exclusive benefit of males. . . .

It will perhaps be sufficient if I confine myself, in the details of my argument, to functions of a public nature: since, if I am successful as to those, it probably will be readily granted that women should be admissible to all other occupations. . . . And here let me begin . . . [with] the suffrage, both parliamentary and municipal. . . .

. . . To have a voice in choosing those by whom one is to be governed, is a means of self-protection due to every one, though he were to remain for ever excluded from the function of governing. . . . Under whatever conditions, and within whatever limits, men are admitted to the suffrage, there is not a shadow of justification for not admitting women under the same. The majority of the women of any class are not likely to differ in political opinion from the majority of the men of the same class, unless the question be one in which the interests of women, as such, are in some way involved; and if they are so, women require the suffrage, as their guarantee of just and equal consideration. . . .

With regard to the fitness of women, not only to participate in elections, but themselves to hold offices or practise professions involving important public responsibilities; I have already observed that this consideration is not essential to the practical question in dispute: since any woman, who succeeds in an open profession, proves by that very fact that she is qualified for it. And in the case of public offices, if the political system of the country is such as to exclude unfit men, it will equally exclude unfit women: while if it is not, there is no additional evil in the fact that the unfit persons whom it admits may be either women or men. . . .

. . . There is no country of Europe in which the ablest men have not frequently experienced, and keenly appreciated, the value of the advice and help of clever and experienced women of the world, in the attainment both of private and of public objects; and there are important matters of public administration to which few men are equally competent with such women; among others, the detailed control of expenditure. But what we are now discussing is not the need which society has of the services of women in public business, but the dull and hopeless life to which it so often condemns them, by forbidding them to exercise the practical abilities which many of them are conscious of, in any wider field than one which to some of them never was, and to others is no longer, open. If there is anything vitally important to the happiness of human beings, it is that they should relish their habitual pursuit [that is, they should be happy in their work]. This requisite of an enjoyable life is very imperfectly granted, or altogether denied, to a large part of mankind; and by its absence many a life is a failure, which is provided, in appearance, with every requisite of success.

The Goncourt Brothers
ON FEMALE INFERIORITY

The brothers Edmund (1822–1896) and Jules (1830–1870) Goncourt were French writers who produced in partnership novels, plays, and art and literary criticism. Starting in December 1851, they kept a journal in which they recorded, often insightfully, the doings of Parisian cultural and social life. In the following entries the Goncourts reveal an extreme bias against women. Even if these sentiments were not shared by all intellectuals, they do show the traditional prejudices confronting French feminists.

13 October, 1855

A conversation about woman, after a couple of tankards of beer at Binding's. Woman is an evil, stupid animal unless she is educated and civilized to a high degree. She is incapable of dreaming, thinking, or loving. Poetry in a woman is never natural but always a product of education. Only the woman of the world is a woman; the rest are females.

Inferiority of the feminine mind to the masculine mind. All the physical beauty, all the strength, and all the development of a woman is concentrated in and as it were directed towards the central and lower parts of the body: the pelvis, the buttocks, the thighs; the beauty of a man is to be found in the upper, nobler parts, the pectoral muscles, the broad shoulders, the high forehead. Venus has a narrow forehead. Dürer's *Three Graces* have flat heads at the back and little shoulders; only their hips are big and beautiful. As regards the inferiority of the feminine mind, consider the self-assurance of a woman, even when she is only a girl, which allows her to be extremely witty with nothing but a little vivacity and a touch of spontaneity. Only man is endowed with the modesty and timidity which woman lacks and which she uses only as weapons.

Woman: the most beautiful and most admirable of laying machines.

21 May, 1857

Men like ourselves need a woman of little breeding and education who is nothing but gaiety and natural wit, because a woman of that sort can charm and please us like an agreeable animal to which we may become quite attached. But if a mistress has acquired a veneer of breeding, art, or literature, and tries to talk to us on an equal footing about our thoughts and our feeling for beauty; if she wants to be a companion and partner in the cultivation of our tastes or the writing of our books, then she becomes for us as unbearable as a piano out of tune—and very soon an object of dislike.

Almroth E. Wright
THE UNEXPURGATED CASE AGAINST WOMAN SUFFRAGE

Sir Almroth Wright (1861–1947) was an eminent physician and one of the founders of modern immunology. He was also a thinker who attempted to construct "a system of Logic which searches for Truth," as he put it.

Wright's opposition to giving women the vote was expressed in letters to *The Times* of London and in a slender book, *The Unexpurgated Case Against Woman Suffrage* (1913). In the extracts that follow, he describes how the disabilities of women make female suffrage impossible, at one point dismissing the suffrage movement as the product of "sex-hostility" caused by the excess population of women without hope of marrying. All told, he found that women's suffrage would be a recipe for social disaster, resulting in unacceptable demands for economic and intellectual equality.

The primordial argument against giving woman the vote is that that vote would not represent physical force.

Now it is by physical force alone and by prestige—which represents physical force in the background—that a nation protects itself against foreign interference, upholds its rule over subject populations, and enforces its own laws. And nothing could in the end more certainly lead to war and revolt than the decline of the military spirit and loss of prestige which would inevitably follow if man admitted woman into political co-partnership. . . .

[A] virile and imperial race will not brook any attempt at forcible control by women. Again, no military foreign nation or native race would ever believe in the stamina and firmness of purpose of any nation that submitted even to the semblance of such control. . . .

The woman voter would be pernicious to the State not only because she could not back her vote by physical force, but also by reason of her intellectual defects.

Woman's mind . . . arrives at conclusions on incomplete evidence; has a very imperfect sense of proportion; accepts the congenial as true, and rejects the uncongenial as false; takes the imaginary which is desired for reality, and treats the undesired reality which is out of sight as nonexistent—building up for itself in this way, when biased by predilections and aversions, a very unreal picture of the external world.

The explanation of this is to be found in all the physiological attachments of woman's mind: in the fact that mental images are in her over-intimately linked up with emotional reflex responses; that yielding to such reflex responses gives gratification; that intellectual analysis and suspense of judgment involve an inhibition of reflex responses which is felt as neural distress; that precipitate judgment brings relief from this physiological strain; and that woman looks upon her mind not as an implement for the pursuit of truth, but as an instrument for providing her with creature comforts in the form of agreeable mental images. . . .

In further illustration of what has been said above, it may be pointed out that woman, even intelligent woman, nurses all sorts of misconceptions about herself. She, for instance, is constantly picturing to herself that she can as a worker lay claim to the same all-round efficiency as a man—forgetting that woman is notoriously unadapted to tasks in which severe physical hardships have to be confronted; and that hardly any one would, if other alternative offered, employ a woman in any work which imposed upon her a combined physical and mental strain, or in any work where emergencies might have to be faced. . . .

Yet a third point has to come into consideration in connexion with the woman voter. This is, that she would be pernicious to the State also by virtue of her defective moral equipment. . . .

It is only a very exceptional woman who would, when put to her election between the claims of a narrow and domestic and a wider or public morality, subordinate the former to the latter.

In ordinary life, at any rate, one finds her following in such a case the suggestions of domestic—I had almost called it animal—morality.

It would be difficult to find any one who would trust a woman to be just to the rights of others in the case where the material interests of her children, or of a devoted husband, were involved. And even to consider the question of being in such a case intellectually just to any one who came into competition with personal belongings like husband and child would, of course, lie quite beyond the moral horizon of ordinary woman. . . . In this matter one would not be very far from the truth if one alleged that there are no good women, but only women who have lived under the influence of good men. . . .

In countries, such as England, where an excess female population [of three million] has made economic difficulties for woman, and where the severe sexual restrictions, which here obtain, have bred in her sex-hostility, the suffrage movement has as its avowed ulterior object the abrogation of all distinctions which depend upon sex; and the achievement of the economic independence of woman.

To secure this economic independence every post, occupation, and Government service is to be thrown open to woman; she is to receive everywhere the same wages as man; male and female are to work side by side; and they are indiscriminately to be put in command the one over the other. Furthermore, legal rights are to be secured to the wife over her husband's property and earnings. The programme is, in fact, to give to woman an economic independence out of the earnings and taxes of man.

Nor does feminist ambition stop short here. It demands that women shall be included in every advisory committee, every governing board, every jury, every judicial bench, every electorate, every parliament, and every ministerial cabinet; further, that every masculine foundation, university, school of learning, academy, trade union, professional corporation, and scientific society shall be converted into an epicene institution [including both male and female]—until we shall have everywhere one vast cock-and-hen show.

The proposal to bring man and woman together everywhere into extremely intimate relationships raises very grave questions. It brings up, first, the question of sexual complications; secondly, the question as to whether the tradition of modesty and reticence between the sexes is to be definitely sacrificed; and, most important of all, the question as to whether [bringing men and women together] would place obstacles in the way of intellectual work. . . .

The matter cannot so lightly be disposed of. It will be necessary for us to find out whether really intimate association with woman on the purely intellectual plane is realisable. And if it is, in fact, unrealisable, it will be necessary to consider whether it is the exclusion of women from masculine corporations; or the perpetual attempt of women to force their way into these, which would deserve to be characterised as *selfish*. . . .

What we have to ask is whether—even if we leave out of regard the whole system of attractions or, as the case may be, repulsions which comes into operation when the sexes are thrown together—purely intellectual intercourse between man and the typical unselected woman is not barred by the intellectual immoralities and limitations which appear to be secondary sexual characters of woman. . . .

Wherever we look we find aversion to compulsory intellectual co-operation with woman. We see it in the sullen attitude which the ordinary male student takes up towards the presence of women students in his classes. We see it in the fact that the older English universities, which have conceded everything else to women, have made a strong stand against making them actual members of the university; for this would impose them on men as intellectual associates. Again we see the aversion in the opposition to the admission of women to the bar.

But we need not look so far afield. Practically every man feels that there is in woman—patent, or hidden away—an element of unreason which, when you come upon it, summarily puts an end to purely intellectual intercourse. One may reflect, for example, upon the way the woman's suffrage controversy has been conducted.

But the feminist will want to argue. She will—taking it as always for granted that woman has a right to all that men's hands or brains have fashioned—argue that it is very important for the intellectual development of woman that she should have exactly the same opportunities as man. And she will, scouting the idea of any differences between the intelligences of man and woman, discourse to you of their intimate affinity. . . .

From these general questions, which affect only the woman with intellectual aspirations, we pass to consider what would be the effect of feminism upon the rank and file of women if it made of these co-partners with man in work. They would suffer, not only because woman's physiological disabilities and the restrictions which arise out of her sex place her at a great disadvantage when she has to enter into competition with man, but also because under feminism man would be less and less disposed to take off woman's shoulders a part of her burden.

And there can be no dispute that the most valuable financial asset of the ordinary woman is the possibility that a man may be willing—and may, if only woman is disposed to fulfil her part of the bargain, be not only willing but anxious—to support her, and to secure for her, if he can, a measure of that freedom which comes from the possession of money.

In view of this every one who has a real fellow-feeling for woman, and who is concerned for her material welfare, as a father is concerned for his daughter's, will above everything else desire to nurture and encourage in man the sentiment of chivalry, and in woman that disposition of mind that makes chivalry possible.

And the woman workers who have to fight the battle of life for themselves would indirectly profit from this fostering of chivalry; for those women who are supported by men do not compete in the limited labour market which is open to the woman worker.

From every point of view, therefore, except perhaps that of the exceptional woman who would be able to hold her own against masculine competition—and men always issue informal letters of [admission] to such an exceptional woman—the woman suffrage which leads up to feminism would be a social disaster.

REVIEW QUESTIONS

1. In John Stuart Mill's view, what was the ultimate origin of the subjection of women?
2. According to Mill, what character qualities did men seek to instill in women?
   Why, according to Mill's argument, should women have the right to participate in politics and public affairs on equal terms with men?
3. In what ways did the Goncourt brothers consider women inferior?
4. Why did Sir Almroth Wright think that women voters would be pernicious to the state?
5. In Wright's view, how were feminist reforms disadvantageous to women?

---

6 Anti-Semitism: Regression to the Irrational

Anti-Semitism, a European phenomenon of long standing, rose to new prominence in the late nineteenth century. Formerly segregated by law into ghettoes, Jews, under the aegis of the Enlightenment and the French Revolution, had gained legal equality in most European lands. In the nineteenth century, Jews participated in the economic and cultural progress of the times and often achieved distinction in business, the professions, and the arts and sciences. However, driven by irrational fears and mythical conceptions that had survived from the Middle Ages, many people regarded Jews as a dangerous race of international conspirators and foreign intruders who threatened their nations.

Throughout the nineteenth century, anti-Semitic outrages occurred in many European lands. Russian anti-Semitism assumed a particularly violent form in the infamous pogroms—murderous mob attacks on Jews—occasionally abetted by government officials. Even in highly civilized France, anti-Semitism proved a powerful force. At the time of the Dreyfus affair—in 1894 Captain Alfred Dreyfus, a Jewish officer appointed to the French General Staff, was convicted on faked evidence of high treason—Catholic and nationalist zealots demanded that Jews be deprived of their civil rights. In Germany, anti-Semitism became associated with the ideological defense of a distinctive German culture, the volkish thought popular in the last part of the nineteenth century. After the foundation of the German Empire in 1871, the pace of economic and cultural change quickened, and with it the cultural disorientation that fanned anti-Semitism. Volkish thinkers, who valued traditional Germany—the landscape, the peasant, and the village—associated Jews with the changes brought about by rapid industrialization and modernization. Compounding the problem was the influx into Germany of Jewish immigrants from the Russian Empire, who were searching for a better life and brought with them their own distinctive culture and religion, which many Germans found offensive. Nationalists and conservatives used anti-Semitism in an effort to gain a mass following.

Racial-nationalist considerations were the decisive force behind modern anti-Semitism. Racists said that the Jews were a wicked race of Asiatics, condemned by their genes; they differed physically, intellectually, and spiritually from Europeans who were descendants of ancient Aryans. (The Aryans emerged some 4,000 years ago, probably between the Caspian Sea and the Hindu Kush Mountains. Intermingling with others, the Aryans lost whatever identity as a people they might have had.) After discovering similarities between core European languages (Greek, Latin, German) and ancient Persian and ancient Sanskrit (the language of the conquerors of India), nineteenth-century scholars believed that these languages all stemmed from a common tongue spoken by the Aryans. From there, some leaped to the conclusion that the Aryans constituted a distinct race endowed with superior racial qualities.

Houston Stewart Chamberlain (1855–1927), an Englishman whose devotion to Germanism led him to adopt German citizenship, pitted Aryans and Jews against each other in a struggle of world historical importance. As agents of a spiritually empty capitalism and divisive liberalism, the Jews, said Chamberlain, were the opposite of the idealistic, heroic, and faithful Germans. Chamberlain denied that Jesus was a Jew, hinting that he was of Aryan stock, and held that the goal of the Jew was "to put his foot upon the neck of all the nations of the world and be lord and possessor of the whole earth." Racial anti-Semitism became a powerful force in European intellectual life, especially in Germany. It was the seedbed of Hitler's movement.

Hermann Ahlwardt
THE SEMITIC VERSUS
THE TEUTONIC RACE

In the following reading, Hermann Ahlwardt (1846–1914), an anti-Semitic member of the Reichstag and author of *The Desperate Struggle Between Aryan and Jew,* addresses the chamber on March 6, 1895, with a plea to close Germany's borders to Jewish immigrants. His speech reflects the anti-Semitic rhetoric popular among German conservatives before World War I. The material in parentheses is by Paul W. Massing, translator and editor.

It is certainly true that there are Jews in our country of whom nothing adverse can be said. Nevertheless, the Jews as a whole must be considered harmful, for the racial traits of this people are of a kind that in the long run do not agree with the racial traits of the Teutons.[1] Every Jew who at this very moment has not as yet transgressed is likely to do so at some future time under given circumstances because his racial characteristics drive him on in that direction. . . .

My political friends do not hold the view that we fight the Jews because of their religion. . . . We would not dream of waging a political struggle against anyone because of his religion. . . . We hold the view that the Jews are a different race, a different people with entirely different character traits.

Experience in all fields of nature shows that innate racial characteristics which have been acquired by the race in the course of many thousands of years are the strongest and most enduring factors that exist, and that therefore we can rid ourselves of the characteristics of our race no more than can the Jews. One need not fight the Jew individually, and we are not doing that, by the way. But, when countless specimens prove the existence of certain racial characteristics and when these characteristics are such as to make impossible a common life, well, then I believe that we who are natives here, who have tilled the soil and defended it against all enemies—that we have a duty to take a stand against the Jews who are of a quite different nature.

We Teutons are rooted in the cultural soil of labor. . . . The Jews do not believe in the culture of labor, they do not want to create values themselves, but want to appropriate, without working, the values which others have created; that is the cardinal difference that guides us in all our considerations. . . .

Herr Deputy Rickert[2] here has just expounded how few Jews we have altogether and that their number is steadily declining. Well, gentlemen, why don't you go to the main business centers and see for yourselves whether the percentages indicated by Herr Rickert prevail there too. Why don't you walk along the Leipzigerstrasse (in Berlin) or the Zeil in Frankfurt and have a look at the shops? Wherever there are opportunities to make money, the Jews have established themselves, but not in order to work—no, they let others work for them and take what the others have produced by their labor.

Deputy Hasse . . . has committed the grave mistake of putting the Jews and other peoples on the same level, and that is the worst mistake that we could possibly make.

The Jews have an attitude toward us which differs totally from that of other peoples. It is one thing when a Pole, a Russian, a Frenchman, a Dane immigrates to our country, and quite another thing when a Jew settles here. . . . Once our (Polish, etc.) guests have lived here for ten, twenty years, they come to resemble us. For they have stood with us on the same cultural soil of labor. . . . After thirty, forty years they have become Germans and their grandchildren would be indistinguishable from us except for the strange-sounding names they still bear. The Jews have lived here for 700, 800 years, but have they become Germans? Have they placed themselves on the cultural soil of labor? They never even dreamed of such a thing; as soon as they arrived, they started to cheat and they have been doing that ever since they have been in Germany. . . .

The Jews should not be admitted, whether or not there is overpopulation, for they do not belong to a productive race, they are exploiters, parasites. . . .

---

[1]"Teutons" refers to the quintessential Germans. The name comes from a German tribe that once defeated a Roman army.

[2]Heinrich Rickert, a leader of the Progressives and an outspoken opponent of anti-Semitism, had pointed out that the Jews constituted only 1.29 percent of the population of Prussia. What enraged the German Right was that the Jews accounted for 9.58 percent of the university students in Prussia.

(Answering Rickert's arguments that . . . it would be a shame if fifty million Germans were afraid of a few Jews, Ahlwardt continued:) . . .

Herr Rickert, who is just as tall as I am, is afraid of one single cholera bacillus—well, gentlemen, the Jews are just that, cholera bacilli!

Gentlemen, the crux of the matter is Jewry's capacity for contagion and exploitation. . . . How many thousands of Germans have perished as a result of this Jewish exploitation, how many may have hanged themselves, shot themselves, drowned themselves, how many may have ended by the wayside as tramps in America or drawn their last breath in the gutter, all of them people who had worked industriously on the soil their fathers had acquired, perhaps in hundreds of years of hard work. . . . Don't you feel any pity for those countless Germans? Are they to perish unsung? Ah, why were they foolish enough to let themselves be cheated? But the Germans are by no means so foolish, they are far more intelligent than the Jews. All inventions, all great ideas come from the Germans and not from the Jews. No, I shall tell you the national difference: The German is fundamentally trusting, his heart is full of loyalty and confidence. The Jew gains this confidence, only to betray it at the proper moment, ruining and pauperizing the German. This abuse of confidence on the part of the Jews is their main weapon. And these Jewish scoundrels are to be defended here! Is there no one to think of all those hundreds of thousands, nor of those millions of workers whose wages grow smaller and smaller because Jewish competition brings the prices down? One always hears: you must be humane toward the Jews. The humanitarianism of our century . . . is our curse. Why aren't you for once humane toward the oppressed? You'd better exterminate those beasts of prey and you'd better start by not letting any more of them into our country. . . .

(Taking issue with the liberals' argument of Jewish achievements in the arts, Ahlwardt declared:)

Art in my opinion is the capacity for expressing one's innermost feelings in such a way as to arouse the same feelings in the other person. Now the Jewish world of emotions (*Gefühlswelt*) and the Teutonic world of emotions are two quite different things. German art can express only German feelings; Jewish art only Jewish feelings. Because Jewry has been thrusting itself forward everywhere, it has also thrust itself forward in the field of art and therefore the art that is now in the foreground is Jewish art. Nowadays the head of a family must be very careful when he decides to take his family to the theater lest his Teutonic feelings be outraged by the infamous Jewish art that has spread everywhere.

The Jew is no German. If you say, the Jew was born in Germany, he was nursed by a German wetnurse, he abides by German laws, he has to serve as a soldier—and what kind of a soldier at that! let's not talk about it—he fulfills all his obligations, he pays his taxes—then I say that all this is not the crucial factor with regard to his nationality; the crucial factor is the race from which he stems. Permit me to make a rather trite comparison which I have already used elsewhere in my speeches: a horse that is born in a cowshed is far from being a cow.

A Jew who was born in Germany does not thereby become a German; he is still a Jew. Therefore it is imperative that we realize that Jewish racial characteristics differ so greatly from ours that a common life of Jews and Germans under the same laws is quite impossible because the Germans will perish. . . .

. . . I beg you from the bottom of my heart not to take this matter[*] lightly but as a very serious thing. It is a question of life and death for our people. . . .

We wouldn't think of going as far as have the Austrian anti-Semites in the Federal Council (*Reichsrat*) and to move that a bounty be paid for every Jew shot or to decree that

---

*Prohibition of Jewish immigration.

he who kills a Jew shall inherit his property. We have no such intention. We shall not go as far as that. What we want is a clear and reasonable separation of the Jews from the Germans. An immediate prerequisite is that we slam the door and see to it that no more of them get in.[†]

[†]At the end of the debate a vote was taken, with 218 representatives present. Of these, 51 voted for, 167 against the motion.

Theodor Herzl
THE JEWISH STATE

Theodor Herzl (1860–1904) was raised in a comfortable Jewish middle-class home. Moving from Budapest, where he was born, to Vienna, the capital of the Austro-Hungarian Empire, he started to practice law, but soon turned to journalism, writing from Paris for the leading Vienna newspaper. A keen observer of the contemporary scene, he vigorously agitated for the ideal of an independent Jewish state. It was not a new idea but one whose time had come. Nationalist ferment was rising everywhere, often combined with virulent anti-Semitism. Under the circumstances, Herzl argued, security for Jews could be guaranteed only by a separate national state for Jews, preferably in Palestine.

In 1896 he published his program in a book, *Der Judenstaat* (The Jewish State), in which he envisaged a glorious future for an independent Jewish state harmoniously cooperating with the local population. In the following year he presided over the first Congress of Zionist Organizations held in Basel (Switzerland), attended mostly by Jews from central and eastern Europe. In its program the congress called for "a publicly guaranteed homeland for the Jewish people in the land of Israel." Subsequently, Herzl negotiated with the German emperor, the British government, and the sultan of the Ottoman Empire (of which Palestine was a part) for diplomatic support. In 1901 the Jewish National Fund was created to help settlers purchase land in Palestine. At his death, Herzl firmly expected a Jewish state to arise sometime in the future. The following excerpts from his book express the main points in his plea for a Jewish state.

We are a people—one people.

We have honestly endeavored everywhere to merge ourselves in the social life of surrounding communities and to preserve the faith of our fathers. We are not permitted to do so. In vain are we loyal patriots, our loyalty in some places running to extremes; in vain do we make the same sacrifices of life and property as our fellow-citizens; in vain do we strive to increase the fame of our native land in science and art, or her wealth by trade and commerce.

In countries where we have lived for centuries we are still cried down as strangers, and often by those whose ancestors were not yet domiciled in the land where Jews had already had experience of suffering. . . . I think we shall not be left in peace.

Oppression and persecution cannot exterminate us. No nation on earth has survived such struggles and sufferings as we have gone through. Jew-baiting has merely stripped off our weaklings; the strong among us were invariably true to their race when persecution broke out against them. . . .

. . . [O]ld prejudices against us still lie deep in the hearts of the people. He who would have proofs of this need only listen to the people where they speak with frankness and simplicity: proverb and fairy-tale are both Anti-Semitic. . . .

No one can deny the gravity of the situation of the Jews. Wherever they live in perceptible numbers, they are more or less persecuted. Their equality before the law, granted by statute, has become practically a dead letter. They are debarred from filling even moderately high positions, either in the army, or in any public or private capacity. And attempts are made to thrust them out of business also: "Don't buy from Jews!"

Attacks in Parliaments, in assemblies, in the press, in the pulpit, in the street, on journeys— for example, their exclusion from certain hotels—even in places of recreation, become daily more numerous. The forms of persecutions varying according to the countries and social circles in which they occur. In Russia, imposts are levied on Jewish villages; in Rumania, a few persons are put to death; in Germany, they get a good beating occasionally; in Austria, Anti-Semites exercise terrorism over all public life; in Algeria, there are travelling agitators; in Paris, the Jews are shut out of the so-called best social circles and excluded from clubs. Shades of anti-Jewish feeling are innumerable. But this is not to be an attempt to make out a doleful category of Jewish hardships.

I do not intend to arouse sympathetic emotions on our behalf. That would be a foolish, futile, and undignified proceeding. I shall content myself with putting the following questions to the Jews: Is it not true that, in countries where we live in perceptible numbers, the position of Jewish lawyers, doctors, technicians, teachers, and employees of all descriptions becomes daily more intolerable? Is it not true that the Jewish middle classes are seriously threatened? Is it not true, that the passions of the mob are incited against our wealthy people? Is it not true, that

our poor endure greater sufferings than any other proletariat? I think that this external pressure makes itself felt everywhere. In our economically upper classes it causes discomfort, in our middle classes continual and grave anxieties, in our lower classes absolute despair.

Everything tends, in fact, to one and the same conclusion, which is clearly enunciated in that classic Berlin phrase: *"Juden Raus!"* (Out with the Jews!)

I shall now put the Question in the briefest possible form: Are we to "get out" now and where to?

Or, may we yet remain? And, how long?

Let us first settle the point of staying where we are. Can we hope for better days, can we possess our souls in patience, can we wait in pious resignation till the princes and peoples of this earth are more mercifully disposed towards us? I say that we cannot hope for a change in the current of feeling. . . . The nations in whose midst Jews live are all either covertly or openly Anti-Semitic. . . .

. . . We might perhaps be able to merge ourselves entirely into surrounding races, if these were to leave us in peace for a period of two generations. But they will not leave us in peace. For a little period they manage to tolerate us, and then their hostility breaks out again and again. . . .

Thus, whether we like it or not, we are now, and shall henceforth remain, a historic group with unmistakable characteristics common to us all.

We are one people—our enemies have made us one without our consent, as repeatedly happens in history. Distress binds us together, and, thus united, we suddenly discover our strength. Yes, we are strong enough to form a State, and, indeed, a model State. We possess all human and material resources necessary for the purpose. . . .

Let the sovereignty be granted us over a portion of the globe large enough to satisfy the rightful requirements of a nation; the rest we shall manage for ourselves.

The creation of a new State is neither ridiculous nor impossible. We have in our day witnessed the process in connection with nations which were not largely members of the middle class, but poorer, less educated, and consequently weaker than ourselves. . . .

Palestine is our ever-memorable historic home. The very name of Palestine would attract our people with a force of marvellous potency. If His Majesty the Sultan were to give us Palestine, we could in return undertake to regulate the whole finances of Turkey. We should there form a portion of a rampart of Europe against Asia, an outpost of civilization as opposed to barbarism. We should as a neutral State remain in contact with all Europe, which would have to guarantee our existence. The sanctuaries of Christendom would be safeguarded by assigning to them an extra-territorial status such as is well-known to the law of nations. We should form a guard of honor about these sanctuaries, answering for the fulfillment of this duty with our existence. This guard of honor would be the great symbol of the solution of the Jewish Question after eighteen centuries of Jewish suffering.

REVIEW QUESTIONS

1. What, according to Hermann Ahlwardt, were the racial characteristics of Jews? What, in contrast, were the racial characteristics of Germans?
2. What, said Ahlwardt, would be the ultimate result if Jewish immigration into Germany were not stopped?
3. How did Ahlwardt's anti-Semitism differ from traditional Christian anti-Semitism?
4. What kind of human needs did anti-Semitism seem to satisfy? What types of people are often attracted to anti-Semitic thinking? How may anti-Semitism be regarded as a regression to mythical modes of thinking?
5. Why did Theodor Herzl believe that the creation of a Jewish state was the only solution to the Jewish question?

---

7 The Spirit of British Imperialism

In 1872 the British statesman Benjamin Disraeli (1804–1881) delivered a famous speech at the Crystal Palace in London that posed a crucial choice for his country: it was either insignificance in world affairs or imperial power with prosperity and global prestige. His speech was soon followed by an outburst of speeches, lectures, and books in which imperialists made claims for British worldwide superiority buttressed by arguments drawn from racist and Darwinian convictions popular at the time. These ideas, illustrated in the following readings, found a receptive audience.

Cecil Rhodes
CONFESSION OF FAITH

One ardent supporter of British expansion was Cecil Rhodes (1853–1902). Raised in a parsonage north of London, Rhodes went to southern Africa at the age of seventeen for his health and to join his brother. Within two years he had established himself in the diamond industry. In the 1870s, he divided his time between Africa and studying at Oxford University. While at Oxford he was inspired by Disraeli's Crystal Palace speech and the views of the prominent Oxford professor John Ruskin (1819–1900), who urged England "to found colonies as fast and as far as she is able, formed of the most energetic and worthiest of men." In this spirit Rhodes wrote, for his own satisfaction, a "Confession of Faith." Composed in 1877, when he was twenty-four years old, it offered a vision of racist expansionism popular before the First World War. It was not published in his lifetime.

His faith propelled him into political and financial prominence in South Africa. In 1889 he became head of the British South African Company, whose territory, twice as large as England, was named Rhodesia six years later (it was renamed Zimbabwe in 1980). He controlled 90 percent of the world's diamond production and a large share of South Africa's gold fields. Never regarding wealth as an end in itself—he endowed the Rhodes Scholarships at Oxford—he sought to extend British influence in East Africa and around the world.

In 1890 he was named prime minister of the British Cape Colony, where government forces were heavily involved in conflict with the original Dutch settlers, the Boers. Driven north by the British, the Boers had set up their own state. Rhodes died during the Boer War (1899–1902), which put the Boers under British rule.

Excerpts follow from the "Confession of Faith" of 1877, included in the appendix of John E. Flint's biography of Cecil Rhodes. Flint reproduced the document "in its original form without any editing of spelling or punctuation."

It often strikes a man to inquire what is the chief good in life; to one the thought comes that it is a happy marriage, to another great wealth, and as each seizes on his idea, for that he more or less works for the rest of his existence. To myself thinking over the same question the wish came to render myself useful to my country. I then asked myself how could I and after reviewing the various methods I have felt that at the present day we are actually limiting our children and perhaps bringing into the world half the human beings we might owing to the lack of country for them to inhabit that if we had retained America there would at this moment be millions more of English living. I contend that we are the finest race in the world and that the more of the world we inhabit the better it is for the human race. Just fancy those parts that are at present inhabited by the most despicable specimens of human beings what an alteration there would be if they were brought under Anglo-Saxon influence, look again at the extra employment a new country added to our dominions gives. I contend that every acre added to our territory means in the future birth to some more of the English race who otherwise would not be brought into existence. Added to this the absorption of the greater portion of the world under our rule simply means the end of all wars. . . .

The idea gleaming and dancing before ones eyes like a will-of-the-wisp at last frames itself into a plan. Why should we not form a secret society with but one object the furtherance of the British Empire and the bringing of the whole uncivilised world under British rule for the recovery of the United States for the making the Anglo-Saxon race but one Empire. What a dream, but yet it is probable, it is possible. I once heard it argued by a fellow in my own college, I am sorry to own it by an Englishman, that it was a good thing for us that we have lost the United States. There are some subjects on which there can be no arguments, and to an Englishman this is one of them, but even from an American's point of view just picture what they have lost, look at their government, are not the frauds that yearly come before the public view a disgrace to any country and especially their's which is the finest in the world. Would they have occurred had they remained under English rule great as they have become how infinitely greater they would have been with the softening and elevating influences of English rule, think of those countless 000's [thousands] of Englishmen that during the last 100 years would have crossed the Atlantic and settled and populated the United States. Would they have not made without any prejudice a finer country of it than the low class Irish and German emigrants? All this we have lost and that country loses owing to whom? Owing to two or three ignorant pig-headed statesmen of the last century, at their door lies the blame. Do you ever feel mad? do you ever feel murderous. I think I do with those men. I bring facts to prove my assertion. Does an English father when his sons wish to emigrate ever think of suggesting emigration to a country under another flag, never—it would seem a disgrace to suggest such a thing I think that we all think that poverty is better under our own flag than wealth under a foreign one.

Put your mind into another train of thought. Fancy Australia discovered and colonised under the French flag. . . . We learn from having lost to cling to what we possess. We know the size of the world we know the total extent. Africa is still lying ready for us it is our duty to take it. It is our duty to seize every opportunity of acquiring more territory and we should keep this one idea steadily before our eyes that more territory simply means more of the Anglo-Saxon race more of the best the most human, most honourable race the world possesses.

To forward such a scheme what a splendid help a secret society would be a society not openly acknowledged but who would work in secret for such an object.

I contend that there are at the present moment numbers of the ablest men in the world who would devote their whole lives to it. . . . What has been the main cause of the success of the Romish Church? The fact that every enthusiast, call it if you like every madman finds employment in it. Let us form the same kind of society a Church for the extension of the British Empire. A society which should have its members in every part of the British Empire working with one object and one idea. . . .

(In every Colonial legislature the Society should attempt to have its members prepared at all times to vote or speak and advocate the closer union of England and the colonies, to crush all disloyalty and every movement for the severance of our Empire. The Society should inspire and even own portions of the press for the press rules the mind of the people. The Society should always be searching for members who might by their position in the world by their energies or character forward the object but the ballot and test for admittance should be severe). . . .[1]

For fear that death might cut me off before the time for attempting its development I leave all my worldly goods in trust to S. G. Shippard and the Secretary for the Colonies at the time of my death to try to form such a Society with such an object.

---

[1]It is not clear why Rhodes placed this paragraph in parentheses.

Joseph Chamberlain
THE BRITISH EMPIRE:
COLONIAL COMMERCE AND
"THE WHITE MAN'S BURDEN"

British imperialists like Joseph Chamberlain (1836–1914) argued that the welfare of Britain depended upon the preservation and extension of the empire, for colonies fostered trade and served as a source of raw materials. In addition, Chamberlain asserted that the British Empire had a sacred duty to carry civilization, Christianity, and British law to the "backward" peoples of Africa and Asia. As a leading statesman, Chamberlain made many speeches, both in Parliament and before local political groups, that endorsed imperialist ventures. Excerpts from these speeches, later collected and published under the title *Foreign and Colonial Speeches* (1897), follow.

June 10, 1896

. . . The Empire, to parody a celebrated expression, is commerce. It was created by commerce, it is founded on commerce, and it could not exist a day without commerce. (Cheers). . . . The fact is history teaches us that no nation has ever achieved real greatness without the aid of commerce, and the greatness of no nation has survived the decay of its trade. Well, then, gentlemen, we have reason to be proud of our commerce and to be resolved to guard it from attack. (Cheers.). . . .

March 31, 1897

. . . We have suffered much in this country from depression of trade. We know how many of our fellow-subjects are at this moment unemployed. Is there any man in his senses who believes that the crowded population of these islands could exist for a single day if we were to cut adrift from us the great dependencies which now look to us for protection and assistance, and which are the natural markets for our trade? (Cheers.) The area of the United Kingdom is only 120,000 miles; the area of the British Empire is over 9,000,000 square miles, of which nearly 500,000 are to be found in the portion of Africa with which we have been dealing. If tomorrow it were possible, as some people apparently desire, to reduce by a stroke of the pen the British Empire to the dimensions of the United Kingdom, half at least of our population would be starved (cheers). . . .

January 22, 1894

We must look this matter in the face, and must recognise that in order that we may have more employment to give we must create more demand. (Hear, hear.) Give me the demand for more goods and then I will undertake to give plenty of employment in making the goods; and the only thing, in my opinion, that the Government can do in order to meet this great difficulty that we are considering, is so to arrange its policy that every inducement shall be given to the demand; that new markets shall be created, and that old markets shall be effectually developed. (Cheers.) . . . I am convinced that it is a necessity as well as a duty for us to uphold the dominion and empire which we now possess. (Loud cheers.) . . . I would never lose the hold which we now have over our great Indian dependency—(hear, hear)—by far the greatest and most valuable of all the customers we have or ever shall have in this country. For the same reasons I approve of the continued occupation of Egypt; and for the same reasons I have urged upon this Government, and upon previous Governments, the necessity for using every legitimate opportunity to extend our influence and control in that great African continent which is now being opened up to civilisation and to commerce; and, lastly, it is for the same reasons that I hold that our navy should be strengthened—(loud cheers)—until its supremacy is so assured that we cannot be shaken in any of the possessions which we hold or may hold hereafter.

Believe me, if in any one of the places to which I have referred any change took place which deprived us of that control and influence of which I have been speaking, the first to suffer would be the working-men of this country. Then, indeed, we should see a distress which would not be temporary, but which would be chronic, and we should find that England was entirely unable to support the enormous population which is now maintained by the aid of her foreign trade. If the working-men of this country understand, as I believe they do—I am one of those who have had good reason through my life to rely upon their intelligence and shrewdness—if they understand their own interests, they will never lend any countenance to the doctrines of those politicians who never lose an opportunity of pouring contempt and abuse upon the brave Englishmen, who, even at this moment, in all parts of the world are carving out new dominions for Britain, and are opening up fresh markets for British commerce, and laying out fresh fields for British labour. (Applause.) . . .

March 31, 1897

. . . We feel now that our rule over these territories can only be justified if we can show that it adds to the happiness and prosperity of the people—(cheers)—and I maintain that our rule does, and has, brought security and peace and comparative prosperity to countries that never knew these blessings before. (Cheers.)

In carrying out this work of civilisation we are fulfilling what I believe to be our national mission, and we are finding scope for the exercise of those faculties and qualities which have made of us a great governing race. (Cheers.) I do not say that our success has been perfect in every case, I do not say that all our methods have been beyond reproach; but I do say that in almost every instance in which the rule of the Queen has been established and the great *Pax Britannica*[1] has been enforced, there has come with it greater security to life and property, and a material improvement in the condition of the bulk of the population. (Cheers.) No doubt, in the first instance, when these conquests have been made, there has been bloodshed, there has been loss of life among the native populations, loss of still more precious lives among those who have been sent out to bring these countries into some kind of disciplined order, but it must be remembered that this is the condition of the mission we have to fulfil. . . .

. . . You cannot have omelettes without breaking eggs; you cannot destroy the practices of barbarism, of slavery, of superstition, which for centuries have desolated the interior of Africa, without the use of force; but if you will fairly contrast the gain to humanity with the price which we are bound to pay for it, I think you may well rejoice in the result of such expeditions as those which have recently been conducted with such signal success—(cheers)—in Nyassaland, Ashanti, Benin, and Nupé [regions in Africa]—expeditions which may have, and indeed have, cost valuable lives, but as to which we may rest assured that for one life lost a hundred will be gained, and the cause of civilisation and the prosperity of the people will in the long run be eminently advanced. (Cheers.) But no doubt such a state of things, such a mission as I have described, involve heavy responsibility . . . and it is a gigantic task that we have undertaken when we

---

[1]*Pax Britannica* means "British Peace" in the tradition of the *Pax Romana*—the peace, stability, and prosperity that characterized the Roman Empire at its height in the first two centuries A.D.

have determined to wield the sceptre of empire. Great is the task, great is the responsibility, but great is the honour—(cheers); and I am convinced that the conscience and the spirit of the country will rise to the height of its obligations, and that we shall have the strength to fulfil the mission which our history and our national character have imposed upon us. (Cheers.)

Karl Pearson
SOCIAL DARWINISM: IMPERIALISM JUSTIFIED BY NATURE

In the last part of the nineteenth century, the spirit of expansionism was buttressed by application of Darwin's theory of evolution to human society. Theorists called Social Darwinists argued that nations and races, like the species of animals, were locked in a struggle for existence in which only the fittest survived and deserved to survive. British and American imperialists employed the language of Social Darwinism to promote and justify Anglo-Saxon expansion and domination of other peoples. Social Darwinist ideas spread to Germany, which was inspired by the examples of British and American expansion. In a lecture given in 1900 and titled "National Life from the Standpoint of Science," Karl Pearson (1857–1936), a British professor of mathematics, expressed the beliefs of Social Darwinists.

What I have said about bad stock seems to me to hold for the lower races of man. How many centuries, how many thousands of years, have the Kaffir [a tribe in southern Africa] or the negro held large districts in Africa undisturbed by the white man? Yet their intertribal struggles have not yet produced a civilization in the least comparable with the Aryan[1] [western European]. Educate and nurture them as you will, I do not believe that you will succeed in modifying the stock. History shows me one way, and one way only, in which a high state of civilization has been produced, namely, the struggle of race with race, and the survival of the physically and mentally fitter race. . . .

. . . Let us suppose we could prevent the white man, if we liked, from going to lands of which the agricultural and mineral resources are not worked to the full; then I should say a thousand times better for him that he should not go than that he should settle down and live alongside the inferior race. The only healthy alternative is that he should go and completely drive out the inferior race. That is practically what the white man has done in North America. . . . But I venture to say that no man calmly judging will wish either that the whites had never gone to America, or would desire that whites and Red Indians were to-day living alongside each other as negro and white in the Southern States, as Kaffir and European in South Africa, still less that they had mixed their blood as Spaniard and Indian in South America. . . . I venture to assert, then, that the struggle for existence between white and red man, painful and even terrible as it was in its details, has given us a good far outbalancing its immediate evil. In place of the red man, contributing practically nothing to the work and thought of the world, we have a great nation, mistress of many arts, and able, with its youth-

[1]Most European languages derive from the Aryan language spoken by people who lived thousands of years ago in the region from the Caspian Sea to the Hindu Kush Mountains. Around 2000 B.C., some Aryan-speaking people migrated to Europe and India. Nineteenth-century racialist thinkers held that Europeans, descendants of the ancient Aryans, were racially superior to other peoples.

ful imagination and fresh, untrammelled impulses, to contribute much to the common stock of civilized man. . . .

But America is but one case in which we have to mark a masterful human progress following an inter-racial struggle. The Australian nation is another case of great civilization supplanting a lower race unable to work to the full the land and its resources. . . . The struggle means suffering, intense suffering, while it is in progress; but that struggle and that suffering have been the stages by which the white man has reached his present stage of development, and they account for the fact that he no longer lives in caves and feeds on roots and nuts. This dependence of progress on the survival of the fitter race, terribly black as it may seem to some of you, gives the struggle for existence its redeeming features; it is the fiery crucible out of which comes the finer metal. You may hope for a time when the sword shall be turned into the ploughshare, when American and German and English traders shall no longer compete in the markets of the world for their raw material and for their food supply, when the white man and the dark shall share the soil between them, and each till it as he lists [pleases]. But, believe me, when that day comes mankind will no longer progress; there will be nothing to check the fertility of inferior stock; the relentless law of heredity will not be controlled and guided by natural selection. Man will stagnate. . . .

The . . . great function of science in national life . . . is to show us what national life means, and how the nation is a vast organism subject . . . to the great forces of evolution. . . . There is a struggle of race against race and of nation against nation. In the early days of that struggle it was a blind, unconscious struggle of barbaric tribes. At the present day, in the case of the civilized white man, it has become more and more the conscious, carefully directed attempt of the nation to fit itself to a continuously changing environment. The nation has to foresee how and where the struggle will be carried on; the maintenance of national position is becoming more and more a conscious preparation for changing conditions, an insight into the needs of coming environments. . . .

. . . If a nation is to maintain its position in this struggle, it must be fully provided with trained brains in every department of national activity, from the government to the factory, and have, if possible, a *reserve of brain and physique* to fall back upon in times of national crisis. . . .

You will see that my view—and I think it may be called the scientific view of a nation— is that of an organized whole, kept up to a high pitch of internal efficiency by insuring that its numbers are substantially recruited from the better stocks, and kept up to a high pitch of external efficiency by contest, chiefly by way of war with inferior races, and with equal races by the struggle for trade-routes and for the sources of raw material and of food supply. This is the natural history view of mankind, and I do not think you can in its main features subvert it. . . .

. . . Is it not a fact that the daily bread of our millions of workers depends on their having somebody to work for? that if we give up the contest for trade-routes and for free markets and for waste lands, we indirectly give up our food-supply? Is it not a fact that our strength depends on these and upon our colonies, and that our colonies have been won by the ejection of inferior races, and are maintained against equal races only by respect for the present power of our empire? . . .

. . . We find that the law of the survival of the fitter is true of mankind, but that the struggle is that of the gregarious animal. A community not knit together by strong social instincts, by sympathy between man and man, and class and class, cannot face the external contest, the competition with other nations, by peace or by war, for the raw material of production and for its food supply. This struggle of tribe with tribe, and nation with nation, may have its mournful side; but we see as a result of it the gradual progress of mankind to higher intellectual and physical efficiency. It is idle to condemn it; we can only see that it exists and recognise what we have gained by it—civilization and social sympathy. But while the statesman has to watch this external struggle, . . . he must be very cautious that the nation is not silently rotting at its core. He must insure that the fertility of the inferior stocks is checked, and that of the superior stocks encouraged; he must regard with suspicion anything that tempts the physically and mentally fitter men and women to remain childless. . . .

. . . The path of progress is strewn with the wrecks of nations; traces are everywhere to be seen of the hecatombs [slaughtered remains] of inferior races, and of victims who found not the narrow way to perfection. Yet these dead people are, in very truth, the stepping stones on which mankind has arisen to the higher intellectual and deeper emotional life of today.

REVIEW QUESTIONS

1. What nationalistic views were expressed in Cecil Rhodes's "Confession of Faith"?
2. What role did the concept of race—the English or Anglo-Saxon—play in the arguments of Rhodes? Compare his views with those advanced by Hermann Ahlwardt on page 146.
3. How did Joseph Chamberlain define the national mission of the "great governing race"? What were the economic benefits of that mission?
4. How did Karl Pearson define the difference between inferior and superior races?
5. What measures did Pearson advocate for keeping a nation such as Britain at its highest potential?

---

8 The Overman and the Will to Power

Few modern thinkers have aroused more controversy than the German philosopher Friedrich Nietzsche (1844–1900). Although scholars pay tribute to Nietzsche's originality and genius, they are often in sharp disagreement over the meaning and influence of his work. Nietzsche was a relentless critic of modern society. He attacked democracy, universal suffrage, equality, and socialism for suppressing a higher type of human existence. Nietzsche was also critical of the Western rational tradition. The theoretical outlook, the excessive intellectualizing of philosophers, he said, smothers the will, thereby stifling creativity and nobility; reason also falsifies life through the claim that it allows apprehension of universal truth, for no such truth exists. Nietzsche was not opposed to the critical use of the intellect, but like the romantics, he focused on the immense vitality of the emotions. He also held that life is a senseless flux devoid of any overarching purpose. There are no moral values revealed by God. Indeed, Nietzsche proclaimed that God is dead. Nor are values and certainties woven into the fabric of nature that can be apprehended by reason—the "natural rights of man," for example. All the values taught by Christian and bourgeois thinkers are without foundation, said Nietzsche. There is only naked man living in a godless and absurd world.

Nietzsche called for the emergence of the *overman* or *superman,* a higher type of man who asserts his will, gives order to chaotic passions, makes great demands on himself, and lives life with a fierce joy. The overman aspires to self-perfection. Without fear or guilt, he creates his own values and defines his own life. In this way, he overcomes nihilism—the belief that there is nothing of ultimate value. It is such rare individuals, the highest specimens of humanity, that concern Nietzsche, not the herdlike masses.

The overman grasps the central reality of human existence—that people instinctively, uncompromisingly, ceaselessly, strive for power. The will to exert power is the determining factor in domestic politics, personal relations, and international affairs. Life is a contest in which the enhancement of power is the ultimate purpose of our actions; it brings supreme enjoyment: "the love of power is the demon of men. Let them have everything—health, food, a place to live, entertainment—they are and remain unhappy and low-spirited: for the demon waits and waits and will be satisfied. Take everything from them and satisfy this and they are almost happy—as happy as men and demons can be."

Friedrich Nietzsche
THE WILL TO POWER
AND *THE ANTICHRIST*

Two of Nietzsche's works—*The Will to Power* and *The Antichrist*—are represented in the following readings. First published in 1901, one year after Nietzsche's death, *The Will to Power* consists of the author's notes written in the years 1883 to 1888. The following passages from this work show Nietzsche's contempt for democracy and socialism and proclaim the will to power.

THE WILL TO POWER
720 (1886–1887)

The most fearful and fundamental desire in man, his drive for power—this drive is called "freedom"—must be held in check the longest. This is why ethics . . . has hitherto aimed at holding the desire for power in check: it disparages the tyrannical individual and with its glorification of social welfare and patriotism emphasizes the power-instinct of the herd.

728 (March–June 1888)

. . . A society that definitely and *instinctively* gives up war and conquest is in decline: it is ripe for democracy and the rule of shopkeepers—In most cases, to be sure, assurances of peace are merely narcotics.

751 (March–June 1888)

"The will to power" is so hated in democratic ages that their entire psychology seems directed toward belittling and defaming it. . . .

752 (1884)

. . . Democracy represents the disbelief in great human beings and an elite society: "Everyone is equal to everyone else." "At bottom we are one and all self-seeking cattle and mob."

753 (1885)

I am opposed to 1. socialism, because it dreams quite naively of "the good, true, and beautiful" and of "equal rights" (—anarchism also desires the same ideal, but in a more brutal fashion); 2. parliamentary government and the press, because these are the means by which the herd animal becomes master.

762 (1885)

European democracy represents a release of forces only to a very small degree. It is above all a release of laziness, of weariness, of *weakness*.

765 (Jan.–Fall 1888)

. . . Another Christian concept, no less crazy, has passed even more deeply into the tissue of modernity: the concept of the "equality of souls before God." This concept furnishes the prototype of all theories of equal rights: mankind was first taught to stammer the proposition of equality in a religious context, and only later was it made into morality: no wonder that man ended by taking it seriously, taking it practically!—that is to say, politically, democratically, socialistically, in the spirit of the pessimism of indignation.

854 (1884)

In the age of *suffrage universel,* i.e., when everyone may sit in judgment on everyone and everything, I feel impelled to reestablish *order of rank.*

855 (Spring–Fall 1887)

What determines rank, sets off rank, is only quanta of power, and nothing else.

857 (Jan.–Fall 1888)

I distinguish between a type of ascending life and another type of decay, disintegration, weakness. Is it credible that the question of the relative rank of these two types still needs to be posed?

858 (Nov. 1887–March 1888)

What determines your rank is the quantum of power you are: the rest is cowardice.

861 (1884)

A declaration of war on the masses by *higher men* is needed! Everywhere the mediocre are combining in order to make themselves master! Everything that makes soft and effeminate, that serves the ends of the "people" or the "feminine," works in favor of *suffrage universel,* i.e., the dominion of *inferior* men. But we should take reprisal and bring this whole affair (which in Europe commenced with Christianity) to light and to the bar of judgment.

862 (1884)

A doctrine is needed powerful enough to work as a breeding agent: strengthening the strong, paralyzing and destructive for the world-weary.

The annihilation of the decaying races. Decay of Europe.—The annihilation of slavish evaluations.—Dominion over the earth as a means of producing a higher type.—The annihilation of the tartuffery [hypocrisy] called "morality." . . . The annihilation of *suffrage universel;* i.e., the system through which the lowest natures prescribe themselves as laws for the higher.—The annihilation of mediocrity and its acceptance. (The onesided, individuals—peoples; to strive for fullness of nature through the pairing of opposites: race mixture to this end).—The new courage—no *a priori* [innate and universal] truths (such truths were sought by those accustomed to faith!), but a *free* subordination to a ruling idea that has its time: e.g., time as a property of space, etc.

870 (1884)

The root of all evil: that the slavish morality of meekness, chastity, selflessness, absolute obedience, has triumphed—ruling natures were thus condemned (1) to hypocrisy, (2) to torments of conscience—creative natures felt like rebels against God, uncertain and inhibited by eternal values. . . .

In summa: the best things have been slandered because the weak or the immoderate swine have cast a bad light on them—and the best men have remained hidden—and have often misunderstood themselves.

874 (1884)

The degeneration of the rulers and the ruling classes has been the cause of the greatest mischief in history! Without the Roman Caesars and Roman society, the insanity of Christianity would never have come to power.

When lesser men begin to doubt whether higher men exist, then the danger is great! And one ends by discovering that there is *virtue* also among the lowly and subjugated, the poor in spirit, and that *before God* men are equal—which has so far been the . . . [height] of nonsense on earth! For ultimately, the higher men measured themselves according to the standard of virtue of slaves—found they were "proud," etc., found all their higher qualities reprehensible.

997 (1884)

I teach: that there are higher and lower men, and that a single individual can under certain circumstances justify the existence of whole millennia—that is, a full, rich, great, whole human being in relation to countless incomplete fragmentary men.

998 (1884)

The highest men live beyond the rulers, freed from all bonds; and in the rulers they have their instruments.

999 (1884)

Order of rank: He who *determines* values and directs the will of millennia by giving direction to the highest natures is the *highest* man.

1001 (1884)

Not "mankind" but *overman* is the goal!

1067 (1885)

. . . This world is the will to power—and nothing besides! And you yourselves are also this will to power—and nothing besides!

Nietzsche regarded Christianity as a life-denying religion that appeals to the masses. Fearful and resentful of their betters, he said, the masses espouse a faith that preaches equality and compassion. He maintained that Christianity has "waged a war to the death against (the) higher type of man." The following passages are from *The Antichrist*, written in 1888.

THE ANTICHRIST

2. What is good?—All that heightens the feeling of power, the will to power, power itself in man.

What is bad?—All that proceeds from weakness.

What is happiness?—The feeling that power *increases*—that a resistance is overcome.

Not contentment, but more power; *not* peace at all, but war; *not* virtue, but proficiency (virtue in the Renaissance style, *virtù*, virtue free of moralic acid).

The weak and ill-constituted shall perish: first principle of *our* philanthropy. And one shall help them to do so.

What is more harmful than any vice?—Active sympathy for the ill-constituted and weak—Christianity. . . .

3. The problem I raise here is not what ought to succeed mankind in the sequence of species (—the human being is an *end*—): but what type of human being one ought to *breed*, ought to *will*, as more valuable, more worthy of life, more certain of the future.

This more valuable type has existed often enough already: but as a lucky accident, as an exception, never as *willed*. He has rather been the most feared, he has hitherto been virtually *the* thing to be feared—and out of fear the reverse type has been willed, bred, *achieved:* the domestic animal, the herd animal, the sick animal man—the Christian. . . .

5. One should not embellish or dress up Christianity: it has waged *a war to the death* against this *higher* type of man, it has excommunicated all the fundamental instincts of this type, it has distilled evil, the *Evil One,* out of these instincts—the strong human being as the type of reprehensibility, as the "outcast." Christianity has taken the side of everything weak, base, ill-constituted, it has made an ideal out of *opposition* to the preservative instincts of strong life; it has depraved the reason even of the intellectually strongest natures by teaching men to feel the supreme values of intellectuality as sinful, as misleading, as *temptations.* The most deplorable example: the depraving of Pascal,[1] who believed his reason had been depraved by original sin while it had only been depraved by his Christianity! . . .

7. Christianity is called the religion of *pity.*—Pity stands in antithesis to the tonic emotions which enhance the energy of the feeling of life: it has a depressive effect. One loses force when one pities. . . .

15. In Christianity neither morality nor religion come into contact with reality at any point. Nothing but imaginary *causes* ("God," "soul," "ego," "spirit," "free will"—or "unfree will"): nothing but imaginary *effects* ("sin," "redemption," "grace," "punishment," "forgiveness of sins"). . . .

18. The Christian conception of God—God as God of the sick, God as spider, God as spirit—is one of the most corrupt conceptions of God arrived at on earth: perhaps it even represents the low-water mark in the descending development of the God type. God degenerated to the *contradiction of life,* instead of being its transfiguration and eternal *Yes!* In God a declaration of hostility towards life, nature, the

will to life! God the formula for every calumny of "this world," for every lie about "the next world"! In God, nothingness deified, the will to nothingness sanctified! . . .

21. In Christianity the instincts of the subjugated and oppressed come into the foreground: it is the lowest classes which seek their salvation in it. . . .

43. The poison of the doctrine "*equal* rights for all"—this has been more thoroughly sowed by Christianity than by anything else; from the most secret recesses of base instincts, Christianity has waged a war to the death against every feeling of reverence and distance between man and man, against, that is, the *precondition* of every elevation, every increase in culture—it has forged out of the [resentment] of the masses its *chief weapon* against *us,* against everything noble, joyful, high-spirited on earth, against our happiness on earth. . . . "Immortality" granted to every Peter and Paul has been the greatest and most malicious outrage on *noble* mankind ever committed.—*And* let us not underestimate the fatality that has crept out of Christianity even into politics! No one any longer possesses today the courage to claim special privileges or the right to rule, the courage to feel a sense of reverence towards himself and towards his equals—the courage for a *pathos of distance.* . . . Our politics is *morbid* from this lack of courage!—The aristocratic outlook has been undermined most deeply by the lie of equality of souls; and if the belief in the "prerogative of the majority" makes revolutions and *will continue to make them*—it is Christianity, let there be no doubt about it, *Christian* value judgement which translates every revolution into mere blood and crime! Christianity is a revolt of everything that crawls along the ground directed against that which is *elevated:* the Gospel of the "lowly" *makes* low. . . .

---

[1]Blaise Pascal (1623–1662) was a French mathematician, philosopher, and eloquent defender of the Christian faith.

REVIEW QUESTIONS

1. Do you agree with Friedrich Nietzsche about a human being's most elemental desire?
2. Why did Nietzsche attack democracy and socialism? How do you respond to his attack?
3. What were Nietzsche's criticisms of Christianity? How do you respond to this attack?
4. How does Nietzsche's philosophy stand in relation to the Enlightenment?

9 The Unconscious

After graduating from medical school in Vienna, Sigmund Freud (1856–1939), the founder of psychoanalysis, specialized in the treatment of nervous disorders. By encouraging his patients to speak to him about their troubles, Freud was able to probe deeper into their minds. These investigations led him to conclude that childhood fears and experiences, often sexual in nature, accounted for neuroses—hysteria, anxiety, depression, obsessions, and so on. So threatening and painful were these childhood emotions and experiences that his patients banished them from conscious memory to the realm of the unconscious. To understand and treat neurotic behavior, Freud said it is necessary to look behind overt symptoms and bring to the surface emotionally charged experiences and fears—childhood traumas—that lie buried in the unconscious. Freud probed the unconscious by urging his patients to say whatever came to their minds. This procedure, called free association, rests on the premise that spontaneous and uninhibited talk reveals a person's underlying preoccupations, his or her inner world. A second avenue to the unconscious is the analysis of dreams; an individual's dreams, said Freud, reveal his or her secret wishes.

Sigmund Freud
CIVILIZATION AND ITS DISCONTENTS

Freud's scientific investigation of psychic development led him to conclude that powerful mental processes hidden from consciousness govern human behavior more than reason does. His exploration of the unconscious produced a new image of the human being that has had a profound impact on twentieth-century thought and beyond. In the tradition of the Enlightenment philosophes, Freud valued reason and science, but he did not share the philosophes' confidence in human goodness and humanity's capacity for future progress. In *Civilization and Its Discontents* (1930), Freud posited the frightening theory that human beings are driven by an inherent aggressiveness that threatens civilized life—that civilization is fighting a losing battle with our aggressive instincts. Although Freud's pessimism was no doubt influenced by the tragedy of World War I, many ideas expressd in *Civilization and Its Discontents* derived from views that he had formulated decades earlier.

CIVILIZATION AND
ITS DISCONTENTS

The element of truth behind all this, which people are so ready to disavow, is that men are not gentle creatures who want to be loved, and who at most can defend themselves if they are attacked; they are, on the contrary, creatures among whose instinctual endowments is to be reckoned a powerful share of aggressiveness. As a result, their neighbour is for them not only a potential helper or sexual object, but also someone who tempts them to satisfy their aggressiveness on him, to exploit his capacity for work without compensation, to use him sexually without his consent, to seize his possessions, to humiliate him, to cause him pain, to torture and to kill him. *Homo homini lupus.* [Man is wolf to man.] Who, in the face of all his experience of life and of history, will have the courage to dispute this assertion? As a rule this cruel aggressiveness waits for some provocation or puts itself at the service of some other purpose, whose goal might also have been reached by milder measures. In circumstances that are favourable to it, when the mental counterforces which ordinarily inhibit it are out of action, it also manifests itself spontaneously and reveals man as a savage beast to whom consideration towards his own kind is something alien. Anyone who calls to mind the atrocities committed during the racial migrations or the invasions of the Huns, or by the people known as Mongols under Jenghiz Khan and Tamerlane, or at the capture of Jerusalem by the pious Crusaders, or even, indeed, the horrors of the recent World War—anyone who calls these things to mind will have to bow humbly before the truth of this view.

The existence of this inclination to aggression, which we can detect in ourselves and justly assume to be present in others, is the factor which disturbs our relations with our neighbour and which forces civilization into such a high expenditure [of energy]. In consequence of this primary mutual hostility of human beings, civilized society is perpetually threatened with disintegration. The interest of work in common would not hold it together; instinctual passions are stronger than reasonable interests. Civilization has to use its utmost efforts in order to set limits to man's aggressive instincts and to hold the manifestations of them in check by psychical reaction-formations. Hence, therefore, the use of methods intended to incite people into identifications and aim-inhibited relationships of love, hence the restriction upon sexual life, and hence too the ideal's commandment to love one's neighbour as oneself—a commandment which is really justified by the fact that nothing else runs so strongly counter to the original nature of man. In spite of every effort, these endeavours of civilization have not so far achieved very much. It hopes to prevent the crudest excesses of brutal violence by itself assuming the right to use violence against criminals, but the law is not able to lay hold of the more cautious and refined manifestations of human aggressiveness. The time comes when each one of us has to give up as illusions the expectations which, in his youth, he pinned upon his fellowmen, and when he may learn how much difficulty and pain has been added to his life by their ill-will. At the same time, it would be unfair to reproach civilization with trying to eliminate strife and competition from human activity. These things are undoubtedly indispensable. But opposition is not necessarily enmity; it is merely misused and made an *occasion* for enmity.

The communists believe that they have found the path to deliverance from our evils. According to them, man is wholly good and is well-disposed to his neighbour; but the institution of private property has corrupted his nature. The ownership of private wealth gives the individual power, and with it the temptation to ill-treat his neighbour; while the man who is excluded from possession is bound to rebel in hostility against his oppressor. If private property were abolished, all wealth held in common, and everyone allowed to share in the enjoyment of it, ill-will and hostility would disappear among men. Since everyone's needs would be satisfied, no one would have any reason to regard another as his enemy; all would willingly undertake the work that was necessary. I have no concern with any economic criticisms of the communist system. . . . But I am able to recognize that the psychological premises on which the system is based are an untenable illusion. In abolishing private property we deprive the human love of aggression of one of its instruments, certainly a strong one, though certainly not the strongest; but we have in no way altered the differences in power and influence which are misused by aggressiveness, nor have we altered anything in its nature. Aggressiveness was not created by property. It reigned almost without limit in primitive times, when property was still very scanty, and it already shows itself in the nursery almost before property has given up its primal, anal form; it forms the basis of every relation of affection and love among people (with the single exception, perhaps, of the mother's relation to her male child). If we do away with personal rights over material wealth, there still remains prerogative in the field of sexual relationships, which is bound to become the source of the strongest dislike and the most violent hostility among men who in other respects are on an equal footing. If we were to remove this factor, too, by allowing complete freedom of sexual life and thus abolishing the family, the germ-cell of civilization, we cannot, it is true, easily foresee what new paths the development of civilization could take; but one thing we can expect, and that is that this indestructible feature of human nature will follow it there.

It is clearly not easy for men to give up the satisfaction of this inclination to aggression. They do not feel comfortable without it. . . .

If civilization imposes such great sacrifices not only on man's sexuality but on his aggressivity, we can understand better why it is hard for him to be happy in that civilization. . . .

In all that follows I adopt the standpoint, therefore, that the inclination to aggression is an original, self-subsisting instinctual disposition in man, and I return to my view that it constitutes the greatest impediment to civilization.

REVIEW QUESTIONS

1. What did Sigmund Freud consider the "greatest impediment to civilization"? Why?
2. How did Freud react to the Marxist view that private property is the source of evil?
3. Compare Freud's view of human nature and reason to that of Enlightenment philosophes.

CHAPTER 7

World War I

WORLD WAR I SOLDIERS charge from trenches in France. *(© Corbis)*

To many Europeans, the opening years of the twentieth century seemed full of promise. Advances in science and technology, the rising standard of living, the expansion of education, and the absence of wars between the Great Powers since the Franco-Prussian War (1870–1871) all contributed to a general feeling of optimism. Yet these accomplishments hid disruptive forces that were propelling Europe toward a cataclysm. On June 28, 1914, Archduke Francis Ferdinand, heir to the throne of Austria-Hungary, was assassinated by Gavrilo Princip, a young Serbian nationalist (and Austrian subject), at Sarajevo in the Austrian province of Bosnia, inhabited largely by South Slavs. The assassination triggered those explosive forces that lay below the surface of European life, and six weeks later, Europe was engulfed in a general war that altered the course of Western civilization.

Belligerent, irrational, and extreme nationalism was a principal cause of World War I. Placing their country above everything, nationalists in various countries fomented hatred of other nationalities and called for the expansion of their nation's borders—attitudes that fostered belligerence in foreign relations. Wedded to nationalism was a militaristic view that regarded war as heroic and as the highest expression of individual and national life.

Yet Europe might have avoided the world war had the nations not been divided into hostile alliance systems. By 1907, the Triple Alliance of Germany, Austria-Hungary, and Italy confronted the loosely organized Triple Entente of France, Russia, and Great Britain. What German chancellor Otto von Bismarck said in 1879 was just as true in 1914: "The great powers of our time are like travellers, unknown to one another, whom chance has brought together in a carriage. They watch each other, and when one of them puts his hand into his pocket, his neighbor gets ready his own revolver in order to be able to fire the first shot."

A danger inherent in an alliance is that a country, knowing that it has the support of allies, may pursue an aggressive foreign policy and may be less likely to compromise during a crisis; also, a war between two states may well draw in the other allied powers. These dangers materialized in 1914.

In the diplomatic furor of July and early August 1914, following the assassination of Francis Ferdinand, several patterns emerged. Austria-Hungary, a multinational empire dominated by Germans and Hungarians, feared the nationalist aspirations of its Slavic minorities. The nationalist yearnings of neighboring Serbia aggravated Austria-Hungary's problems, for the Serbs, a South Slav people, wanted to create a Greater Serbia by uniting with South Slavs of Austria-Hungary. If Slavic nationalism gained in intensity, the Austro-Hungarian (or Hapsburg) Empire would be broken into states based on nationality. Fearing disintegration, Austria-Hungary decided to use the assassination as justification for crushing Serbia.

The system of alliances escalated the tensions between Austria-Hungary and Serbia into a general European war. Germany saw itself threatened by the Triple Entente (a conviction based more on paranoia than on objective fact) and regarded Austria-Hungary as its only reliable ally. Holding that at all costs its ally must be kept strong, German officials supported Austria-Hungary's decision to crush Serbia. Fearing that Germany and Austria-Hungary aimed to extend their power into southeastern Europe, Russia would not permit the destruction of Serbia. With the support of France, Russia began to mobilize, and when it moved to full mobilization, Germany declared war. As German battle plans, drawn up years before, called for a war with both France and Russia, France was drawn into the conflict; Germany's invasion of neutral Belgium brought Great Britain into the war.

Most European statesmen and military men believed the war would be over in a few months. Virtually no one anticipated that it would last more than four years and that the casualties would number in the millions.

World War I was a turning point in Western history. In Russia, it led to the downfall of the tsarist autocracy and the rise of the Soviet state. The war created unsettling conditions that led to the emergence of fascist movements in Italy and Germany, and it shattered, perhaps forever, the Enlightenment belief in the inevitable and perpetual progress of Western civilization.

1 Militarism

Historians regard a surging militarism as an underlying cause of World War I. One sign of militarism was the rapid increase in expenditures for armaments in the years prior to 1914. Between 1910 and 1914, both Austria-Hungary and Germany, for example, doubled their military budgets. The arms race intensified suspicion among the Great Powers. A second danger was the increased power of the military in policymaking, particularly in Austria-Hungary and Germany. In the crisis following the assassination, generals tended to press for a military solution. The few dissenting voices raised against militarism were all but drowned out in this martial atmosphere.

Heinrich von Treitschke
THE GREATNESS OF WAR

Coupled with the military's influence on state decisions was a romantic glorification of the nation and war, an attitude shared by both the elite and the masses.

Although militarism generally pervaded Europe, it was particularly strong in Germany. In the following reading from *Politics* (1899–1900), the influential German historian Heinrich von Treitschke (1834–1896) glorified warfare.

. . . One must say with the greatest determination: War is for an afflicted people the only remedy. When the State exclaims: My very existence is at stake! then social self-seeking must disappear and all party hatred be silent. The individual must forget his own *ego* and feel himself a member of the whole, he must recognize how negligible is his life compared with the good of the whole. Therein lies the greatness of war that the little man completely vanishes before the great thought of the State. The sacrifice of nationalities for one another is nowhere invested with such beauty as in war. At such a time the corn is separated from the chaff. All who lived through 1870 [the Franco-Prussian war] will understand the saying of Niebuhr[1] with regard to the year 1813, that he then experienced the "bliss of sharing with all his fellow citizens, with the scholar and the ignorant, the one common feeling—no man who enjoyed this experience will to his dying day forget how loving, friendly and strong he felt."

It is indeed political idealism which fosters war, whereas materialism rejects it. What a perversion of morality to want to banish heroism from human life. The heroes of a people are the personalities who fill the youthful souls with delight and enthusiasm, and amongst authors we as boys and youths admire most those whose words sound like a flourish of trumpets. He who cannot take pleasure therein, is too cowardly to take up arms himself for his fatherland. All appeal to Christianity in this matter is perverted. The Bible states expressly that the man in authority shall wield the sword; it states likewise that: "Greater love hath no man than this: that he giveth his life for his friend." Those who preach the nonsense about everlasting peace do not understand the life of the Aryan race, the Aryans are before all brave. They have always been men enough to protect by the sword what they had won by the intellect. . . .

To the historian who lives in the realms of the Will, it is quite clear that the furtherance of an everlasting peace is fundamentally reactionary. He sees that to banish war from history would be to banish all progress and becoming. It is only the periods of exhaustion, weariness and mental stagnation that have dallied with the dream of everlasting peace. . . . The living God will see to it that war returns again and again as a terrible medicine for humanity.

---

[1]Barthold G. Niebuhr (1776–1831) was a Prussian historian. The passage refers to the German War of Liberation against Napoleon, which German patriots regarded as a glorious episode in their national history.

Friedrich von Bernhardi
GERMANY AND THE NEXT WAR

Friedrich von Bernhardi (1849–1930), a German general and influential military writer, considered war "a biological necessity of the first importance." The following excerpt comes from his work *Germany and the Next War* (1911), which was immensely popular in his country.

. . . War is a biological necessity of the first importance, a regulative element in the life of mankind which cannot be dispensed with, since without it an unhealthy development will follow, which excludes every advancement of the race, and therefore all real civilization. "War is the father of all things." The sages of antiquity long before Darwin recognized this.

The struggle for existence is, in the life of Nature, the basis of all healthy development. . . . The law of the stronger holds good everywhere. Those forms survive which are able to procure themselves the most favourable conditions of life, and to assert themselves in the universal economy of Nature. The weaker succumb. . . .

Struggle is, therefore, a universal law of Nature, and the instinct of self-preservation which leads to struggle is acknowledged to be a natural condition of existence.

Strong, healthy, and flourishing nations increase in numbers. From a given moment they require a continual expansion of their frontiers, they require new territory for the accommodation of their surplus population. Since almost every part of the globe is inhabited, new territory must, as a rule, be obtained at the cost of its possessors—that is to say, by conquest, which thus becomes a law of necessity.

The right of conquest is universally acknowledged.

. . . Vast territories inhabited by uncivilized masses are occupied by more highly civilized States, and made subject to their rule. Higher civilization and the correspondingly greater power are the foundations of the right to annexation. . . .

Lastly, in all times the right of conquest by war has been admitted. It may be that a growing people cannot win colonies from civilized races, and yet the State wishes to retain the surplus population which the mother-country can no longer feed. Then the only course left is to acquire the necessary territory by war. Thus the instinct of self-preservation leads inevitably to war, and the conquest of foreign soil. It is not the possessor, but the victor, who then has the right. . . .

In such cases might gives the right to occupy or to conquer. Might is at once the supreme right, and the dispute as to what is right is decided by war. War gives a biologically just decision, since its decisions rest on the very nature of things. . . .

The knowledge, therefore, that war depends on biological laws leads to the conclusion that every attempt to exclude it from international relations must be demonstrably untenable.

REVIEW QUESTIONS

1. Why did Heinrich von Treitschke regard war as a far more desirable condition than peace?
2. According to Treitschke, what is the individual's highest responsibility?
3. According to Treitschke, what function does the hero serve in national life?
4. What conclusions did Friedrich von Bernhardi draw from his premise that war was "a biological necessity"?

2 Pan-Serbism: Nationalism and Terrorism

The conspiracy to assassinate Archduke Francis Ferdinand was organized by a secret Serbian society called Union or Death, more popularly known as the Black Hand. Founded in 1911, the Black Hand aspired to create a Greater Serbia by uniting with their kinsmen, the South Slavs dwelling in Austria-Hungary. Thus, Austrian officials regarded the aspirations of Pan-Serbs as a significant threat to the Hapsburg Empire.

THE BLACK HAND

In 1914, the Black Hand had some 2,500 members, most of them army officers. The society indoctrinated members with a fanatic nationalism and trained them in terrorist methods. The initiation ceremony, designed to strengthen a new member's commitment to the cause and to foster obedience to the society's leaders, had the appearance of a sacred rite. The candidate entered a dark room in which a table stood covered with a black cloth; resting on the table were a dagger, a revolver, and a crucifix. When the candidate declared his readiness to take the oath of allegiance, a masked member of the society's elite entered the room and stood in silence. After the initiate pronounced the oath, the masked man shook his hand and departed without uttering a word. Excerpts of the Black Hand's by-laws, including the oath of allegiance, follow.

BY-LAWS OF THE ORGANIZATION UNION OR DEATH

Article 1. This organization is created for the purpose of realizing the national ideal: the union of all Serbs. Membership is open to every Serb, without distinction of sex, religion, or place of birth, and to all those who are sincerely devoted to this cause.

Article 2. This organization prefers terrorist action to intellectual propaganda, and for this reason it must remain absolutely secret.

Article 3. The organization bears the name *Ujedinjenje ili Smirt* (Union or Death).

Article 4. To fulfill its purpose, the organization will do the following:

1. Exercise influence on government circles, on the various social classes, and on the entire social life of the kingdom of Serbia, which is considered the Piedmont[1] of the Serbian nation;

2. Organize revolutionary action in all territories inhabited by Serbs;

3. Beyond the frontiers of Serbia, fight with all means the enemies of the Serbian national idea;

4. Maintain amicable relations with all states, peoples, organizations, and individuals who support Serbia and the Serbian element;

5. Assist those nations and organizations that are fighting for their own national liberation and unification. . . .

---

[1]The Piedmont was the Italian state that served as the nucleus for the unification of Italy.

Article 24. Every member has a duty to recruit new members, but the member shall guarantee with his life those whom he introduces into the organization.

Article 25. Members of the organization are forbidden to know each other personally. Only members of the central committee are known to each other.

Article 26. In the organization itself, the members are designated by numbers. Only the central committee in Belgrade knows their names.

Article 27. Members of the organization must obey absolutely the commands given to them by their superiors.

Article 28. Each member has a duty to communicate to the central committee at Belgrade all information that may be of interest to the organization.

Article 29. The interests of the organization stand above all other interests.

Article 30. On entering the organization, each member must know that he loses his own personality, that he can expect neither personal glory nor personal profit, material or moral. Consequently, any member who endeavors to exploit the organization for personal, social, or party motives, will be punished. If by his acts he harms the organization itself, his punishment will be death.

Article 31. Those who enter the organization may never leave it, and no one has the authority to accept a member's resignation.

Article 32. Each member must aid the organization, with weekly contributions. If need be, the organization may procure funds through coercion. . . .

Article 33. When the central committee of Belgrade pronounces a death sentence the only thing that matters is that the execution is carried out unfailingly. The method of execution is of little importance.

Article 34. The organization's seal is composed as follows. On the center of the seal a powerful arm holds in its hand an unfurled flag. On the flag, as a coat of arms, are a skull and crossed bones; by the side of the flag are a knife, a bomb and poison. Around, in a circle, are inscribed the following words reading from left to right: "Unification or Death," and at the base "The Supreme Central Directorate."

Article 35. On joining the organization, the recruit takes the following oath:

"I (name), in becoming a member of the organization, 'Unification or Death,' do swear by the sun that shines on me, by the earth that nourishes me, by God, by the blood of my ancestors, on my honor and my life that from this moment until my death, I shall be faithful to the regulations of the organization and that I will be prepared to make any sacrifice for it. I swear before God, on my honor and on my life, that I shall carry with me to the grave the organization's secrets. May God condemn me and my comrades judge me if I violate or do not respect, consciously or not, my oath."

Article 36. These regulations come into force immediately.

Article 37. These regulations must not be changed.

Belgrade, 9 May 1911.

REVIEW QUESTIONS

1. How did Union or Death seek to accomplish its goal of uniting all Serbs?
2. What type of people do you think were attracted to the objectives and methods of the Black Hand?

3   War as Celebration: The Mood in European Capitals

An outpouring of patriotism greeted the proclamation of war. Huge crowds thronged the avenues and squares of capital cities to express their devotion to their nations and their willingness to bear arms. Many Europeans regarded war as a sacred moment that held the promise of adventure and an escape from a humdrum and purposeless daily existence. Going to war seemed to satisfy a yearning to surrender oneself to a noble cause: the greatness of the nation. The image of the nation united in a spirit of fraternity and self-sacrifice was immensely appealing.

Roland Doregelès
PARIS: "THAT FABULOUS DAY"

In "After Fifty Years," Roland Doregelès (1886–1973), a distinguished French writer, recalls the mood in Paris at the outbreak of the war.

"It's come!* It's posted at the district mayor's office," a passerby shouted to me as he ran.

I reached the Rue Drouot in one leap and shouldered through the mob that already filled the courtyard to approach the fascinating white sheet pasted to the door. I read the message at a glance, then reread it slowly, word for word, to convince myself that it was true:

> THE FIRST DAY OF
> MOBILIZATION WILL BE
> SUNDAY, AUGUST 2

Only three lines, written hastily by a hand that trembled. It was an announcement to a million and a half Frenchmen.

The people who had read it moved away, stunned, while others crowded in, but this silent numbness did not last. Suddenly a heroic wind lifted their heads. What? War, was it? Well, then, let's go! Without any signal, the "Marseillaise" poured from thousands of throats, sheafs of flags appeared at windows, and howling processions rolled out on the boulevards. Each column brandished a placard: AL-SACE VOLUNTEERS, JEWISH VOLUNTEERS, POLISH VOLUNTEERS. They hailed one another above the bravos of the crowd, and this human torrent, swelling at every corner, moved on to circle around the Place de la Concorde, before the statue of Strasbourg banked with flowers, then flowed toward the Place de la République, where mobs from Belleville and the Faubourg St. Antoine yelled themselves hoarse on the refrain from the great days, *"Aux armes, citoyens!"* (To arms, citizens!) But this time it was better than a song.

To gather the news for my paper, I ran around the city in every direction. At the Cours la Reine I saw the fabled cuirassiers [cavalry] in their horsetail plumes march by, and at the Rue La Fayette footsoldiers in battle garb with women throwing flowers and kisses to them. In a marshaling yard I saw guns being loaded, their long, thin barrels twined around with branches and laurel leaves, while troops in red breeches piled gaily into delivery vans

---

*Translated from the French by Sally Abeles.

# # # # # #

# #

they were scrawling with challenges and caricatures. Young and old, civilians and military men burned with the same excitement. It was like a Brotherhood Day.

Dead tired but still exhilarated, I got back to *L'Homme libre* and burst into the office of Georges Clemenceau, our chief.[†]

"What is Paris saying?" he asked me.

"It's singing, sir!"

"Then everything will be all right. . . ."

His old patriot's heart was not wrong; no cloud marred that fabulous day. . . .

Less than twenty-four hours later, seeing their old dreams of peace crumble [socialist workers] would stream out into the boulevards . . . [but] they would break into the "Marseillaise," not the "Internationale" [anthem of international communism]; they would cry, "To Berlin!," not "Down with war!"

What did they have to defend, these black-nailed patriots? Not even a shack, an acre to till, indeed hardly a patch of ground reserved at the Pantin Cemetery; yet they would depart, like their rivals of yesterday, a heroic song on their lips and a flower in their guns. No more poor or rich, proletarians or bourgeois, right-wingers or militant leftists; there were only Frenchmen.

[†]*L'Homme libre* (The Free Man) was but one of several periodicals Clemenceau founded and directed during his long political career.—Tr.

Beginning the next day, thousands of men eager to fight would jostle one another outside recruiting offices, waiting to join up. Men who could have stayed home, with their wives and children or an imploring mama. But no. The word "duty" had a meaning for them, and the word "country" had regained its splendor.

I close my eyes, and they appear to me, those volunteers on the great day; then I see them again in the old kepi [military cap] or blue helmet, shouting, "Here!" when somebody called for men for a raid, or hurling themselves into an attack with fixed bayonets, and I wonder, and I question their bloody [ghosts].

Tell me, comrades in eternal silence, would you have besieged the enlistment offices with the same enthusiasm, would you have fought such a courageous fight had you known that fifty years later those men in gray knit caps or steel helmets you were ordered to kill would no longer be enemies and that we would have to open our arms to them? Wouldn't the heroic "Let's go!" you shouted as you cleared the parapets have stuck in your throats? Deep in the grave where you dwell, don't you regret your sacrifice? "Why did we fight? Why did we let ourselves get killed?" This is the murmur of a million and a half voices rising from the bowels of the earth, and we, the survivors, do not know what to answer.

Stefan Zweig
VIENNA: "THE RUSHING FEELING OF FRATERNITY"

Some intellectuals viewed the war as a way of regenerating the nation; nobility and fraternity would triumph over life's petty concerns. In the following reading, Stefan Zweig (1881–1942), a prominent Austrian literary figure, recalled the scene in Vienna, the capital of the Austro-Hungarian Empire, at the outbreak of World War I. This passage comes from Zweig's autobiography, *The World of Yesterday,* written in 1941.

The next morning I was in Austria. In every station placards had been put up announcing general mobilization. The trains were filled with fresh recruits, banners were flying, music sounded, and in Vienna I found the entire city in a tumult. The first shock at the news of war—the war that no one, people or government, had wanted—the war which had slipped, much against their will, out of the clumsy hands of the diplomats who had been bluffing and toying with it, had suddenly been transformed into enthusiasm. There were parades in the street, flags, ribbons, and music burst forth everywhere, young recruits were marching triumphantly, their faces lighting up at the cheering—they, the John Does and Richard Roes who usually go unnoticed and uncelebrated.

And to be truthful, I must acknowledge that there was a majestic, rapturous, and even seductive something in this first outbreak of the people from which one could escape only with difficulty. And in spite of all my hatred and aversion for war, I should not like to have missed the memory of those first days. As never before, thousands and hundreds of thousands felt what they should have felt in peace time, that they belonged together. A city of two million, a country of nearly fifty million, in that hour felt that they were participating in world history, in a moment which would never recur, and that each one was called upon to cast his infinitesimal self into the glowing mass, there to be purified of all selfishness. All differences of class, rank, and language were flooded over at that moment by the rushing feeling of fraternity. Strangers spoke to one another in the streets, people who had avoided each other for years shook hands, everywhere one saw excited faces. Each individual experienced an exaltation of his ego, he was no longer the isolated person of former times, he had been incorporated into the mass, he was part of the people, and his person, his hitherto unnoticed person, had been given meaning. The petty mail clerk, who ordinarily sorted letters early and late, who sorted constantly, who sorted from Monday until Saturday without interruption; the clerk, the cobbler, had suddenly achieved a romantic possibility in life: he could become a hero, and everyone who wore a uniform was already being cheered by the women, and greeted beforehand with this romantic [image] by those who had to remain behind. They acknowledged the unknown power which had lifted them out of their everyday existence. Even mothers with their grief, and women with their fears, were ashamed to manifest their quite natural emotions in the face of this first transformation. But it is quite possible that a deeper, more secret power was at work in this frenzy. So deeply, so quickly did the tide break over humanity that, foaming over the surface, it churned up the depths, the subconscious primitive instincts of the human animal—that which Freud so meaningfully calls "the revulsion from culture," the desire to break out of the conventional bourgeois world of codes and statutes, and to permit the primitive instincts of the blood to rage at will. It is also possible that these powers of darkness had their share in the wild frenzy into which everything was thrown—self-sacrifice and alcohol, the spirit of adventure and the spirit of pure faith, the old magic of flags and patriotic slogans, that mysterious frenzy of the millions which can hardly be described in words, but which, for the moment, gave a wild and almost rapturous impetus to the greatest crime of our time. . . .

. . . What did the great mass know of war in 1914, after nearly half a century of peace? They did not know war, they had hardly given it a thought. It had become legendary, and distance had made it seem romantic and heroic. They still saw it in the perspective of their school readers and of paintings in museums; brilliant cavalry attacks in glittering uniforms, the fatal shot always straight through the heart, the entire campaign a resounding march of victory— "We'll be home at Christmas," the recruits shouted laughingly to their mothers in August of 1914. Who in the villages and the cities of Austria remembered "real" war? A few ancients at best, who in 1866 had fought against Prussia, which was now their ally. But what a quick, bloodless far-off war that had been, a campaign that had ended in three weeks with few victims and before it had well started! A rapid excursion into the romantic, a wild, manly adventure—that is how the war of 1914 was painted in the imagination of the simple man, and the young people were honestly afraid that they might miss this most wonderful and exciting experience of their lives; that is why they hurried and thronged to the colors, and that is why they shouted and sang in the trains that carried them to the slaughter; wildly and feverishly the red wave of blood coursed through the veins of the entire nation.

REVIEW QUESTIONS

1. Why was war welcomed as a positive event by so many different peoples?
2. Do you think human beings are aggressive by nature? Explain your answer.

4 Trench Warfare

In 1914 the young men of European nations marched off to war believing that they were embarking on a glorious and chivalrous adventure. They were eager to serve their countries, to demonstrate personal valor, and to experience life at its most intense moments. But in the trenches, where unseen enemies fired machine guns and artillery that killed indiscriminately and relentlessly, this romantic illusion about combat disintegrated.

Erich Maria Remarque
ALL QUIET ON THE WESTERN FRONT

The following reading is taken from Erich Maria Remarque's novel *All Quiet on the Western Front* (1929), the most famous literary work to emerge from World War I. A veteran of the trenches himself, Remarque (1898–1970) graphically described the slaughter that robbed Europe of its young men. His narrator is a young German soldier.

We wake up in the middle of the night. The earth booms. Heavy fire is falling on us. We crouch into corners. We distinguish shells of every calibre.

Each man lays hold of his things and looks again every minute to reassure himself that they are still there. The dug-out heaves, the night roars and flashes. We look at each other in the momentary flashes of light, and with pale faces and pressed lips shake our heads.

Every man is aware of the heavy shells tearing down the parapet, rooting up the embankment and demolishing the upper layers of concrete. When a shell lands in the trench we note how the hollow, furious blast is like a blow from the paw of a raging beast of prey. Already by morning a few of the recruits are green and vomiting. They are too inexperienced. . . .

The bombardment does not diminish. It is falling in the rear too. As far as one can see spout fountains of mud and iron. A wide belt is being raked.

The attack does not come, but the bombardment continues. We are gradually benumbed. Hardly a man speaks. We cannot make ourselves understood.

Our trench is almost gone. At many places it is only eighteen inches high, it is broken by holes, and craters, and mountains of earth. A shell lands square in front of our post. At once it is dark. We are buried and must dig ourselves out. . . .

Towards morning, while it is still dark, there is some excitement. Through the entrance rushes in a swarm of fleeing rats that try to storm the walls. Torches light up the confusion. Everyone yells and curses and slaughters. The madness and despair of many hours unloads itself in this outburst. Faces are distorted, arms strike out, the beasts scream; we just stop in time to avoid attacking one another. . . .

Suddenly it howls and flashes terrifically, the dug-out cracks in all its joints under a direct hit, fortunately only a light one that the concrete blocks are able to withstand. It rings metallically, the walls reel, rifles, helmets, earth, mud, and dust fly everywhere. Sulphur fumes pour in.

If we were in one of those light dug-outs that they have been building lately instead of this deeper one, none of us would be alive.

But the effect is bad enough even so. The recruit starts to rave again and two others follow suit. One jumps up and rushes out, we have trouble with the other two. I start after the one who escapes and wonder whether to shoot him in the leg—then it shrieks again, I fling myself down and when I stand up the wall of the trench is plastered with smoking splinters, lumps of flesh, and bits of uniform. I scramble back.

The first recruit seems actually to have gone insane. He butts his head against the wall like a goat. We must try to-night to take him to the rear. Meanwhile we bind him, but in such a way that in case of attack he can be released at once. . . .

Suddenly the nearer explosions cease. The shelling continues but it has lifted and falls behind us, our trench is free. We seize the hand-grenades, pitch them out in front of the dug-out and jump after them. The bombardment has stopped and a heavy barrage now falls behind us. The attack has come.

No one would believe that in this howling waste there could still be men; but steel helmets now appear on all sides out of the trench, and fifty yards from us a machine-gun is already in position and barking.

The wire entanglements are torn to pieces. Yet they offer some obstacle. We see the storm-troops coming. Our artillery opens fire. Machine-guns rattle, rifles crack. The charge works its way across. Haie and Kropp begin with the hand-grenades. They throw as fast as they can, others pass them, the handles with the strings already pulled. Haie throws seventy-five yards, Kropp sixty, it has been measured, the distance is important. The enemy as they run cannot do much before they are within forty yards.

We recognize the smooth distorted faces, the helmets: they are French. They have already suffered heavily when they reach the remnants of the barbed wire entanglements. A whole line has gone down before our machine-guns; then we have a lot of stoppages and they come nearer.

I see one of them, his face upturned, fall into a wire cradle. His body collapses, his hands remain suspended as though he were praying. Then his body drops clean away and only his hands with the stumps of his arms, shot off, now hang in the wire.

The moment we are about to retreat three faces rise up from the ground in front of us. Under one of the helmets a dark pointed beard and two eyes that are fastened on me. I raise my hand, but I cannot throw into those strange eyes; for one mad moment the whole slaughter whirls like a circus round me, and these two eyes alone are motionless; then the head rises up, a hand, a movement, and my hand-grenade flies through the air and into him.

We make for the rear, pull wire cradles into the trench and leave bombs behind us with the strings pulled, which ensures us a fiery retreat. The machine-guns are already firing from the next position.

We have become wild beasts. We do not fight, we defend ourselves against annihilation. It is not against men that we fling our bombs, what do we know of men in this moment when Death is hunting us down—now, for the first time in three days we can see his face, now for the first time in three days we can oppose him; we feel a mad anger. No longer do we lie helpless, waiting on the scaffold, we can destroy and kill, to save ourselves, to save ourselves and to be revenged.

We crouch behind every corner, behind every barrier of barbed wire, and hurl heaps of explosives at the feet of the advancing enemy before we run. The blast of the hand-grenades impinges powerfully on our arms and legs; crouching like cats we run on, overwhelmed by this wave that bears us along, that fills us with ferocity, turns us into thugs, into murderers, into God only knows what devils; this wave that multiplies our strength with fear and madness and greed of life, seeking and fighting for nothing but our deliverance. If your own father came over with them you would not hesitate to fling a bomb at him.

The forward trenches have been abandoned. Are they still trenches? They are blown to pieces, annihilated—there are only broken bits of trenches, holes linked by cracks, nests of craters, that is all. But the enemy's casualties increase. They did not count on so much resistance.

————

It is nearly noon. The sun blazes hotly, the sweat stings in our eyes, we wipe it off on our sleeves and often blood with it. At last we reach a trench that is in a somewhat better condition. It is manned and ready for the counter-attack, it receives us. Our guns open in full blast and cut off the enemy attack.

The lines behind us stop. They can advance no farther. The attack is crushed by our artillery. We watch. The fire lifts a hundred yards and we break forward. Beside me a lance-corporal has his head torn off. He runs a few steps more while the blood spouts from his neck like a fountain.

It does not come quite to hand-to-hand fighting; they are driven back. We arrive once again at our shattered trench and pass on beyond it. . . .

We have lost all feeling for one another. We can hardly control ourselves when our glance lights on the form of some other man. We are insensible, dead men, who through some trick, some dreadful magic, are still able to run and to kill.

A young Frenchman lags behind, he is overtaken, he puts up his hands, in one he still holds his revolver—does he mean to shoot or to give himself up!—a blow from a spade cleaves through his face. A second sees it and tries to run farther; a bayonet jabs into his back. He leaps in the air, his arms thrown wide, his mouth wide open, yelling; he staggers, in his back the bayonet quivers. A third throws away his rifle, cowers down with his hands before his eyes. He is left behind with a few other prisoners to carry off the wounded.

Suddenly in the pursuit we reach the enemy line.

We are so close on the heels of our retreating enemies that we reach it almost at the same time as they. In this way we suffer few casualties. A machine-gun barks, but is silenced with a bomb. Nevertheless, the couple of seconds has sufficed to give us five stomach wounds. With the butt of his rifle Kat smashes to pulp the face of one of the unwounded machine-gunners. We bayonet the others before they have time to get out their bombs. Then thirstily we drink the water they have for cooling the gun.

Everywhere wire-cutters are snapping, planks are thrown across the entanglements, we jump through the narrow entrances into the trenches. Haie strikes his spade into the neck of a gigantic Frenchman and throws the first hand-grenade; we duck behind a breastwork for a few seconds, then the straight bit of trench ahead of us is empty. The next throw whizzes obliquely over the corner and clears a passage; as we run past we toss handfuls down into the dug-outs, the earth shudders, it crashes, smokes and groans, we stumble over slippery lumps of flesh, over yielding bodies; I fall into an open belly on which lies a clean, new officer's cap.

The fight ceases. We lose touch with the enemy. We cannot stay here long but must retire under cover of our artillery to our own posi-

tion. No sooner do we know this than we dive into the nearest dug-outs, and with the utmost haste seize on whatever provisions we can see, especially the tins of corned beef and butter, before we clear out.

We get back pretty well. There is no further attack by the enemy. We lie for an hour panting and resting before anyone speaks. We are so completely played out that in spite of our great hunger we do not think of the provisions. Then gradually we become something like men again.

REVIEW QUESTIONS

1. In Erich Maria Remarque's account, how did the soldiers in the trenches react to artillery bombardment?
2. What ordeal did the attacking soldiers encounter as they neared the enemy trenches?

---

5   The Paris Peace Conference

The most terrible war the world had experienced ended in November 1918; in January 1919, representatives of the victorious powers assembled in Paris to draw up a peace settlement. The principal figures at the Paris Peace Conference were Woodrow Wilson (1856–1924), president of the United States; David Lloyd George (1863–1945), prime minister of Great Britain; Georges Clemenceau (1841–1929), premier of France; and Vittorio Orlando (1860–1952), premier of Italy. Disillusioned intellectuals and the war-weary masses turned to Wilson as the prince of peace who would fashion a new and better world based on democratic and Christian ideals and international cooperation.

Georges Clemenceau
FRENCH DEMANDS FOR SECURITY AND REVENGE

Wilson's promised new world clashed with French demands for security and revenge. Almost all the fighting on the war's western front had taken place in France; its industries and farmlands lay in ruins, and many of its young men had perished. France had been invaded by Germany in 1870 as well as in 1914, so the French believed that only by crippling Germany could they gain security. Premier Georges Clemenceau, who was called "the Tiger," dismissed Wilson's vision of a new world as mere noble sentiment divorced from reality, and he fought tenaciously to gain security for France. Clemenceau's profound hatred and mistrust of Germany are revealed in his book *Grandeur and Misery of Victory* (1930), written a decade after the Paris Peace Conference.

For the catastrophe of 1914 the Germans are responsible. Only a professional liar would deny this. . . .

What after all is this war, prepared, undertaken, and waged by the German people, who flung aside every scruple of conscience to let it loose, hoping for a peace of enslavement under the yoke of a militarism destructive of all human dignity? It is simply the continuance, the recrudescence, of those never-ending acts of violence by which the first savage tribes carried out their depredations with all the resources of barbarism. The means improve with the ages. The ends remain the same. . . .

Germany, in this matter, was unfortunate enough to allow herself (in spite of her skill at dissimulation) to be betrayed into an excess of candour by her characteristic tendency to go to extremes. *Deutschland über alles. Germany above everything!* That, and nothing less, is what she asks, and when once her demand is satisfied she will let you enjoy a peace under the yoke. Not only does she make no secret of her aim, but the intolerable arrogance of the German aristocracy, the servile good nature of the intellectual and the scholar, the gross vanity of the most competent leaders in industry, and the wide-spread influence of a violent popular poetry conspire to shatter throughout the world all the time-honoured traditions of individual, as well as international, dignity. . . .

On November 11, 1918, the fighting ceased.

It is not I who will dispute the German soldier's qualities of endurance. But he had been promised a *fresh and frolicsome war,* and for four years he had been pinned down between the anvil and the hammer. . . . Our defeat would have resulted in a relapse of human civilization into violence and bloodshed. . . .

Outrages against human civilization are in the long run defeated by their own excess, and thus I discern in the peculiar mentality of the German soldier, with his *"Deutschland über alles,"* the cause of the premature exhaustion that brought him to beg for an armistice before the French soldier, who was fighting for his independence. . . .

And what is this "Germanic civilization," this monstrous explosion of the will to power, which threatens openly to do away entirely with the diversities established by many evolutions, to set in their place the implacable mastery of a race whose lordly part would be to substitute itself, by force of arms, for all national developments? We need only read [General Friedrich von] Bernhardi's famous pamphlet *Our Future,* in which it is alleged that Germany sums up within herself, as the historian Treitschke asserts, the greatest manifestation of human supremacy, and finds herself condemned, by her very greatness, either to absorb all nations in herself or to return to nothingness. . . . Ought we not all to feel menaced in our very vitals by this mad doctrine of universal Germanic supremacy over England, France, America, and every other country? . . .

What document more suitable to reveal the direction of "German culture" than the famous manifesto of the ninety-three super-intellectuals of Germany,[1] issued to justify the bloodiest and the least excusable of military aggressions against the great centres of civilization? At the moment . . . violated Belgium lay beneath the heel of the malefactor (October 1914) . . . [and German troops were] razing . . . great historical buildings to the ground [and] burning down . . . libraries. It would need a whole book to tell of the infamous treatment inflicted upon noncombatants, to reckon up those who were shot down, or put to death, or deported, or condemned to forced labour. . . .

Well, this was the hour chosen by German intellectuals to make themselves heard. Let all the nations give ear! . . .

. . . Their learning made of them merely Germans better than all others qualified to formulate, on their own account, the extravagances of Germanic arrogance. The only difference is that they speak louder than the common people, those docile automatons. The fact is that they really believe themselves to be

---

[1]Shortly after the outbreak of war, ninety-three leading German scholars and scientists addressed a letter to the world, defending Germany's actions.

the representatives of a privileged *"culture"* that sets them above the errors of the human race, and confers on them the prerogative of a superior power. . . .

The whole document is nothing but denials without the support of a single proof. *"It is not true* that Germany wanted the War." [Kaiser] William II had for years been *"mocked at by his adversaries of today on account of his unshakable love of peace."* They neglect to tell us whence they got this lie. They forget that from 1871 till 1914 we received from Germany a series of war threats in the course of which Queen Victoria and also the Czar had to intervene with the *Kaiser* direct for the maintenance of peace.

I have already recalled how our German intellectuals account for the violation of the Belgian frontier:

> *It is not true that we criminally violated Belgian neutrality. It can be proved that France and England had made up their minds to violate it. It can be proved that Belgium was willing. It would have been suicide not to forestall them. . . .*

. . . And when a great chemist such as Ostwald tells us, with his colleagues, that our struggle *"against the so-called German militarism"* is really directed *"against German culture,"* we must remember that *this same savant published a history of chemistry* IN WHICH THE NAME OF [eighteenth-century French chemist Antoine] LAVOISIER WAS NOT MENTIONED.

The "intellectuals" take their place in public opinion as the most ardent propagandists of the thesis which makes Germany the very model of the *"chosen people."* The same Professor Ostwald had already written, *"Germany has reached a higher stage of civilization than the other peoples, and the result of the War will be an organization of Europe under German leadership."* Professor Haeckel had demanded *the conquest of London, the division of Belgium between Germany and Holland, the annexation of North-east France, of Poland, the Baltic Provinces, the Congo, and a great part of the English colonies.* Professor Lasson went further still:

We are morally and intellectually superior to all men. We are peerless. So too are our organizations and our institutions. *Germany is the most perfect creation known in history,* and the Imperial Chancellor, Herr von Bethmann-Hollweg, is *the most eminent of living men.*

Ordinary laymen who talked in this strain would be taken off to some safe asylum. Coming from duly hallmarked professors, such statements explain all German warfare by alleging that Germany's destiny is universal domination, and that for this very reason she is bound either to disappear altogether or to exercise violence on all nations with a view to their own betterment. . . .

May I further recall, since we have to emphasize the point, that on September 17, 1914, Erzberger, the well-known German statesman, an eminent member of the Catholic Party, wrote to the Minister of War, General von Falkenhayn, *"We must not worry about committing an offence against the rights of nations nor about violating the laws of humanity. Such feelings today are of secondary importance"*? A month later, on October 21, 1914, he wrote in *Der Tag*, *"If a way was found of entirely wiping out the whole of London it would be more humane to employ it* than to allow the blood of A SINGLE GERMAN SOLDIER to be shed on the battlefield!". . .

. . . General von Bernhardi himself, the best pupil, as I have already said, of the historian Treitschke, whose ideas are law in Germany, has just preached the doctrine of "World power or Downfall" at us. So there is nothing left for other nations, as a way of salvation, but to be conquered by Germany. . . .

I have sometimes penetrated into the sacred cave of the Germanic cult, which is, as every one knows, the *Bierhaus* [beer hall]. A great aisle of massive humanity where there accumulate, amid the fumes of tobacco and beer, the popular rumblings of a nationalism upheld by the sonorous brasses blaring to the heavens the supreme voice of Germany, *"Deutschland über alles!"* Men, women, and children, all petrified in reverence before the divine stoneware pot, brows furrowed with irrepressible power, eyes lost in a dream of infinity, mouths twisted by the intensity of will-power, drink in long draughts the celestial hope of vague expecta- tions. These only remain to be realized pres- ently when the chief marked out by Destiny shall have given the word. There you have the ultimate framework of an old but childish race.

REVIEW QUESTIONS

1. What accusations did Georges Clemenceau make against the German national character? What contrasts did he draw between the Germans and the French?
2. How did Clemenceau respond to the manifesto of the German intellectuals?
3. Why, more than a decade after the war, did Clemenceau believe that Germany should still be feared?

6 The Bolshevik Revolution

In March 1917, in the middle of World War I, Russians were demoralized. The army, poorly trained, inadequately equipped, and incompetently led, had suf- fered staggering losses; everywhere soldiers were deserting. Food shortages and low wages drove workers to desperation; the loss of fathers and sons at the front embittered peasants. Discontent was keenest in Petrograd, where on March 9, two hundred thousand striking workers shouting "Down with autoc- racy!" packed the streets. After some bloodshed, government troops refused to fire on them. Faced with a broad and debilitating crisis—violence and anarchy in the capital, breakdown of transport, uncertain food and fuel supplies, and general disorder—Tsar Nicholas II was forced to turn over authority to a provi- sional government, thereby ending three centuries of tsarist rule under the Ro- manov dynasty.

The Provisional Government, after July 1917 guided by Aleksandr Kerensky (1881–1970), sought to transform Russia into a Western-style liberal state, but the government failed to comprehend the urgency with which the Russian peasants wanted the landlords' land, and soldiers and the masses wanted peace. Resentment spiraled. Kerensky's increasing unpopularity and the magnitude of popular unrest seemed to the Bolsheviks' leader, Vladimir Ilyich Lenin (1870–1924), then in hiding, to offer the long-expected opportunity for the Bol- sheviks to seize power and bring about a socialist revolution.

N. N. Sukhanov
TROTSKY AROUSES THE PEOPLE

Playing a crucial role in the Bolshevik seizure of power on November 7, 1917, was Leon Trotsky (1879–1940). Born Lev Davidovich Bronstein, the son of a prosperous Jewish farmer in Ukraine, Trotsky was attracted early to the ranks of the revolutionaries, and he shared their fate. Exiled to Siberia in 1902, he escaped to Switzerland with a faked passport in the name of Leon Trotsky. Back in Russia for the Revolution of 1905, he was again exiled and again escaped. After a period abroad, he returned to Russia after the overthrow of the tsar in March 1917 and soon assumed a leading role among the Bolsheviks. In September 1917, as the moderate regime of Kerensky began to totter, Trotsky was elected chairman of the Petrograd soviet; soon afterward he masterminded the Military-Revolutionary Committee, the Bolshevik strike force.

On the evening of November 4, Trotsky delivered a rousing speech at the Peoples' House, a popular theater much used for working-class meetings. His speech is described by an eyewitness, the Menshevik (a Social Democratic moderate) leader N. N. Sukhanov, in his 1917 book, *The Russian Revolution.*

The mood of the people, more than 3,000, who filled the hall was definitely tense; they were all silently waiting for something. The audience was of course primarily workers and soldiers, but more than a few typically lower-middle-class men's and women's figures were visible.

Trotsky's ovation seemed to be cut short prematurely, out of curiosity and impatience: what was he going to say? Trotsky at once began to heat up the atmosphere, with his skill and brilliance. I remember that at length and with extraordinary power he drew a picture of the suffering of the trenches. Thoughts flashed through my mind of the inevitable incongruity of the parts in this oratorical whole. But Trotsky knew what he was doing. The whole point lay in the mood. The political conclusions had long been familiar. They could be condensed, as long as there were enough highlights.

Trotsky did this—with enough highlights. The Soviet regime was not only called upon to put an end to the suffering of the trenches. It would give land and heal the internal disorder. Once again the recipes against hunger were repeated: a soldier, a sailor, and a working girl, who would requisition bread from those who had it and distribute it gratis to the cities and front. But Trotsky went even further on this decisive "Day of the Petersburg Soviet."

"The Soviet Government will give everything the country contains to the poor and the men in the trenches. You, bourgeois, have got two fur caps!—give one of them to the soldier, who's freezing in the trenches. Have you got warm boots? Stay at home. The worker needs your boots. . . ."

These were very good and just ideas. They could not but excite the enthusiasm of a crowd who had been reared on the Tsarist whip. In any case, I certify as a direct witness that this was what was said on this last day.

All round me was a mood bordering on ecstasy. It seemed as though the crowd, spontaneously and of its own accord, would break into some religious hymn. Trotsky formulated a brief and general resolution, or pronounced some general formula like "we will defend the worker-peasant cause to the last drop of our blood."

Who was—for? The crowd of thousands, as one man, raised their hands. I saw the raised hands and burning eyes of men, women, youths, soldiers, peasants, and typically lower-middle-class faces. Were they in spiritual transport? Did they see, through the raised curtain, a corner of the "righteous land" of their longing? Or were they penetrated by a consciousness of the *political occasion,* under the influence of the political agitation of a *Socialist?* Ask no questions! Accept it as it was. . . .

Trotsky went on speaking. The innumerable crowd went on holding their hands up. Trotsky rapped out the words: "Let this vote of yours be your vow—with all your strength and at any sacrifice to support the Soviet that has taken on itself the glorious burden of bringing to a conclusion the victory of the revolution and of giving land, bread, and peace!"

The vast crowd was holding up its hands. It agreed. It vowed. Once again, accept this as it was. With an unusual feeling of oppression I looked on at this really magnificent scene.

Trotsky finished. Someone else went out on to the stage. But there was no point in waiting and looking any more.

Throughout Petersburg more or less the same thing was going on. Everywhere there were final reviews and final vows. Thousands, tens of thousands and hundreds of thousands of people . . . This, actually, was already an insurrection. Things had started. . . .

V. I. Lenin
THE CALL TO POWER

On November 6 (October 24 by the old-style calendar then in use in Russia), Lenin urged immediate action, as the following document reveals.

. . . The situation is critical in the extreme. In fact it is now absolutely clear that to delay the uprising would be fatal.

With all my might I urge comrades to realise that everything now hangs by a thread; that we are confronted by problems which are not to be solved by conferences or congresses (even congresses of Soviets), but exclusively by peoples, by the masses, by the struggle of the armed people. The bourgeois onslaught of the Kornilovites [followers of General Kornilov, who tried to establish a military dictatorship] show that we must not wait. We must at all costs, this very evening, this very night, arrest the government, having first disarmed the officer cadets (defeating them, if they resist), and so on.

We must not wait! We may lose everything! Who must take power?

That is not important at present. Let the Revolutionary Military Committee [Bolshevik organization working within the army and navy] do it, or "some other institution" which will declare that it will relinquish power only to the true representatives of the interests of the people, the interests of the army (the immediate proposal of peace), the interests of the peasants (the land to be taken immediately and private property abolished), the interests of the starving.

All districts, all regiments, all forces must be mobilised at once and must immediately send their delegations to the Revolutionary Military Committee and to the Central Committee of the Bolsheviks [governing organization of the Bolshevik party] with the insistent demand that under no circumstances should power be left in the hands of Kerensky and Co. . . . not under any circumstances; the matter must be decided without fail this very evening, or this very night.

History will not forgive revolutionaries for procrastinating when they could be victorious today (and they certainly will be victorious today), while they risk losing much tomorrow, in fact, they risk losing everything.

If we seize power today, we seize it not in opposition to the Soviets but on their behalf.

The seizure of power is the business of the uprising; its political purpose will become clear after the seizure. . . .

. . . It would be an infinite crime on the part of the revolutionaries were they to let the chance slip, knowing that the *salvation of the revolution,* the offer of peace, the salvation of Petrograd, salvation from famine, the transfer of the land to the peasants depend upon them.

The government is tottering. It must be *given the death-blow* at all costs.

To delay action is fatal.

REVIEW QUESTIONS

1. With what issues and what promises did Leon Trotsky arouse the masses in support of the Bolshevik seizure of power?
2. What promises did V. I. Lenin hold out to his supporters should the revolution succeed?
3. How would you define, from the evidence here offered, a revolutionary situation? What factors create it?

---

7   The War and European Consciousness

World War I caused many intellectuals to have grave doubts about the Enlightenment tradition and the future of Western civilization. More than ever the belief in human goodness, reason, and the progress of humanity seemed an illusion. Despite its many accomplishments, intellectuals contended that Western civilization was flawed and perishable.

Paul Valéry
DISILLUSIONMENT

Shortly after World War I, Paul Valéry (1871–1945), a prominent French writer, expressed the mood of disillusionment that gripped many intellectuals. The following reading was written in 1919; the second reading is from a 1922 speech. Both were published in *Variety*, a collection of some of Valéry's works.

We modern civilizations have learned to recognize that we are mortal like the others.

We had heard tell of whole worlds vanished, of empires foundered with all their men and all their engines, sunk to the inexplorable depths of the centuries with their gods and laws, their academies and their pure and applied sciences, their grammars, dictionaries, classics, romantics, symbolists, their critics and the critics of their critics. We knew that all the apparent earth is made of ashes, and that ashes have a meaning. We perceived, through the misty bulk of history, the phantoms of huge vessels once laden with riches and learning. We could not count them. But these wrecks, after all, were no concern of ours.

Elam, Nineveh, Babylon were vague and splendid names; the total ruin of these worlds, for us, meant as little as did their existence. But *France, England, Russia* . . . these names, too, are splendid. . . . And now we see that the abyss of history is deep enough to bury all the world. We feel that a civilization is fragile as a life. The circumstances which will send the works of [John] Keats [English poet] and the works of [Charles] Baudelaire [French poet] to join those of Menander[1] are not at all inconceivable; they are found in the daily papers.

---
[1]Menander was an ancient Greek poet whose works were lost until fragments were found in Egypt at the end of the nineteenth century.

The following passage is from an address that Valéry delivered at the University of Zurich on November 15, 1922.

The storm has died away, and still we are restless, uneasy, as if the storm were about to break. Almost all the affairs of men remain in a terrible uncertainty. We think of what has disappeared, we are almost destroyed by what has been destroyed; we do not know what will be born, and we fear the future, not without reason. We hope vaguely, we dread precisely; our fears are infinitely more precise than our hopes; we confess that the charm of life is behind us, abundance is behind us, but doubt and disorder are in us and with us. There is no thinking man, however shrewd or learned he may be, who can hope to dominate this anxiety, to escape from this impression of darkness, to measure the probable duration of this period when the vital relations of humanity are disturbed profoundly.

We are a very unfortunate generation, whose lot has been to see the moment of our passage through life coincide with the arrival of great and terrifying events, the echo of which will resound through all our lives.

One can say that all the fundamentals of the world have been affected by the war, or more exactly, by the circumstances of the war; something deeper has been worn away than the renewable parts of the machine. You know how greatly the general economic situation has been disturbed, and the polity of states, and the very life of the individual; you are familiar with the universal discomfort, hesitation, apprehension. *But among all these injured things is the Mind.* The Mind has indeed been cruelly wounded; its complaint is heard in the hearts of intellectual man; it passes a mournful judgment on itself. It doubts itself profoundly.

Erich Maria Remarque
THE LOST GENERATION

In Erich Maria Remarque's *All Quiet on the Western Front,* a wounded German soldier reflects on the war and his future. He sees himself as part of a lost generation.

Gradually a few of us are allowed to get up. And I am given crutches to hobble around on. But I do not make much use of them; I cannot bear Albert's gaze as I move about the room. His eyes always follow me with such a strange look. So I sometimes escape to the corridor;—there I can move about more freely.

On the next floor below are the abdominal and spine cases, head wounds and double amputations. On the right side of the wing are the jaw wounds, gas cases, nose, ear, and neck wounds. On the left the blind and the lung wounds, pelvis wounds, wounds in the joints, wounds in the kidneys, wounds in the testicles, wounds in the intestines. Here a man realizes for the first time in how many places a man can get hit.

Two fellows die of tetanus. Their skin turns pale, their limbs stiffen, at last only their eyes live—stubbornly. Many of the wounded have their shattered limbs hanging free in the air from a gallows; underneath the wound a basin is placed into which drips the pus. Every two or three hours the vessel is emptied. Other men lie in stretching bandages with heavy weights hanging from the end of the bed. I see intestine wounds that are constantly full of excreta. The surgeon's clerk shows me X-ray photographs of completely smashed hip-bones, knees, and shoulders.

A man cannot realize that above such shattered bodies there are still human faces in which life goes its daily round. And this is only one hospital, one single station; there are hundreds of thousands in Germany, hundreds of thousands in France, hundreds of thousands in Russia. How senseless is everything that can ever be written, done, or thought, when such things are possible. It must be all lies and of no account when the culture of a thousand years could not prevent this stream of blood being poured out, these torture-chambers in their hundreds of thousands. A hospital alone shows what war is.

I am young, I am twenty years old; yet I know nothing of life but despair, death, fear, and fatuous superficiality cast over an abyss of sorrow. I see how peoples are set against one another, and in silence, unknowingly, foolishly, obediently, innocently slay one another. I see that the keenest brains of the world invent weapons and words to make it yet more refined and enduring. And all men of my age, here and over there, throughout the whole world see these things; all my generation is experiencing these things with me. What would our fathers do if we suddenly stood up and came before them and [told our story]? What do they expect of us if a time ever comes when the war is over? Through the years our business has been killing;—it was our first calling in life. Our knowledge of life is limited to death. What will happen afterwards? And what shall come out of us?

REVIEW QUESTIONS

1. What did Paul Valéry mean in saying that the mind of Europe doubted itself profoundly?
2. Why do you think many veterans felt that they were part of a lost generation?

CHAPTER 8
Era of Totalitarianism

ADOLF HITLER before his Labor Service at Nuremberg, September 1938. German Nazis designed their mass rallies, replete with pageantry and marching battalions, to arouse the emotions of the public and thereby open them to manipulation. *(UPI/Corbis-Bettmann)*

Following World War I, fascist movements arose in Italy, Germany, and many other European countries. Although these movements differed—each a product of separate national histories and the outlook of its leader—they shared a hatred of liberalism, democracy, and communism; a commitment to aggressive nationalism; and a glorification of the party leader. Fascist leaders cleverly utilized myths, rituals, and pageantry to mobilize and manipulate the masses.

Several conditions fostered the rise of fascism. One factor was the fear of communism among the middle and upper classes. Inspired by the success of the Bolsheviks in Russia, communists in other lands were calling for the establishment of Soviet-style republics. Increasingly afraid of a communist takeover, industrialists, landowners, government officials, army leaders, professionals, and shopkeepers were attracted to fascist movements that promised to protect their nation from this threat. A second factor contributing to the growth of fascism was the disillusionment of World War I veterans and the mood of violence bred by the war. The thousands of veterans facing unemployment and poverty made ideal recruits for fascist parties that glorified combat and organized private armies. A third contributing factor was the inability of democratic parliamentary governments to cope with the problems that burdened postwar Europe. Having lost confidence in the procedures and values of democracy, many people joined fascist movements that promised strong leadership, an end to party conflicts, and a unified national will.

Fascism's appeal to nationalist feelings also drew people into the movement. In a sense, fascism expressed the aggressive racial nationalism that had emerged in the late nineteenth century. Fascists saw themselves as dedicated idealists engaged in a heroic struggle to rescue their nations from domestic and foreign enemies; they aspired to regain lands lost by their countries in World War I or to acquire lands denied them by the Paris Peace Conference.

Fascists glorified instinct, will, and blood as the true forces of life; they openly attacked the ideals of reason, liberty, and equality—the legacies of the Enlightenment and the French Revolution. At the center of German fascism (National Socialism or Nazism) was a bizarre racial mythology that preached the superiority of the German race and the inferiority of others, particularly Jews and Slavs.

In the 1930s, the term *totalitarianism* was used to describe the Fascist regime in Italy, the National Socialist regime in Germany, and the communist regime in the Soviet Union. To a degree that far exceeds the ancient tyrannies and early modern autocratic states, these dictatorships aspired to and, with varying degrees of success, attained control over the individual's consciousness and behavior and all phases of political, social, and cultural life. To many people it seemed that a crises-riddled democracy was dying and that the future belonged to these dynamic totalitarian movements.

Totalitarianism was a twentieth-century phenomenon, for such all-embracing control over the individual and society could have been achieved only in an age of modern ideology, technology, and bureaucracy. The ideological aims and social and economic policies of Hitler and Stalin differed fundamentally. However, both Soviet Russia and Nazi Germany shared the totalitarian goal of monolithic unity and total domination, and both employed similar methods to achieve it. Mussolini's Italy is more accurately called authoritarian, for the party-state either did not intend to control all phases of life or lacked the means to do so. Moreover, Mussolini hesitated to use the ruthless methods that Hitler and Stalin employed so readily.

Striving for total unity, control, and obedience, the totalitarian dictatorship is the antithesis of liberal democracy. It abolishes all competing political parties, suppresses individual liberty, eliminates or regulates private institutions, and utilizes the modern state's bureaucracy and technology to impose its ideology and enforce its commands. The party-state determines what people should believe—what values they should hold. There is no room for individual thinking, private moral judgment, or individual conscience. The individual possesses no natural rights that the state must respect.

Like a religion, the totalitarian ideology provides its adherents with beliefs that make society and history intelligible, that explain all of existence in an emotionally gratifying way. Again like a religion, it creates true believers, who feel that they are participating in a great cause—a heroic fight against evil—that gives meaning to their lives.

Not only did the totalitarian religion-ideology supply followers with a cause that claimed absolute goodness; it also provided a Devil. For the Soviets, the source of evil and the cause of all the people's hardships were the degenerate capitalists, the traitorous Trotskyites, or the saboteurs and foreign agents, who impeded the realization of the socialist society. For the Nazis, the Devil was the conspirator Jew. These "evil" ones must be eliminated in order to realize the totalitarian movement's vision of the future. Thus, totalitarian regimes liquidate large segments of the population designated as "enemies of the people." Historical necessity or a higher purpose demands and justifies their liquidation. The appeal to historical necessity has all the power of a great myth. Presented as a world-historical struggle between the forces of good and the forces of evil, the myth incites fanaticism and numbs the conscience. Seemingly decent people engage in terrible acts of brutality with no remorse, convinced that they are waging a righteous war.

1   Modernize or Perish

Joseph Stalin (1879–1953) was the Communist leader who made the Soviet Union into a superpower. He was born Iosif Vissarionovich Dzhugashvili in Trans-Caucasus Georgia. A rebel from childhood, he was one of Lenin's favored professional revolutionaries, trained in the tough schools of underground agitation, tsarist prisons, and Siberian exile. Unscrupulous, energetic, and endowed with a keen nose for the realities of power within the party and the country as a whole, Stalin surpassed his political rivals in strength of will and organizational astuteness. After he was appointed secretary-general of the Communist party (then considered a minor post) in 1922, he concentrated on building, amid the disorganization caused by war, revolution, and civil war, an effective party organization adapted to the temper of the Russian people. With this structure's help, he established himself as Lenin's successor. Stalin, more powerful and more ruthless than Lenin, was determined to force his country to overcome the economic and political weakness that had led to defeat and ruin in 1917. After Lenin's death, Stalin preached the "Leninist style of work," which combined "Russian revolutionary sweep" with "American efficiency."

Joseph Stalin
THE HARD LINE

Firmly entrenched in power by 1929, Stalin started a second revolution (called the Stalin revolution), mobilizing at top speed the economic potential of the country, however limited the human and material resources available, whatever the obstacles, and whatever the human price. The alternative, he was sure, was foreign domination that would totally destroy his country's independence. In this spirit, he addressed a gathering of industrial managers in 1931, talking to them not in Marxist-Leninist jargon, but in terms of hard-line Russian nationalism.

It is sometimes asked whether it is not possible to slow down the tempo a bit, to put a check on the movement. No, comrades, it is not possible! The tempo must not be reduced! On the contrary, we must increase it as much as is within our powers and possibilities. This is dictated to us by our obligations to the workers and peasants of the U.S.S.R. This is dictated to us by our obligations to the working class of the whole world.

To slacken the tempo would mean falling behind. And those who fall behind get beaten. But we do not want to be beaten. No, we refuse to be beaten! One feature of the history of old Russia was the continual beatings she suffered for falling behind, for her backwardness. She was beaten by the Mongol Khans. She was beaten by the Turkish beys. She was beaten by the Swedish feudal lords. She was beaten by the Polish and Lithuanian gentry. She was beaten by the British and French capitalists. She was beaten by the Japanese barons. All beat her—for her backwardness: for military backwardness, for cultural backwardness, for political backwardness, for industrial backwardness, for agricultural backwardness. She was beaten because to do so was profitable and could be done with impunity. Do you remember the words of the pre-revolutionary poet [Nikolai Nekrassov]: "You are poor and abundant, mighty and impotent, Mother Russia." These words of the old poet were well learned by those gentlemen. They beat her, saying: "You are abundant," so one can enrich oneself at your expense. They beat her, saying: "You are poor and impotent," so you can be beaten and plundered with impunity. Such is the law of the exploiters—to beat the backward and the weak. It is the jungle law of capitalism. You are backward, you are weak—therefore you are wrong; hence, you can be beaten and enslaved. You are mighty—therefore you are right; hence, we must be wary of you.

That is why we must no longer lag behind. In the past we had no fatherland, nor could we have one. But now that we have overthrown capitalism and power is in the hands of the working class, we have a fatherland, and we will defend its independence. Do you want our socialist fatherland to be beaten and to lose its independence? If you do not want this you must put an end to its backwardness in the shortest possible time and develop genuine Bolshevik tempo in building up its socialist system of economy. There is no other way. That is why Lenin said during the October Revolution: "Either perish, or overtake and outstrip the advanced capitalist countries."

We are fifty or a hundred years behind the advanced countries. We must make good this distance in ten years. Either we do it, or they crush us.

This is what our obligations to the workers and peasants of the U.S.S.R. dictate to us.

REVIEW QUESTIONS

1. Why did Joseph Stalin argue that the tempo of industrialization could not be slowed down?
2. How important is the idea of "fatherland" to Stalin?

---

2 Forced Collectivization

The forced collectivization of agriculture from 1929 to 1933 was an integral part of the Stalin revolution. His argument in favor of it was simple: an economy divided against itself cannot stand—planned industrial mobilization was incompatible with small-scale private agriculture in the traditional manner. Collectivization meant combining many small peasant holdings into a single large unit run in theory by the peasants (now called collective farmers), but run in practice by the collective farm chairman and guided by the government's Five-Year Plan, which was designed to industrialize the country rapidly. Collectivization also meant liquidating the Kulaks—the more prosperous peasants.

Lev Kopelev
TERROR IN THE COUNTRYSIDE

The liquidation of the kulaks began in late 1929, extending through the length and breadth of the country during the winter. The confiscation of kulak property, the deportations, and the killing rose to a brutal climax in the following spring and continued for another two years, by which time the bulk of the private farms had been eliminated. By some estimates, almost five million people were liquidated. Some were driven from their huts, deprived of all possessions, and left destitute in the dead of winter; the men were sent to forced labor and their families left abandoned. Others killed themselves or were killed outright, sometimes in pitched battles involving a whole village— men, women, and children.

The upheaval destroyed agricultural production in these years; farm animals died or were killed in huge numbers; fields lay barren. In 1932 and 1933, famine stalked the south and southeast, killing additional millions. The vast tragedy caused by collectivization did not deter Stalin from pursuing his goals: the establishment of state farms run like factories and the subordination of the rebellious and willful peasantry to state authority.

Here a militant participant in the collectivization drive, Lev Kopelev, recalls some of his experiences. These passages are from his memoirs published in 1978. Kopelev (1912–1997), raised in a Ukrainian middle-class Jewish family, evolved from a youthful Stalinist into a tolerant, gentle person in later years. After trying to keep Russian soldiers from raping and pillaging in German territory in 1945, he was given a ten-year sentence for antistate crimes. Subsequently out of favor because of his literary protests against the inhumanities of the Soviet system, he was exiled from the Soviet Union to West Germany in 1980.

The grain front! Stalin said the struggle for grain was the struggle for socialism. I was convinced that we were warriors on an invisible front, fighting against kulak sabotage for the grain which was needed by the country, by the five-year plan. Above all, for the grain, but also for the souls of these peasants who were mired in unconscientiousness, in ignorance, who succumbed to enemy agitation, who did not understand the great truth of communism. . . .

The highest measure of coercion on the hardcore holdouts was "undisputed confiscation."

A team consisting of several young kolkhozniks [collective farmers] and members of the village soviet . . . would search the hut, barn, yard, and take away all the stores of seed, lead away the cow, the horse, the pigs.

In some cases they would be merciful and leave some potatoes, peas, corn for feeding the family. But the stricter ones would make a clean sweep. They would take not only the food and livestock, but also "all valuables and surpluses of clothing," including icons in their frames, samovars, painted carpets and even

metal kitchen utensils which might be silver. And any money they found stashed away. Special instructions ordered the removal of gold, silver and currency. . . .

Several times Volodya and I were present at such plundering raids. We even took part: we were entrusted to draw up inventories of the confiscated goods. . . . The women howled hysterically, clinging to the bags.

"Oy, that's the last thing we have! That was for the children's kasha [cereal]! Honest to God, the children will starve!"

They wailed, falling on their trunks:

"Oy, that's a keepsake from my dead mama! People, come to my aid, this is my trousseau, never e'en put on!"

I heard the children echoing them with screams, choking, coughing with screams. And I saw the looks of the men: frightened, pleading, hateful, dully impassive, extinguished with despair or flaring up with half-mad, daring ferocity.

"Take it. Take it away. Take everything away. There's still a pot of borscht on the stove. It's plain, got no meat. But still it's got beets, taters 'n' cabbage. And it's salted! Better take it, comrade citizens! Here, hang on, I'll take off my shoes. They're patched and re-patched, but maybe they'll have some use for the proletariat, for our dear Soviet power."

It was excruciating to see and hear all this. And even worse to take part in it. . . . And I persuaded myself, explained to myself. I mustn't give in to debilitating pity. We were realizing historical necessity. We were performing our revolutionary duty. We were obtaining grain for the socialist fatherland. For the five-year plan. . . .

I have always remembered the winter of the last grain collections, the weeks of the great famine. And I have always told about it. But I did not begin to write it down until many years later. . . .

How could all this have happened?

Who was guilty of the famine which destroyed millions of lives?

How could I have participated in it?. . .

We were raised as the fanatical [believers] of a new creed, the only true *religion* of scientific socialism. The party became our church militant, bequeathing to all mankind eternal salvation, eternal peace and the bliss of an earthly paradise. It victoriously surmounted all other churches, schisms and heresies. The works of Marx, Engels and Lenin were accepted as holy writ, and Stalin was the infallible high priest.

. . . Stalin was the most perspicacious, the most wise (at that time they hadn't yet started calling him "great" and "brilliant"). He said: "The struggle for grain is the struggle for socialism." And we believed him unconditionally. And later we believed that unconditional collectivization was unavoidable if we were to overcome the capriciousness and uncertainty of the market and the backwardness of individual farming, to guarantee a steady supply of grain, milk and meat to the cities. And also if we were to reeducate millions of peasants, those petty landowners and hence potential bourgeoisie, potential kulaks, to transform them into laborers with a social conscience, to liberate them from

"the idiocy of country life," from ignorance and prejudice, and to accustom them to culture, to all the boons of socialism. . . .

In the following passage Kopelev reflects, even more searchingly, on his own motivation and state of mind as a participant in Stalin's collectivization drive.

With the rest of my generation I firmly believed that the ends justified the means. Our great goal was the universal triumph of Communism, and for the sake of that goal everything was permissible—to lie, to steal, to destroy hundreds of thousands and even millions of people, all those who were hindering our work or could hinder it, everyone who stood in the way. And to hesitate or doubt about all this was to give in to "intellectual squeamishness" and "stupid liberalism," the attributes of people who "could not see the forest for the trees."

That was how I had reasoned, and everyone like me, even when I did have my doubts, when I saw what "total collectivization" meant—how . . . mercilessly they stripped the peasants in the winter of 1932–33. I took part in this myself, scouring the countryside, searching for hidden grain, testing the earth with an iron rod for loose spots that might lead to buried grain. With the others, I emptied out the old folks' storage chests, stopping my ears to the children's crying and the women's wails. For I was convinced that I was accomplishing the great and necessary transformation of the countryside; that in the days to come the people who lived there would be better off for it; that their distress and suffering were a result of their own ignorance or the machinations of the class enemy; that those who sent me—and I myself—knew better than the peasants how they should live, what they should sow and when they should plow.

In the terrible spring of 1933 I saw people dying from hunger. I saw women and children with distended bellies, turning blue, still breathing but with vacant, lifeless eyes. And corpses— corpses in ragged sheepskin coats and cheap felt boots; corpses in peasant huts, in the melting snow of old Vologda, under the bridges of Kharkov. . . . I saw all this and did not go out of my mind or commit suicide. Nor did I curse those who had sent me to take away the peasants' grain in the winter, and in the spring to persuade the barely walking, skeleton-thin or sickly-swollen people to go into the fields in order to "fulfill the Bolshevik sowing plan in shock-worker style."

Nor did I lose my faith. As before, I believed because I wanted to believe. Thus from time immemorial men have believed when possessed by a desire to serve powers and values above and beyond humanity: gods, emperors, states; ideals of virtue, freedom, nation, race, class, party. . . .

Any single-minded attempt to realize these ideals exacts its toll of human sacrifice. In the name of the noblest visions promising eternal happiness to their descendants, such men bring merciless ruin on their contemporaries. Bestowing paradise on the dead, they maim and destroy the living. They become unprincipled liars and unrelenting executioners, all the while seeing themselves as virtuous and honorable militants—convinced that if they are forced into villainy, it is for the sake of future good, and that if they have to lie, it is in the name of eternal truths. . . .

That was how we thought and acted—we, the fanatical disciples of the all-saving ideals of Communism. When we saw the base and cruel acts that were committed in the name of our exalted notions of good, and when we ourselves took part in those actions, what we feared most was to lose our heads, fall into doubt or heresy and forfeit our unbounded faith. . . . The concepts of conscience, honor, humaneness we dismissed as idealistic prejudices, "intellectual" or "bourgeois," and hence, perverse.

REVIEW QUESTIONS

1. How would you characterize the motivation of the young Lev Kopelev and his associates in carrying out the collectivization of agriculture?
2. How, in retrospect, did Kopelev explain his role in the collectivization drive?

3   Soviet Indoctrination

Pressed by the necessity to transform their country into a modern state, the communist leaders used every opportunity to force the population to adopt the attitudes and motivation necessary to effect such a transformation. Education, from nursery school to university, provided special opportunities to mold attitudes. The Soviet regime made impressive gains in promoting education among its diverse people; it also used education to foster dedication to hard work, disciplined social cooperation, and pride in the nation. For a backward country that, as Lenin had said, must "either perish or overtake and outstrip the advanced capitalist countries," such changes were considered essential, even though they were contrary to traditional Russian attitudes. To ensure their implementation, the Soviet regime employed terror and indoctrination.

During the Stalin era, artists and writers were compelled to promote the ideals of the Stalin revolution. In the style of "socialist realism," their heroes were factory workers and farmers who labored tirelessly and enthusiastically to build a new society. Even romance served a political purpose. Novelists wrote love stories following limited, prosaic themes. For example, a young girl might lose her heart to a co-worker who is a leader in the communist youth organization and who outproduces his comrades at his job; as the newly married couple is needed at the factory, they choose to forgo a honeymoon.

A. O. Avdienko
THE CULT OF STALIN

Among a people so deeply divided by ethnicity and petty localism and limited by a pervasive narrowness of perspective, building countrywide unity and consensus was a crucial challenge for the government. In the Russian past the worship of saints and the veneration of the tsar had served that purpose. The political mobilization of the masses during the revolution required an intensification of that tradition. It led to the "cult of personality," the deliberate fixation of individual dedication and loyalty on the all-powerful leader, whose personality exemplified the challenge of extraordinary times. The following selection, written in 1936, illustrates by what emotional bonds the individual was tied to Stalin, and through Stalin to the prodigious transformation of Russian state and society that he was attempting.

Thank you, Stalin. Thank you because I am joyful. Thank you because I am well. No matter how old I become, I shall never forget how we received Stalin two days ago. Centuries will pass, and the generations still to come will regard us as the happiest of mortals, as the most fortunate of men, because we lived in the century of centuries, because we were privileged to see Stalin, our inspired leader. Yes, and we regard ourselves as the happiest of mortals because we are the contemporaries of a man who never had an equal in world history.

The men of all ages will call on thy name, which is strong, beautiful, wise and marvellous. Thy name is engraven on every factory, every machine, every place on the earth, and in the hearts of all men.

Every time I have found myself in his presence I have been subjugated by his strength, his charm, his grandeur. I have experienced a great desire to sing, to cry out, to shout with joy and happiness. And now see me—me!—on the same platform where the Great Stalin stood a year ago. In what country, in what part of the world could such a thing happen.

I write books. I am an author. All thanks to thee, O great educator, Stalin. I love a young woman with a renewed love and shall perpetuate myself in my children—all thanks to thee, great educator, Stalin. I shall be eternally happy and joyous, all thanks to thee, great educator, Stalin. Everything belongs to thee, chief of our great country. And when the woman I love presents me with a child the first word it shall utter will be: Stalin.

O great Stalin, O leader of the peoples,
Thou who broughtest man to birth.
Thou who fructifiest the earth,
Thou who restorest the centuries,
Thou who makest bloom the spring,
Thou who makest vibrate the musical
    chords. . .
Thou, splendour of my spring, O Thou,
Sun reflected by millions of hearts. . .

Yevgeny Yevtushenko
LITERATURE AS PROPAGANDA

After Stalin's death in 1953, Soviet intellectuals breathed more freely, and they protested against the rigid Stalinist controls. In the following extract from his *Precocious Autobiography* (1963), Russian poet Yevgeny Yevtushenko (b. 1933) looks back to the raw days of intellectual repression under Stalin.

Blankly smiling workers and collective farmers looked out from the covers of books. Almost every novel and short story had a happy ending. Painters more and more often took as their subject state banquets, weddings, solemn public meetings, and parades.

The apotheosis of this trend was a movie which in its grand finale showed thousands of collective farmers having a gargantuan feast against the background of a new power station.

Recently I had a talk with its producer, a gifted and intelligent man.

"How could you produce such a film?" I asked. "It is true that I also once wrote verses in that vein, but I was still wet behind the ears, whereas you were adult and mature."

The producer smiled a sad smile. "You know, the strangest thing to me is that I was absolutely sincere. I thought all this was a necessary part of building communism. And then I believed Stalin."

So when we talk about "the cult of personality," we should not be too hasty in accusing all those who, one way or another, were involved in it, debasing themselves with their flattery. There were of course sycophants [servile flatterers] who used the situation for their own ends. But that many people connected with the arts sang Stalin's praises was often not vice but tragedy.

How was it possible for even gifted and intelligent people to be deceived?

To begin with, Stalin was a strong and vivid personality. When he wanted to, Stalin knew how to charm people. He charmed Gorky and Barbusse. In 1937, the cruelest year of the purges, he managed to charm that tough and experienced observer, Lion Feuchtwanger.[1]

In the second place, in the minds of the Soviet people, Stalin's name was indissolubly linked with Lenin's. Stalin knew how popular Lenin was and saw to it that history was rewritten in such a way as to make his own relations with Lenin seem much more friendly than they had been in fact. The rewriting was so thorough that perhaps Stalin himself believed his own version in the end.

There can be no doubt of Stalin's love for Lenin. His speech on Lenin's death, beginning with the words, "In leaving us, Comrade Lenin has bequeathed . . ." reads like a poem in prose. He wanted to stand as Lenin's heir not only in other people's eyes, but in his own eyes too. He deceived himself as well as the others. Even [Boris] Pasternak put the two names side by side:

> Laughter in the village,
> Voice behind the plow,
> Lenin and Stalin,
> And these verses now . . .

In reality, however, Stalin distorted Lenin's ideas, because to Lenin—and this was the whole meaning of his work—communism was to serve man, whereas under Stalin it appeared that man served communism.

Stalin's theory that people were the little cogwheels of communism was put into practice

---

[1]Gorky was a prominent Russian writer; Barbusse and Feuchtwanger were well-known western European writers.

and with horrifying results. . . . Russian poets, who had produced some fine works during the war, turned dull again. If a good poem did appear now and then, it was likely to be about the war—this was simpler to write about.

Poets visited factories and construction sites but wrote more about machines than about the men who made them work. If machines could read, they might have found such poems interesting. Human beings did not.

The size of a printing was not determined by demand but by the poet's official standing. As a result bookstores were cluttered up with books of poetry which no one wanted. . . . A simple, touching poem by the young poet Vanshenkin, about a boy's first love, caused almost a sensation against this background of industrial-agricultural verse. Vinokurov's first poems, handsomely disheveled among the general sleekness, were avidly seized upon—they had human warmth. But the general situation was unchanged. Poetry remained unpopular. The older poets were silent, and when they did break their silence, it was even worse. The generation of poets that had been spawned by the war and that had raised so many hopes had petered out. Life in peacetime turned out to be more complicated than life at the front. Two of the greatest Russian poets, Zabolotsky and Smelyakov, were in concentration camps. The young poet Mandel (Korzhavin) had been deported. I don't know if Mandel's name will be remembered in the history of Russian poets but it will certainly be remembered in the history of Russian social thought.

He was the only poet who openly wrote and recited verses against Stalin while Stalin was alive. That he recited them seems to be what saved his life, for the authorities evidently thought him insane. In one poem he wrote of Stalin:

There in Moscow, in whirling darkness,
Wrapped in his military coat,
Not understanding Pasternak,
A hard and cruel man stared at the snow.

. . . Now that ten years have gone by, I realize that Stalin's greatest crime was not the arrests and the shootings he ordered. His greatest crime was the corruption of the human spirit.

REVIEW QUESTIONS

1. In light of the A. O. Avdienko reading, how would you say communists were supposed to feel about Stalin?
2. What were Yevgeny Yevtushenko's reasons for denouncing Stalin?
3. What do you think Yevtushenko meant by the "corruption of the human spirit" under Stalin?

4 Stalin's Terror

The victims of Stalin's terror number in the many millions. Stalin had no qualms about sacrificing multitudes of people to build up the Soviet Union's strength and to make it a powerful factor in world politics. In addition, he felt entitled to settle his own private scores as well as national ones against secessionist Ukrainians. The Soviet government's first acknowledgment of Stalin's terror was made by Khrushchev.

Nikita S. Khrushchev
KHRUSHCHEV'S SECRET SPEECH

Nikita Khrushchev (1894–1971), first secretary of the Communist party (1953–1964) and premier of the Soviet Union (1958–1964), delivered a famous speech to an unofficial, closed session of the twentieth Party Congress on February 25, 1956. Although the speech was considered confidential, it was soon leaked to outsiders. While safeguarding the moral authority of Lenin, Khrushchev attacked Stalin, who had died three years earlier, revealing some of the crimes committed by him and his closest associates in the 1930s. The following passages from the speech draw on evidence collected by a special commission of inquiry.

We have to consider seriously and analyze correctly this matter [the crimes of the Stalin era] in order that we may preclude any possibility of a repetition in any form whatever of what took place during the life of Stalin, who absolutely did not tolerate collegiality in leadership and in work, and who practiced brutal violence, not only toward everything which opposed him, but also toward that which seemed to his capricious and despotic character, contrary to his concepts.

Stalin acted not through persuasion, explanation, and patient co-operation with people, but by imposing his concepts and demanding absolute submission to his opinion. Whoever opposed this concept or tried to prove his viewpoint, and the correctness of his position, was doomed to removal from the leading collective and to subsequent moral and physical annihilation. This was especially true during the period following the XVIIth Party Congress [1934], when many prominent Party leaders and rank-and-file Party workers, honest and dedicated to the cause of Communism, fell victim to Stalin's despotism. . . .

Stalin originated the concept "enemy of the people." This term automatically rendered it unnecessary that the ideological errors of a man or men engaged in a controversy be proven; this term made possible the usage of the most cruel repression, violating all norms of revolutionary legality, against anyone who in any way disagreed with Stalin, against those who were only suspected of hostile intent, against those who had bad reputations. This concept, "enemy of the people," actually eliminated the possibility of any kind of ideological fight or the making of one's views known on this or that issue, even those of a practical character. In the main, and in actuality, the only proof of guilt used, against all norms of current legal science, was the "confession" of the accused himself; and, as subsequent probing proved, "confessions" were acquired through physical pressures against the accused.

This led to glaring violations of revolutionary legality, and to the fact that many entirely innocent persons, who in the past had defended the Party line, became victims. . . .

The Commission [of Inquiry] has become acquainted with a large quantity of materials in the NKVD [secret police, forerunner to the KGB] archives and with other documents and has established many facts pertaining to the fabrication of cases against Communists, to false accusations, to glaring abuses of socialist legality—which resulted in the death of innocent people. It became apparent that many Party, Soviet and economic activists who were branded in 1937–1938 as "enemies" were actually never enemies, spies, wreckers, etc., but were always honest Communists; they were only so stigmatized, and often, no longer able to bear barbaric tortures, they charged themselves (at the order of the investigative judges—falsifiers) with all kinds of grave and unlikely crimes. . . .

Lenin used severe methods only in the most necessary cases, when the exploiting classes were still in existence and were vigorously opposing the revolution, when the struggle for survival was decidedly assuming the sharpest forms, even including a civil war.

Stalin, on the other hand, used extreme methods and mass repressions at a time when the revolution was already victorious, when the Soviet state was strengthened, when the exploiting classes were already liquidated and Socialist relations were rooted solidly in all phases of national economy, when our Party was politically consolidated and had strengthened itself both numerically and ideologically. It is clear that here Stalin showed in a whole series of cases his intolerance, his brutality and his abuse of power. Instead of proving his political correctness and mobilizing the masses, he often chose the path of repression and physical annihilation, not only against actual enemies, but also against individuals who had not committed any crimes against the Party and the Soviet government. . . .

An example of vile provocation, of odious falsification and of criminal violation of revolutionary legality is the case of the former candidate for the Central Committee Political Bureau, one of the most eminent workers of the Party and of the Soviet government, Comrade Eikhe, who was a Party member since 1905. *(Commotion in the hall.)*

Comrade Eikhe was arrested on April 29, 1938, on the basis of slanderous materials, without the sanction of the Prosecutor of the USSR, which was finally received 15 months after the arrest.

Investigation of Eikhe's case was made in a manner which most brutally violated Soviet legality and was accompanied by willfulness and falsification.

Eikhe was forced under torture to sign ahead of time a protocol of his confession prepared by the investigative judges, in which he and several other eminent Party workers were accused of anti-Soviet activity.

On October 1, 1939, Eikhe sent his declaration to Stalin in which he categorically denied his guilt and asked for an examination of his case. In the declaration he wrote: "There is no more bitter misery than to sit in the jail of a government for which I have always fought."

A second declaration of Eikhe has been preserved which he sent to Stalin on October 27, 1939; in it he cited facts very convincingly and countered the slanderous accusations made against him, arguing that his provocatory accusation was on the one hand the work of real Trotskyites [supporters of Leon Trotsky killed in Mexico on Stalin's orders] whose arrests he had sanctioned as First Secretary of the West Siberian Krai [local] Party Committee and who conspired in order to take revenge on him, and, on the other hand, the result of the base falsification of materials by the investigative judges. . . .

It would appear that such an important declaration was worth an examination by the Central Committee. This, however, was not done and the declaration was transmitted to Beria [head of the NKVD] while the terrible maltreatment of the Political Bureau candidate, Comrade Eikhe, continued.

On February 2, 1940, Eikhe was brought before the court. Here he did not confess any guilt and said as follows:

> In all the so-called confessions of mine there is not one letter written by me with the exception of my signatures under the protocols which were forced from me. I have made my confession under pressure from the investigative judge who from the time of my arrest tormented me. After that I began to write all this nonsense. . . . The most important thing for me is to tell the court, the Party and Stalin that I am not guilty. I have never been guilty of any conspiracy. I will die believing in the truth of Party policy as I have believed in it during my whole life.

On February 4 Eikhe was shot. *(Indignation in the hall.)*

Lev Razgon
TRUE STORIES

"Corrective labor" was part of Stalin's efforts to terrorize the peoples of the Soviet Union into compliance with his plan to modernize the country's economy and society. All those accused of disloyalty to the party and not killed outright ended up in one of the *gulags. Gulag* is the Russian term for the Soviet forced-labor camps, scattered, like islands in an archipelago, over the entire Soviet Union. The inhabitants of that archipelago were the *zeks,* as the political prisoners were called. Their labor served a double purpose. It was designed as punishment for their alleged crimes and as a means of obtaining vital raw materials—including lumber and minerals—from areas too inhospitable for, or outright hostile to, regular labor. Forced labor also built the canal linking the Leningrad area with the White Sea in the far north.

In 1988, Lev Razgon, a survivor of Stalin's camps, published an account of his experiences, which appeared in English under the title *True Stories* in 1997. Razgon was a journalist who married the daughter of a high-ranking member of the Soviet secret police. Gaining access to the Soviet elite, in 1934 he attended the Seventeenth Party Congress. In 1937, his father-in-law was arrested for "counter-revolutionary" activities, along with many family friends; the following year the police came for Razgon and his wife. She perished in a transit prison en route to a northern camp, and Razgon spent the next seven years in a labor camp. Released in 1945, he was confined to various provincial towns, but in 1949 was rearrested and returned to the camps. Finally, he was released again in 1956 after Stalin's death.

Over the years Razgon began to write down his prison experiences for his desk drawer, with the specific intent of preserving the memory of fellow prisoners who did not survive. As the Soviet Union began to crumble, Razgon was able to publish his stories. The following extracts from *True Stories* reveal the brutality and irrationality of the Soviet prison system under Stalin. In the first selection, Razgon reproduces a discussion he had with a former prison guard, whom he met by chance in a hospital ward in 1977. The guard described to Razgon his role as an executioner of political prisoners.

THE ROUTINE OF EXECUTION

"It was like this. In the morning we'd hand everything over to the new shift and go into the guardhouse. We'd collect our weapons, and then and there they'd give us each a shot glass of vodka. After that we'd take the list and go round with the senior warder to pick them up from the cells and take them out to the truck."

"What kind of truck?"

"A closed van. Six of them and four of us in each one."

"How many trucks would leave at the same time?"

"Three or four."

"Did they know where they were going? Did someone read them their death sentence before, or what?"

"No, no sentences were announced. No one even spoke, just, 'Come out, then straight ahead, into the van—fast!'"

"Were they in handcuffs?"

"No, we didn't have any."

"How did they behave, once they were in the van?"

"The men, well, they kept quiet. But the women would start crying, they'd say: 'What are you doing, we're not guilty of anything, comrades, what are you doing?' and things like that."

"They used to take men and women together?"

"No, always separately."

"Were the women young? Were there a lot of them?"

"Not so many, about two vanloads a week. No very young ones but there were some about twenty-five or thirty. Most were older, and some even elderly."

"Did you drive them far?"

"Twelve kilometers or so, to the hill. The Distant Hill, it was called. There were hills all around and that's where we unloaded them."

"So you would unload them, and then tell them their sentence?"

"What was there to tell them?! No, we yelled, 'Out! Stand still!' They scrambled down and there was already a trench dug in front of them. They clambered down, clung together and right away we got to work. . . ."

"They didn't make any noise?"

"Some didn't, others began shouting, 'We're Communists, we are being wrongly executed,' that type of thing. But the women would only cry and cling to each other. So we just got on with it. . . ."

"Did you have a doctor with you?"

"What for? We would shoot them, and those still wriggling got another bullet and then we were off back to the van. The work team from the Dalag camps was already nearby, waiting."

"What work team was that?"

"There was a team of criminal inmates from Dalag who lived in a separate compound. They were the trusties[1] at Bikin and they also had to dig and fill in the pits. As soon as we left they would fill in that pit and dig a new one for the next day. When they finished their work, they went back to the compound. They got time off their sentence for it and were well fed. It was easy work, not like felling timber."

"And what about you?"

"We would arrive back at the camp, hand in our weapons at the guardhouse and then we could have as much to drink as we wanted. The others used to lap it up—it didn't cost them a kopeck. I always had my shot, went off to the canteen for a hot meal, and then back to sleep in the barracks."

"And did you sleep well? Didn't you feel bad or anything?"

"Why should I?"

"Well, that you had just killed other people. Didn't you feel sorry for them?"

"No, not at all. I didn't give it a thought. No, I slept well and then I'd go for a walk outside the camp. There's some beautiful places around there. Boring, though, with no women."

"Were any of you married?"

"No, they didn't take married men. Of course, the bosses made out all right. There were some real lookers on the Dalag work team! Your head would spin! Cooks, dishwashers, floor cleaners—the bosses had them all. We went without. It was better not to even think about it. . . ."

"Grigory Ivanovich, did you know that the people you were shooting were not guilty at all, that they hadn't done anything wrong?"

"Well, we didn't think about that then. Later, yes. We were summoned to the procurators [officials] and they asked us questions. They explained that those had been innocent people. There had been mistakes, they said, and—what was the word?—excesses. But they told us that it was nothing to do with us, we were not guilty of anything."

---

[1]Trusties were convicts regarded as trustworthy, who were given special duties and privileges.

"Well, I understand, then you were under orders and you shot people. But when you learned that you had been killing men and women who were not guilty at all, didn't your conscience begin to bother you?"

"Conscience? No, Naum'ich, it didn't bother me. I never think about all that now, and when I do remember something . . . no, nothing at all, as if nothing had happened. You know, I've become so soft-hearted that one look at an old man suffering today and I feel so much pity that I even cry sometimes. But those ones, no, I'm not sorry for them. Not at all, it's just like they never existed. . . ."

The "special operation" at Bikin existed for almost three years. Well, two and a half, to be more exact. It also probably had its holidays and weekends—perhaps no one was shot on Sundays, May Day, Revolution Day and the Day of the Soviet Constitution. Even so, that means that it functioned for a total of 770 days. Every morning on each of those days four trucks set out from Bikin compound for the Distant Hill. Six people in each truck, a total of 24. It took 25–30 minutes for them to reach the waiting pit. The "special operation" thus disposed of 15,000 to 18,000 people during its existence. Yet it was of a standard design, just like any transit camp. The well-tried, well-planned machinery operated without interruption, functioning regularly and efficiently, filling the ready-made pits with bodies—in the hills of the Far East, in the Siberian forests, and in the glades of the Tambov woods or the Meshchera nature reserve. They existed everywhere, yet nothing remains of them now. There are no terrible museums as there are today at Auschwitz, or at Mauthausen in Austria. There are no solemn and funereal memorials like those that testify to the Nazi atrocities at Khatyn* . . . or

Lidice.[2] Thousands of unnamed graves, in which there lie mingled the bones of hundreds of thousands of victims, have now been overgrown by bushes, thick luxuriant grass and young new forest. Not exactly the same as the Germans, it must be admitted. The men and women were buried separately here. Our regime made sure that even at that point no moral laxity might occur.

And the murderers? They are still alive.

. . . There were a great many, of course, who took part in these shootings. There were yet more, however, who never made the regular journey to the Distant Hill or the other killing grounds. Only in bourgeois society are the procurator and others obliged to attend an execution. Under our regime, thank God, that was not necessary. There were many, many more involved in these murders than those who simply pulled the trigger. For them a university degree, often in the "humanities," was more common than the rudimentary education of the Niyazovs [the former guard Razgon questioned]. They drafted the instructions and decisions; they signed beneath the words "agreed," "confirmed," "to be sentenced to . . ." Today they are all retired and most of them receive large individual pensions. They sit in the squares and enjoy watching the children play. They go to concerts and are moved by the music. We meet them when we attend a meeting, visit friends, or find ourselves sitting at the same table, celebrating with our common acquaintances. They are alive, and there are many of them.

COLLECTIVE GUILT

In the most general terms, paragraph 17 [of the Soviet criminal code] said that each member of a criminal group (and membership in that

---

*In 1942 German forces massacred all the inhabitants of the Belorussian village of Khatyn. (Not to be confused with Katyn . . . where in 1940 23,500 Polish officers were murdered by the [Soviet] NKVD.)

[2]After Czech resistance fighters assassinated Richard Heydrich, Chief of the Security Police, the Germans took savage revenge on the little Czech village of Lidice. They massacred all the men and deported the women and children to concentration camps (some children with suitable "Aryan features" were sent to live with German families and to be reared as Germans). The Nazis then burned, dynamited, and leveled the village.

group was expressed by knowledge of its existence and failure to report it) was responsible not only for his own individual criminal deeds but also for the deeds of the criminal group as a whole and for each of its individual members, taken separately. It did not matter that the individual in question might not know the other members of the group, might be unaware what they were up to, and might not have any idea at all what the group he belonged to was doing. The purpose of the "doctrine of complicity" was to alleviate the exhausting labors of the interrogators. Undoubtedly, however, it also lightened the burden of those under investigation. The techniques of cross-examination became far simpler. Several dozen people were linked together in a group and then one of them, the weakest, was beaten almost to death in order to obtain confessions of espionage, sabotage, subversion and, of course, attempts on the life of "one of the leaders of the Party and the government." The others could be more gently treated, only requiring beating until they admitted they knew the individual who had given a "complete and full confession." Then the same crimes, in accordance with paragraph 17, were automatically attributed to them as well. What this sounded like during a court hearing I can describe from the words of a man I came to know in the camps.

Yefim Shatalov was a very high-ranking manager and for years he headed the State Cement Administration. Why they needed to send him to prison, God only knows! He had no political interests or involvements and did not wish to have any, since he was always prepared to serve his immediate superior faithfully and truthfully, and was unquestionably loyal to his ultimate chief, Comrade Stalin. Furthermore, he was incredibly circumspect and every step he took was protected by an entire system of safety measures. When he was baldly accused of sabotage he conducted himself so aggressively in court that the judge, in panic, deferred the hearing of his case. Some time after, Shatalov was presented with a new charge sheet and within an hour he was summoned to appear before a new sitting of

the Military Tribunal. The chairman now was Ulrich himself. For the defendant Vasya Ulrich was an old, dear and kind acquaintance. For many years they had always sat at the same table at the Party elite's sanatorium, The Pines; they went for walks together, shared a drink or two, and exchanged men's jokes. Evidently the chairman was observing the old principles that justice must be rapid, fair and clement in his conduct of this hearing. What follows includes almost everything that was said, as recalled by Yefim Shatalov.

ULRICH (in a business-like, quiet, and jaded voice): Defendant! you have read the charge sheet? Do you recognize your guilt?

SHATALOV (with all the force of his love and loyalty to the judge): No! I am not guilty in any respect!

ULRICH: Did you know that there was a counter-revolutionary Right-Trotskyist organization in the People's Commissariat of Heavy Industry?

SHATALOV (throwing up his arms): I had no idea whatsoever. I had no suspicion there was such a hostile gang of saboteurs and terrorists there.

ULRICH (gazing with affectionate attention at his former drinking companion): You were not in prison during the last trial of the Right-Trotskyist center, were you?

SHATALOV: No, I was not.

ULRICH: You were reading the newspapers then?

SHATALOV (slowly, trying to grasp the purpose of such a strange question): I did. . . .

ULRICH: So you read Pyatakov's testimony that there was a counter-revolutionary organization in the People's Commissariat of Heavy Industry?

SHATALOV (uncertainly): Of course, of course.

ULRICH (triumphantly): Well, there we are! So you knew there was a counter-revolutionary organization in the People's Commissariat of Heavy Industry. (Turning to the secretary of the court.) Write down: the defendant acknowledges that he knew about the existence of Pyatakov's organization. . . .

SHATALOV (shouts passionately, stuttering from horror): But it was from the newspapers, the newspapers, that I learnt there was an organization there!

ULRICH (calm and satisfied): But to the court it is not important where you found out. You knew! (Hurriedly, like a priest at a poorly-paid funeral.) Any questions? No. You want to say a last word? No need for repetition, we've heard it already! (Nodding right and left at his assessors.) I pronounce sentence. Mmmh . . . 15 years. . . .

I shall not insist that this trial strictly met the requirement for fairness. Yet compared to others it was clement, leaving Shatalov among the living. And it was indisputably rapid. Evidently the speed was typical. In the late 1950s I attended a memorial evening at the Museum of the Revolution for Kosarev, the 1930s Kommsomol leader executed by Stalin. The head of the Central Committee administrative department told me that Khrushchev had entrusted him to re-examine Kosarev's case: "The hearing began at 11.00 a.m.," read the record of the trial, "and ended at 11.10 a.m."

THE HEARTLESS BUREAUCRACY

Auntie Pasha, a kindly middle-aged woman, washed the floors in the camp office. She pitied the office workers because they were so helpless and impractical: and she darned and sewed patches on the trousers and quilt jackets of the "trusties" who were not yet privileged to wear first-hand clothing. The story of her life was simple. Auntie Pasha came from Zlatoust in the Urals. Her husband, a furnace man, died during an accident at work and she was left with two teenage sons. Their life was predictably hard. Someone taught Auntie Pasha to go to Chelyabinsk to buy stockings and then sell them (naturally, at a suitably higher price) in Zlatoust where they were not to be found. The rest was recorded in the charge sheet and the sentence passed by the court. "For the purposes of speculation" she had "obtained 72 pairs of knitted stockings in Chelyabinsk which she

then tried to resell at the market in Zlatoust." Auntie Pasha was reported, arrested, tried and sentenced to seven years imprisonment with confiscation of all her property. The children were taken in by acquaintances and, besides, they were almost old enough to take up any profession at the trade school. Five years passed, the war began, and Auntie Pasha's boys had reached the age when they could defend the Motherland. So off they went to fight. First Auntie Pasha was informed that her younger son had been killed. Staying behind in the office at night to wash the floors, she moaned and beat her head against the table.

Then one evening she came up to me with a glassy-eyed expression and handed over a thick package which she had been given in Records and Distribution. This contained several medical reports and the decisions of various commissions. To these was added a letter to Auntie Pasha from the hospital administrator. It concerned her elder son. He had been severely wounded and was in the hospital. The doctors had done all within their power and he was, as they put it in his medical history, "fit, to all intents and purposes"—apart, that is, from having lost both arms and one leg. He could be discharged from the hospital if there was some close relation to look after him. Evidently the son had explained where she was because the administrator advised the mother of this wounded soldier to send an appeal to the USSR Procurator General's Office, including the enclosed documents, after which they would release her and she could come and fetch him.

"Manuilich, dear heart," Auntie Pasha said, starting to cry, "You write for me."

So I wrote, and very persuasively. I attached all the documents and handed in the letter. Two or three months passed, and each day I reassured Auntie Pasha: they received a great many such appeals, I told her, and it would take time to process her release. I described in detail the lengthy procedures as her application passed from one level to another. Auntie Pasha wept, but believed me and each day I gave her paper on which to write her son a letter.

One day I went into Records and Distribution myself. A great pile of mail lay on the table, already sorted out to be handed over, or its contents communicated, to the prisoners. Auntie Pasha's surname caught my eye. I picked up the flimsy sheet of headed paper from the USSR Procurator General's Office and read it through. A public procurator of a certain rank or class informed Auntie Pasha that her application had been examined and her request for early release turned down because there were "no grounds." I carefully placed the single sheet on the table and went out onto the verandah, terrified that I might suddenly meet Auntie Pasha. . . . Everywhere, in the barracks and in the office, there were people I did not want to see. I ran to the latrines and there, clinging to the stinking walls, started to shake uncontrollably. Only two times in my prison life did this happen. Why was I crying? Then I understood: I felt ashamed, terribly ashamed, before Auntie Pasha.

She had already served five years for 72 pairs of stockings. She had given the state her two sons. Now, there it was, there were "no grounds.". . .

REVIEW QUESTIONS

1. Why was Nikita Khrushchev careful to distinguish Stalin from Lenin?
2. What charges against Stalin did Khrushchev highlight in his speech?
3. What image of Stalin did Khrushchev draw?
4. From a reading of these passages from Lev Razgon's book, what do you think motivated the behavior of Stalin's bureaucrats who committed these terrible crimes?

5 The Rise of Italian Fascism

Benito Mussolini (1883–1945) started his political life as a socialist and in 1912 was appointed editor of *Avanti,* the leading socialist newspaper. During World War I, Mussolini was expelled from the Socialist party for advocating Italy's entry into the conflict. Immediately after the war, he organized the Fascist party. Exploiting labor unrest, fear of communism, and thwarted nationalist hopes, Mussolini gained followers among veterans and the middle class. Powerful industrialists and landowners, viewing the Fascists as a bulwark against communism, helped to finance the young movement. An opportunist, Mussolini organized a march on Rome in 1922 to bring down the government. King Victor Emmanuel, fearful of civil war, appointed the Fascist leader prime minister. Had Italian liberals and the king taken a firm stand, the government could have crushed the 20,000 lightly armed marchers.

Benito Mussolini
FASCIST DOCTRINES

Ten years after he seized power, Mussolini, assisted by philosopher Giovanni Gentile (1875–1944), contributed an article to the *Italian Encyclopedia* in which he discussed fascist political and social doctrines. In this piece, Mussolini lauded

violence as a positive experience; attacked Marxism for denying idealism by subjecting human beings to economic laws and for dividing the nation into warring
classes; and denounced liberal democracy for promoting individual selfishness
at the expense of the national community and for being unable to solve the nation's problems. The fascist state, he said, required unity and power, not individual freedom. The following excerpts are from Mussolini's article.

. . . Above all, Fascism, the more it considers and observes the future and the development of humanity quite apart from political considerations of the moment, believes neither in the possibility nor the utility of perpetual peace. It thus repudiates the doctrine of Pacifism—born of a renunciation of the struggle and an act of cowardice in the face of sacrifice. War alone brings up to its highest tension all human energy and puts the stamp of nobility upon the peoples who have the courage to meet it. All other trials are substitutes, which never really put men into the position where they have to make the great decision—the alternative of life or death. Thus a doctrine which is founded upon this harmful postulate of peace is hostile to Fascism. And thus hostile to the spirit of Fascism, though accepted for what use they can be in dealing with particular political situations, are all the inter-national leagues and societies which, as history will show, can be scattered to the winds when once strong national feeling is aroused by any motive—sentimental, ideal, or practical. This anti-pacifist spirit is carried by Fascism even into the life of the individual; the proud motto of the *Squadrista* [early Fascist paramilitary units], "Me ne frego" [It doesn't matter], writ-ten on the bandage of the wound, is an act of philosophy not only stoic, the summary of a doctrine not only political—it is the education to combat, the acceptation of the risks which combat implies, and a new way of life for Italy. Thus the Fascist accepts life and loves it, know-ing nothing of and despising suicide: he rather conceives of life as duty and struggle and con-quest, life which should be high and full, lived for oneself, but above all for others—those who are at hand and those who are far distant, con-temporaries, and those who will come after. . . .

. . . Fascism [is] the complete opposite of . . . Marxian Socialism, the materialist conception of history; according to which the history of human civilization can be explained simply through the conflict of interests among the var-ious social groups and by the change and devel-opment in the means and instruments of production. That the changes in the economic field—new discoveries of raw materials, new methods of working them, and the inventions of science—have their importance no one can deny; but that these factors are sufficient to ex-plain the history of humanity excluding all oth-ers is an absurd delusion. Fascism, now and always, believes in holiness and in heroism; that is to say, in actions influenced by no economic motive, direct or indirect. And if the economic conception of history be denied, according to which theory men are no more than puppets, carried to and fro by the waves of chance, while the real directing forces are quite out of their control, it follows that the existence of an un-changeable and unchanging class-war is also denied—the natural progeny of the economic conception of history. And above all Fascism denies that class-war can be the preponderant force in the transformation of society. . . .

After Socialism, Fascism combats the whole complex system of democratic ideology, and repudiates it, whether in its theoretical prem-ises or in its practical application. Fascism de-nies that the majority, by the simple fact that it is a majority, can direct human society; it de-nies that numbers alone can govern by means of a periodical consultation, and it affirms the immutable, beneficial, and fruitful inequality of mankind, which can never be permanently leveled through the mere operation of a me-chanical process such as universal suffrage. . . .

. . . Fascism denies, in democracy, the absurd conventional untruth of political equality dressed out in the garb of collective irresponsibility, and the myth of "happiness" and indefinite progress. . . .

. . . Given that the nineteenth century was the century of Socialism, of Liberalism, and of Democracy, it does not necessarily follow that the twentieth century must also be a century of Socialism, Liberalism, and Democracy: political doctrines pass, but humanity remains; and it may rather be expected that this will be a century of authority, . . . a century of Fascism. For if the nineteenth century was a century of individualism (Liberalism always signifying individualism) it may be expected that this will be the century of collectivism, and hence the century of the State. . . .

The foundation of Fascism is the conception of the State, its character, its duty, and its aim. Fascism conceives of the State as an absolute, in comparison with which all individuals or groups are relative, only to be conceived of in their relation to the State. The conception of the Liberal State is not that of a directing force, guiding the play and development, both material and spiritual, of a collective body, but merely a force limited to the function of recording results: on the other hand, the Fascist State is itself conscious and has itself a will and a personality—thus it may be called the "ethic" State. . . .

. . . The Fascist State organizes the nation, but leaves a sufficient margin of liberty to the individual; the latter is deprived of all useless and possibly harmful freedom, but retains what is essential; the deciding power in this question cannot be the individual, but the State alone. . . .

. . . For Fascism, the growth of empire, that is to say the expansion of the nation, is an essential manifestation of vitality, and its opposite a sign of decadence. Peoples which are rising, or rising again after a period of decadence, are always imperialist; any renunciation is a sign of decay and of death. Fascism is the doctrine best adapted to represent the tendencies and the aspirations of a people, like the people of Italy, who are rising again after many centuries of abasement and foreign servitude. But empire demands discipline, the coordination of all forces and a deeply felt sense of duty and sacrifice: this fact explains many aspects of the practical working of the régime, the character of many forces in the State, and the necessarily severe measures which must be taken against those who would oppose this spontaneous and inevitable movement of Italy in the twentieth century, and would oppose it by recalling the outworn ideology of the nineteenth century—repudiated wheresoever there has been the courage to undertake great experiments of social and political transformation; for never before has the nation stood more in need of authority, of direction, and of order. If every age has its own characteristic doctrine, there are a thousand signs which point to Fascism as the characteristic doctrine of our time. For if a doctrine must be a living thing, this is proved by the fact that Fascism has created a living faith; and that this faith is very powerful in the minds of men is demonstrated by those who have suffered and died for it.

REVIEW QUESTIONS

1. Why did Benito Mussolini consider pacifism to be the enemy of fascism?
2. Why did Mussolini attack Marxism?
3. How did Mussolini view majority rule and equality?
4. What relationship did Mussolini see between the individual and the state?

6 The Rise of Nazism

Many extreme racist-nationalist and paramilitary organizations sprang up in postwar Germany. Adolf Hitler (1889–1945), a veteran of World War I, joined one of these organizations, which became known as the National Socialist German Worker's Party (commonly called the Nazi Party). Hitler's uncanny insight into the state of mind of postwar Germans, along with his extraordinary oratorical gifts, enabled him to gain control of the party. Had it not been for the Great Depression that began in late 1929, the National Socialists might have remained a relatively small and insignificant party, a minor irritant outside the mainstream of German politics. In 1928 the Nazis had 810,000 votes; in 1930, during the Depression, their share of votes soared to 6,400,000. To many Germans, the Depression was final evidence that the Weimar Republic had failed.

Adolf Hitler
MEIN KAMPF

In the "Beer Hall Putsch" of November 1923, Hitler attempted to overthrow the state government in Bavaria as the first step in bringing down the Weimar Republic. But the Nazis quickly scattered when the Bavarian police opened fire. Hitler was arrested and sentenced to five years' imprisonment—he served only nine months. While in prison, Hitler wrote *Mein Kampf (My Struggle)* (1925–1926), in which he presented his views. The book came to be regarded as an authoritative expression of the Nazi world-view and served as a kind of sacred writing for the Nazi movement.

Hitler's thought—a patchwork of nineteenth-century anti-Semitic, Volkish, Social Darwinist, and anti-Marxist ideas—contrasted sharply with the core values of both the Judeo-Christian and the Enlightenment traditions. Central to Hitler's world-view was racial mythology: a heroic Germanic race that was descended from the ancient Aryans, who once swept across Europe, and was battling for survival against racial inferiors. In the following passages excerpted from *Mein Kampf,* Hitler presents his views of race, of propaganda, and of the National Socialist territorial goals.

THE PRIMACY OF RACE

Nature does not want a pairing of weaker individuals with stronger ones; it wants even less a mating of a higher race with a weaker one. Otherwise its routine labors of promoting a higher breed lasting perhaps over hundreds of thousands of years would be wiped out.

History offers much evidence for this process. It proves with terrifying clarity that any genetic mixture of Aryan blood with people of a lower quality undermines the culturally superior people. The population of North America consists to a large extent of Germanic elements, which have mixed very little with inferior people of color. Central and South America shows a different humanity and culture; here Latin immigrants mixed with the aborigines, sometimes on a large scale. This example alone allows a clear recognition of the effects of racial mixtures. Remaining racially pure the Germans of North America rose to be masters of their continent; they will remain masters as long as they do not defile their blood.

The result of mixing races in short is: a) lowering the cultural level of the higher race; b) physical and spiritual retrogression and thus the beginning of a slow but progressive decline.

To promote such a development means no less than committing sin against the will of the eternal creator. . . .

Everything that we admire on earth—science, technology, invention—is the creative product of only a few people, and perhaps originally of only *one* race; our whole culture depends upon them. If they perish, the beauties of the earth will be buried. . . .

All great cultures of the past perished because the original creative race was destroyed by the poisoning of its blood.

Such collapse always happened because people forgot that all cultures depend on human beings. In order to preserve a given culture it is necessary to preserve the human beings who created it. Cultural preservation in this world is tied to the iron law of necessity and the right to victory of the stronger and better. . . .

If we divide humanity into three categories: into founders of culture, bearers of culture, and destroyers of culture, the Aryan would undoubtedly rate first. He established the foundations and walls of all human progress. . . .

The mixing of blood and the resulting lowering of racial cohesion is the sole reason why cultures perish. People do not perish by defeat in war, but by losing the power of resistance inherent in pure blood.

All that is not pure race in this world is chaff. . . .

A state which in the age of racial poisoning dedicates itself to the cultivation of its best racial elements will one day become master of the world.

Modern anti-Semitism was a powerful legacy of the Middle Ages and the unsettling changes brought about by rapid industrialization; it was linked to racist doctrines that asserted the Jews were inherently wicked and bore dangerous racial qualities. Hitler grasped the political potential of anti-Semitism: by concentrating all evil in one enemy, he could provide non-Jews with an emotionally satisfying explanation for all their misfortunes and thus manipulate and unify the German people.

ANTI-SEMITISM

The Jew offers the most powerful contrast to the Aryan. . . . Despite all their seemingly intellectual qualities the Jewish people are without true culture, and especially without a culture of their own. What Jews seem to possess as culture is the property of others, for the most part corrupted in their hands.

In judging the Jewish position in regard to human culture, we have to keep in mind their essential characteristics. There never was—and still is no—Jewish art. The Jewish people made no original contribution to the two queen goddesses of all arts: architecture and music. What they have contributed is patchwork or spiritual theft. Which proves that Jews lack the very qualities distinguishing creative and culturally blessed races. . . .

The first and biggest lie of Jews is that Jewishness is not a matter of race but of religion, from which inevitably follow even more lies. One of them refers to the language of Jews. It is not a means of expressing their thoughts, but of hiding them. While speaking French a Jew thinks Jewish, and while he cobbles together some German verse, he merely expresses the mentality of his people.

As long as the Jew is not master of other peoples, he must for better or worse speak their languages. Yet as soon as the others have become his servants, then all should learn a universal language (Esperanto for instance), so that by these means the Jews can rule more easily. . . .

For hours the blackhaired Jewish boy lies in wait, with satanic joy on his face, for the unsuspecting girl whom he disgraces with his blood and thereby robs her from her people. He tries by all means possible to destroy the racial foundations of the people he wants to subjugate.

But a people of pure race conscious of its blood can never be enslaved by the Jew; he remains forever a ruler of bastards.

Thus he systematically attempts to lower racial purity by racially poisoning individuals.

In politics he begins to replace the idea of democracy with the idea of the dictatorship of the proletariat.

He found his weapon in the organized Marxist masses, which avoid democracy and instead help him to subjugate and govern people dictatorially with his brutal fists.

Systematically he works toward a double revolution, in economics and politics.

With the help of his international contacts he enmeshes people who effectively resist his attacks from within in a net of external enemies whom he incites to war, and, if necessary, goes on to unfurling the red flag of revolution over the battlefield.

He batters the national economies until the ruined state enterprises are privatized and subject to his financial control.

In politics he refuses to give the state the means for its self-preservation, destroys the bases of any national self-determination and defense, wipes out the faith in leadership, denigrates the historic past, and pulls everything truly great into the gutter.

In cultural affairs he pollutes art, literature, theatre, befuddles national sentiment, subverts all concepts of beauty and grandeur, of nobleness and goodness, and reduces people to their lowest nature.

Religion is made ridiculous, custom and morals are declared outdated, until the last props of national character in the battle for survival have collapsed. . . .

Thus the Jew is the big rabble-rouser for the complete destruction of Germany. Wherever in the world we read about attacks on Germany, Jews are the source, just as in peace and during the war the newspapers of both the Jewish stock market and the Marxists systematically incited hatred against Germany. Country after country gave up its neutrality and joined the world war coalition in disregard of the true interest of the people.

Jewish thinking in all this is clear. The Bolshevization of Germany, i.e., the destruction of the German national people-oriented intelligentsia and thereby the exploitation of German labor under the yoke of Jewish global finance are but the prelude for the expansion of the Jewish tendency to conquer the world. As so often in history, Germany is the turning point in this mighty struggle. If our people and our state become the victims of blood-thirsty and money-thirsty Jewish tyrants, the whole world will be enmeshed in the tentacles of this octopus. If, however, Germany liberates itself from this yoke, we can be sure that the greatest threat to all humanity has been broken. . . .

Hitler was a master propagandist and advanced his ideas on propaganda techniques in *Mein Kampf*. He mocked the learned and book-oriented German liberals and socialists who he felt were entirely unsuited for modern mass politics. The successful leader, he said, must win over the masses through the use of simple ideas and images, constantly repeated, to control the mind by evoking primitive feelings. Hitler contended that mass meetings were the most effective means of winning followers. What counted most at these demonstrations, he said, was will power, strength, and unflagging determination radiating from the speaker to every single individual in the crowd.

PROPAGANDA AND MASS RALLIES

The task of propaganda does not lie in the scientific training of individuals, but in directing the masses toward certain facts, events, necessities, etc., whose significance is to be brought to their attention.

The essential skill consists in doing this so well that you convince people about the reality of a fact, about the necessity of an event, about the correctness of something necessary, etc. . . . You always have to appeal to the emotions and far less to the so-called intellect. . . .

The art of propaganda lies in sensing the emotional temper of the broad masses, so that you, in psychologically effective form, can catch their attention and move their hearts. . . .

The attention span of the masses is very short, their understanding limited; they easily forget. For that reason all effective propaganda has to concentrate on very few points and drive them home through simple slogans, until even the simplest can grasp what you have in mind. As soon as you give up this principle and become too complex, you will lose your effectiveness, because the masses cannot digest and retain what you have offered. You thereby weaken your case and in the end lose it altogether.

The larger the scope of your case, the more psychologically correct must be the method of your presentation. . . .

The task of propaganda lies not in weighing right and wrong, but in driving home your own point of view. You cannot objectively explore the facts that favor others and present them in doctrinaire sincerity to the masses. You have to push relentlessly your own case. . . .

Even the most brilliant propaganda will not produce the desired results unless it follows this fundamental rule: You must stick to limiting yourself to essentials and repeat them endlessly. Persistence on this point, as in so many other cases in the world, is the first and most important precondition for success. . . .

Propaganda does not exist to furnish interesting diversions to blasé young dandies, but to convince above all the masses. In their clumsiness they always require a long time before they are ready to take notice. Only by thousandfold repetition will the simplest concepts stick in their memories.

No variation of your presentation should change the content of your propaganda; you always have to come to the same conclusion. You may want to highlight your slogans from various sides, but at the end you always have to reaffirm it. Only consistent and uniform propaganda will succeed. . . .

Every advertisement, whether in business or politics, derives its success from its persistence and uniformity. . . .

The mass meeting is . . . necessary because an incipient supporter of a new political movement will feel lonely and anxiously isolated. He needs at the start a sense of a larger community which among most people produces vitality and courage. The same man as member of a military company or battalion and surrounded by his comrades will more light-heartedly join an attack than if he were all by himself. In a crowd he feels more sheltered, even if reality were a thousandfold against him.

The sense of community in a mass demonstration not only empowers the individual, but also promotes an esprit de corps. The person who in his business or workshop is the first to represent a new political creed is likely to be exposed to heavy discrimination. He needs the reassurance that comes from the conviction of being a member and a fighter in a large comprehensive organization. The sense of this organization comes first to him in a mass demonstration. When he for the first time goes from a petty workshop or from a large factory, where he feels insignificant, to a mass demonstration surrounded by thousands and thousands of like-minded fellows—when he as a seeker is gripped by the intoxicating surge of enthusiasm among three or four thousand others—when the visible success and the consensus of thousands of others prove the correctness of his new political creed and for the first time arouse doubts about his previous political convictions—then he submits to the miraculous influence of what we call "mass suggestion." The will, the yearning, and also the power of thousands of fellow citizens now fill every individual. The man who full of doubts and uncertain enters such a gathering, leaves it inwardly strengthened; he has become a member of a community. . . .

Hitler was an extreme nationalist who wanted a reawakened, racially united Germany to expand eastward at the expense of the Slavs, whom he viewed as racially inferior.

LEBENSRAUM

A people gains its freedom of existence only by occupying a sufficiently large space on earth. . . .

If the National Socialist movement really wants to achieve a hallowed mission in history for our people, it must, in painful awareness of its position in the world, boldly and methodically fight against the aimlessness and incapacity which have hitherto guided the foreign policy of the German people. It must then, without respect for "tradition" and prejudice, find the courage to rally the German people to a forceful advance on the road which leads from their present cramped living space to new territories. In this manner they will be liberated from the danger of perishing or being enslaved in service to others.

The National Socialist movement must try to end the disproportion between our numerous population and its limited living space, the source of our food as well as the base of our power—between our historic past and the hopelessness of our present impotence. . . .

The demand for restoring the boundaries of 1914 is a political nonsense with consequences so huge as to make it appear a crime—quite apart from the fact that our pre-war boundaries were anything but logical. They neither united all people of German nationality nor served strategic-political necessity. . . .

In the light of this fact we National Socialists must resolutely stick to our foreign policy goals, namely *to secure for the German people the territorial base to which they are entitled.* This is the only goal which before God and our German posterity justifies shedding our blood. . . .

Just as our forebears did not receive the soil on which we live as a gift from heaven—they had to risk their lives for it—so in future we will not secure the living space for our people by divine grace, but by the might of the victorious sword.

However much all of us recognize the necessity of a reckoning with France, it would remain ineffectual if we thereby limited the scope of our foreign policy. It makes sense only if we consider it as a rear-guard action for expanding our living space elsewhere in Europe. . . .

If we speak today about gaining territory in Europe, we think primarily of Russia and its border states. . . .

Kurt G. W. Ludecke
THE DEMAGOGIC ORATOR

Nazi popularity grew partly due to Hitler's power as an orator to play on the dissatisfactions of postwar Germans with the Weimar Republic. In the following selection from *I Knew Hitler—The Story of a Nazi Who Escaped the Blood Purge* (1937), Kurt G. W. Ludecke, an early supporter of Hitler who later broke with the Nazis, describes Hitler's ability to mesmerize his audience.

. . . [W]hen the Nazis marched into the Koenigsplatz with banners flying, their bands playing stirring German marches, they were greeted with tremendous cheers. An excited, expectant crowd was now filling the beautiful square to the last inch and overflowing into surrounding streets. They were well over a hundred thousand. . . . I was close enough to see Hitler's face, watch every change in his expression, hear every word he said.

When the man stepped forward on the platform, there was almost no applause. He stood silent for a moment. Then he began to speak, quietly and ingratiatingly at first. Before long his voice had risen to a hoarse shriek that gave an extraordinary effect of an intensity of feeling. There were many high-pitched, rasping notes. . . .

Critically I studied this slight, pale man, his brown hair parted on one side and falling again and again over his sweating brow. Threatening and beseeching, with small, pleading hands and flaming, steel-blue eyes, he had the look of a fanatic.

Presently my critical faculty was swept away. Leaning from the [platform] as if he were trying to impel his inner self into the consciousness of all these thousands, he was holding the masses, and me with them, under a hypnotic spell by the sheer force of his conviction.

He urged the revival of German honor and manhood with a blast of words that seemed to cleanse. "Bavaria is now the most German land in Germany!" he shouted, to roaring applause. Then, plunging into sarcasm, he indicted the leaders in Berlin as "November Criminals" (see page 220), daring to put into words thoughts that Germans were now almost afraid to think and certainly to voice.

It was clear that Hitler was feeling the exaltation of the emotional response now surging up toward him from his thousands of hearers.

His voice rising to passionate climaxes, he finished his speech with an anthem of hate against the "Novemberlings" and a pledge of undying love for the Fatherland. "Germany must be free!" was his final defiant slogan. Then two last words that were like the sting of a lash: *"Deutschland Erwache!"*

Awake, Germany! There was thunderous applause. Then the masses took a solemn oath "to save Germany in Bavaria from Bolshevism."

I do not know how to describe the emotions that swept over me as I heard this man. His words were like a scourge [a whip's lash]. When he spoke of the disgrace of Germany, I felt ready to spring on any enemy. His appeal to German manhood was like a call to arms, the gospel he preached a sacred truth. He seemed another Luther. I forgot everything but the man; then, glancing round, I saw that his magnetism was holding these thousands as one.

Of course I was ripe for this experience. I was a man of thirty-two, weary of disgust and disillusionment, a wanderer seeking a cause; a patriot without a channel for his patriotism, a yearner after the heroic without a hero. The intense will of the man, the passion of his sincerity seemed to flow from him into me. I experienced an exaltation that could be likened only to religious conversion.

I felt sure that no one who had heard Hitler that afternoon could doubt that he was the man of destiny, the vitalizing force in the future of Germany. The masses who had streamed into the Koenigsplatz with a stern sense of national humiliation seemed to be going forth renewed.

The bands struck up, the thousands began to move away. I knew my search was ended. I had found myself, my leader, and my cause.

REVIEW QUESTIONS

1. How did Adolf Hitler account for cultural greatness? Cultural decline?
2. What comparisons did Hitler draw between Aryans and Jews?
3. What kind of evidence did Hitler offer for his anti-Semitic arguments?
4. Theodor Mommsen, a nineteenth-century German historian, said that anti-Semites do not listen to "logic and ethical arguments. . . . They listen only to their own envy and hatred, to the meanest instincts." Discuss this statement.
5. What insights did Hitler have into mass psychology and propaganda?
6. What foreign policy goals did Hitler have for Germany? How did he expect them to be achieved?
7. How did Hitler mesmerize his audience?

7   The Leader-State

Adolf Hitler came to power by legal means, appointed chancellor by President Paul von Hindenburg on January 30, 1933, according to the constitution of the Weimar Republic. Thereafter, however, he proceeded to dismantle the legal structure of the Weimar system and replace it with an inflexible dictatorship that revolved around his person. Quickly reacting to the popular confusion caused by the suspicious Reichstag fire, Hitler issued a decree on February 28 that suspended all guarantees of civil and individual freedom. In March, the Reichstag adopted the Enabling Act, which vested all legislative powers in his hands. Then Hitler proceeded to destroy the autonomy of the federal states, dissolve the trade unions, outlaw other political parties, and end freedom of the press. By the time he eliminated party rivals in a blood purge on June 30, 1934, the consolidation of power was complete. Meanwhile, much of Germany's public and institutional life fell under Nazi Party control in a process known as the *Gleichschaltung,* or coordination. The Third Reich was organized as a leader-state, in which Hitler the *Führer* (leader) embodied and expressed the real will of the German people, commanded the supreme loyalty of the nation, and had unlimited authority.

Ernst Huber
"THE AUTHORITY OF THE FÜHRER IS . . . ALL-INCLUSIVE AND UNLIMITED"

In *Verfassungsrecht des grossdeutschen Reiches* (Constitutional Law of the Greater German Reich) (1939), legal scholar Ernst Rudolf Huber (1903–1990) offered a classic explication of the basic principles of National Socialism. The following excerpts from that work describe the nature of Hitler's political authority.

The Führer-Reich of the [German] people is founded on the recognition that the true will of the people cannot be disclosed through parliamentary votes and plebiscites but that the will of the people in its pure and uncorrupted form can only be expressed through the Führer. Thus a distinction must be drawn between the supposed will of the people in a parliamentary democracy, which merely reflects the conflict of the various social interests, and the true will of the people in the Führer-state, in which the collective will of the real political unit is manifested. . . .

It would be impossible for a law to be introduced and acted upon in the Reichstag which had not originated with the Führer or, at least, received his approval. The procedure is similar to that of the plebiscite: The lawgiving power does not rest in the Reichstag; it merely proclaims through its decision its agreement with the will of the Führer, who is the lawgiver of the German people.

The Führer unites in himself all the sovereign authority of the Reich; all public authority in the state as well as in the [Nazi] movement is derived from the authority of the Führer. We must speak not of the state's authority but of the Führer's authority if we wish to designate the character of the political authority within the Reich correctly. The state does not hold political authority as an impersonal unit but receives it from the Führer as the executor of the national will. The authority of the Führer is complete and all-embracing; it unites in itself all the means of political direction; it extends into all fields of national life; it embraces the entire people, which is bound to the Führer in loyalty and obedience. The authority of the Führer is not limited by checks and controls, by special autonomous bodies or individual rights, but it is free and independent, all-inclusive and unlimited. It is not, however, self-seeking or arbitrary. . . . It is derived from the people; that is, it is entrusted to the Führer by the people. It exists for the people and has its justification in the people; it is free of all outward ties because it is in its innermost nature firmly bound up with the fate, the welfare, the mission, and the honor of the people.

Führung [leadership] is not, like government, the highest organ of the state, which has grown out of the order of the state, but it receives its legitimation, its call, and its mission from the people. . . .

The people cannot as a rule announce its will by means of majority vote but only through its embodiment in one man, or in a few men. The principle of the *identity* of the ruler and those who are ruled, of the government and those who are governed has been very forcibly represented as the principle of democracy. But this identity . . . becomes mechanistic and superficial if one seeks to establish it in the theory that the people are at once the governors and the governed. . . . A true organic identity is only possible when the great mass of the people recognizes its embodiment in one man and feels itself to be one nature with him.

---

8   The Nazification of Culture and Society

The Nazis aspired to more than political power; they also wanted to have the German people view the world in accordance with National Socialist ideology. Toward this end, the Nazis strictly regulated cultural life. Believing that the struggle of racial forces occupied the center of world history, Nazi ideologists tried to strengthen the racial consciousness of the German people. Numerous courses in "race science" introduced in schools and universities emphasized the superiority of the Nordic soul as well as the worthlessness of Jews and their threat to the nation.

Johannes Stark
"JEWISH SCIENCE" VERSUS "GERMAN SCIENCE"

Several prominent German scientists endorsed the new regime and tried to make science conform to Nazi ideology. In 1934, Johannes Stark (1874–1957), who had won a Nobel Prize for his work in electromagnetism, requested fellow German Nobel Prize winners to sign a declaration supporting "Adolf Hitler . . . the savior and leader of the German people." In the following passage, Stark makes the peculiar assertion that "German science" was based on an objective analysis of nature, whereas "Jewish science" (German Jews had distinguished themselves in science and medicine) sacrificed objectivity to self-interest and a subjective viewpoint.

But aside from this fundamental National Socialist demand, the slogan of the international character of science is based on an untruth, insofar as it asserts that the type and the success of scientific activity are independent of membership in a national group. Nobody can seriously assert that art is international. It is similar with science. Insofar as scientific work is not merely imitation but actual creation, like any other creative activity it is conditioned by the spiritual and characterological endowments of its practitioners. Since the individual members of a people have a common endowment, the creative activity of the scientists of a nation, as much as that of its artists and poets, thus assumes the stamp of a distinctive Volkish type. No, science is not international; it is just as national as art. This can be shown by the example of Germans and Jews in the natural sciences.

Science is the knowledge of the uniform interconnection of facts; the purpose of natural science in particular is the investigation of bodies and processes outside of the human mind, through observation and, insofar as possible, through the setting up of planned experiments. The spirit of the German enables him to observe things outside himself exactly as they are, without the interpolation of his own ideas and wishes, and his body does not shrink from the effort which the investigation of nature demands of him. The German's love of nature and his aptitude for natural science are based on this endowment. Thus it is understandable that natural science is overwhelmingly a creation of the Nordic-Germanic blood component of the Aryan peoples. Anyone who, in Lenard's classic work *Grosse Naturforscher (Great Investigators of Nature),* compares the faces of the outstanding natural scientists will find this common Nordic-Germanic feature in almost all of them. The ability to observe and respect facts, in complete disregard of the "I," is the most characteristic feature of the scientific activity of Germanic types. In addition, there is the joy and satisfaction the German derives from the acquisition of scientific knowledge, since it is principally this with which he is concerned. It is only under pressure that he decides to make his findings public, and the propaganda for them and their commercial exploitation appear to him as degradations of his scientific work.

The Jewish spirit is wholly different in its orientation: above everything else it is focused upon its own ego, its own conception, and its self-interest—and behind its egocentric conception stands its strong will to win recognition for itself and its interests. In accordance with this natural orientation the Jewish spirit strives to heed facts only to the extent that they do not hamper its opinions and purposes, and to bring them in such a connection with each other as is expedient for effecting its opinions and purposes. The Jew, therefore, is the born advocate who, unencumbered by regard for truth, mixes facts and imputations topsy-turvy in the endeavor to secure the court decision he desires. On the other hand, because of these characteristics, the Jewish spirit has little aptitude for creative activity in the sciences because it takes the individual's thinking and will as the measure of things, whereas science demands observation and respect for the facts.

It is true, however, that the Jewish spirit, thanks to the flexibility of its intellect, is capable, through imitation of Germanic examples, of producing noteworthy accomplishments, but it is not able to rise to authentic creative work, to great discoveries in the natural sciences. In recent times the Jews have frequently invoked the name of Heinrich Hertz as a counter-argument to this thesis. True, Heinrich Hertz made the great discovery of electromagnetic waves, but he was not a full-blooded Jew. He had a German mother, from whose side his spiritual endowment may well have been conditioned. When the Jew in natural science abandons the Germanic example and engages in scientific work according to his own spiritual particularity, he turns to theory. His main object is not the observation of facts and their true-to-reality presentation, but the view which he forms about them and the formal exposition to which he subjects them. In the interest of his theory he will suppress facts that are not in keeping with it and likewise, still in the interest of his theory, he will engage in propaganda on its behalf.

Jakob Graf
HEREDITY AND RACIAL BIOLOGY FOR STUDENTS

The following assignments from a textbook entitled *Heredity and Racial Biology for Students* (1935) show how young people were indoctrinated with racist teachings.

HOW WE CAN LEARN TO RECOGNIZE A PERSON'S RACE
Assignments

1. Summarize the spiritual characteristics of the individual races.

2. Collect from stories, essays, and poems examples of ethnological illustrations. Underline those terms which describe the type and mode of the expression of the soul.

3. What are the expressions, gestures, and movements which allow us to make conclusions as to the attitude of the racial soul?

4. Determine also the physical features which go hand in hand with the specific racial soul characteristics of the individual figures.

5. Try to discover the intrinsic nature of the racial soul through the characters in stories and poetical works in terms of their inner attitude. Apply this mode of observation to persons in your own environment.

6. Collect propaganda posters and caricatures for your race book and arrange them according to a racial scheme. What image of beauty is emphasized by the artist (a) in posters publicizing sports and travel? (b) in publicity for cosmetics? How are hunters, mountain climbers, and shepherds drawn?

7. Collect from illustrated magazines, newspapers, etc., pictures of great scholars, statesmen, artists, and others who distinguish themselves by their special accomplishments (for example, in economic life, politics, sports). Determine the preponderant race and admixture, according to physical characteristics. Repeat this exercise with the pictures of great men of all nations and times.

8. When viewing monuments, busts, etc., be sure to pay attention to the race of the person portrayed with respect to figure, bearing, and physical characteristics. Try to harmonize these determinations with the features of the racial soul.

9. Observe people whose special racial features have drawn your attention, also with respect to their bearing when moving or when speaking. Observe their expressions and gestures.

10. Observe the Jew: his way of walking, his bearing, gestures, and movements when talking.

11. What strikes you about the way a Jew talks and sings?

Louis P. Lochner
BOOK BURNING

The anti-intellectualism of the Nazis was demonstrated on May 10, 1933, when the principal German student body organized students for a book-burning festival. In university towns, students consigned to the flames books that were considered a threat to the Germanic spirit, many of them written by prominent

Jewish authors. Louis P. Lochner (1887–1975), head of the Associated Press Bureau in Berlin, gave an eyewitness account of the scene in the German capital in *The Goebbels Diaries 1942–43* (1948).

The whole civilized world was shocked when on the evening of May 10, 1933, the books of authors displeasing to the Nazis, including even those of our own Helen Keller, were solemnly burned on the immense Franz Joseph Platz between the University of Berlin and the State Opera on Unter den Linden. I was a witness to the scene.

All afternoon Nazi raiding parties had gone into public and private libraries, throwing onto the streets such books as Dr. [Joseph] Goebbels [Nazi Progaganda Minister] in his supreme wisdom had decided were unfit for Nazi Germany. From the streets Nazi columns of beerhall fighters had picked up these discarded volumes and taken them to the square above referred to.

Here the heap grew higher and higher, and every few minutes another howling mob arrived, adding more books to the impressive pyre. Then, as night fell, students from the university, mobilized by the little doctor, performed veritable Indian dances and incantations as the flames began to soar skyward.

When the orgy was at its height, a cavalcade of cars drove into sight. It was the Propaganda Minister himself, accompanied by his bodyguard and a number of fellow torch bearers of the new Nazi *Kultur.*

"Fellow students, German men and women!" he said as he stepped before a microphone for all Germany to hear him. "The age of extreme Jewish intellectualism has now ended, and the success of the German revolution has again given the right of way to the German spirit. . . .

"You are doing the right thing in committing the evil spirit of the past to the flames at this late hour of the night. It is a strong, great, and symbolic act—an act that is to bear witness before all the world to the fact that the spiritual foundation of the November Republic has disappeared. From the ashes there will rise the phoenix of a new spirit. . . .

"The past is lying in flames. The future will rise from the flames within our own hearts. . . . Brightened by these flames our vow shall be: The Reich and the Nation and our Fuehrer Adolf Hitler: *Heil! Heil! Heil!*"

The few foreign correspondents who had taken the trouble to view this "symbolic act" were stunned. What had happened to the "Land of Thinkers and Poets?" they wondered.

REVIEW QUESTIONS

1. What, in Johannes Stark's view, made the Nordic, Aryan people especially fitted for scientific creativity? What disqualified the non-Nordic, especially the Jewish, people from achievement in science?
2. What was Jakob Graf's purpose in teaching students how to recognize a person's race?
3. Why do you think the Nazis made the burning of books a public event? Why does book burning have such potent symbolism?

9 Persecution of the Jews

The Nazis deprived Jews of their German citizenship and instituted many anti-Jewish measures designed to make them outcasts. Thousands of Jewish doctors, lawyers, musicians, artists, and professors were barred from practicing their professions, and Jewish members of the civil service were dismissed. A series of laws tightened the screws of humiliation and persecution. Marriages or sexual encounters between Germans and Jews were forbidden. Universities, schools, restaurants, pharmacies, hospitals, theaters, museums, and athletic fields were gradually closed to Jews.

In November 1938, using as a pretext the assassination of a German official in Paris by a seventeen-year-old Jewish youth whose family had been mistreated by the Nazis, the Nazis organized an extensive pogrom. Nazi gangs murdered scores of Jews and burned and looted thousands of Jewish businesses, homes, and synagogues all over Germany—an event that became known as the Night of the Broken Glass *(Kristallnacht).* Twenty thousand Jews were thrown into concentration camps. The Reich then imposed on the Jewish community a fine of 1 billion marks. By the outbreak of the war in September 1939, approximately one-half of Germany's six hundred thousand Jews had fled the country. Those who stayed behind would fall victim to the last stage of the Nazi anti-Jewish campaign—the Final Solution.

Marta Appel
MEMOIRS OF A GERMAN JEWISH WOMAN

Marta Appel and her husband, Dr. Ernst Appel, a rabbi in the city of Dortmund, fled Germany in 1937. In 1940–1941, while in the United States, she wrote her memoirs, which described conditions in Dortmund after the Nazis took power.

The children had been advised not to come to school on April 1, 1933, the day of the boycott {of Jewish businesses}. Even the principal of the school thought Jewish children's lives were no longer safe. One night they placed big signs on every store or house owned by Jewish people. In front of our temple, on every square and corner, billboards were scoffing at us. Everywhere, and on all occasions, we read and heard that we were vermin and had caused the ruin of the German people. No Jewish store was closed on that day, none was willing to show fear in the face of the boycott. The only building which did not open its door as usual, since it was Saturday, was the temple. We did not want this holy place desecrated by any trouble.

I even went downtown that day to see what was going on in the city. There was no cheering crowd as the Nazis had expected, no running

and smashing of Jewish businesses. I heard only words of anger and disapproval. People were massed before the Jewish stores to watch the Nazi guards who were posted there to prevent anyone from entering to buy. And there were many courageous enough to enter, although they were called rude names by the Nazi guards, and their pictures were taken to show them as enemies of the German people in the daily papers. . . .

Our gentile friends and neighbors, even people whom we had scarcely known before, came to assure us of their friendship and to tell us that these horrors could not last very long. But after some months of a regime of terror, fidelity and friendship had lost their meaning, and fear and treachery had replaced them. For the sake of our gentile friends, we turned our heads so as not to greet them in the streets, for we did not want to bring upon them the danger of imprisonment for being considered a friend of Jews.

With each day of the Nazi regime, the abyss between us and our fellow citizens grew larger. Friends whom we had loved for years did not know us anymore. They suddenly saw that we were different from themselves. Of course we were different, since we were bearing the stigma of Nazi hatred, since we were hunted like deer. Through the prominent position of my husband we were in constant danger. Often we were warned to stay away from home. We were no longer safe, wherever we went.

How much our life changed in those days! Often it seemed to me I could not bear it any longer, but thinking of my children, I knew we had to be strong to make it easier for them. From then on I hated to go out, since on every corner I saw signs that the Jews were the misfortune of the people. . . .

In the evenings we sat at home at the radio listening fearfully to all the new and outrageous restrictions and laws which almost daily brought further suffering to Jewish people. . . .

Since I had lived in Dortmund, I had met every four weeks with a group of women, all of whom were born in Metz, my beloved home city. We all had been pupils or teachers in the same high school. After the Nazis came, I was afraid to go to the meetings. I did not want the presence of a Jewess to bring any trouble, since we always met publicly in a café. One day on the street, I met one of my old teachers, and with tears in her eyes she begged me: "Come again to us; we miss you; we feel ashamed that you must think we do not want you anymore. Not one of us has changed in her feeling toward you." She tried to convince me that they were still my friends, and tried to take away my doubts. I decided to go to the next meeting. It was a hard decision, and I had not slept the night before. I was afraid for my gentile friends. For nothing in the world did I wish to bring them trouble by my attendance, and I was also afraid for myself. I knew I would watch them, noticing the slightest expression of embarrassment in their eyes when I came. I knew they could not deceive me;

I would be aware of every change in their voices. Would they be afraid to talk to me?

It was not necessary for me to read their eyes or listen to the change in their voices. The empty table in the little alcove which always had been reserved for us spoke the clearest language. It was even unnecessary for the waiter to come and say that a lady phoned that morning not to reserve the table thereafter. I could not blame them. Why should they risk losing a position only to prove to me that we still had friends in Germany?

I, personally, did not mind all those disappointments, but when my children had to face them, and were not spared being offended everywhere, my heart was filled with anguish. It required a great deal of inner strength, of love and harmony among the Jewish families, to make our children strong enough to bear all that persecution and hatred. . . . My heart was broken when I saw tears in my younger child's eyes when she had been sent home from school while all the others had been taken to a show or some other pleasure. It was not because she was denied going to the show that my little girl was weeping—she knew her Mommy always could take her—but because she had to stay apart, as if she were not good enough to associate with her comrades any longer. It was this that made it hard and bitter for her. I think that even the Nazi teacher sometimes felt ashamed when she looked into the sad eyes of my little girl, since several times, when the class was going out for pleasure, she phoned not to send her to school. Maybe it was not right to hate this teacher so much, since everything she did had been upon orders, but it was she who brought so much bitterness to my child, and never can I forget it.

Almost every lesson began to be a torture for Jewish children. There was not one subject anymore which was not used to bring up the Jewish question. And in the presence of Jewish children the teachers denounced all the Jews, without exception, as scoundrels and as the most destructive force in every country where they were living. My children were not permitted to leave the room during such a talk; they were compelled to stay and to listen; they had to feel all the other children's eyes looking and staring at them, the examples of an outcast race.

Every day they had to face another degrading and offensive incident. As Mother's Day came near, the children were practicing songs at school to celebrate that day. Every year on that occasion the whole school gathered in a joint festival. It was the day before when my girls were ordered to see the music teacher. "You have to be present for the festival," the teacher told them, "but since you are Jewish, you are not allowed to join in the songs." "Why can't we sing?" my children protested with tears in their eyes. "We have a mother too, and we wish to sing for her." But it seemed the teacher did not want to understand the children's feelings. Curtly she rebuked their protest. "I know you have a mother," she said haughtily, "but she is only a Jewish mother." At that the girls had no reply; there was no use to speak any longer to the teacher, but seldom had they been so much disturbed as when they came from school that day, when someone had tried to condemn their mother. . . .

One day, for the first time in a long while, I saw my children coming back from school with shining eyes, laughing and giggling together. Most of the classes had been gathered that morning in the big hall, since an official of the new *Rasseamt,* the office of races, had come to give a talk about the differences of races. "I asked the teacher if I could go home," my daughter was saying, "but she told me she had orders not to dismiss anyone. You may imagine it was an awful talk. He said that there are two groups of races, a high group and a low one. The high and upper race that was destined to rule the world was the Teutonic, the German race, while one of the lowest races was the Jewish race. And then, Mommy, he looked around and asked one of the girls to

come to him." The children again began to giggle about their experience. "First we did not know," my girl continued, "what he intended, and we were very afraid when he picked out Eva. Then he began, and he was pointing at Eva, 'Look here, the small head of this girl, her long forehead, her very blue eyes, and blond hair,' and he was lifting one of her long blond braids. 'And look,' he said, 'at her tall and slender figure. These are the unequivocal marks of a pure and unmixed Teutonic race.' Mommy, you should have heard how at this moment all the girls burst into laughter. Even Eva could not help laughing. Then from all sides of the hall there was shouting, 'She is a Jewess!' You should have seen the officer's face! I guess he was lucky that the principal got up so quickly and, with a sign to the pupils, stopped the laughing and shouting and dismissed the man, thanking him for his interesting and very enlightening talk. At that we began again to laugh, but he stopped us immediately. Oh, I was so glad that the teacher had not dismissed me and I was there to hear it."

When my husband came home, they told him and enjoyed it again and again. And we were thankful to know that they still had not completely forgotten how to laugh and to act like happy children.

"If only I could take my children out of here!" That thought was occupying my mind more and more. I no longer hoped for any change as did my husband. Besides, even a changed Germany could not make me forget that all our friends, the whole nation, had abandoned us in our need. It was no longer the same country for me. Everything had changed, not people alone—the city, the forest, the river—the whole country looked different in my eyes.

REVIEW QUESTION

1. What was the purpose of the humiliation inflicted on German Jews in the first few years of the Nazi regime?

CHAPTER 9

World War II

"GRIEF." Photographed in the Kerch Peninsula, Russia, January 1942. (© *Dmitry Battermants/Sovfoto/ Eastfoto*)

From the early days of his political career, Hitler dreamed of forging a vast German empire in central and eastern Europe. He believed that only by waging a war of conquest against Russia could the German nation gain the living space and security it required and, as a superior race, deserved. War was an essential component of National Socialist ideology; it also accorded with Hitler's temperament. For the former corporal from the trenches, the Great War had never ended. Hitler aspired to political power because he wanted to mobilize the material and human resources of the German nation for war and conquest. Whereas historians may debate the question of responsibility for World War I, few would disagree with French historian Pierre Renouvin that World War II was Hitler's war:

> It appears to be an almost incontrovertible fact that the Second World War was brought on by the actions of the Hitler government, that these actions were the expression of a policy laid down well in advance in *Mein Kampf,* and that this war could have been averted up until the last moment if the German government had so wished.

Western statesmen had sufficient warning that Hitler was a threat to peace and the essential values of Western civilization, but they failed to rally their people and take a stand until Germany had greatly increased its capacity to wage aggressive war.

World War II was the most destructive war in history. Estimates of the number of dead range as high as 50 million, including 25 million Russians, who sacrificed more than the other participants in both population and material resources. The consciousness of Europe, already profoundly damaged by World War I, was again grievously wounded. Nazi racial theories showed that even in an age of sophisticated science the mind remains attracted to irrational beliefs and mythical imagery. Nazi atrocities proved that people will torture and kill with religious zeal and machinelike indifference. The Nazi assault on reason and freedom demonstrated anew the precariousness of Western civilization. This assault would forever cast doubt on the Enlightenment conception of human goodness, secular rationality, and the progress of civilization through advances in science and technology.

1 The Anschluss, March 1938

One of Hitler's aims was the incorporation of Austria into the Third Reich. The Treaty of Versailles had expressly prohibited the union of the two countries, but in *Mein Kampf,* Hitler had insisted that an Anschluss was necessary for German *Lebensraum* (living space). In February 1938, under intense pressure from Hitler, Austrian Chancellor Kurt von Schuschnigg promised to accept Austrian Nazis in his cabinet and agreed to closer relations with Germany. Austrian independence was slipping away, and increasingly, Austrian Nazis undermined Schuschnigg's authority. Seeking to gain his people's support, Schuschnigg made plans for a plebiscite on the issue of preserving Austrian independence. An enraged Hitler ordered his generals to draw up plans for an invasion of Austria. Hitler then demanded Schuschnigg's resignation and the formation of a new government headed by Arthur Seyss-Inquart, an Austrian Nazi.

Believing that Austria was not worth a war, Britain and France informed the embattled chancellor that they would not help in the event of a German invasion. Schuschnigg then resigned, and Austrian Nazis began to take control of the government. Under the pretext of preventing violence, Hitler ordered his troops to cross into Austria, and on March 13, 1938, Austrian leaders declared that Austria was a province of the German Reich.

The Anschluss was supported by many Austrians: Nazis and their sympathizers, average people who hoped it would bring improved material conditions, and opportunists who had their eyes set on social and economic advancement by working with the Nazis. Even many opponents of the Nazis felt that Austrian unity with Germany was fated to be accomplished, even as they lamented that it meant incorporation into Hitler's regime.

In the first days after the Anschluss, anti-Nazis, particularly Social Democrats, were incarcerated; a wave of dissidents, politicians, and intellectuals fled the country; and Jews were subjected to torment and humiliation. Austrian Nazis, often with the approval of their fellow citizens, plundered Jewish shops, pulled elderly Orthodox Jews around by their beards, and made Jews scour pro-Schuschnigg slogans off the streets with toothbrushes or their bare hands. One eyewitness recalled years later: "I saw in the crowd a well-dressed woman . . . holding up a little girl, a blond lovely little girl with these curls, so that the girl could see better how a . . . Nazi Storm Trooper kicked an old Jew who fell down because he wasn't allowed to kneel. He had to scrub and just bend down sort of, and he fell and he kicked him. And they all laughed and she laughed as well—it was wonderful entertainment—and that shook me."

Stefan Zweig
THE WORLD OF YESTERDAY

One of modern German-speaking Europe's most important authors, Stefan Zweig (see page 175) was born into a well-to-do Viennese Jewish household, came of age during the waning years of the monarchy, and witnessed both the devastation of World War I and the chaos of the interwar years. A passionate European and a convinced Austrian patriot, Zweig was disgusted by national chauvinisms, particularly the virulent German nationalism clearly discernible in Austria after the collapse of the Hapsburg monarchy. His *World of Yesterday*

(1943) both laments the loss of European cosmopolitanism and offers biting criticism of the inability, or unwillingness, of many Austrians to come to terms with the violent intolerance in their own society and the spreading danger of Nazism. Zweig's despair was all-consuming; he took his own life in South American exile, unable to reconcile himself to the changes in his beloved Europe and his Austrian homeland.

In the following selection from his autobiography, Zweig describes the orgy of hate that engulfed Vienna immediately after the Anschluss.

I thought that I had foreboded all the terror that would come to pass when Hitler's dream of hate would come true and he would triumphantly occupy Vienna, the city which had turned him off, poor and a failure, in his youth. But how timid, how petty, how lamentable my imagination, all human imagination, in the light of the inhumanity which discharged itself on that March 13, 1938, that day when Austria and Europe with it fell prey to sheer violence! The mask was off. The other States having plainly shown their fear, there was no further need to check moral inhibitions or to employ hypocritical pretexts about "Marxists" having to be politically liquidated. Who cared for England, France, for the whole world! Now there was no longer mere robbery and theft, but every private lust for revenge was given free rein. University professors were obliged to scrub the streets with their naked hands, pious white-bearded Jews were dragged into the synagogue by hooting youths and forced to do knee-exercises and to shout "Heil Hitler" in chorus. Innocent people in the streets were trapped like rabbits and herded off to clean the latrines in the S. A. barracks. All the sickly, unclean fantasies of hate that had been conceived in many orgiastic nights found raging expression in bright daylight. Breaking into homes and tearing earrings from trembling women may well have happened in the looting of cities, hundreds of years ago during medieval wars; what was new, however, was the shameless delight in public tortures, in spiritual martyrization, in the refinements of humiliation. All this has been recorded not by one but by thousands who suffered it; and a more peaceful day—not one already morally fatigued as ours is—will shudder to read what a single hate-crazed man perpetrated in that city of culture in the twentieth century. For amidst his military and political victories Hitler's most diabolic triumph was that he succeeded through progressive excesses in blunting every sense of law and order. Before this "New Order," the murder of a single man without legal process and without apparent reason would have shocked the world; torture was considered unthinkable in the twentieth century, expropriations were known by the old names, theft and robbery. But now after successive [murderous] nights the daily mortal tortures in the S. A. prisons and behind barbed wire, what did a single injustice or earthly suffering signify? In 1938, after Austria, our universe had become accustomed to inhumanity, to lawlessness, and brutality as never in centuries before. In a former day the occurrences in unhappy Vienna alone would have been sufficient to cause international proscription, but in 1938 the world conscience was silent or merely muttered surlily before it forgot and forgave.

Those days, marked by daily cries for help from the homeland when one knew close friends to be kidnapped and humiliated and one trembled helplessly for every loved one, were among the most terrible of my life. These times have so perverted our hearts that I am not ashamed to say that I was not shocked and did not mourn upon learning of the death of my mother in Vienna; on the contrary, I even felt something like composure in the knowledge that she was now safe from suffering and danger. Eighty-four years old, almost completely deaf, she occupied rooms in our old home and thus could not, even under the new "Aryan" code, be evicted for the time being and we had hoped somehow to get her abroad after a while. One of the first Viennese ordinances had hit her hard. At her advanced age she was a little shaky on her legs and was accustomed, when on her daily laborious walk, to rest on a bench in the Ringstrasse or in the park, every five or ten minutes. Hitler had not been master of the city for a week when the bestial order forbidding Jews to sit on public benches was issued—one of those orders obviously thought up only for the sadistic purpose of malicious torture. There was logic and reason in robbing Jews for with the booty from factories, the home furnishings, the villas, and the jobs compulsorily vacated they could feather their followers' nests, reward their satellites; after all, Goering's[1] picture-gallery owes its splendor mainly to this generously exercised practice. But to deny an aged woman or an exhausted old man a few minutes on a park bench to catch his breath—this remained reserved to the twentieth century and to the man whom millions worshipped as the greatest in our day.

Fortunately, my mother was spared suffering such brutality and humiliation for long. She died a few months after the occupation of Vienna and I cannot forbear to write about an episode in connection with her passing; it seems important to me to record just such details for a time in which such things will again seem impossible.

One morning the eighty-four-year-old woman suddenly lost consciousness. The doctor who was called declared that she could hardly live through the night and engaged a nurse, a woman of about forty, to attend her deathbed. Neither my brother nor I, her only children, was there nor could we have come back, because a return to the deathbed of a mother would have been counted a misdeed by the representatives of German culture. A cousin of ours undertook to spend the night in the apartment so that at least one of the family might be present at her death. He was then a man of sixty, and in poor health; in fact he too died about a year later. As he was uncovering his bed in an adjoining room the nurse appeared and declared her regret that because of the new National-Socialist laws it was impossible for her to stay overnight with the dying woman. To her credit be it said that she was rather shamefaced about it. My cousin being a Jew and she a woman under fifty, she was not permitted to spend a night under the same roof with him, even at a deathbed, because according to the [vile Nazi] mentality, it must be a Jew's first thought to practice race defilement upon her. Of course the regulation was extremely embarrassing, but she would have to obey the law. So my sixty-year-old cousin had to leave the house in the evening so that the nurse could stay with my dying mother; it will be intelligible, then, why I considered her almost lucky not to have to live on among such people.

REVIEW QUESTIONS

1. What was the underlying purpose of the various anti-Jewish ordinances in Vienna that Stefan Zweig refers to? How might they have paved the way for even harsher actions?
2. Zweig accurately predicted that people in "a more peaceful day" would later "shudder to read what a single hate-crazed man perpetrated in that city of culture in the twentieth century." Why do you think so many of Zweig's contemporaries failed to feel the same dismay and horror as these events unfolded?

---

[1]Head of the German air force, Hermann Goering (1893–1946), was notorious for looting conquered lands of their art treasures for his own personal collection.

2 The Munich Agreement

Hitler sought power to build a great German empire in Europe, a goal that he revealed in *Mein Kampf*. In 1935, Hitler declared that Germany was no longer bound by the Versailles Treaty and would restore military conscription. Germany remilitarized the Rhineland in 1936 and incorporated Austria into the Third Reich in 1938. Although these actions violated the Versailles Treaty, Britain and France offered no resistance.

In 1938, Hitler also threatened war if Czechoslovakia did not cede to Germany the Sudetenland with its large German population—of the 3.5 million people living in the Czech Sudetenland, some 2.8 million were Germans. In September 1938, Hitler met with other European leaders at Munich. Prime Minister Neville Chamberlain (1869–1940) of Great Britain and Prime Minister Édouard Daladier (1884–1970) of France agreed to Hitler's demands, despite France's mutual assistance pact with Czechoslovakia and the Czechs' expressed determination to resist the dismemberment of their country. Both Chamberlain and Daladier were praised by their compatriots for ensuring, as Chamberlain said, "peace in our time."

Neville Chamberlain
IN DEFENSE OF APPEASEMENT

Britain and France pursued a policy of appeasement—giving in to Germany in the hope that a satisfied Hitler would not drag Europe into another war. Appeasement expressed the widespread British desire to heal the wounds of World War I and to correct what many British officials regarded as the injustices of the Versailles Treaty. Some officials, lauding Hitler's anticommunism, regarded a powerful Germany as a bulwark against the Soviet Union. Britain's lack of military preparedness was another compelling reason for not resisting Hitler. On September 27, 1938, when negotiations between Hitler and Chamberlain reached a tense moment, the British prime minister addressed his nation. Excerpts of this speech and of another before the House of Commons, which appeared in his *In Search of Peace* (1939), follow.

First of all I must say something to those who have written to my wife or myself in these last weeks to tell us of their gratitude for my efforts and to assure us of their prayers for my success. Most of these letters have come from women—mothers or sisters of our own countrymen. But there are countless others besides—from France, from Belgium, from Italy, even from Germany, and it has been heartbreaking to read of the growing anxiety they reveal and their intense relief when they thought, too soon, that the danger of war was past.

If I felt my responsibility heavy before, to read such letters has made it seem almost overwhelming. How horrible, fantastic, incredible it is that we should be digging trenches and trying on gas masks here because of a quarrel in a far-away country between people of whom we know nothing. It seems still more impossible that a quarrel which has already been settled in principle should be the subject of war.

I can well understand the reasons why the Czech Government have felt unable to accept the terms which have been put before them in the German memorandum. Yet I believe after my talks with Herr Hitler that, if only time were allowed, it ought to be possible for the arrangements for transferring the territory that the Czech Government has agreed to give to Germany to be settled by agreement under conditions which would assure fair treatment to the population concerned. . . .

However much we may sympathise with a small nation confronted by a big and powerful neighbour, we cannot in all circumstances undertake to involve the whole British Empire in war simply on her account. If we have to fight it must be on larger issues than that. I am myself a man of peace to the depths of my soul. Armed conflict between nations is a nightmare to me; but if I were convinced that any nation had made up its mind to dominate the world by fear of its force, I should feel that it must be resisted. Under such a domination life for people who believe in liberty would not be worth living; but war is a fearful thing, and we must be very clear, before we embark on it, that it is really the great issues that are at stake, and that the call to risk everything in their defence, when all the consequences are weighed, is irresistible.

For the present I ask you to await as calmly as you can the events of the next few days. As long as war has not begun, there is always hope that it may be prevented, and you know that I am going to work for peace to the last moment. Good night. . . .

On October 6, 1938, in a speech to Britain's House of Commons, Chamberlain defended the Munich agreement signed on September 30.

Since I first went to Berchtesgaden [to confer with Hitler in Germany] more than 20,000 letters and telegrams have come to No. 10, Downing Street [British prime minister's residence]. Of course, I have only been able to look at a tiny fraction of them, but I have seen enough to know that the people who wrote did not feel that they had such a cause for which to fight, if they were asked to go to war in order that the Sudeten Germans might not join the Reich. That is how they are feeling. That is my answer to those who say that we should have told Germany weeks ago that, if her army crossed the border of Czechoslovakia, we should be at war with her. We had no treaty obligations and no legal obligations to Czechoslovakia and if we had said that, we feel that we should have received no support from the people of this country. . . .

. . . When we were convinced, as we became convinced, that nothing any longer would keep the Sudetenland within the Czechoslovakian State, we urged the Czech Government as strongly as we could to agree to the cession of territory, and to agree promptly. The Czech Government, through the wisdom and courage of President Benes, accepted the advice of the French Government and ourselves. It was a hard decision for anyone who loved his country to take, but to accuse us of having by that advice betrayed the Czechoslovakian State is simply preposterous. What we did was to save her from annihilation and give her a chance of new life as a new State, which involves the loss of territory and fortifications, but may perhaps enable her to enjoy in the future and develop a national existence under a neutrality and security comparable to that which we see in Switzerland to-day. Therefore, I think the Government deserve the approval of this House for their conduct of affairs in this recent crisis which has saved Czechoslovakia from destruction and Europe from Armageddon.

Does the experience of the Great War and of the years that followed it give us reasonable hope that, if some new war started, that would end war any more than the last one did? . . .

One good thing, at any rate, has come out of this emergency through which we have passed.

It has thrown a vivid light upon our preparations for defence, on their strength and on their weakness. I should not think we were doing our duty if we had not already ordered that a prompt and thorough inquiry should be made to cover the whole of our preparations, military and civil, in order to see, in the light of what has happened during these hectic days, what further steps may be necessary to make good our deficiencies in the shortest possible time.

Winston Churchill
"A DISASTER OF THE FIRST MAGNITUDE"

On October 5, 1938, Britain's elder statesman Winston Churchill (1874–1965) delivered a speech in the House of Commons attacking the Munich agreement and British policy toward Nazi Germany.

... I will begin by saying what everybody would like to ignore or forget but which must nevertheless be stated, namely, that we have sustained a total and unmitigated defeat, and that France has suffered even more than we have....

... And I will say this, that I believe the Czechs, left to themselves and told they were going to get no help from the Western Powers, would have been able to make better terms than they have got—they could hardly have worse—after all this tremendous perturbation [agitation]....

... I have always held the view that the maintenance of peace depends upon the accumulation of deterrents against the aggressor, coupled with a sincere effort to redress grievances.... After [Hitler's] seizure of Austria in March ... I ventured to appeal to the Government ... to give a pledge that in conjunction with France and other Powers they would guarantee the security of Czechoslovakia while the Sudeten-Deutsch question was being examined either by a League of Nations Commission or some other impartial body, and I still believe that if that course had been followed events would not have fallen into this disastrous state....

France and Great Britain together, especially if they had maintained a close contact with Russia, which certainly was not done, would have been able in those days in the summer, when they had the prestige, to influence many of the smaller States of Europe, and I believe they could have determined the attitude of Poland. Such a combination, prepared at a time when the German dictator was not deeply and irrevocably committed to his new adventure, would, I believe, have given strength to all those forces in Germany which resisted this departure, this new design. They were varying forces, those of a military character which declared that Germany was not ready to undertake a world war, and all that mass of moderate opinion and popular opinion which dreaded war, and some elements of which still have some influence upon the German Government. Such action would have given strength to all that intense desire for peace which the helpless German masses share with their British and French fellow men....

... I do not think it is fair to charge those who wished to see this course followed, and followed consistently and resolutely, with having wished for an immediate war. Between submission and immediate war there was this third alternative, which gave a hope not only of peace but of justice. It is quite true that such a policy in order to succeed demanded that

Britain should declare straight out and a long time beforehand that she would, with others, join to defend Czechoslovakia against an unprovoked aggression. His Majesty's Government refused to give that guarantee when it would have saved the situation. . . .

All is over. Silent, mournful, abandoned, broken, Czechoslovakia recedes into the darkness. She has suffered in every respect by her association with the Western democracies and with the League of Nations, of which she has always been an obedient servant. She has suffered in particular from her association with France, under whose guidance and policy she has been actuated for so long. . . .

We in this country, as in other Liberal and democratic countries, have a perfect right to exalt the principle of self-determination, but it comes ill out of the mouths of those in totalitarian States who deny even the smallest element of toleration to every section and creed within their bounds. . . .

What is the remaining position of Czechoslovakia? Not only are they politically mutilated, but, economically and financially, they are in complete confusion. Their banking, their railway arrangements, are severed and broken, their industries are curtailed, and the movement of their population is most cruel. The Sudeten miners, who are all Czechs and whose families have lived in that area for centuries, must now flee into an area where there are hardly any mines left for them to work. It is a tragedy which has occurred. . . .

I venture to think that in future the Czechoslovak State cannot be maintained as an independent entity. You will find that in a period of time which may be measured by years, but may be measured only by months, Czechoslovakia will be engulfed in the Nazi régime. Perhaps they may join it in despair or in revenge. At any rate, that story is over and told. But we cannot consider the abandonment and ruin of Czechoslovakia in the light only of what happened only last month. It is the most grievous consequence which we have yet experienced of what we have done and of what we have left undone in the last five years—five years of futile good

intention, five years of eager search for the line of least resistance, five years of uninterrupted retreat of British power, five years of neglect of our air defences. Those are the features which I stand here to declare and which marked an improvident [incautious] stewardship for which Great Britain and France have dearly to pay. We have been reduced in those five years from a position of security so overwhelming and so unchallengeable that we never cared to think about it. We have been reduced from a position where the very word "war" was considered one which would be used only by persons qualifying for a lunatic asylum. We have been reduced from a position of safety and power—power to do good, power to be generous to a beaten foe, power to make terms with Germany, power to give her proper redress for her grievances, power to stop her arming if we chose, power to take any step in strength or mercy or justice which we thought right—reduced in five years from a position safe and unchallenged to where we stand now.

When I think of the fair hopes of a long peace which still lay before Europe at the beginning of 1933 when Herr Hitler first obtained power, and of all the opportunities of arresting the growth of the Nazi power which have been thrown away, when I think of the immense combinations and resources which have been neglected or squandered, I cannot believe that a parallel exists in the whole course of history. So far as this country is concerned the responsibility must rest with those who have the undisputed control of our political affairs. They neither prevented Germany from rearming, nor did they rearm ourselves in time. . . . They neglected to make alliances and combinations which might have repaired previous errors, and thus they left us in the hour of trial without adequate national defence or effective international security. . . .

We are in the presence of a disaster of the first magnitude which has befallen Great Britain and France. Do not let us blind ourselves to that. It must now be accepted that all the countries of Central and Eastern Europe will make the best terms they can with the triumphant Nazi Power. The system of alliances in Central Europe upon which France has relied for her safety has been swept away, and I can see no means by which it can be reconstituted. . . .

. . . If the Nazi dictator should choose to look westward, as he may, bitterly will France and England regret the loss of that fine army of ancient Bohemia [Czechoslovakia] which was estimated last week to require not fewer than 30 German divisions for its destruction. . . .

. . . Many people, no doubt, honestly believe that they are only giving away the interests of Czechoslovakia, whereas I fear we shall find that we have deeply compromised, and perhaps fatally endangered, the safety and even the independence of Great Britain and France. . . . [T]here can never be friendship between the British democracy and the Nazi Power, that Power which spurns Christian ethics, which cheers its onward course by a barbarous paganism, which vaunts the spirit of aggression and conquest, which derives strength and perverted pleasure from persecution, and uses, as we have seen, with pitiless brutality the threat of murderous force. That Power cannot ever be the trusted friend of the British democracy. . . .

. . . [O]ur loyal, brave people . . . should know the truth. They should know that there has been gross neglect and deficiency in our defences; they should know that we have sustained a defeat without a war, the consequences of which will travel far with us along our road; they should know that we have passed an awful milestone in our history, when the whole equilibrium of Europe has been deranged, and that the terrible words have for the time being been pronounced against the Western democracies:

Thou art weighed in the balance and found wanting.

And do not suppose that this is the end. This is only the beginning of the reckoning. This is only the first sip, the first foretaste of a bitter cup which will be proffered [offered] to us year by year unless by a supreme recovery of moral health and martial vigour, we arise again and take our stand for freedom as in the olden time.

REVIEW QUESTIONS

1. In Neville Chamberlain's view, how did the British people regard a war with Germany over the Sudetenland?
2. How did Chamberlain respond to the accusation that Britain and France had betrayed Czechoslovakia?
3. What did Chamberlain consider to be the "one good thing" to come out of the Sudetenland crisis?
4. Why did Winston Churchill believe that "there [could] never be friendship between the British democracy and the Nazi Power"?
5. Why did Churchill believe that the Munich agreement was "a disaster of the first magnitude" for Britain and France?

3 World War II Begins

After Czechoslovakia, Hitler turned to Poland. In the middle of June 1939, the army presented him with a battle plan for an invasion of Poland, and on August 22, Hitler informed his leading generals that war with Poland was necessary. The following day, Nazi Germany signed a nonaggression pact with Communist Russia, which blocked Britain and France from duplicating their World

War I alliance against Germany. The Nazi–Soviet pact was the green light for an attack on Poland. At dawn on September 1, German forces, striking with co-ordinated speed and power, invaded Poland, starting World War II.

Adolf Hitler
"POLAND WILL BE DEPOPULATED AND SETTLED WITH GERMANS"

An American journalist was given a copy of Hitler's speech to his generals at the August 22 conference. Probably the supplier was an official close to Admiral Canaris, an opponent of Hitler who had attended the conference. The journalist then gave it to the British ambassador. The speech is reproduced below.

Decision to attack Poland was arrived at in spring. Originally there was fear that because of the political constellation we would have to strike at the same time against England, France, Russia and Poland. This risk too we should have had to take. Goering (see footnote on page 228) had demonstrated to us that his Four-Year Plan is a failure and that we are at the end of our strength, if we do not achieve victory in a coming war.

Since the autumn of 1938 and since I have realised that Japan will not go with us unconditionally and that Mussolini is endangered by that nitwit of a King and the treacherous scoundrel of a Crown Prince, I decided to go with Stalin. After all there are only three great statesmen in the world, Stalin, I and Mussolini. Mussolini is the weakest, for he has been able to break the power neither of the crown nor of the Church. Stalin and I are the only ones who visualise the future. So in a few weeks hence I shall stretch out my hand to Stalin at the common German-Russian frontier and with him undertake to re-distribute the world.

Our strength lies in our quickness and in our brutality; Genghis Khan has sent millions of women and children into death knowingly and with a light heart. History sees in him only the great founder of States. As to what the weak Western European civilisation asserts about me, that is of no account. I have given the command and I shall shoot everyone who

utters one word of criticism, for the goal to be obtained in the war is not that of reaching certain lines but of physically demolishing the opponent. And so for the present only in the East I have put my death-head formations[1] in place with the command relentlessly and without compassion to send into death many women and children of Polish origin and language. Only thus we can gain the living space that we need. Who after all is today speaking about the destruction of the Armenians?

Colonel-General von Brauchitsch has promised me to bring the war against Poland to a close within a few weeks. Had he reported to me that he needs two years or even only one year, I should not have given the command to march and should have allied myself temporarily with England instead of Russia for we cannot conduct a long war. To be sure a new situation has arisen. I experienced those poor worms Daladier and Chamberlain in Munich. They will be too cowardly to attack. They won't go beyond a blockade. Against that we have our autarchy [absolute self-sufficiency] and the Russian raw materials.

Poland will be depopulated and settled with Germans. My pact with the Poles was merely

---

[1]The S.S. Head's Head formations were principally employed in peacetime in guarding concentration camps. With the S.S. Verfügungstruppen they formed the nucleus of the Waffen S.S.

conceived of as a gaining of time. As for the rest, gentlemen, the fate of Russia will be exactly the same as I am now going through with in the case of Poland. After Stalin's death—he is a very sick man—we will break the Soviet Union. Then there will begin the dawn of the German rule of the earth. . . .

The opportunity is as favourable as never before. I have but one worry, namely that Chamberlain or some other such pig of a fellow ("Saukerl") will come at the last moment with proposals or with ratting ("Umfall"). He will fly down the stairs, even if I shall personally have to trample on his belly in the eyes of the photographers.

No, it is too late for this. The attack upon and the destruction of Poland begins Saturday[2] early. I shall let a few companies in Polish uniform attack in Upper Silesia or in the Protectorate. Whether the world believes it is quite indifferent ("Scheissegal"). The world believes only in success.

For you, gentlemen, fame and honour are beginning as they have not since centuries. Be hard, be without mercy, act more quickly and brutally than the others. The citizens of Western Europe must tremble with horror. That is

the most human way of conducting a war. For it scares the others off.

The new method of conducting war corresponds to the new drawing of the frontiers. A war extending from Reval, Lublin, Kaschau to the mouth of the Danube. The rest will be given to the Russians. Ribbentrop has orders to make every offer and to accept every demand. In the West I reserve to myself the right to determine the strategically best line. Here one will be able to work with Protectorate regions, such as Holland, Belgium and French Lorraine.

And now, on to the enemy, in Warsaw we will celebrate our reunion.

The speech was received with enthusiasm. Göring jumped on a table, thanked bloodthirstily and made bloodthirsty promises. He danced like a wild man. The few that had misgivings remained quiet. (Here a line of the memorandum is missing in order no doubt to protect the source of information.)[3]

During the meal which followed Hitler said he must act this year as he was not likely to live very long. His successor however would no longer be able to carry this out. Besides, the situation would be a hopeless one in two years at the most.

---

[2]August 26.

[3]This sentence in parentheses forms part of the original typescript.

---

4 The Fall of France

On May 10, 1940, Hitler launched his offensive in the west with an invasion of neutral Belgium, Holland, and Luxembourg. French troops rushed to Belgium to prevent a breakthrough, but the greater menace lay to the south, on the French frontier. Meeting almost no resistance, German panzer divisions had moved through the narrow mountain passes of Luxembourg and the dense Forest of the Ardennes in southern Belgium. On May 12, German units were on French soil near Sedan. Thinking that the Forest of the Ardennes could not be penetrated by a major German force, the French had only lightly fortified the western extension of the Maginot Line, the immense fortifications designed to hold back a German invasion.

The battle for France turned into a rout. Whole French divisions were cut off or in retreat. On June 10, Mussolini also declared war on France. With authority breaking down and resistance dying, the French cabinet appealed for an armistice, which was signed on June 22 in the same railway car in which Germany had agreed to the armistice ending World War I.

Several reasons explain the collapse of France. It is likely that the Germans and the French (including the British planes based in France) had some three thousand planes each. But many French planes—in what still remains a mystery—stayed on the airfields. The planes were available, but the high command either did not use them or did not deploy them properly. Unlike the Germans, the French did not comprehend or appreciate the use of aviation in modern warfare. As for tanks, the French had as many as the Germans, and some were superior. Nor was German manpower overwhelming. France met disaster largely because its military leaders, unlike the Germans, had not mastered the psychology and technology of motorized warfare. "The French commanders, trained in the slow-motion methods of 1918, were mentally unfitted to cope with Panzer pace, and it produced a spreading paralysis among them," says British military expert Sir Basil Liddell Hart. One also senses a loss of will among the French people: a consequence of internal political disputes dividing the nation, poor leadership, the years of appeasement and lost opportunities, and German propaganda, which depicted Nazism as irresistible and the Führer as a man of destiny. It was France's darkest hour.

Heinz Guderian
"FRENCH LEADERSHIP . . . COULD NOT GRASP THE SIGNIFICANCE OF THE TANK IN MOBILE WARFARE"

After the war, General Heinz Guderian (1888–1954), whose panzer divisions formed the vanguard of the attack through the Ardennes into France, analyzed the reasons for France's collapse in *Panzer Leader* (1952).

The First World War on the Western Front, after being for a short time a war of movement, soon settled down to positional warfare. No massing of war material, on no matter how vast a scale, had succeeded in getting the armies moving again until, in November 1916, the enemy's tanks appeared on the battlefield. With their armour plating, their tracks, their guns and their machine-guns, they succeeded in carrying their crews, alive and capable of fighting, through artillery barrages and wire entanglements, over trench systems and shell craters, into the centre of the German lines.

The power of the offensive had come back into its own.

The true importance of tanks was proved by the fact that the Versailles Treaty forbade Germany the possession or construction of armoured vehicles, tanks or any similar equipment which might be employed in war, under pain of punishment.

So our enemies regarded the tank as a decisive weapon which we must not be allowed to have. I therefore decided carefully to study the history of this decisive weapon and to follow its future development. For someone observing tank theory from afar, unburdened by tradition, there were lessons to be learned in the employment, organisation and construction of armour and of armoured units that went beyond the doctrines then accepted abroad. After years of hard struggle, I had succeeded in putting my theories into practice before the other armies had arrived at the same conclusions. The advance we had made in the organisation and employment of tanks was the primary factor on which my belief in our forthcoming success was based. Even in 1940 this belief was shared by scarcely anybody in the German Army.

A profound study of the First World War had given me considerable insight into the psychology of the combatants. I already, from personal experience, knew a considerable amount about our own army. I had also formed certain opinions about our Western adversaries which the events of 1940 were to prove correct. Despite the tank weapons to which our enemies owed in large measure their 1918 victory, they were preoccupied with the concepts of positional warfare.

France possessed the strongest land army in Western Europe. France possessed the numerically strongest tank force in Western Europe.

The combined Anglo-French forces in the West in May 1940 consisted of some 4,000 armoured vehicles: the German Army at that time had 2,800, including armoured reconnaissance cars, and when the attack was launched only 2,200 of these were available for the operation. We thus faced superiority in numbers, to which was added the fact that the French tanks were superior to the German ones both in armour and in gun-calibre, though admittedly inferior in control facilities and in speed. Despite possessing the strongest forces for mobile warfare the French had also built the strongest line of fortifications in the world, the Maginot Line. Why was the money spent on the construction of those fortifications not used for the modernisation and strengthening of France's mobile forces?

The proposals of de Gaulle, Daladier and others along these lines had been ignored. From

this it must be concluded that the highest French leadership either would not or could not grasp the significance of the tank in mobile warfare. In any case all the manœuvres and large-scale exercises of which I had heard led to the conclusion that the French command wanted its troops to be trained in such a way that careful movement and planned measures for attack or for defence could be based on definite, prearranged circumstances. They wanted a complete picture of the enemy's order of battle and intentions before deciding on any undertaking. Once the decision was taken it would be carried out according to plan, one might almost say methodically, not only during the approach march and the deployment of troops, but also during the artillery preparation and the launching of the attack or the construction of the defence as the case might be. This mania for planned control, in which nothing should be left to chance, led to the organisation of the armoured forces within the army in a form that would destroy the general scheme, that is to say their assignment in detail to the infantry divisions. Only a fraction of the French armour was organised for operational employment.

So far as the French were concerned the German leadership could safely rely on the defence of France being systematically based on fortifications and carried out according to a rigid doctrine: this doctrine was the result of the lessons that the French had learned from the First World War, their experience of positional warfare, of the high value they attached to fire power, and of their underestimation of movement.

These French strategic and tactical principles, well known to us in 1940 and the exact contrary of my own theories of warfare, were the second factor on which my belief in victory was founded.

By the spring of 1940 we Germans had gained a clear picture of the enemy's dispositions, and of his fortifications. We knew that somewhere between Montmédy and Sedan the Maginot Line changed from being very strong indeed to being rather weaker. We called the fortifications from Sedan to the Channel "the prolonged Maginot Line." We knew about the locations and, usually, about the strength of the Belgian and Dutch fortifications. They all faced only towards Germany.

While the Maginot Line was thinly held, the mass of the French army together with the British Expeditionary Force was assembled in Flanders, between the Meuse and the English Channel, facing northeast; the Belgian and Dutch troops, on the other hand, were deployed to defend their frontiers against an attack from the east.

From their order of battle it was plain that the enemy expected the Germans to attempt the Schlieffen Plan[1] once again, and that they intended to bring the bulk of the allied armies against this anticipated outflanking movement through Holland and Belgium. A sufficient safeguard of the hinge of their proposed advance into Belgium by reserve units—in the area, say, of Charleville and Verdun—was not apparent. It seemed that the French High Command did not regard any alternative to the old Schlieffen Plan as even conceivable.

Our knowledge of the enemy's order of battle and of his predictable reactions at the beginning of the German advance was the third factor that contributed to my belief in victory.

In addition there were a number of other aspects in our general evaluation of the enemy which, though of less reliability, were still worth taking into consideration.

We knew and respected the French soldier from the First World War as a brave and tough fighter who had defended his country with stubborn energy. We did not doubt that he would show the same spirit this time. But so far as the French leaders were concerned, we were amazed that they had not taken advantage of their favourable situation during the autumn of 1939 to attack, while the bulk of the German forces, including the entire armoured force, was engaged in Poland. Their reasons for such restraint were at the time hard to see. We could only guess. Be that as it may, the caution shown by the French leaders led us to believe that our adversaries hoped somehow to avoid a serious clash of arms. The rather inactive behavior of the French during the winter of 1939–40 seemed to indicate a limited enthusiasm for the war on their part.

From all this I concluded that a determined and forcibly led attack by strong armoured forces through Sedan and Amiens, with the Atlantic coast as its objective, would hit the enemy deep in the flank of his forces advancing into Belgium; I did not think that he disposed of sufficient reserves to parry this thrust; and I therefore believed it had a great chance of succeeding and, if the initial success were fully exploited, might lead to the cutting off of all the main enemy forces moving up into Belgium.

REVIEW QUESTIONS

1. According to Heinz Guderian, why was it an error for French military strategy to rely so heavily on the Maginot Line?
2. How did World War I demonstrate the importance of tanks in modern warfare?
3. What mistaken lessons did the French draw from their experience in World War I?

5 The Battle of Britain

Hitler expected that after his stunning victories in the West, Britain would make peace. The British, however, continued to reject Hitler's overtures, for they envisioned a bleak future if Nazi Germany dominated the Continent. With

[1]Drawn up by General Alfred von Schlieffen prior to World War I, the plan called for the German army to swing through Belgium, outflank, envelop, and destroy the French forces, and isolate Paris, compelling France to surrender.

Britain unwilling to come to terms, Hitler proceeded in earnest with invasion plans. A successful crossing of the English Channel and the establishment of beachheads on the English coast depended on control of the skies. In early August 1940, the Luftwaffe began massive attacks on British air and naval installations. Virtually every day during the Battle of Britain, hundreds of planes fought in the sky above Britain as British pilots rose to the challenge. On September 15, the Royal Air Force (RAF) shot down sixty aircraft; two days later Hitler postponed the invasion of Britain "until further notice." The development of radar by British scientists, the skill and courage of British fighter pilots, and the inability of Germany to make up its losses in planes saved Britain in its struggle for survival. With the invasion of Britain called off, the Luftwaffe concentrated on bombing English cities, industrial centers, and ports. Almost every night for months, the inhabitants of London sought shelter in subways and cellars to escape German bombs, while British planes rose time after time to make the Luftwaffe pay the price. British morale never broke during the "Blitz."

Winston Churchill
"BLOOD, TOIL, TEARS, AND SWEAT"

Churchill, at the age of sixty-six, proved to be an undaunted leader, sharing the perils faced by all and able by example and by speeches to rally British morale. When he first addressed Parliament as prime minister on May 13, 1940, he left no doubt about the grim realities that lay ahead. Excerpts from his speeches in 1940 follow.

May 13, 1940

I would say to the House, as I said to those who have joined this Government: "I have nothing to offer but blood, toil, tears, and sweat." We have before us an ordeal of the most grievous kind. We have before us many, many long months of struggle and suffering. You ask: "What is our policy?" I will say: "It is to wage war by sea, land, and air with all our might, and with all the strength that God can give us; to wage war against a monstrous tyranny, never surpassed in the dark lamentable catalogue of human crime." That is our policy.

You ask: "What is our aim?" I can answer in one word: "Victory!" Victory at all costs, victory in spite of all terror, victory however long and hard the road may be; for without victory there is no survival.

When Churchill spoke next, on May 19, the Dutch had surrendered to the Germans, and the French and British armies were in retreat. Still, Churchill promised that "conquer we shall."

May 19, 1940

This is one of the most awe-striking periods in the long history of France and Britain. It is also beyond doubt the most sublime. Side by side, unaided except by their kith and kin in the great Dominions and by the wide Empires which rest beneath their shield—side by side, the British and French peoples have advanced to rescue not only Europe but mankind from the foulest and most soul-destroying tyranny which has ever darkened and stained the pages of history. Behind them—behind us—behind the armies and fleets of Britain and France—gather a group of shattered states and bludgeoned races: the Czechs, the Poles, the Norwegians, the Danes, the Dutch, the Belgians—upon all of whom the long night of barbarism will descend unbroken even by a star of hope, unless we conquer, as conquer we must; as conquer we shall.

By early June the Belgians had surrendered to the Germans, and the last units of the British Expeditionary Force in France had been evacuated from Dunkirk; the French armies were in full flight. Again Churchill spoke out in defiance of events across the Channel.

June 4, 1940

We shall not flag or fail. We shall go on to the end. We shall fight in France, we shall fight on the seas and oceans, we shall fight with growing confidence and growing strength in the air. We shall defend our island, whatever the cost may be. We shall fight on the beaches, we shall fight on the landing-grounds, we shall fight in the fields and in the streets, we shall fight in the hills. We shall never surrender; and even if, which I do not for a moment believe, this island or a large part of it were subjugated and starving, then our Empire beyond the seas, armed and guarded by the British Fleet, would carry on the struggle, until, in God's good time, the New World, with all its power and might, steps forth to the rescue and liberation of the Old.

By June 18 the battle of France was lost; on June 22 France surrendered. Now Britain itself was under siege. Churchill again found the right words to sustain his people.

June 18, 1940

What General [Maxime] Weygand [commander of the French army] called the Battle of France is over. . . . The Battle of Britain is about to begin. Upon this battle depends the survival of Christian civilization. Upon it depends our own British life and the long continuity of our institutions and our Empire. The whole fury and might of the enemy must very soon be turned upon us. Hitler knows that he will have to break us in this island or lose the war.

If we can stand up to him, all Europe may be free and the life of the world may move forward into broad sunlit uplands. But if we fail, then the whole world, including the United States, including all that we have known and cared for, will sink into the abyss of a new Dark Age made more sinister and perhaps more prolonged by the lights of a perverted science.

Let us therefore brace ourselves to our duty and so bear ourselves that if the British Empire and Commonwealth last for a thousand years, men will still say, "This was their finest hour."

While the Battle of Britain raged, Churchill lauded the courage of British airmen who rose to the challenge.

August 20, 1940

The gratitude of every home in our island, in our Empire, and indeed throughout the world, except in the abodes of the guilty, goes out to the British airmen who, undaunted by odds, unwearied in their constant challenge and mortal danger, are turning the tide of world war by their prowess and by their devotion. Never in the field of human conflict was so much owed by so many to so few. All hearts go out to the fighter pilots whose brilliant actions we see with our own eyes day after day.

REVIEW QUESTIONS

1. According to Winston Churchill, what would a Nazi victory mean for Europe?
2. On whose help did Churchill ultimately count for the liberation of Europe?
3. Both Hitler and Churchill were gifted orators. Compare their styles.

6 Nazi Propaganda: For Volk, Führer, and Fatherland

After World War II, Germans maintained that the Wehrmacht (the German army) was an apolitical professional fighting force that remained free of Nazi ideology and was uninvolved in criminal acts perpetrated by Heinrich Himmler's SS, the elite units responsible for the extermination of Jews. It is now known that units of the German army assisted the SS in the rounding up of Jews and at times participated in mass murder. Recently historians have also argued that the regular army, far from being apolitical, was imbued with Nazi ideology, and that many German officers and soldiers, succumbing to Nazi indoctrination, viewed the war, particularly on the eastern front, as a titanic struggle against evil and subhuman Jewish-led Bolsheviks who threatened the very existence of the German Volk.

THE INDOCTRINATION OF THE GERMAN SOLDIER

The following excerpts from German army propaganda and letters written by soldiers show how Nazi ideology influenced ordinary German troops. The first is a news-sheet published by the High Command of the Armed Forces in the spring of 1940, and distributed to all army units, which expressed quasi-religious fervor for the Führer.

THE FÜHRER AS SAVIOR

Behind the battle of annihilation of May 1940 stands in lone greatness the name of the Führer.

All that has been accomplished since he has taken the fate of our people into his strong hands!

. . . He gave the people back its unity, smashed the parties and destroyed the hydra of the organizations . . . he decontaminated the body of our people from the Jewish subversion, created a stock-proud, race-conscious *Volk,* which had overcome the racial death of diminishing births and was granted renewed [abundance of childbirths] as a carrier of the great future of the Fatherland. He subdued the terrible plight of unemployment and granted to millions of people who had already despaired of the *Volk* a new belief in the *Volksgemeinschaft* [community of the people] and happiness in a new Fatherland. . . .

His genius, in which the whole strength of Germandom is embodied with ancient powers, has animated the souls of 80,000,000 Germans, has filled them with strength and will, with the storm and stress *{Sturm und Drang}* of a renewed young people; and, himself the first soldier of Germany, he has entered the name of the German soldier into the book of immortality.

All this we were allowed to experience. Our great duty in this year of decision is that we do not accept it as observers, but that we, enchanted, and with all the passion of which we are capable, sacrifice ourselves to this Führer and strive to be worthy of the historical epoch molded by a heaven-storming will.

This same religious devotion to Hitler and Nazi ideology was expressed in literature given to company commanders to assist them in indoctrinating their troops.

Only the Führer could carry out what had not been achieved for a thousand years. . . . [He has] brought together all the German stock . . . for the struggle for freedom and living space . . . [and] directed all his thoughts and efforts toward the National Socialist education of the *Volk,* the inner cohesion of the state, the armament and offensive capability of the Wehrmacht. . . . When the German Eastern Armies fought an unparalleled battle during the winter of 1941–42 in the snow and ice of the Russian winter, he said: "Any weakling can put up with victories. Only the strong can stand firm in battles of destiny. But heaven gives the ultimate and highest prize only to those who are capable of withstanding battles of destiny." In the difficult winter of 1942–43 the strength of the Führer was demonstrated once more, when . . . he called upon the German *Volk* at the front and in the homeland to stand firm and make the supreme effort. The Führer . . . clearly sees the goal ahead: a strong German Reich as the power of order in Europe and a firm root of the German *Lebensraum.* This goal will be achieved if the whole *Volk* remains loyal to him even in difficult times and as long as we soldiers do our duty.

Such words were not without their impact on German soldiers. In November 1940, one soldier expressed his feelings about Hitler in a letter home.

The last words of the Führer's radio address are over and a new strength streams through our veins. It is as if he spoke to each individual, to everyone of us, as if he wanted to give everyone new strength. With loyalty and a sense of duty, we must fight for our principles and endure to the end. Our Führer represents our united German Fatherland. . . . What we do for him, we do for all of you; what we sacrifice in foreign lands, we sacrifice for our loved ones. When the Führer speaks on these festive occasions, I feel deep in my soul that you at home also feel that we must be ready to make all sacrifices. . . . German victory is as certain as

our love for each other. Just as we believe in our love, so we believe in our final victory and in the future of our people and our Fatherland.

Similar sentiments were voiced by a private in a letter to his brother.

The Führer has grown into the greatest figure of the century, in his hand lies the destiny of the world and of culturally-perceptive humanity. May his pure sword strike down the Satanic monster. Yes, the blows are still hard, but the horror will be forced into the shadows through the inexorable Need, through the command which derives from our National Socialist idea. This [battle] is for a new ideology, a new belief, a new life! I am glad that I can participate, even if as a tiny cog, in this war of light against darkness.

BOLSHEVIKS AND JEWS AS DEVILS

German propaganda described Jews and Russian communists in racial and religious terms, calling them a morally depraved form of humanity in the service of Satan. A tract from SS headquarters illustrates the mythical nature of Nazi ideology.

Just as night rises up against the day, just as light and darkness are eternal enemies, so the greatest enemy of world-dominating man is man himself. The sub-man—that creature which looks as though biologically it were of absolutely the same kind, endowed by Nature with hands, feet and a sort of brain, with eyes and mouth—is nevertheless a totally different, a fearful creature, is only an attempt at a human being, with a quasi-human face, yet in mind and spirit lower than any animal. Inside this being a cruel chaos of wild, unchecked passions: a nameless will to destruction, the most primitive lusts, the most undisguised vileness. A sub-man—nothing else! . . . Never has the sub-man granted peace, never has he permitted rest. . . . To preserve himself he needed mud, he needed hell, but not the sun. And this underworld of sub-men found its leader: the eternal Jew!

The news-sheet distributed to regular army units used similar language.

Anyone who has ever looked at the face of a red commissar knows what the Bolsheviks are like. Here there is no need for theoretical expressions. We would insult the animals if we described these mostly Jewish men as beasts. They are the embodiment of the Satanic and insane hatred against the whole of noble humanity. The shape of these commissars reveals to us the rebellion of the *Untermenschen* [sub-men] against noble blood. The masses, whom they have sent to their deaths [in this war against Germany] by making use of all means at their disposal such as ice-cold terror and insane incitement, would have brought an end to all meaningful life, had this eruption not been dammed at the last moment.

In October 1941, Walter von Reichenau, commander of the Sixth Army, appealed to his men in the language of Nazi racial ideology.

The essential goal of the campaign against the Jewish-Bolshevik system is the complete destruction of its power instruments and the eradication of the Asiatic influence on the European cultural sphere. . . . Therefore the soldier must have *complete* understanding for the necessity of the harsh, but just atonement of Jewish subhumanity.

In November 1941, General von Manstein, commander of the Eleventh Army, used much the same language.

Since 22 June the German *Volk* is in the midst of a battle for life and death against the Bolshevik system. This battle is conducted against the Soviet army not only in a conventional manner according to the rules of European warfare. . . .

Judaism constitutes the mediator between the enemy in the rear and the still fighting remnants of the Red Army and the Red leadership. It has a stronger hold [in the Soviet Union] than in Europe on all key positions of the political leadership and administration, it occupies commerce and trade and further forms cells for all the disturbances and possible rebellions.

The Jewish-Bolshevik system must be eradicated once and for all. Never again may it interfere in our European living space.

The German soldier is therefore not only charged with the task of destroying the power instrument of this system. He marches forth also as a carrier of a racial conception and as an avenger of all the atrocities which have been committed against him and the German people.

The soldier must show understanding for the harsh atonement of Judaism, the spiritual carrier of the Bolshevik terror.

And in that same month, Colonel-General Hoth also interpreted the war as a struggle between racial superiors and inferiors.

It has become increasingly clear to us this summer, that here in the East spiritually unbridgeable conceptions are fighting each other: German sense of honor and race, and a soldierly tradition of many centuries, against an Asiatic mode of thinking and primitive instincts, whipped up by a small number of mostly Jewish intellectuals: fear of the knout [whip used for flogging], disregard of moral values, levelling down, throwing away of one's worthless life.

More than ever we are filled with the thought of a new era, in which the strength of the German people's racial superiority and achievements entrust it with the leadership of Europe. We clearly recognize our mission to save European culture from the advancing Asiatic barbarism. We now know that we have to fight against an incensed and tough opponent. This battle can only end with the destruction of one or the other; a compromise is out of the question.

The frontline soldier was affected by ideological propaganda.

I have received the "Stürmer" [a notoriously anti-Semitic newspaper] now for the third time. It makes me happy with all my heart. . . . You could not have made me happier. . . . I recognized the Jewish poison in our people long ago; how far it might have gone with us, this we see only now in this campaign. What the Jewish-regime has done in Russia, we see every day, and even the last doubters are cured here in view of the facts. We must and we will liberate the world from this plague, this is why the German soldier protects the Eastern Front, and we shall not return before we have uprooted all evil and destroyed the center of the Jewish-Bolshevik "world-do-gooders."

REVIEW QUESTIONS

1. How did Nazi propaganda depict Hitler? Germans? Jews? Russians?
2. Why was such propaganda effective?

---

7   Stalingrad: A Turning Point

In July 1942, the Germans resumed their advance into the U.S.S.R., begun the previous summer, seeking to conquer Stalingrad, a vital transportation center located on the Volga River. Germans and Russians battled with dogged ferocity over every part of the city; 99 percent of Stalingrad was reduced to rubble. A Russian counteroffensive in November trapped the German Sixth Army. Realizing that the Sixth Army, exhausted and short of weapons, ammunition, food, and medical supplies, faced annihilation, German generals pleaded in vain with Hitler to permit withdrawal before the Russians closed the ring. On February 2, 1943, the remnants of the Sixth Army surrendered. More than a million people—Russian civilians and soldiers, Germans and their Italian, Hungarian, and Romanian allies—perished in the epic struggle for Stalingrad. The Russian victory was a major turning point in the war.

William Hoffman
DIARY OF A GERMAN SOLDIER

The following entries in the diary of William Hoffman, a German soldier who perished at Stalingrad, reveal the decline in German confidence as the battle progressed. While the German army was penetrating deeply into Russia, he believed that victory was not far away and dreamed of returning home with medals. Then the terrible struggles in Stalingrad made him curse the war.

Today, after we'd had a bath, the company commander told us that if our future operations are as successful, we'll soon reach the Volga, take Stalingrad and then the war will inevitably soon be over. Perhaps we'll be home by Christmas.

July 29 1942. . . . The company commander says the Russian troops are completely broken, and cannot hold out any longer. To reach the Volga and take Stalingrad is not so difficult for us. The Führer knows where the Russians' weak point is. Victory is not far away. . . .

August 2. . . . What great spaces the Soviets occupy, what rich fields there are to be had here after the war's over! Only let's get it over with quickly. I believe that the Führer will carry the thing through to a successful end.

August 10. . . . The Führer's orders were read out to us. He expects victory of us. We are all convinced that they can't stop us.

August 12. We are advancing towards Stalingrad along the railway line. Yesterday Russian "katyushi" [small rocket launchers] and then tanks halted our regiment. "The Russians are throwing in their last forces," Captain Werner explained to me. Large-scale help is coming up for us, and the Russians will be beaten.

This morning outstanding soldiers were presented with decorations. . . . Will I really go back to Elsa without a decoration? I believe that for Stalingrad the Führer will decorate even me. . . .

August 23. Splendid news—north of Stalingrad our troops have reached the Volga and captured part of the city. The Russians have two alternatives, either to flee across the Volga or give themselves up. Our company's interpreter has interrogated a captured Russian officer. He was wounded, but asserted that the Russians would fight for Stalingrad to the last round. Something incomprehensible is, in fact, going on. In the north our troops capture a

part of Stalingrad and reach the Volga, but in the south the doomed divisions are continuing to resist bitterly. Fanaticism. . . .

August 27. A continuous cannonade on all sides. We are slowly advancing. Less than twenty miles to go to Stalingrad. In the daytime we can see the smoke of fires, at night-time the bright glow. They say that the city is on fire; on the Führer's orders our Luftwaffe [air force] has sent it up in flames. That's what the Russians need, to stop them from resisting. . . .

September 4. We are being sent northward along the front towards Stalingrad. We marched all night and by dawn had reached Voroponovo Station. We can already see the smoking town. It's a happy thought that the end of the war is getting nearer. That's what everyone is saying. If only the days and nights would pass more quickly. . . .

September 5. Our regiment has been ordered to attack Sadovaya station—that's nearly in Stalingrad. Are the Russians really thinking of holding out in the city itself? We had no peace all night from the Russian artillery and aeroplanes. Lots of wounded are being brought by. God protect me. . . .

September 8. Two days of non-stop fighting. The Russians are defending themselves with insane stubbornness. Our regiment has lost many men from the "katyushi," which belch out terrible fire. I have been sent to work at battalion H.Q. It must be mother's prayers that have taken me away from the company's trenches. . . .

September 11. Our battalion is fighting in the suburbs of Stalingrad. We can already see the Volga; firing is going on all the time. Wherever you look is fire and flames. . . . Russian cannon and machine-guns are firing out of the burning city. Fanatics. . . .

September 13. An unlucky number. This morning "katyushi" attacks caused the company heavy losses: twenty-seven dead and fifty wounded. The Russians are fighting desperately like wild beasts, don't give themselves up, but come up close and then throw grenades. Lieutenant Kraus was killed yesterday, and there is no company commander.

September 16. Our battalion, plus tanks, is attacking the [grain storage] elevator, from which smoke is pouring—the grain in it is burning, the Russians seem to have set light to it themselves. Barbarism. The battalion is suffering heavy losses. There are not more than sixty men left in each company. The elevator is occupied not by men but by devils that no flames or bullets can destroy.

September 18. Fighting is going on inside the elevator. The Russians inside are condemned men; the battalion commander says: "The commissars have ordered those men to die in the elevator."

If all the buildings of Stalingrad are defended like this then none of our soldiers will get back to Germany. I had a letter from Elsa today. She's expecting me home when victory's won.

September 20. The battle for the elevator is still going on. The Russians are firing on all sides. We stay in our cellar; you can't go out into the street. Sergeant-Major Nuschke was killed today running across a street. Poor fellow, he's got three children.

September 22. Russian resistance in the elevator has been broken. Our troops are advancing towards the Volga. . . .

. . . Our old soldiers have never experienced such bitter fighting before.

September 26. Our regiment is involved in constant heavy fighting. After the elevator was taken the Russians continued to defend themselves just as stubbornly. You don't see them at all, they have established themselves in houses and cellars and are firing on all sides, including

from our rear—barbarians, they use gangster methods.

In the blocks captured two days ago Russian soldiers appeared from somewhere or other and fighting has flared up with fresh vigour. Our men are being killed not only in the firing line, but in the rear, in buildings we have already occupied.

The Russians have stopped surrendering at all. If we take any prisoners it's because they are hopelessly wounded, and can't move by themselves. Stalingrad is hell. Those who are merely wounded are lucky; they will doubtless be at home and celebrate victory with their families. . . .

September 28. Our regiment, and the whole division, are today celebrating victory. Together with our tank crews we have taken the southern part of the city and reached the Volga. We paid dearly for our victory. In three weeks we have occupied about five and a half square miles. The commander has congratulated us on our victory. . . .

October 3. After marching through the night we have established ourselves in a shrub-covered gully. We are apparently going to attack the factories, the chimneys of which we can see clearly. Behind them is the Volga. We have entered a new area. It was night but we saw many crosses with our helmets on top. Have we really lost so many men? Damn this Stalingrad!

October 4. Our regiment is attacking the Barrikady settlement. A lot of Russian tommy [machine]-gunners have appeared. Where are they bringing them from?

October 5. Our battalion has gone into the attack four times, and got stopped each time. Russian snipers hit anyone who shows himself carelessly from behind shelter.

October 10. The Russians are so close to us that our planes cannot bomb them. We are preparing for a decisive attack. The Führer has ordered the whole of Stalingrad to be taken as rapidly as possible.

October 14. It has been fantastic since morning: our aeroplanes and artillery have been hammering the Russian positions for hours on end; everything in sight is being blotted from the face of the earth. . . .

October 22. Our regiment has failed to break into the factory. We have lost many men; every time you move you have to jump over bodies. You can scarcely breathe in the daytime: there is nowhere and no one to remove the bodies, so they are left there to rot. Who would have thought three months ago that instead of the joy of victory we would have to endure such sacrifice and torture, the end of which is nowhere in sight? . . .

The soldiers are calling Stalingrad the mass grave of the Wehrmacht [German army]. There are very few men left in the companies. We have been told we are soon going to be withdrawn to be brought back up to strength.

October 27. Our troops have captured the whole of the Barrikady factory, but we cannot break through to the Volga. The Russians are not men, but some kind of cast-iron creatures; they never get tired and are not afraid of fire. We are absolutely exhausted; our regiment now has barely the strength of a company. The Russian artillery at the other side of the Volga won't let you lift your head. . . .

October 28. Every soldier sees himself as a condemned man. The only hope is to be wounded and taken back to the rear. . . .

November 3. In the last few days our battalion has several times tried to attack the Russian positions, . . . to no avail. On this sector also the Russians won't let you lift your head. There have been a number of cases of self-inflicted wounds and malingering among the men. Every day I write two or three reports about them.

November 10. A letter from Elsa today. Everyone expects us home for Christmas. In Germany everyone believes we already hold Stalingrad. How wrong they are. If they could only see what Stalingrad has done to our army.

November 18. Our attack with tanks yesterday had no success. After our attack the field was littered with dead.

November 21. The Russians have gone over to the offensive along the whole front. Fierce fighting is going on. So, there it is—the Volga, victory and soon home to our families! We shall obviously be seeing them next in the other world.

November 29. We are encircled. It was announced this morning that the Führer has said: "The army can trust me to do everything necessary to ensure supplies and rapidly break the encirclement."

December 3. We are on hunger rations and waiting for the rescue that the Führer promised.

I send letters home, but there is no reply.

December 7. Rations have been cut to such an extent that the soldiers are suffering terribly from hunger; they are issuing one loaf of stale bread for five men.

December 11. Three questions are obsessing every soldier and officer: When will the Russians stop firing and let us sleep in peace, if only for one night? How and with what are we going to fill our empty stomachs, which, apart from 3½–7 ozs of bread, receive virtually nothing at all? And when will Hitler take any decisive steps to free our armies from encirclement?

December 14. Everybody is racked with hunger. Frozen potatoes are the best meal, but to get them out of the ice-covered ground under fire from Russian bullets is not so easy.

December 18. The officers today told the soldiers to be prepared for action. General Manstein is approaching Stalingrad from the south with strong forces. This news brought hope to the soldiers' hearts. God, let it be!

December 21. We are waiting for the order, but for some reason or other it has been a long time coming. Can it be that it is not true about Manstein? This is worse than any torture.

December 23. Still no orders. It was all a bluff with Manstein. Or has he been defeated at the approaches to Stalingrad?

December 25. The Russian radio has announced the defeat of Manstein. Ahead of us is either death or captivity.

December 26. The horses have already been eaten. I would eat a cat; they say its meat is also tasty. The soldiers look like corpses or lunatics, looking for something to put in their mouths. They no longer take cover from Russian shells; they haven't the strength to walk, run away and hide. A curse on this war! . . .

Joachim Wieder
MEMORIES AND REASSESSMENTS

In 1962, Joachim Wieder, a German officer who had survived Stalingrad and Russian captivity, wrote *Stalingrad: Memories and Reassessments,* in which he described his feelings as the Russians closed the ring on the trapped Sixth Army. Wieder recalled his outrage at Hitler's refusal to allow the Sixth Army to break out when it still had a chance. As the German army faced decimation, he reflected on the misery and death the invading German forces had inflicted on other people and the terrible retribution Germany would suffer.

A foreboding I had long held grew into a terrible certainty. What was happening here in Stalingrad was a tragic, senseless self-sacrifice, a scarcely credible betrayal of the final commitment and devotion of brave soldiers. Our innocent trust had been misused in the most despicable manner by those responsible for the catastrophe. We had been betrayed, led astray and condemned. The men of Stalingrad were dying in betrayed belief and in betrayed trust. In my heart the bitter feeling of ". . . and all for nothing" became ever more torturing.

In my soul arose again the whole abysmal disaster of the war itself. More clearly than ever before I appreciated the full measure of misery and wretchedness of the other countries in Europe to which German soldiers and German arms had brought boundless misfortune. Had

not we, so far the victors, been all too prone to close our eyes and our hearts and to forget that always and everywhere, the issues were living human beings, their possessions and their happiness?

Probably only a few among us had entertained the thought that the suffering and dying being caused by our sorry profession of war would one day be inflicted upon us. We had carried our total war into one region of Europe after another and thereby destructively interfered in the destinies of foreign nations. Far too little had we asked the reason why, the necessities and the justifications for what was happening or reflected on the immeasurability of our political responsibility that these entailed. Misery and death had been initiated by us and now they were inexorably coming home to roost. The steppe on the

Don and the Volga had drunk streams of precious human blood. Here in their hundreds of thousands had Germans, Roumanians, Italians, Russians and members of other Soviet peoples found their common grave.

The Russians were certainly also making cruelly high blood sacrifices in the murderous battle of Stalingrad. But they, who were defending their country against a foreign aggressor, knew better than we why they were risking their lives.

Several thousand Red Army prisoners suffering hunger and misery behind barbed wire at Voroponovo and doomed to share our downfall were particularly to be pitied. In my broodings which constantly haunted and tortured me, I began to realise just how much our feelings had atrophied towards the continual boundless disregard and violation of human dignity and human life. At the same time my horror and revulsion of the Moloch[1] of war, to whom ethical-religious conscience had stood in irreconcilable opposition from the very beginning, grew.

And so as the last days of our army were drawing to a close, a deep moral misery gnawed at the hearts of the men helplessly doomed to destruction. Added to their indescribable external suffering were the violent internal conflicts caused by the voice of conscience, and not only with regard to the question of the unconditional duty to obey. Wherever I went and observed I saw the same picture. And what I learned about the matter later on only confirmed the impressions I had gained. Whoever was still unclear about the contexts and reasons for the catastrophe sensed them in dark despair.

Many officers and commanders now began to oppose the insane orders emanating from Führer Headquarters and being passed on by Army Command. By this time they began to reject the long eroded military concepts of honour and discipline to which the Army leadership had

clung until the end. In the unconditional obedience, such as was fatally being upheld here at Stalingrad, they no longer saw a soldierly stance but rather a lack of responsibility. . . .

How shocked had we been then at the very outset of the eastern campaign, about two inhumane orders of the day that had been in open breach of international law and of true, decent German soldiery itself! These were the unethical "commissar order" that required the physical extermination of the regulators of the Bolshevik ideology in the Red Army, and the "Barbarossa order" dealing with military tribunals, that abolished mandatory prosecution of crimes by German soldiers against civilians in the eastern theatre. Even if these orders had only been acknowledged by our staffs on the front and evaded as far as possible, was it not guilt enough to have accepted and tolerated them in silence like so much else?

And what had gone on in the rear of the fighting troops? Many an ugly rumour had come to one's ears, many an ugly picture had come before one's eyes. I had heard of brutal acts of retribution which had struck the innocent with the guilty. On a drive through the occupied area I had on one occasion seen in Minsk, with its dozens of public gallows, scenes of shameful inhumanity. Were all these excesses and evils not bound to rebound on us sooner or later? . . .

Now, faced with the imminently impending final catastrophe, the question about the sense of what was happening that had plagued me so often during the war seized me again with cruel force. Hundreds of thousands of flowering human lives were suddenly being senselessly snuffed out here in Stalingrad. What an immeasurable wealth of human happiness, human plans, hopes, talents, fertile possibilities for the future were thereby being destroyed for ever! The criminal insanity of an irresponsible war management with its superstitious belief in technology and its utter lack of feeling for the life, value and dignity of man, had here prepared a hell on earth for us. Of what importance was the individual in his uniqueness and

---

[1]In the Old Testament Moloch was the god of the Ammonites and the Phoenicians to whom children were sacrificed.

distinctiveness? He felt himself as if extinguished and used up as raw material in a demonic machine of destruction. Here war showed itself in its unmasked brutality. Stalingrad appeared to me as an unsurpassed violation and degeneration of the human essence. I felt myself to be locked into a gigantic, inhuman mechanism that was running on with deadly precision to its own dissolution and destruction. . . .

In the sad events on the Volga I saw not only the military turning-point of the war. In the experiences behind me I felt and apprehended something else as well; the anticipation of the final catastrophe towards which the whole nation was reeling. In my mind's eye I suddenly saw a second Stalingrad, a repetition of the tragedy just lived through, but of much greater, more terrible proportions. It was a vast pocket battle on German soil with the whole German nation fighting for life or death inside. And were the issues not the same as those of the final months of our Sixth Army? In the sacrifice thus already ordained, would insight, the power of decision and the strength either to break out or to surrender be able to mature?

In our helpless abandonment, to feel our own fate and destruction breaking in on our country, was a crushing mental burden that was to become virtually unbearable in the times ahead.

REVIEW QUESTIONS

1. What were the expectations of William Hoffman as he marched with the German army in July and August? How did he view Hitler and the war?
2. How did the hard fighting at Stalingrad alter Hoffman's conception of the war and his attitude toward the Russians?
3. What kinds of doubts attacked Joachim Wieder when the Sixth Army was trapped at Stalingrad?

8 The Holocaust

Over conquered Europe the Nazis imposed a "New Order" marked by exploitation, torture, and mass murder. The Germans took some 5.5 million Russian prisoners of war, of whom more than 3.5 million perished; many of these prisoners were deliberately starved to death. The Germans imprisoned and executed many Polish intellectuals and priests and slaughtered vast numbers of Gypsies. Using the modern state's organizational capacities and the instruments of modern technology, the Nazis murdered six million Jews, including one and a half million children—two-thirds of the Jewish population of Europe. Gripped by the mythical, perverted world-view of Nazism, the SS, Hitler's elite guard, carried out these murders with dedication and idealism; they believed that they were exterminating subhumans who threatened the German nation.

Hermann Graebe
SLAUGHTER OF JEWS IN THE UKRAINE

While the regular German army penetrated deeply into Russia, special SS units, the *Einsatzgruppen,* rounded up Jews for mass executions. Aided by Ukrainian, Lithuanian, and Latvian auxiliaries, and contingents from the Romanian army, the Einsatzgruppen massacred 1 to 1.4 million Jews. Hermann Graebe, a German construction engineer, saw such a mass slaughter in Dubno in the Ukraine. He gave a sworn affidavit before the Nuremberg tribunal, a court at which the Allies tried Nazi war criminals after the end of World War II.

Graebe had joined the Nazi Party in 1931 but later renounced his membership, and during the war he rescued Jews from the SS. Graebe was the only German citizen to volunteer to testify at the Nuremberg trials, an act that earned him the enmity of his compatriots. Socially ostracized, Graebe emigrated to the United States, where he died in 1986 at the age of eighty-five.

On October 5, 1942, when I visited the building office at Dubno, my foreman told me that in the vicinity of the site, Jews from Dubno had been shot in three large pits, each about 30 metres long and 3 metres deep. About 1,500 persons had been killed daily. All the 5,000 Jews who had still been living in Dubno before the pogrom were to be liquidated. As the shooting had taken place in his presence, he was still much upset.

Thereupon, I drove to the site accompanied by my foreman and saw near it great mounds of earth, about 30 metres long and 2 metres high. Several trucks stood in front of the mounds. Armed Ukrainian militia drove the people off the trucks under the supervision of an S.S. man. The militiamen acted as guards on the trucks and drove them to and from the pit. All these people had the regulation yellow patches on the front and back of their clothes, and thus could be recognized as Jews.

My foreman and I went directly to the pits. Nobody bothered us. Now I heard rifle shots in quick succession from behind one of the earth mounds. The people who had got off the trucks—men, women and children of all ages—had to undress upon the orders of an S.S. man, who carried a riding or dog whip. They had to put down their clothes in fixed places, sorted according to shoes, top clothing and underclothing. I saw a heap of shoes of about 800 to 1,000 pairs, great piles of underlinen and clothing.

Without screaming or weeping, these people undressed, stood around in family groups, kissed each other, said farewells, and waited for a sign from another S.S. man, who stood near the pit, also with a whip in his hand. During the fifteen minutes that I stood near I heard no complaint or plea for mercy. I watched a family of about eight persons, a man and a woman both about fifty with their children of about one, eight and ten, and two grown-up daughters of about twenty to twenty-nine. An old woman with snow-white hair was holding the one-year-old child in her arms and singing to it and tickling it. The child was cooing with delight. The couple were looking on with tears in their eyes. The father was holding the hand of a boy about ten years old and speaking to him softly; the boy was fighting his tears. The father pointed to the sky, stroked his head, and seemed to explain something to him.

At that moment the S.S. man at the pit shouted something to his comrade. The latter counted off about twenty persons and instructed them to go behind the earth mound. Among them was the family which I have mentioned. I well remember a girl, slim and with black hair, who, as she passed close to me, pointed to herself and said "23." I walked around the mound and found myself confronted by a tremendous grave. People were closely wedged together and lying on top of each other so that only their heads were visible. Nearly all had blood running over their shoulders from their heads. Some of the people shot were still moving. Some were lifting their arms and turning their heads to show that they were still alive. The pit was already two-thirds full. I estimated that it already contained about 1,000 people.

I looked for the man who did the shooting. He was an S.S. man, who sat at the edge of the narrow end of the pit, his feet dangling into the pit. He had a tommy-gun on his knees and was smoking a cigarette. The people, completely naked, went down some steps which were cut in the clay wall of the pit and clambered over the heads of the people lying there, to the place to which the S.S. man directed them. They lay down in front of the dead or injured people; some caressed those who were still alive and spoke to them in a low voice.

Then I heard a series of shots. I looked into the pit and saw that the bodies were twitching or the heads lying motionless on top of the bodies which lay before them. Blood was running from their necks. I was surprised that I was not ordered away, but I saw that there were two or three postmen in uniform nearby. The next batch was approaching already. They went down into the pit, lined themselves up against the previous victims and were shot.

When I walked back round the mound, I noticed another truckload of people which had just arrived. This time it included sick and infirm persons. An old, very thin woman with terribly thin legs was undressed by others who were already naked, while two people held her up. The woman appeared to be paralyzed. The naked people carried the woman around the mound. I left with my foreman and drove in my car back to Dubno.

On the morning of the next day, when I again visited the site, I saw about thirty naked people lying near the pit—about 30 to 50 metres away from it. Some of them were still alive; they looked straight in front of them with a fixed stare and seemed to notice neither the chilliness of the morning nor the workers of my firm who stood around. A girl of about twenty spoke to me and asked me to give her clothes and help her escape. At that moment we heard a fast car approach and I noticed that it was an S.S. detail. I moved away to my site. Ten minutes later we heard shots from the vicinity of the pit. The Jews alive had been ordered to throw the corpses into the pit, then they had themselves to lie down in it to be shot in the neck.

Rudolf Hoess
COMMANDANT OF AUSCHWITZ

To speed up the "final solution of the Jewish problem," the SS established death camps in Poland. Jews from all over Europe were crammed into cattle cars and shipped to these camps to be gassed or worked to death. At Auschwitz, the most notorious of the concentration camps, the SS used five gas chambers to kill as many as 9,000 people a day. Special squads of prisoners, called *Sonderkommandos,* were forced to pick over the corpses for gold teeth, jewelry, and anything else of value for the German war effort. Some 1.3 million Jews perished at Auschwitz. In the following passage from *Commandant of Auschwitz* (1962), Rudolf Hoess (1900–1947), who commanded the camp and was executed by Poland after the war, recalled the murder process when he was in a Polish prison.

In the spring of 1942 the first transports of Jews, all earmarked for extermination, arrived from Upper Silesia.

They were taken from the detraining platform to the "cottage"—to bunker I—across the meadows where later building site II was located. The transport was conducted by Aumeier and Palitzsch and some of the block leaders. They talked with the Jews about general topics, inquiring concerning their qualifications and trades, with a view to misleading them. On arrival at the "cottage," they were told to undress. At first they went calmly into the rooms where they were supposed to be disinfected. But some of them showed signs of alarm, and spoke of death by suffocation and of annihilation. A sort of panic set in at once. Immediately all the Jews still outside were pushed into the chambers, and the doors were screwed shut. With subsequent transports the difficult individuals were picked out early and most carefully supervised. At the first signs of unrest, those responsible were unobtrusively led behind the building and killed with a small-caliber gun, that was inaudible to the others. The presence and calm behavior of the Special Detachment [of *Sonderkommandos*] served to reassure those who were worried or who suspected what was about to happen. A further calming effect was obtained by members of the Special Detachment accompanying them into the rooms and remaining with them until the last moment, while an SS man also stood in the doorway until the end.

It was most important that the whole business of arriving and undressing should take place in an atmosphere of the greatest possible calm. People reluctant to take off their clothes had to be helped by those of their companions who had already undressed, or by men of the Special Detachment.

The refractory ones were calmed down and encouraged to undress. The prisoners of the Special Detachment also saw to it that the process of undressing was carried out quickly, so that the victims would have little time to wonder what was happening. . . .

Many of the women hid their babies among the piles of clothing. The men of the Special Detachment were particularly on the lookout for this, and would speak words of encouragement to the woman until they had persuaded her to take the child with her. The women believed that the disinfectant might be bad for their smaller children, hence their efforts to conceal them.

The smaller children usually cried because of the strangeness of being undressed in this fashion, but when their mothers or members of the Special Detachment comforted them, they became calm and entered the gas chambers, playing or joking with one another and carrying their toys.

I noticed that women who either guessed or knew what awaited them nevertheless found the courage to joke with the children to encourage them, despite the mortal terror visible in their own eyes.

One woman approached me as she walked past and, pointing to her four children who were manfully helping the smallest ones over the rough ground, whispered:

"How can you bring yourself to kill such beautiful, darling children? Have you no heart at all?"

One old man, as he passed by me, hissed:

"Germany will pay a heavy penance for this mass murder of the Jews."

His eyes glowed with hatred as he said this. Nevertheless he walked calmly into the gas chamber, without worrying about the others.

One young woman caught my attention particularly as she ran busily hither and thither, helping the smallest children and the old women to undress. During the selection she had had two small children with her, and her agitated behavior and appearance had brought her to my notice at once. She did not look in the least like a Jewess. Now her children were no longer with her. She waited until the end, helping the women who were not undressed and who had several children with them, encouraging them and calming the children. She went with the very last ones into the gas chamber. Standing in the doorway, she said:

"I knew all the time that we were being brought to Auschwitz to be gassed. When the selection took place I avoided being put with the able-bodied ones, as I wished to look after the children. I wanted to go through it all, fully conscious of what was happening. I hope that it will be quick. Goodbye!"

From time to time women would suddenly give the most terrible shrieks while undressing, or tear their hair, or scream like maniacs. These were immediately led away behind the building and shot in the back of the neck with a small-caliber weapon.

It sometimes happened that, as the men of the Special Detachment left the gas chamber, the women would suddenly realize what was happening, and would call down every imaginable curse upon our heads.

I remember, too, a woman who tried to throw her children out of the gas chamber, just as the door was closing. Weeping, she called out:

"At least let my precious children live."

There were many such shattering scenes, which affected all who witnessed them.

During the spring of 1942 hundreds of vigorous men and women walked all unsuspecting to their death in the gas chambers, under the blossom-laden fruit trees of the "cottage" orchard. This picture of death in the midst of life remains with me to this day.

The process of selection, which took place on the unloading platforms, was in itself rich in incident.

The breaking up of families, and the separation of the men from the women and children, caused much agitation and spread anxiety throughout the whole transport. This was increased by the further separation from the others of those capable of work. Families wished at all costs to remain together. Those who had been selected ran back to rejoin their relations. Mothers with children tried to join their husbands, or old people attempted to find those of their children who had been selected for work, and who had been led away.

Often the confusion was so great that the selections had to be begun all over again. The limited area of standing room did not permit better sorting arrangements. All attempts to pacify these agitated mobs were useless. It was often necessary to use force to restore order.

As I have already frequently said, the Jews have strongly developed family feelings. They stick together like limpets. . . .

Then the bodies had to be taken from the gas chambers, and after the gold teeth had been extracted, and the hair cut off, they had to be dragged to the pits or to the crematoria. Then the fires in the pits had to be stoked, the surplus fat drained off, and the mountain of burning corpses constantly turned over so that the draught might fan the flames. . . .

It happened repeatedly that Jews of the Special Detachment would come upon the bodies of close relatives among the corpses, and even among the living as they entered the gas chambers. They were obviously affected by this, but it never led to any incident.[1]

---

[1]On October 7, 1944, the *Sonderkommandos* attacked the SS. Some SS guards were killed, and one crematorium was burned. Most of the prisoners who escaped were caught and killed.

Y. Pfeffer
CONCENTRATION CAMP LIFE AND DEATH

Jews not immediately selected for extermination faced a living death in the concentration camp, which also included non-Jewish inmates, many of them opponents of the Nazi regime. The SS, who ran the camps, took sadistic pleasure in humiliating and brutalizing their helpless Jewish victims. In 1946,

Y. Pfeffer, a Jewish survivor of Majdanek concentration camp in Poland, described the world created by the SS and Nazi ideology.

You get up at 3 A.M. You have to dress quickly, and make the "bed" so that it looks like a matchbox. For the slightest irregularity in bed-making the punishment was 25 lashes, after which it was impossible to lie or sit for a whole month.

Everyone had to leave the barracks immediately. Outside it is still dark—or else the moon is shining. People are trembling because of lack of sleep and the cold. In order to warm up a bit, groups of ten to twenty people stand together, back to back so as to rub against each other.

There was what was called a wash-room, where everyone in the camp was supposed to wash—there were only a few faucets—and we were 4,500 people in that section (no. 3). Of course there was neither soap nor towel or even a handkerchief, so that washing was theoretical rather than practical. . . . In one day, a person there [be]came a lowly person indeed.

At 5 A.M. we used to get half a litre of black, bitter coffee. That was all we got for what was called "breakfast." At 6 A.M.—a headcount (*Appell* in German). We all had to stand at attention, in fives, according to the barracks, of which there were 22 in each section. We stood there until the SS men had satisfied their game-playing instincts by "humorous" orders to take off and put on caps. Then they received their report, and counted us. After the headcount—work.

We went in groups—some to build railway tracks or a road, some to the quarries to carry stones or coal, some to take out manure, or for potato-digging, latrine-cleaning, barracks—or sewer—repairs. All this took place inside the camp enclosure. During work the SS men beat up the prisoners mercilessly, inhumanly and for no reason.

They were like wild beasts and, having found their victim, ordered him to present his backside, and beat him with a stick or a whip, usually until the stick broke.

The victim screamed only after the first blows, afterwards he fell unconscious and the SS man then kicked at the ribs, the face, at the most sensitive parts of a man's body, and then, finally convinced that the victim was at the end of his strength, he ordered another Jew to pour one pail of water after the other over the beaten person until he woke and got up.

A favorite sport of the SS men was to make a "boxing sack" out of a Jew. This was done in the following way: Two Jews were stood up, one being forced to hold the other by the collar, and an SS man trained giving him a knockout. Of course, after the first blow, the poor victim was likely to fall, and this was prevented by the other Jew holding him up. After the fat, Hitlerite murderer had "trained" in this way for 15 minutes, and only after the poor victim was completely shattered, covered in blood, his teeth knocked out, his nose broken, his eyes hit, they released him and ordered a doctor to treat his wounds. That was their way of taking care and being generous.

Another customary SS habit was to kick a Jew with a heavy boot. The Jew was forced to stand to attention, and all the while the SS man kicked him until he broke some bones. People who stood near enough to such a victim, often heard the breaking of the bones. The pain was so terrible that people, having undergone that treatment, died in agony.

Apart from the SS men there were other expert hangmen. These were the so-called Capos. The name was an abbreviation for "barracks police." The Capos were German criminals who were also camp inmates. However, although they belonged to "us," they were privileged. They had a special, better barracks of their own, they had better food, better, almost normal clothes, they wore special red or green riding pants, high leather boots, and fulfilled the functions of camp guards. They were worse even than the SS men. One of them, older than the others and the worst murderer of them all, when he descended on a victim, would not revive him later with water but would choke him to death. Once, this murderer caught a boy of 13 (in the presence of his father) and hit his head so that the poor child died instantly. This "camp elder" later boasted in front of his peers, with a smile on his beast's face and with pride, that he managed to kill a Jew with one blow.

In each section stood a gallows. For being late for the headcount, or similar crimes, the "camp elder" hanged the offenders.

Work was actually unproductive, and its purpose was exhaustion and torture.

At 12 noon there was a break for a meal. Standing in line, we received half a litre of soup each. Usually it was cabbage soup, or some other watery liquid, without fats, tasteless. That was lunch. It was eaten—in all weather—under the open sky, never in the barracks. No spoons were allowed, though wooden spoons lay on each bunk—probably for show, for Red Cross committees. One had to drink the soup out of the bowl and lick it like a dog.

From 1 P.M. till 6 P.M. there was work again. I must emphasize that if we were lucky we got a 12 o'clock meal. There were "days of punishment"—when lunch was given together with the evening meal, and it was cold and sour, so that our stomach was empty for a whole day.

Afternoon work was the same: blows, and blows again. Until 6 P.M.

At 6 there was the evening headcount. Again we were forced to stand at attention. Counting, receiving the report. Usually we were left standing at attention for an hour or two, while some prisoners were called up for "punishment parade"—they were those who in the Germans' eyes had transgressed in some way during the day, or had not been punctilious in their performance. They were stripped naked publicly, laid out on specially constructed benches, and whipped with 25 or 50 lashes.

The brutal beating and the heart-rending cries—all this the prisoners had to watch and hear.

REVIEW QUESTIONS

1. What do the accounts of Hermann Graebe, Rudolf Hoess, and Y. Pfeffer reveal about the capacity of people to inflict oppression? How did the SS view their victims?
2. What do these accounts reveal about the ways in which people respond to overwhelmingly hopeless oppression?

9 D-Day, June 6, 1944

On June 6, 1944, the Allied forces launched their invasion of Nazi-occupied France. The invasion, called Operation Overlord, had been planned with meticulous care. Under the supreme command of General Dwight D. Eisenhower (1890–1969), the Allies organized the biggest amphibious operation of the war. It involved 5,000 ships of all kinds, 11,000 aircraft, and 2 million soldiers, 1.5 million of them Americans, all equipped with the latest military gear. Two artificial harbors and several oil pipelines stood ready to supply the troops once the invasion was under way.

Historical Division, War Department
OMAHA BEACHHEAD

Allied control of the air was an important factor in the success of D-Day. A second factor was the fact that the Germans were caught by surprise. Although expecting an invasion, they did not believe that it would take place in the Normandy area of France, and they dismissed June 6 as a possible date because weather conditions were unfavorable.

Ultimately the invasion's success depended on what happened during the first few hours. If the Allies had failed to secure beachheads, the operation would have ended in disaster. As the following reading illustrates, some of the hardest fighting took place on Omaha Beach, which was attacked by the Americans. The extract, published in 1945, comes from a study prepared in the field by the 2nd Information and Historical Service attached to the First Army, and by the Historical Section, European Theater of Operations.

As expected, few of the LCVP's and LCA's [amphibious landing craft] carrying assault infantry were able to make dry landings. Most of them grounded on sandbars 50 to 100 yards out, and in some cases the water was neck deep. Under fire as they came within a quarter-mile of the shore, the infantry met their worst experiences of the day and suffered their heaviest casualties just after touchdown. Small-arms fire, mortars, and artillery concentrated on the landing area, but the worst hazard was produced by converging fires from automatic weapons. Survivors from some craft report hearing the fire beat on the ramps before they were lowered, and then seeing the hail of bullets whip the surf just in front of the lowered ramps. Some men dove under water or went over the side to escape the beaten zone of the machine guns. Stiff, weakened from seasickness, and often heavily loaded, the debarking troops had little chance of moving fast in water that was knee deep or higher, and their progress was made more difficult by uneven footing in the runnels crossing the tidal flat. Many men were exhausted before they reached shore, where they faced 200 yards or more of open sand to cross before reaching cover at the sea wall or shingle bank. Most men who reached that cover made it by walking, and under increasing enemy fire. Troops who stopped to organize, rest, or take shelter behind obstacles or tanks merely prolonged their difficulties and suffered heavier losses. . . .

Perhaps the worst area on the beach was Dog Green, directly in front of strongpoints guarding the Vierville draw [gully] and under heavy flanking fire from emplacements to the west, near Pointe de la Percée. Company A of the 116th was due to land on this sector with Company C of the 2d Rangers on its right flank, and both units came in on their targets. One of the six LCA's carrying Company A foundered about a thousand yards off shore, and passing Rangers saw men jumping overboard and being dragged down by their loads. At H+6[1] minutes the remaining craft grounded in water 4 to 6 feet deep, about 30 yards short of the outward band of obstacles. Starting off the craft in three files, center file first and the flank files peeling right and left, the men were enveloped in accurate and intense fire from automatic weapons. Order was quickly lost as the troops attempted to dive under water or

---

[1]H indicates the start of an operation.

dropped over the sides into surf over their heads. Mortar fire scored four direct hits on one LCA, which "disintegrated." Casualties were suffered all the way to the sand, but when the survivors got there, some found they could not hold and came back into the water for cover, while others took refuge behind the nearest obstacles. Remnants of one boat team on the right flank organized a small firing line on the first yards of sand, in full exposure to the enemy. In short order every officer of the company, including Capt. Taylor N. Fellers, was a casualty, and most of the sergeants were killed or wounded. The leaderless men gave up any attempt to move forward and confined their efforts to saving the wounded, many of whom drowned in the rising tide. Some troops were later able to make the sea wall by staying in the edge of the water and going up the beach with the tide. Fifteen minutes after landing, Company A was out of action for the day. Estimates of its casualties range as high as two-thirds. . . .

As headquarters groups arrived from 0730 on, they found much the same picture at whatever sector they landed. Along 6,000 yards of beach, behind sea wall or shingle [stone] embankment, elements of the assault force were immobilized in what might well appear to be hopeless confusion. As a result of mislandings, many companies were so scattered that they could not be organized as tactical units. At some places, notably in front of the German strongpoints guarding [gulleys], losses in officers and noncommissioned officers were so high that remnants of units were practically leaderless. . . .

There was, definitely, a problem of morale. The survivors of the beach crossing, many of whom were experiencing their first enemy fire, had seen heavy losses among their comrades or in neighboring units. No action could be fought in circumstances more calculated to heighten the moral effects of such losses. Behind them, the tide was drowning wounded men who had been cut down on the sands and was carrying bodies ashore just below the shin-

gle. Disasters to the later landing waves were still occurring, to remind of the potency of enemy fire. . . .

At 0800, German observers on the bluff sizing up the grim picture below them might well have felt that the invasion was stopped at the edge of the water. Actually, at three or four places on the four-mile beachfront, U.S. troops were already breaking through the shallow crust of enemy defenses.

The outstanding fact about these first two hours of action is that despite heavy casualties, loss of equipment, disorganization, and all the other discouraging features of the landings, the assault troops did not stay pinned down behind the sea wall and embankment. At half-a-dozen or more points on the long stretch, they found the necessary drive to leave their cover and move out over the open beach flat toward the bluffs. Prevented by circumstance of mislandings from using carefully rehearsed tactics, they improvised assault methods to deal with what defenses they found before them. In nearly every case where advance was attempted, it carried through the enemy beach defenses. . . .

Various factors, some of them difficult to evaluate, played a part in the success of these advances. . . . But the decisive factor was leadership. Wherever an advance was made, it depended on the presence of some few individuals, officers and noncommissioned officers, who inspired, encouraged, or bullied their men forward, often by making the first forward moves. On Easy Red a lieutenant and a wounded sergeant of divisional engineers stood up under fire and walked over to inspect the wire obstacles just beyond the embankment. The lieutenant came back and, hands on hips, looked down disgustedly at the men lying behind the shingle bank. "Are you going to lay there and get killed, or get up and do something about it?" Nobody stirred, so the sergeant and the officer got the materials and blew the wire. On the same sector, where a group advancing across the flat was held up by a marshy area suspected of being mined, it was a lieutenant of engineers who crawled ahead through the mud on his belly, probing for mines with a hunting knife in the absence of other equipment. When remnants of an isolated boat section of Company B, 116th Infantry, were stopped by fire from a well-concealed emplacement, the lieutenant in charge went after it single-handed. In trying to grenade the rifle pit he was hit by three rifle bullets and eight grenade fragments, including some from his own grenade. He turned his map and compass over to a sergeant and ordered his group to press on inland. . . .

. . . Col. George A. Taylor arrived in the second section at 0815 and found plenty to do on the beach. Men were still hugging the embankment, disorganized, and suffering casualties from mortar and artillery fire. Colonel Taylor summed up the situation in terse phrase: "Two kinds of people are staying on this beach, the dead and those who are going to die—now let's get the hell out of here." Small groups of men were collected without regard to units, put under charge of the nearest noncommissioned officer, and sent on through the wire and across the flat, while engineers worked hard to widen gaps in the wire and to mark lanes through the minefields.

REVIEW QUESTIONS

1. What disadvantages did Allied troops face while attempting the amphibious landing at Omaha Beach? Why were casualties so heavy?
2. According to the Historical Division study, many of the Allied soldiers at Omaha Beach were experiencing their first enemy fire. How did the officers who survived manage to rally these shaken and demoralized soldiers?

CHAPTER 10

Western Europe:
The Dawn of a New Era

WHEN THE WAR IN EUROPE ENDED in May 1945, many areas lay devastated, none more so than the once-picturesque German city of Dresden, in which some 50,000 people had perished in a terror bombing by Allied planes in February 1945. Europe was faced with the awesome task of reconstructing a continent in ruins. *(Sovfoto/Eastfoto)*

At the end of World War II, Winston Churchill lamented: "What is Europe now? A rubble heap, a charnel house [a place for corpses], a breeding ground for pestilence and hate." Everywhere the survivors counted their dead. War casualties were relatively light in Western Europe. Britain and the Commonwealth suffered 460,000 casualties; France, 570,000; and Italy, 450,000. War casualties were heavier in the east: 5 million people in Germany, 6 million in Poland (including 3 million Jews), 1 million in Yugoslavia, and more than 25 million in the Soviet Union. The material destruction had been unprecedentedly heavy in the battle zones of northwestern Europe, northern Italy, and Germany, growing worse farther east, where Hitler's and Stalin's armies had fought without mercy to people, animals, or the environment. Industry, transportation, and communication had come to a virtual standstill. Now members of families searched for each other; prisoners of war made their way home; Jews from extermination camps or from hiding places returned to open life; and displaced persons by the millions sought refuge. Yet Europe did recover from this blight, and with astonishing speed.

The war produced a shift in power arrangements. The United States and the Soviet Union emerged as the two most powerful states in the world. The traditional Great Powers—Britain, France, and Germany—were now dwarfed by these superpowers. The United States had the atomic bomb and immense industrial might; the Soviet Union had the largest army in the world and was extending its dominion over Eastern Europe. With Germany defeated, the principal incentive for Soviet-American cooperation had evaporated.

After World War I, nationalist passions intensified. After World War II, Western Europeans progressed toward unity. The Hitler years convinced many Europeans of the dangers inherent in extreme nationalism, and fear of the Soviet Union prodded them toward greater cooperation.

Some intellectuals, shocked by the irrationality and horrors of the Hitler era, drifted into despair. To these thinkers, life was absurd, without meaning; human beings could neither comprehend nor control it. In 1945, only the naive could have faith in continuous progress or believe in the essential goodness of the individual. The future envisioned by the philosophes seemed more distant than ever. Nevertheless, this profound disillusionment was tempered by hope. Democracy had, in fact, prevailed over Nazi totalitarianism and terror. Moreover, fewer intellectuals were now attracted to antidemocratic thought. The Nazi dictatorship convinced many of them, even some who had wavered in previous decades, that freedom and human dignity were precious ideals and that liberal constitutional government, despite its imperfections, was the best means of preserving these ideals. Perhaps, then, democratic institutions and values would spread throughout the globe, and the newly established United Nations would promote world peace.

1   The Aftermath: Devastation and Demoralization

In 1945 European cities everywhere were in rubble; bridges, railway systems, waterways, and harbors destroyed; farmlands laid waste; livestock killed; coal mines wrecked. Homeless and hungry people wandered the streets and roads. Europe faced the gigantic task of rebuilding.

Stephen Spender
EUROPEAN WITNESS

The English poet and critic Stephen Spender (1909–1995) traveled through Germany (with a side trip to France) in the summer and fall of 1945. His mission was to assess German intellectual life and to inquire into the conditions in German libraries. His book *European Witness,* based on a journal he kept during his travels, was published in 1946. It offers an eyewitness account of the ruined country and its demoralized people under Allied occupation.

In the selection below, Spender describes the devastation of the heavily bombed city of Cologne.

My first impression on passing through [Cologne] was of there being not a single house left. There are plenty of walls but these walls are a thin mask in front of the damp, hollow, stinking emptiness of gutted interiors. Whole streets with nothing but the walls left standing are worse than streets flattened. They are more sinister and oppressive.

Actually, there are a few habitable buildings left in Cologne; three hundred in all, I am told. One passes through street after street of houses whose windows look hollow and blackened—like the open mouth of a charred corpse; behind these windows there is nothing except floors, furniture, bits of rag, books, all dropped to the bottom of the building to form there a sodden mass.

Through the streets of Cologne thousands of people trudge all day long. These are crowds who a few years ago were shop-gazing in their city, or waiting to go to the cinema or to the opera, or stopping taxis. They are the same people who once were the ordinary inhabitants of a great city when by what now seems an un-believable magical feat of reconstruction in time, this putrescent corpse-city was the hub of the Rhineland, with a great shopping centre, acres of plate-glass, restaurants, a massive business street containing the head offices of many banks and firms, an excellent opera, theatres, cinemas, lights in the streets at night.

Now it requires a real effort of the imagination to think back to that Cologne which I knew well ten years ago. Everything has gone. In this the destruction of Germany is quite different from even the worst that has happened in England (though not different from Poland and from parts of Russia). In England there are holes, gaps and wounds, but the surrounding life of the people themselves has filled them up, creating a scar which will heal. In towns such as Cologne and those of the Ruhr, something quite different has happened. The external destruction is so great that it cannot be healed and the surrounding life of the rest of the country cannot flow into and resuscitate the city which is not only battered but also dismembered and cut off from the rest of Germany and from Europe. The ruin of the city is reflected in the internal ruin of its inhabitants who, instead of being lives that can form a scar over the city's wounds, are parasites sucking at a dead [carcass], digging among the ruins for hidden food, doing business at their black market near the cathedral—the commerce of destruction instead of production.

The people who live there seem quite dissociated from Cologne. They resemble rather a tribe of wanderers who have discovered a ruined city in a desert and who are camping there, living in the cellars and hunting amongst the ruins for the booty, relics of a dead civilization.

The great city looks like a corpse and stinks like one also, with all the garbage which has not been cleared away, all the bodies still buried under heaps of stones and iron. Although the streets have been partly cleared, they still have many holes in them and some of the side streets are impassable. The general impression is that very little has been cleared away. There are landscapes of untouched ruin still left.

. . . But it is the comparatively undamaged cathedral which gives Cologne what it still retains of character. One sees that this is and was a great city, it is uplifted by the spire of the cathedral from being a mere heap of rubble and a collection of walls, like the towns of the Ruhr. Large buildings round the cathedral have been scratched and torn, and, forming a kind of cliff beneath the spires, they have a certain dignity like the cliffs and rocks under a church close to the sea.

. . . In the destroyed German towns one often feels haunted by the ghost of a tremendous noise. It is impossible not to imagine the rocking explosions, the hammering of the sky upon the earth, which must have caused all this.

The effect of these corpse-towns is a grave discouragement which influences everyone living and working in Germany, the Occupying Forces as much as the German. The destruction is *serious* in more senses than one. It is a climax of deliberate effort, an achievement of our civilization, the most striking result of co-operation between nations in the twentieth century. It is the shape created by our century as the Gothic cathedral is the shape created by the Middle Ages. Everything has stopped here, that fusion of the past within the present, integrated into architecture, which forms the organic life of a city, a life quite distinct from that of the inhabitants who are, after all, only using a city as a waiting-room on their journey through time: that long, gigantic life of a city has been killed. The city is dead and the inhabitants only haunt the cellars and basements. Without their city they are rats in the cellars, or bats wheeling around the towers of the cathedral. The citizens go on existing with a base mechanical kind of life like that of insects in the crannies of walls who are too creepy and ignoble to be destroyed when the wall is torn down. The destruction of the city itself, with all its past as well as its present, is like a reproach to the people who go on living there. The sermons in the stones of Germany preach nihilism.

REVIEW QUESTIONS

1. How did the destruction that Stephen Spender witnessed in Cologne differ from what he had seen in England?
2. What examples did Spender provide to use to illustrate "the internal ruin" of Cologne's inhabitants?

2 The Cold War

After World War II the first Western statesman to express his alarm over Soviet expansionism was Winston Churchill, the doughty and articulate wartime leader of Great Britain. While noting, on a visit to America, that the United States stood "at the pinnacle of world power," he warned of the Soviet challenge. It threatened the liberties that were a traditional part of Western democracy. Prompted by the failure of the attempt to appease Hitler and by the war experience, he urged military strength and political cooperation between Western Europe and the United States in order to stem the communist advance.

In the United States, George Kennan, a foreign service officer with extensive experience in Eastern Europe and Moscow, soon followed Churchill's lead, advocating the thwarting of Soviet ambitions by a policy of containment. Churchill and Kennan formulated the Western outlook in what came to be called "the Cold War."

Winston Churchill
THE "IRON CURTAIN"

In a famous speech at Fulton, Missouri, on March 5, 1946, when he was no longer in office, Churchill (1874–1965) articulated his views on the duty of Western democracies in the face of Soviet expansion. Significant passages from that speech, in which the term *iron curtain* was first used, follow.

A shadow has fallen upon the scenes so lately lighted by the Allied victory. Nobody knows what Soviet Russia and its Communist international organization intends to do in the immediate future, or what are the limits, if any, to their expansive and proselytizing tendencies. I have a strong admiration and regard for the valiant Russian people and for my wartime comrade, Marshal Stalin. There is sympathy and good will in Britain—and I doubt not here also—toward the peoples of all the Russias and a resolve to persevere through many differences and rebuffs in establishing lasting friendships. We understand the Russian need to be secure on her western frontiers from all renewal of German aggression. We welcome

her to her rightful place among the leading nations of the world. Above all we welcome constant, frequent and growing contacts between the Russian people and our own people on both sides of the Atlantic. It is my duty, however, to place before you certain facts about the present position in Europe—I am sure I do not wish to, but it is my duty, I feel, to present them to you.

From Stettin in the Baltic to Trieste in the Adriatic, an iron curtain has descended across the Continent. Behind that line lie all the capitals of the ancient states of central and eastern Europe. Warsaw, Berlin, Prague, Vienna, Budapest, Belgrade, Bucharest and Sofia, all these famous cities and the populations around them lie in the Soviet sphere and all are subject in one form or another, not only to Soviet influence but to a very high and increasing measure of control from Moscow. . . . The Communist parties, which were very small in all these eastern states of Europe, have been raised to preeminence and power far beyond their numbers and are seeking everywhere to obtain totalitarian control. Police governments are prevailing in nearly every case. . . . Turkey and Persia are both profoundly alarmed and disturbed at the claims which are made upon them and at the pressure being exerted by the Moscow government. An attempt is being made by the Russians in Berlin to build up a quasi-Communist party in their zone of occupied Germany. . . . Whatever conclusions may be drawn from these facts—and facts they are—this is certainly not the liberated Europe we fought to build up. Nor is it one which contains the essentials of permanent peace. . . . What we have to consider here today while time remains, is the permanent prevention of war and the es-

tablishment of conditions of freedom and democracy as rapidly as possible in all countries. Our difficulties and dangers will not be removed by closing our eyes to them. They will not be removed by mere waiting to see what happens; nor will they be relieved by a policy of appeasement. What is needed is a settlement and the longer this is delayed the more difficult it will be and the greater our dangers will become. From what I have seen of our Russian friends and allies during the war, I am convinced that there is nothing they admire so much as strength, and there is nothing for which they have less respect than for military weakness. . . . If the western democracies stand together in strict adherence to the principles of the United Nations Charter, their influence for furthering these principles will be immense and no one is likely to molest them. If, however, they become divided or falter in their duty, and if these all-important years are allowed to slip away, then indeed catastrophe may overwhelm us all.

REVIEW QUESTIONS

1. Where did Winston Churchill observe evidence of Soviet expansionism? Find on a map of Europe and Asia the areas he mentioned.
2. What were Churchill's recommendations for countering Soviet expansionism?

3 Communist Repression

When at the end of World War II the Soviet armies pursued the retreating Germans deep into central Europe, they subjected Eastern Europe to Soviet domination. By 1948 all countries except Yugoslavia had fallen under Stalin's iron grip. Soviet domination was buttressed by the Warsaw Pact, the military alliance of all countries within the Soviet bloc formed in 1955 to counter the North Atlantic Treaty Organization (NATO). It was further strengthened by the Council for Mutual Economic Assistance (COMECON), created in 1958 in response to the emerging European Economic Community; it tried to weld the disparate economies of Eastern Europe into a viable unit for the benefit of the Soviet boss.

Yet Soviet rule did not take firm root. The peoples under Soviet domination traditionally had looked westward, benefiting from economic, religious, and cultural ties with Western Europe. They also carried over from their past a strong nationalist ambition for independence. As Western Europe recovered from World War II, the discrepancy between the poverty of the Soviet bloc and the prosperity of its Western neighbors, especially the Federal Republic of Germany, added a further source of anti-Soviet agitation.

Inevitably the craving for independence and freedom caused mounting tensions in Soviet-controlled Eastern Europe. Within each country Soviet lackeys struggled against the reformers who were asserting, however cautiously, the yearnings of their peoples. Tensions occasionally erupted in dramatic protests, as evidenced in Hungary in 1956.

Milovan Djilas
THE NEW CLASS

Milovan Djilas's book *The New Class: An Analysis of the Communist System* (1957), from which the following excerpts are taken, provides helpful insights into the explosion of discontent in Hungary, Czechoslovakia, and Poland under Soviet control. Djilas (1911–1995), a Yugoslav author and political commentator, became a communist after finishing his studies in 1933. Although he began as a close friend of Marshal Tito, the all-powerful leader of Yugoslavia, in 1953 he turned critic, not only of his friend, but also of communist practice and ideology. Jailed for his heresies in 1956, he wrote his assessment of the communist system, showing its connection to the unprecedented new class of political bureaucrats dominating state and society. Under communism the state did not wither away, as early theorists had expected. On the contrary, it grew more powerful, thanks to that highly privileged "exploiting and governing class." Aware of the dynamics of nationalism at work underneath each communist regime, Djilas pointed to the weaknesses of communist rule and the growing desire for national self-assertion among the peoples of the Soviet satellite states.

Earlier revolutions, particularly the so-called bourgeois ones, attached considerable significance to the establishment of individual freedoms immediately following cessation of the revolutionary terror. Even the revolutionaries considered it important to assure the legal status of the citizenry. Independent administration of justice was an inevitable final result of all these revolutions. The Communist regime in the U.S.S.R. is still remote from independent administration of justice after forty years of tenure. The final results of earlier revolutions were often greater legal security and greater civil rights. This cannot be said of the Communist revolution. . . .

In contrast to earlier revolutions, the Communist revolution, conducted in the name of doing away with classes, has resulted in the most complete authority of any single new class. Everything else is sham and an illusion. . . .

This new class, the bureaucracy, or more accurately the political bureaucracy, has all the characteristics of earlier ones as well as some new characteristics of its own. Its origin had its special characteristics also, even though in essence it was similar to the beginnings of other classes. . . . The new class may be said to be made up of those who have special privileges and economic preference because of the administrative monopoly they hold. . . .

The mechanism of Communist power is perhaps the simplest which can be conceived, although it leads to the most refined tyranny and the most brutal exploitation. The simplicity of this mechanism originates from the fact that one party alone, the Communist Party, is the backbone of the entire political, economic, and ideological activity. The entire public life is at a standstill or moves ahead, falls behind or turns around according to what happens in the party forums. . . .

. . . Communist control of the social machine . . . restricts certain government posts to party members. These jobs, which are essential in any government but especially in a Communist one, include assignments with police, especially the secret police; and the diplomatic and officers corps, especially positions in the information and political services. In the judiciary only top positions have until now been in the hands of Communists. . . .

Only in a Communist state are a number of both specified and unspecified positions reserved for members of the party. The Communist government, although a class structure, is a party government; the Communist army is a party army; and the state is a party state. More precisely, Communists tend to treat the army and the state as their exclusive weapons.

The exclusive, if unwritten, law that only party members can become policemen, officers, diplomats, and hold similar positions, or that only they can exercise actual authority, creates a special privileged group of bureaucrats. . . .

The entire governmental structure is organized in this manner. Political positions are reserved exclusively for party members. Even in non-political governmental bodies Communists hold the strategic positions or oversee administration. Calling a meeting at the party center or publishing an article is sufficient to cause the entire state and social mechanism to begin functioning. If difficulties occur anywhere, the party and the police very quickly correct the "error." . . .

The classes and masses do not exercise authority, but the party does so in their name. In every party, including the most democratic, leaders play an important role to the extent that the party's authority becomes the authority of the leaders. The so-called "dictatorship of the proletariat," which is the beginning of and under the best circumstances becomes the authority of the party, inevitably evolves into the dictatorship of the leaders. In a totalitarian government of this type, the dictatorship of the proletariat is a theoretical justification, or ideological mask at best, for the authority of some oligarchs. . . .

Freedoms are formally recognized in Communist regimes, but one decisive condition is a prerequisite for exercising them: freedoms must be utilized only in the interest of the system of "socialism," which the Communist leaders represent, or to buttress their rule. This practice, contrary as it is to legal regulations, inevitably had to result in the use of exceptionally severe and unscrupulous methods by police and party bodies. . . .

. . . It has been impossible in practice to separate police authority from judicial authority. Those who arrest also judge and enforce punishments. The circle is closed: the executive, the legislative, the investigating, the court, and the punishing bodies are one and the same. . . .

Communist parliaments are not in a position to make decisions on anything important. Selected in advance as they are, flattered that they have been thus selected, representatives do not have the power or the courage to debate even if they wanted to do so. Besides, since their mandate does not depend on the voters, representatives do not feel that they are answerable to them. Communist parliaments are justifiably called "mausoleums" for the representatives who compose them. Their right and role consist of unanimously approving from time to time that which has already been decided for them from the wings. . . .

Though history has no record of any other system so successful in *checking* its opposition as the Communist dictatorship, none ever has *provoked* such profound and far-reaching discontent. It seems that the more the conscience is crushed and the less the opportunities for establishing an organization exist, the greater the discontent. . . .

In addition to being motivated by the historical need for rapid industrialization, the Communist bureaucracy has been compelled to establish a type of economic system designed to insure the perpetuation of its own power. Allegedly for the sake of a classless society and for the abolition of exploitation, it has created a closed economic system, with forms of property which facilitate the party's domination and its monopoly. At first, the Communists had to turn to this "collectivistic" form for objective reasons. Now they continue to strengthen this form—without considering whether or not it is in the interest of the national economy and of further industrialization—for their own sake, for an exclusive Communist class aim. They first administered and controlled the entire economy for so-called ideal goals; later they did it for the purpose of maintaining their absolute control and domination. That is the real reason for such far-reaching and inflexible political measures in the Communist economy. . . .

A citizen in the Communist system lives oppressed by the constant pangs of his conscience, and the fear that he has transgressed. He is always fearful that he will have to demonstrate that he is not an enemy of socialism, just as in the Middle Ages a man constantly had to show his devotion to the Church. . . .

. . . Tyranny over the mind is the most complete and most brutal type of tyranny; every other tyranny begins and ends with it. . . .

History will pardon Communists for much, establishing that they were forced into many brutal acts because of circumstances and the need to defend their existence. But the stifling of every divergent thought, the exclusive monopoly over thinking for the purpose of defending their personal interests, will nail the Communists to a cross of shame in history. . . .

In essence, Communism is only one thing, but it is realized in different degrees and manners in every country. Therefore it is possible to speak of various Communist systems, i.e., of various forms of the same manifestation.

The differences which exist between Communist states—differences that Stalin attempted futilely to remove by force—are the result, above all, of diverse historical backgrounds. . . . When ascending to power, the Communists face in the various countries different cultural and technical levels and varying social relationships, and are faced with different national intellectual characters. . . . Of the former international proletariat, only words and empty dogmas remained. Behind them stood the naked national and international interests, aspirations, and plans of the various Communist oligarchies, comfortably entrenched. . . .

. . . The Communist East European countries did not become satellites of the U.S.S.R. because they benefited from it, but because they were too weak to prevent it. As soon as they become stronger, or as soon as favorable conditions are created, a yearning for independence and for protection of "their own people" from Soviet hegemony will rise among them.

The subordinate Communist governments in East Europe can, in fact must, declare their independence from the Soviet government. No one can say how far this aspiration for independence will go and what disagreements will result. The result depends on numerous unforeseen internal and external circumstances. However, there is no doubt that a national Communist bureaucracy aspires to more complete authority for itself. This is demonstrated . . . by the current unconcealed emphasis on "one's own path to socialism," which has recently come to light sharply in Poland and Hungary. The central Soviet government has found itself in difficulty because of the nationalism existing even in those governments which it installed in the Soviet republics (Ukraine, Caucasia), and still more so with regard to those governments installed in the East European countries. Playing an important role in all of this is the fact that the Soviet Union was unable, and will not be able in the future, to assimilate the economies of the East European countries.

The aspirations toward national independence must of course have greater impetus. These aspirations can be retarded and even made dormant by external pressure or by fear on the part of the Communists of "imperialism" and the "bourgeoisie," but they cannot be removed. On the contrary, their strength will grow.

Andor Heller
THE HUNGARIAN REVOLUTION, 1956

After Stalin's death in 1953, the rigid political controls in Hungary were relaxed, leading to an unstable balance between Soviet-oriented hard-liners and patriotic reformers willing to grant greater freedom to the spirit of nationalism and individual enterprise stirring among the people. In 1956, the year of Khrushchev's attack on Stalin, the Hungarian yearning for escape from Soviet domination exploded. On October 23 a student demonstration in Budapest, the capital, provided the spark. Throughout the country, communist officials were ousted and the Soviet troops forced to withdraw. A coalition government under Imre Nagy was formed to restore Hungary's independence; it even appeared that the country would withdraw from the newly formed Warsaw Pact controlled by Moscow. In Budapest especially, the popular excitement over the country's liberation from the Soviet yoke knew no bounds, as is described in the eyewitness account that follows. The author, Andor Heller, was a Hungarian news photographer. He fled to Western Europe with photographs of the invasion and published them in his book *No More Comrades* (1957).

Deep dejection followed the anger caused by the Soviet counterattack that killed thousands of people and drove 200,000 into exile. A new "peasant-worker government" under János Kádár boasted of having saved the country from "fascist counter-revolution." Subsequently, however, Kádár transformed his country's economy. Dubbed "goulash communism" for its mixture of state and private enterprise, Hungary became the freest in the Soviet bloc and a model for Gorbachev's *perestroika* (restructuring).

I saw freedom rise from the ashes of Communism in Hungary: a freedom that flickered and then blazed before it was beaten down—but not extinguished—by masses of Russian tanks and troops.

I saw young students, who had known nothing but a life under Communist and Russian control, die for a freedom about which they had only heard from others or from their own hearts.

I saw workers, who had been pushed to the limit of endurance by their hopeless existence under Communism, lay down their tools and take up arms in a desperate bid to win back freedom for our country.

I saw a girl of fourteen blow up a Russian tank, and grandmothers walk up to Russian cannons.

I watched a whole nation—old and young, men and women, artists and engineers and doctors, clerks and peasants and factory workers—become heroes overnight as they rose up in history's first successful revolt against Communism.

Tuesday, October 23, 1956

No Hungarian will forget this day. . . .

. . . In spite of the cold and fog, students are on the streets early in the morning, marching and singing. No one shows up for classes at the universities. After a decade of Communist control over our country, we are going to show our feelings spontaneously, in our own way—something never allowed under Communist rules.

The students carry signs with slogans that until now we have never dared express except to members of our own family—and not in every family. The slogans read:

RUSSIANS GO HOME!

LET HUNGARY BE INDEPENDENT!

BRING RAKOSI [A NOTORIOUS STALINIST] TO JUSTICE!

WE WANT A NEW LEADERSHIP!

SOLIDARITY WITH THE POLISH PEOPLE!

WE TRUST IMRE NAGY—BRING IMRE NAGY INTO THE GOVERNMENT!

The walls of Budapest are plastered with leaflets put up by the students during the night. They list the fourteen demands adopted at the stormy meetings held at the universities:

1. Withdrawal of all Soviet troops from Hungary.
2. Complete economic and political equality with the Soviet Union, with no interference in Hungary's internal affairs.
3. Publication of Hungary's trade agreements, and a public report on Hungary's reparations payments to the U.S.S.R.
4. Information on Hungary's uranium resources, their exploitation, and the concessions given to the U.S.S.R.
5. The calling of a Hungarian Communist Party congress to elect a new leadership.
6. Reorganization of the government, with Imre Nagy as Premier.

7. A public trial of Mihaly Farkas and Matyas Rakosi [notorious Stalinists].
8. A secret general multi-party election.
9. The reorganization of Hungary's economy on the basis of her actual resources.
10. Revision of the workers' output quotas, and recognition of the right to strike.
11. Revision of the system of compulsory agricultural quotas.
12. Equal rights for individual farmers and co-operative members.
13. Restoration of Hungary's traditional national emblem and the traditional Hungarian army uniforms.
14. Destruction of the giant statue of Stalin.

During the morning a radio announcement from the Ministry of Interior bans all public meetings and demonstrations "until further notice," and word is sent to the universities that the student demonstrations cannot be held. At that moment the students decide that the will to freedom is greater than the fear of the A.V.H.—the Russian-controlled Hungarian secret police. The meeting will be held! . . .

At 3 P.M. there are 25,000 of us at the Petofi Monument. We weep as Imre Sinkovits, a young actor, declaims the *Nemzeti Dal* ("National Song"), Sandor Petofi's [a great Hungarian poet and revolutionary hero in the anti-Austrian rebellion of 1848–1849] ode to Hungary and our 1848 "freedom revolution." With tears in our eyes, we repeat the refrain with Sinkovits: . . .

"We swear, we swear, we will no longer remain slaves."

The student voices are tense with feeling. No policeman or Communist official is in sight. The young people are keeping order on their own.

. . . [W]e have swelled to some 60,000. Someone grabs a Hungarian flag and cuts out the hated hammer and sickle that the Communists had placed at its center.

One after another of the purified Hungarian flags appear. Suddenly someone remembers to put the old Kossuth [Lajos Kossuth was the leader of the Hungarian uprising of 1848–1849] coat-of-arms on the flag, in place of the Communist emblem.

We have created a new flag of freedom!

Meantime we all sing the . . . *Appeal to the Nation,* and the *Hungarian National Hymn* that begins "God Bless the Magyar"—both of which had been banned under the Communist rule.

We cannot get enough. The actor Ferenc Bessenyei recites the *National Song* again, and follows once more with *Appeal to the Nation.* Peter Veres, the head of the Hungarian Writers' Federation, leaps to the top of a car equipped with a loudspeaker. He reads the Hungarian writers' demands for more freedom—many of them the same as those in the fourteen points of the students.

The day is ending. We begin to march toward the Parliament Building. The crowds are peaceful, marching in orderly lines. We carry the new Hungarian flag.

As we march we are joined by workers leaving their jobs. By the time we arrive in Kossuth Lajos Square there are at least 150,000 of us, in front of the Parliament Building. On the square, the traffic stops. . . .

Suddenly everyone makes torches of newspapers, and lights them. It is a marvelous spectacle—ten thousand torches burning in the Square before the Parliament Building. . . .

But finally, Imre Nagy appears on the balcony. "Comrades!" he begins, but the crowd interrupts him with a roar: "There are no more comrades! We are all Hungarians!" . . .

The crowd grows still bigger, and we head for the Stalin statue. Now the demonstration has spread so large that it is going on simultaneously in three places: at the Parliament Building; in Stalin Square, where the crowd is trying to pull down the huge Stalin statue with tractors and ropes; and at the building of Radio Budapest, where part of the crowd has gone to demand the right of patriots to be heard over the air. . . .

I go with the group that heads for Stalin Square. Some of the workers have got hold of acetylene torches. They and the students are trying to cut down the dictator's twenty-five-foot metal figure. At the edge of the crowd the first Russian tanks appear, but at the moment they are only onlookers. The crowd pulls hard at the cables that have been attached to the Stalin statue. It leans forward, but is still held by its boots—a symbol, we feel. The cables are now being pulled by tractors, and the men with the torches work feverishly. The statue, though still in one piece, begins to bend at the knees. The crowds burst into cheers. . . .

. . . [W]e watch the Stalin statue, cut off at the knees, fall to the ground with a thunderous crash. . . .

Suddenly shooting breaks out from all sides. The security police—the A.V.H.—are firing into the crowds. In minutes the streets are strewn with the dying and wounded. News of the A.V.H. attack spreads. All over Budapest the workers and students are battling the hated A.V.H.

The peaceful demonstrations of the youth and the workers have been turned by Communist guns into a revolution for national freedom.

For four days—from October 31 to November 3, 1956—Hungary was free. Although the Russian forces were still in our country, they had withdrawn from the cities and the fighting had stopped. The whole nation recognized the Imre Nagy government, which, knowing it had no other alternative, was ready to carry out the will of the people. . . .

On November 3, Radio Free Kossuth summed up: "The over-whelming weight of Hungarian public opinion sees the result of the revolution as the establishment of a neutral, independent and democratic country, and just as it was ready to sweep out Stalinist tyranny, so it will protect with the same determination and firmness its regained democratic achievement." . . .

In those four days of freedom, political liberty came quickly to life. . . .

Before October 23 there had been only five newspapers in Budapest, all under complete

Communist control. On November 4 there were twenty-five. Neither news nor opinions could be suppressed any longer.

Plans for a free general election were speeded.

Religious freedom, like political freedom, came back to strong life in those four days. . . .

In the countryside, the peasants and their spokesmen were mapping the changes of the farm laws and regulations. All were agreed on the goal of a free farm economy based on the individual working farmers and peasants. Peasants would be free to join or leave the farm collectives. If the collectives were dissolved, the land, tools and stock were to be distributed to the individual peasants. Compulsory deliveries at government fixed prices were abolished.

The factory committees and workers' groups were putting forward the needs and demands of the workers, not the government. The right to strike—a criminal act under the Communists—was upheld. Wages, prices, pension rights, working conditions were eagerly discussed and debated.

The economy was slowly getting on its feet. Everyone wanted to be on the streets together. . . .

Return of the Russians

At dawn on November 4, 1956, Soviet Russia attacked Hungary with 6,000 tanks, thousands of guns and armored cars, squadrons of light bombers, 200,000 soldiers—and a tidal wave of lies.

REVIEW QUESTIONS

1. How did Milovan Djilas characterize the "new class"? What were its qualities? How did it wield its power?
2. Why, according to Djilas, would the communist governments in Eastern Europe sooner or later declare their independence from the Soviet government?
3. What would you say was the climax of the Budapest demonstration on October 23?
4. What was at stake for the workers and farmers of Hungary in the anti-Soviet uprising?
5. How did the Hungarians in those crucial October days assert their freedom? What evidence of nationalism did you observe in the anti-Soviet demonstrations?

---

4 Germany Confronts Its Past

In the years immediately following World War II, Germans were too preoccupied with rebuilding their devastated country to reflect on the horrific crimes committed by the Third Reich and bring the criminals to justice. Indeed, many Germans either failed to comprehend the enormity of these crimes or found the subject uncomfortable, for only a few years earlier they had faithfully served the Nazi regime and embraced its ideology. They simply wanted to sweep the extermination of European Jewry from memory. However, the public trials of war criminals starting in the 1960s and the greater attention given to the topic in books and the media, including an American television miniseries that dramatized and personalized the Jewish tragedy, stimulated open discussion and reflection within Germany.

Hannah Vogt
THE BURDEN OF GUILT

Until the 1960s, German secondary school history courses generally ended with the beginning of the twentieth century. Few teachers discussed the Nazi regime, and appropriate books about Nazism and the Holocaust were lacking. Moreover, teachers who had previously endorsed Hitler were not eager to discuss the Holocaust with their students. Distressed by a sudden outburst of anti-Semitic incidents that afflicted Germany in 1959, notably desecrated cemeteries and swastikas smeared on the walls of synagogues, German educational authorities made a concerted effort to teach young people about the Nazi past. These same anti-Semitic outrages moved Hannah Vogt, a civil servant concerned principally with education, to write a book for students about the Nazi past. Published in 1961, *The Burden of Guilt* became a widely used text in secondary schools. In the Preface, Vogt stated the book's purpose:

> [S]elf-examination and a repudiation of false political principles are the only means we have of winning new trust among those peoples who were forced to suffer fearful things under Hitler's brutal policy of force. . . . Only if we draw the right conclusions from the mistakes of the past and apply them to our thought and action can we win new trust. . . . Anyone who makes an effort to understand recent political history will learn that in politics not every means is just [and] that law and the dignity of man are not empty phrases.

The book's conclusion, excerpted below, showed a sincere effort of German schools to come to grips with the darkest period in German history.

A nation is made up of individuals whose ideas—right or wrong—determine their actions, their decisions, and their common life, and for this reason a nation, too, can look back at its history and learn from it. As Germans, we should not find it too difficult to understand the meaning of the fourteen years of the Weimar Republic and the twelve years of the Hitler regime.

The ancient Greeks already knew and taught that no state can remain free without free citizens. If the citizens of a commonwealth are not prepared to make sacrifices for their liberty, to take matters into their own hands and participate in public affairs, they deliver themselves into the hands of a tyrant. They do not deserve anything but tyrannical rule: "A class which fails to make sacrifices for political affairs may not make demands on political life.

It renounces its will to rule, and must therefore be ruled." These words of a German liberal about the educated class are valid for people everywhere.

The Greeks called a man who abstained from politics "idiotēs." The Oxford English Dictionary translates this as "private person," "ignorant," "layman," or "not professionally learned." And what are we to call those who have learned nothing from our recent history but the foolish slogan "without me" *(Ohne mich)*? Are they not like fish who expect to improve their condition by jumping from the frying pan into the fire?

We have paid dearly once before for the folly of believing that democracy, being an ideal political arrangement, must function automatically while the citizens sit in their parlors berating it, or worrying about their money.

Everybody must share in the responsibility and must be prepared to make sacrifices. He must also respect the opinions of others and must curb his hates, which are too blinding to be good guides for action. In addition, we need to be patient, we must have confidence in small advances and abandon the belief in political miracles and panaceas.

Only if the citizens are thoroughly imbued with democratic attitudes can we put into practice those principles of political life which were achieved through centuries of experience, and which we disregarded to our great sorrow. The first such principle is the need for a continuous and vigilant control of power. For this, we need not only a free and courageous press but also some mechanism for shaping a vital political opinion in associations, parties, and other organizations. Equally necessary are clearly drawn lines of political responsibility, and a strong and respected political opposition. Interest groups must not be diffused too widely but must aim at maximum cohesiveness. Present developments appear to indicate that we are deeply aware of at least this necessity.

More than anything else we must base our concept of law on the idea of justice. We have had the sad experience that the principle "the law is the law" does not suffice, if the laws are being abused to cover up for crimes and to wrap injustices in a tissue of legality. Our actions must once again be guided by that idea which is the basis of just life: no man must be used as a means to an end.

This principle must also be applied to our relationships with other nations. Although, on the international scene, there is as yet no all-inclusive legal body that would have enough power to solve all conflicts peacefully, still there are legal norms in international affairs which are not at all the "sound and smoke" (Faust) Hitler had presumed them to be. In no other matter was he as divorced from reality as in his belief that it was shrewd to conclude treaties today and "to break them in cold blood tomorrow," and that he could undo 2000 years of legal evolution without having such action

recoil upon him. He considered force the one and only means of politics, while, in reality, it had always been the worst. Hitler's so-called *Realpolitik* was terrifyingly unreal, and brought about a catastrophe which has undone the gains Bismarck had made through moderation. Bismarck gave Germany its unity. Hitler, goaded by his limitless drive for world power, divided Germany and destroyed the work of generations.

Thus we are now faced with the difficult task of regaining, by peaceful means, the German unity that Hitler has gambled away. We must strive for it tirelessly, even though it may take decades. At the same time, we must establish a new relationship, based on trust, with the peoples of Europe and the nations of the world. Our word must again be believed, our commitment to freedom and humanity again be trusted. Our name has been used too much for lies and treachery. We cannot simply stretch out our hands and hope that all will be forgotten.

These are the questions which should touch the younger generation most deeply: What position could and should we have among the nations? Can we restore honor to the German name? Can we shape a new and better future? Or shall we be burdened with the crimes of the Hitler regime for generations to come?

However contradictory the problem may look at first sight, there can be no shilly-shallying, but only a clear Yes to these questions. The past cannot be erased, but the future is free. It is not predetermined. We have the power to re-examine our decisions and mend our wrong ways; we can renounce force and place our trust in peaceful and gradual progress; we can reject racial pride. Instead of impressing the world with war and aggression, we can strive for world prestige through the peaceful solution of conflicts, as the Swiss and the Scandinavians have done for centuries to their national glory. For us, the choice is open to condemn Hitler's deluded destructiveness and to embrace Albert Schweitzer's message— respect for life.

If we are really serious about this new respect for life, it must also extend to the victims of the unspeakable policy of extermination. Ever since human beings have existed, respect for life has included respect for the dead. Everywhere it is the duty of the living to preserve the memory of the dead. Should we listen to insinuations that the time has come to forget crimes and victims because nobody must incriminate himself? Is it not, rather, cowardly, mean, and miserable to deny even now the dead the honor they deserve, and to forget them as quickly as possible?

We owe it to ourselves to examine our consciences sincerely and to face the naked truth, instead of minimizing it or glossing over it. This is also the only way we can regain respect in the world. Covering up or minimizing crimes will suggest that we secretly approve of them. Who will believe that we want to respect all that is human if we treat the death of nearly six million Jews as a "small error" to be forgotten after a few years?

The test of our change of heart should be not only the dead but the living. There are 30,000 Jewish fellow-citizens living among us. Many of them have returned only recently from emigration, overwhelmed with a desire for their old homeland. It is up to all of us to make sure that they live among us in peace and without being abused, that their new trust in us, won after much effort, is not destroyed by desecrated cemeteries, gutter slogans, or hate songs. Those who will never learn must not be allowed to take refuge in the freedom of opinion. A higher value is at stake here, the honor of the dead, and respect for the living. But it is not up to the public prosecutor to imbue our lives with new and more humane principles. This is everybody's business. It concerns us all! It will determine our future.

REVIEW QUESTIONS

1. According to Hannah Vogt, what lessons should Germans learn from the Nazi era?
2. How did she suggest that Germans now confront the Holocaust?

CHAPTER 11

The West in an Age of Globalism

WORLD TRADE CENTER TOWERS burn after terrorist attack on September 11, 2001. (© *Jason Szenes/CORBIS/Sygma*)

The most important developments in recent European history were the collapse of communism and the end of the Cold War. With the decline of Soviet power and the discrediting of Marxism, the countries of Eastern Europe, and Russia itself, struggled to adapt to Western democratic forms and the free market. The transition to laissez-faire capitalism proved particularly difficult in Russia, which remained plagued with corruption, organized crime, and a declining standard of living.

In the closing decades of the twentieth century, ethnic conflicts grew more acute. Throughout Europe right-wing parties protested against immigration, particularly from African, Middle Eastern, and Asian lands, complaining that the essential character of their nation was being destroyed. At times, right-wing extremists, often neo-Nazis, employed violence against immigrants. Yugoslavia was torn apart by the worst ethnic violence since World War II.

In the twenty-first century, globalization continues relentlessly; the world is being knit ever closer together by the spread of Western ideals, popular culture (particularly American), free market capitalism, and technology. Government officials and business and professional people all over the world dress in Western clothes. Women follow Western fashions in dress and makeup. People line up to eat at McDonalds, see a Hollywood movie, or attend a rock concert. Everywhere people are eager to adopt the latest technology that originated in the West but is now also manufactured in other, particularly Asian, lands.

Advanced technology intensifies the means of communication, not only through television and radio, but also with faxes, e-mail, cellular phones, and the Internet—all means of instantaneous individual communication that have become commonplace in the past two decades.

These developments promote shared interests among individuals and businesses, some of them multinational corporations, throughout the globe, reducing the importance of national frontiers. All these factors combined are reshaping non-Western societies in a relentless adjustment that causes both deep hardships and possibilities for a better life.

The ideals of freedom and democracy, historical accomplishments of Western civilization, exert a powerful influence worldwide; they are also part of the process of westernization. Unlike technology, they cannot easily be put into practice outside the countries of their origin. However, they inspire human ambitions everywhere. They have even become part of the rhetoric of dictatorships.

At the same time, strong cultural traditions still divide the world. The hatred of radical Muslims for the West, which they see as a threat to traditional Islam, is a striking example of the clash of cultures. These Muslim militants, organized in an international network, Al Qaeda, with well-financed cells in dozens of countries, including the United States, were behind appalling attacks in Africa, Asia, and Europe as well as the bombing of the World Trade Center and the Pentagon, the worst terrorist attack in history. Their ultimate aims are the destruction of Western civilization, which they see as immoral and an affront to God, the restoration of the Islamic empire that existed in the Middle Ages, and the imposition of strict Islamic law in all Islamic lands. Often fortified by a fundamentalist theology, these militants represent a radical attack on freedom and secularism, two hallmarks of modernity.

1 The Collapse of Communism

Throughout the 1970s and early 1980s the discrepancy between Soviet ambition and deteriorating economic conditions became apparent in the Soviet Union and satellite countries of Eastern Europe. Economic productivity declined just when increasing contact with democratic and prosperous Western countries raised consumer expectations. In addition, loyalty toward the Soviet Union in the satellite countries had been steadily eroded by nationalist resentment against communist repression.

The reforms instituted by Mikhail Gorbachev in the Soviet Union in 1986 led to a groundswell of support for liberation in Eastern Europe. Agitation for self-determination, democracy, and the end of communist rule spread and was not suppressed as it had been in the past. During 1989, Soviet power crumbled as one by one, the Eastern European countries declared their sovereignty and ousted their communist governments. By the end of the year, all communist regimes there, except in Albania, had been overthrown. (Communist rule in Albania ended in 1991.) In the Soviet Union itself the communist empire collapsed at the end of 1991. Within three years, the once-mighty superpower had disintegrated unexpectedly and in a remarkably peaceful manner. The Cold War was over.

Vaclav Havel
THE FAILURE OF COMMUNISM

Established as a sovereign state at the end of World War I, Czechoslovakia enjoyed two decades of independence until it fell under Hitler's rule in 1938–1939; in World War II it was brutally occupied by the German army. After Czechoslovakia's liberation by Soviet soldiers, Stalin ruthlessly turned it into a communist state in 1948.

In 1968, enlightened party members, with the support of the Czech people, sought to loosen the oppressive restraints of the communist order and reestablish ties with Western Europe. Under the leadership of Alexander Dubček the country was intoxicated with the air of freedom. Seeking a humane version of Marxism, the reformers rehabilitated the victims of the Stalinist past and stopped censorship.

Suddenly, on August 21, 1968, Soviet troops invaded the country. Although they avoided the bloodshed that had accompanied their suppression of the Hungarian uprising in 1956, the Soviet leaders stopped Dubček's reforms; liberalization in Czechoslovakia endangered their own political system. "Socialism with a human face," as Dubček's program was called, came to an end.

Yet twenty years later, in December 1989, the communist regime dissolved in the "Velvet Revolution." Vaclav Havel, a frequently imprisoned dissident playwright and a lively intellectual, was elected president. In his 1990 New Year's Day address, excerpted below, Havel told the Czech people how the communist regime had abused its power.

THE TRUTH, UNVARNISHED

For 40 years you have heard on this day from the mouths of my predecessors, in a number of variations, the same thing: how our country is flourishing, how many more millions of tons of steel we have produced, how we are all happy, how we believe in our Government and what beautiful prospects are opening ahead of us. I assume you have not named me to this office so that I, too, should lie to you.

Our country is not flourishing. The great creative and spiritual potential of our nation is not being applied meaningfully. Entire branches of industry are producing things for which there is no demand while we are short of things we need.

The state, which calls itself a state of workers, is humiliating and exploiting them instead. Our outmoded economy wastes energy, which we have in short supply. The country, which could once be proud of the education of its people, is spending so little on education that today, in that respect, we rank 72d in the world. We have spoiled our land, rivers and forests, inherited from our ancestors, and we have, today, the worst environment in the whole of Europe. Adults die here earlier than in the majority of European countries. . . .

LEARNING TO BELIEVE AGAIN

The worst of it is that we live in a spoiled moral environment. We have become morally ill because we are used to saying one thing and thinking another. We have learned not to believe in anything, not to care about each other, to worry only about ourselves. The concepts of love, friendship, mercy, humility or forgiveness have lost their depths and dimension, and for many of us they represent only some sort of psychological curiosity or they appear as long-lost wanderers from faraway times, somewhat ludicrous in the era of computers and space ships. . . .

COGS NO LONGER

The previous regime, armed with a proud and intolerant ideology, reduced people into the means of production, and nature into its tools. So it attacked their very essence, and their mutual relations. . . . Out of talented and responsible people, ingeniously husbanding their land, it made cogs of some sort of great, monstrous, thudding, smelly machine, with an unclear purpose. All it can do is slowly but irresistibly, wear itself out, with all its cogs.

If I speak about a spoiled moral atmosphere I don't refer only to our masters. . . . I'm speaking about all of us. For all of us have grown used to the totalitarian system and accepted it as an immutable fact, and thereby actually helped keep it going. None of us are only its victims; we are all also responsible for it.

It would be very unwise to think of the sad heritage of the last 40 years only as something foreign; something inherited from a distant relative. On the contrary, we must accept this heritage as something we have inflicted on ourselves. If we accept it in such a way, we shall come to understand it is up to all of us to do something about it.

Let us make no mistake: even the best Government, the best Parliament and the best President cannot do much by themselves. Freedom and democracy, after all, mean joint participation and shared responsibility. If we realize this, then all the horrors that the new Czechoslovak democracy inherited cease to be so horrific. If we realize this, then hope will return to our hearts.

Everywhere in the world, people were surprised how these malleable, humiliated, cynical citizens of Czechoslovakia, who seemingly believed in nothing, found the tremendous strength within a few weeks to cast off the totalitarian system, in an entirely peaceful and dignified manner. We ourselves are surprised at it.

And we ask: Where did young people who had never known another system get their longing for truth, their love of freedom, their political imagination, their civic courage and civic responsibility? How did their parents, precisely the generation thought to have been lost, join them? How is it possible that so many people immediately understood what to do and that none of them needed any advice or instructions? . . .

RECALLING RUINED LIVES

Naturally we too had to pay for our present-day freedom. Many of our citizens died in prison in the 1950's. Many were executed. Thousands of human lives were destroyed. Hundreds of thousands of talented people were driven abroad. . . . Those who fought against totalitarianism during the war were also persecuted. . . . Nobody who paid in one way or another for our freedom could be forgotten.

Independent courts should justly evaluate the possible guilt of those responsible, so that the full truth about our recent past should be exposed.

But we should also not forget that other nations paid an even harsher price for their present freedom, and paid indirectly for ours as well. All human suffering concerns each human being. . . . Without changes in the Soviet Union, Poland, Hungary, and the German Democratic Republic, what happened here could hardly have taken place, and certainly not in such a calm and peaceful way.

Now it depends only on us whether this hope will be fulfilled, whether our civic, national and political self-respect will be revived. Only a man or nation with self-respect, in the best sense of the word, is capable of listening to the voices of others, while accepting them as equals, of forgiving enemies and of expiating sins. . . .

A HUMANE REPUBLIC

Perhaps you are asking what kind of republic I am dreaming about. I will answer you: a republic that is independent, free, democratic, a republic with economic prosperity and also social justice, a humane republic that serves man and that for that reason also has the hope that man will serve it. . . .

THE PEOPLE HOLD SWAY

My most important predecessor started his first speech by quoting from Comenius.[1] Permit me to end my own first speech by my own paraphrase. Your Government, my people, has returned to you.

---

[1]Comenius was a Czech theologian and educator of the seventeenth century. The quotation was used by Tomáš Masaryk (1850–1937), the first president of Czechoslovakia, which was created after World War I. "I, too, believe before God that, when the storms of wrath have passed, to thee shall return the rule over thine own things, O Czech people."

REVIEW QUESTION

1. What did Vaclav Havel mean when he said the Czechs had lived in a "spoiled moral environment" for the past forty years?

2   Globalization: Patterns and Problems

The interaction between the West and the non-Western world initiated during the Age of Exploration in the fifteenth and sixteenth centuries accelerated with the emergence of European imperialism in the late nineteenth century. Today the world is being knit ever closer together by the spread of Western ideals, free-market capitalism, and technology, particularly telecommunications (satellites and the Internet). The breakthrough in information technology, says Thomas L. Friedman, foreign affairs columnist for *The New York Times,* has enabled companies "to locate different parts of their production, research, and marketing in different countries, but still tie them together through computers and teleconferencing as though they were in one place." And it allows individuals all over the world to communicate with each other instantly and inexpensively, overcoming national borders. A distinguishing feature of globalization is the elimination of barriers to free trade and the interconnectedness of national economies. Proponents of these trends argue convincingly, as does economist Jagdish Bhagwati, that expanded international "trade enhances growth, and the growth reduces poverty." The economic growth facilitated by globalization, continues Bhagwati, also alleviates social distress, including female oppression, child labor, and illiteracy.

> Let me add that growth is also a powerful mechanism that brings to life social legislation aimed at helping the poor and peripheral groups. Thus, rights and benefits for women may be guaranteed by legislation that prohibits dowry, proscribes polygamy, mandates primary enrollment for all children (including girls), and much else. But it will often amount to a hill of beans unless a growing economy gives women the economic independence to walk out and even to sue at the risk of being discarded. A battered wife who cannot find a new job is less likely to take advantage of legislation that says a husband cannot beat his wife.

Moreover, Bhagwati argues that even if the state requires primary school education, necessity will often compel impoverished parents to send their children to work rather than to school. However, as the parents' income increases because of economic growth they are likely to send their children to school.

But globalization has also created a backlash among people who regard westernization as a threat to revered traditions. The most dramatic and dangerous reaction against Western values has occurred in Muslim lands, which have witnessed a surge of religious fundamentalism designed to counter Western influence. In their struggle against modernization and westernization. Radical Islamic fundamentalists have resorted to terrorism, culminating in the attack on the World Trade Center and the Pentagon on September 11, 2001.

Fareed Zakaria
"DEMOCRACY HAS ITS DARK SIDES"

In the following selection from his book *The Future of Freedom* (2003), Fareed Zakaria, editor of *Newsweek International,* discusses the implications of the spread of democracy throughout much of the globe. In many countries, he observes, the adoption of democratic procedures—parliaments and the ballot—has enabled dictators to gain and retain power.

We live in a democratic age. Over the last century the world has been shaped by one trend above all others—the rise of democracy. In 1900 not a single country had what we would today consider democracy: a government created by elections in which every adult citizen could vote. Today 119 do, comprising 62 percent of all countries in the world. What was once a peculiar practice of a handful of states around the North Atlantic has become the standard form of government for humankind. Monarchies are antique, fascism and communism utterly discredited. Even Islamic theocracy appeals only to a fanatical few. For the vast majority of the world, democracy is the sole surviving source of political legitimacy. Dictators such as Egypt's Hosni Mubarak and Zimbabwe's Robert Mugabe go to great effort and expense to organize national elections—which, of course, they win handily. When the enemies of democracy mouth its rhetoric and ape its rituals, you know it has won the war.

We live in a democratic age in an even broader sense. From its Greek root, "democracy" means "the rule of the people." And everywhere we are witnessing the shift of power downward. I call this "democratization," even though it goes far beyond politics, because the process is similar: hierarchies are breaking down, closed systems are opening up, and pressures from the masses are now the primary engine of social change. Democracy has gone from being a form of government to a way of life.

Consider the economic realm. What is truly distinctive and new about today's capitalism is not that it is global or information-rich or tech-nologically driven—all that has been true at earlier points in history—but rather that it is *democratic.* Over the last half-century economic growth has enriched hundreds of millions in the industrial world, turning consumption, saving, and investing into a mass phenomenon. This has forced the social structures of societies to adapt. Economic power, which was for centuries held by small groups of businessmen, bankers, and bureaucrats, has, as a result, been shifting downward. Today most companies—indeed most countries—woo not the handful that are rich but the many that are middle class. And rightly so, for the assets of the most exclusive investment group are dwarfed by those of a fund of workers' pensions.

Culture has also been democratized. What was once called "high culture" continues to flourish, of course, but as a niche product for the elderly set, no longer at the center of society's cultural life, which is now defined and dominated by popular music, blockbuster movies, and prime-time television. Those three make up the canon of the modern age, the set of cultural references with which everyone in society is familiar. The democratic revolution coursing through society has changed our very definiton of culture. The key to the reputation of, say, a singer in an old order would have been *who* liked her. The key to fame today is *how many* like her. And by that yardstick Madonna will always trump [opera singer] Jessye Norman. Quantity has become quality.

What has produced this dramatic shift? As with any large-scale social phenomenon, many forces have helped produce the democratic wave—a technological revolution, growing middle-class wealth, and the collapse of alternative systems and ideologies that organized society. To these grand systemic causes add another: America. The rise and dominance of America—a country whose politics and culture are deeply democratic—has made democratization seem inevitable. Whatever its causes, the democratic wave is having predictable effects in every area. It is breaking down hierarchies, empowering individuals, and transforming societies well beyond their politics. Indeed much of what is distinctive about the world we live in is a consequence of the democratic idea.

We often read during the roaring 1990s that technology and information had been democratized. This is a relatively new phenomenon. In the past, technology helped reinforce centralization and hierarchy. For example, the last great information revolution—in the 1920s involving radio, television, movies, megaphones—had a centralizing effect. It gave the person or group with access to that technology the power to reach the rest of society. That's why the first step in a twentieth-century coup or revolution was always to take control of the country's television or radio station. But today's information revolution has produced thousands of outlets for news that make central control impossible and dissent easy. The Internet has taken this process another huge step forward, being a system where, in the columnist Thomas Friedman's words, "everyone is connected but no one is in control."

The democratization of technology and information means that most anyone can get his hands on anything. Like weapons of mass destruction. We now know that Osama bin Laden was working on a serious biological-weapon program during the 1990s. But what is most astonishing is that the scientific information and manuals found in Al Qaeda's Kabul safe houses were not secrets stolen from government laboratories. They were documents downloaded from the Internet. Today if you want to find sources for anthrax, recipes for poison, or methods to weaponize chemicals, all you need is a good search engine. These same open sources will, unfortunately, soon help someone build a dirty bomb. The components are easier to get than ever before. Mostly what you need is knowledge, and that has been widely disseminated over the last decade. Even nuclear technology is now commonly available. It is, after all, fifty-year-old know-how, part of the world of AM radios and black-and-white television. Call it the democratization of violence.

It's more than a catchy phrase. The democratization of violence is one of the fundamental—and terrifying—features of the world today. For centuries the state has had a monopoly over the legitimate use of force in human societies. This inequality of power between the state and the citizen created order and was part of the glue that held modern civilization together. But over the last few decades the state's advantage has been weakened; now small groups of people can do dreadful things. And while terrorism is the most serious blow to state authority, central governments have been under siege in other ways as well. Capital markets, private businesses, local governments, nongovernmental organizations have all been gaining strength, sapping the authority of the state. The illegal flow of people, drugs, money, and weapons rising around the world attests to its weakness. This diffusion of power will continue because it is fueled by broad technological, social, and economic changes. In the post–September 11 world the state has returned, with renewed power and legitimacy. This too will endure. The age of terror will thus be marked by a tension, between the forces that drive the democratization of authority on the one hand and the state on the other.

To discuss these problems is not to say that democracy is a bad thing. Overwhelmingly it has had wonderful consequences. Who among us would want to go back to an age with fewer choices and less individual power and autonomy? But like any broad transformation, democracy has its dark sides. Yet we rarely speak about them. To do so would be to provoke instant criticism that you are "out of sync" with the times. But this means that we never really stop to understand these times. Silenced by fears of being branded "antidemocratic" we have no way to understand what might be troubling about the ever-increasing democratization of our lives. We asssume that no problem could ever be caused by democracy, so when we see social, political, and economic maladies we shift blame here and there, deflecting problems, avoiding answers, but never talking about the great transformation that is at the center of our political, economic, and social lives.

DEMOCRACY AND LIBERTY

"Suppose elections are free and fair and those elected are racists, fascists, separatists," said the American diplomat Richard Holbrooke about Yugoslavia in the 1990s. "That is the dilemma." Indeed it is, and not merely in Yugoslavia's past but in the world's present. Consider, for example, the challenge we face across the Islamic world. We recognize the need for democracy in those often-repressive countries. But what if democracy produces an Islamic theocracy or something like it? It is not an idle concern. Across the globe, democratically elected regimes, often ones that have been re-elected or reaffirmed through referenda, are routinely ignoring constitutional limits on their power and depriving their citizens of basic rights. This disturbing phenomenon—visible from Peru to the Palestinian territories, from Ghana to Venezuela—could be called "illiberal democracy."

For people in the West, democracy means "liberal domocracy": a political system marked not only by free and fair elections but also by the rule of law, a separation of powers, and the protection of basic liberties of speech, assembly, religion, and property. But this bundle of freedoms—what might be termed "constitutional liberalism"—has nothing intrinsically to do with democracy and the two have not always gone together, even in the West. After all, Adolf Hitler became chancellor of Germany via free elections. Over the last half-century in the West, democracy and liberty have merged. But today the two strands of liberal democracy, interwoven in the Western political fabric, are coming apart across the globe. Democracy is flourishing; liberty is not.

In some places, such as Central Asia, elections have paved the way for dictatorships. In others, they have exacerbated group conflict and ethnic tensions. Both Yugoslavia and Indonesia, for example, were far more tolerant and secular when they were ruled by strongmen (Tito and Suharto, respectively) than they are now as democracies. And in many non-democracies, elections would not improve matters much. Across the Arab world elections held tomorrow would probably bring to power regimes that are more intolerant, reactionary, anti-Western, and anti-Semitic than the dictatorships currently in place.

In a world that is increasingly democratic, regimes that resist the trend produce dysfunctional societies—as in the Arab world. Their people sense the deprivation of liberty more strongly than ever before because they know the alternatives; they can see them on CNN, BBC, and Al-Jazeera. But yet, newly democratic countries too often become sham democracies, which produces disenchantment, disarray, violence, and new forms of tyranny. Look at Iran and Venezuela. This is not a reason to stop holding elections, of course, but surely it should make us ask, What is at the root of this troubling development? Why do so many developing countries have so much difficulty creating stable, genuinely democratic societies? Were we to embark on the vast challenge of building democracy in Iraq, how would we make sure that we succeed?

REVIEW QUESTION

1. According to Fareed Zakaria, how has the contemporary world been shaped by democracy? What does he see as the "dark sides" of democracy?

3   Radical Islamic Terrorists

On September 11, 2001, nineteen Muslim Arabs, most of them from Saudi Arabia, hijacked four planes: two of them they crashed into the World Trade Center in New York, bringing down both towers; a third plane rammed into the Pentagon in Washington, D.C., causing severe damage; the fourth plane, apparently headed for the White House, crashed in a field in Pennsylvania when passengers attacked the hijackers. In all, about three thousand people perished in the worst terrorist attack in history. The meticulously planned operation was the work of Al Qaeda, an international terrorist network of militant Muslims, or Islamists as they call themselves.

The leader of Al Qaeda, Osama bin Laden, scion of an immensely wealthy Saudi family, operated from Afghanistan with the protection of the radical fundamentalist Taliban, who ruled the country, transforming it into a repressive regime based on a rigid interpretation of Islamic law.

When Taliban leaders refused to turn bin Laden over to the United States, President George W. Bush, supported by an international coalition, launched a military campaign whose ultimate goal was the destruction of international terrorism. Local Afghan forces opposed to the Taliban, assisted by American airpower—which proved decisive—defeated the Taliban in a few weeks. The new leaders of Afghanistan no longer permitted their country to serve as a haven and training center for radical Islamic terrorists. But Taliban fighters, who found refuge in Pakistan, continue to wage guerrilla war against the American-backed government.

Seething discontent in the Muslim world, particularly among Arabs, provides Al Qaeda with recruits, including zealots willing to inflict maximum casualties on civilians, even if doing so means blowing themselves up in the process. After September 11, several Al Qaeda operations were thwarted, including attempts to explode airplanes. But terrorists, either loosely or directly affiliated with Al Qaeda, succeeded in other operations, including the bombing of a nightclub in Bali, Indonesia, that killed more than 200 people, most of them Australian tourists; a series of truck-bomb explosions in Istanbul that wrecked two Jewish synagogues, the British consulate, and a British bank, killing more than fifty people and wounding hundreds; and the blowing up of a crowded train in Madrid that killed 191 people and wounded more than a thousand.

Abbas Amanat
"EMPOWERED THROUGH VIOLENCE: THE REINVENTION OF ISLAMIC EXTREMISM"

Bin Laden and his followers view their struggle against the United States as a holy war against the infidel. Their goal is the creation of an Islamic world-state governed by Islamic law, a revival of the medieval caliphate. A religious fanatic and absolutist who cannot tolerate pluralism, bin Laden wants to drive westerners and Western values out of Islamic lands; he is also a theocrat who would use the state's power to impose a narrow, intolerant version of Islam on the Muslim world. He and his followers are zealots who are convinced that they are doing God's will. Recruits for suicide missions are equally convinced that they are waging holy war against the enemies of God and their centers of evil, for which they will be richly rewarded in Paradise. The hatred of radical Muslims for the West shows that in an age of globalism the world is still divided by strong cultural traditons. In the following selection, Abbas Amanat, specialist in Middle East history, analyzes the roots of Islamic radicalism, focusing on the resentment many Muslims have against the West.

To this author, a historian of the Middle East who grew up in that part of the world, bin Laden's message of violence comes as a sobering reminder of what has become of the Middle East. This is not only because an outrage of unprecedented magnitude has been committed by some Middle Easterners against the U.S., which is both demonized in that region and seductive to many who live there. Nor is it because such an act confirmed the worst stereotypes of violence and fanaticism long associated with Islam and the Middle East. It was also because the outrage revealed much about the undeniable and alarming growth of religious extremism in the Muslim world, a trend that has been deeply intertwined with the tortured historical experience of becoming modern. . . .

1.

The emergence of the construct we call Islamic extremism, with its penchant for defiance, resentment, and violence, has its roots in the history of the Muslim sense of decline and its unhappy encounter with the dominant West. It is sobering to remind ourselves how frequently the Middle East, as one part of the Muslim world, has been visited by waves of violence in its recent history. Since the end of the Second World War, the area extending from Egypt and Turkey in the west to Afghanistan in the northwest and Yemen in the south has suffered at least ten major wars—and that's not counting the U.S. engagement in Afghanistan

after September 11. Casualties have run into millions. Populations have been uprooted, societies torn up by their roots, political structures demolished—all on a massive scale. Three of the region's wars were fought with Western powers (Britain's and France's attacks on Egypt during the Suez crisis in 1956; the Soviet Union's long, losing effort to subjugate Afghanistan in the 1980s; the American-led campaign to liberate Kuwait from Iraq in 1990–91); Israel and its Arab neighbors waged five wars (1948, 1956, 1967, 1973 and 1982); Yemen and Lebanon have suffered prolonged civil wars; and Iraq and Iran fought for eight years. The transforming effects of these crises haunted the last several generations in the Middle East. Throughout the region people have become ever more disillusioned with the deeply-entrenched dictatorships in their own countries, with the collapse of democratic institutions, hollow nationalistic rhetoric, and with their failing economies.

In the minds of many, Western powers shared the blame, both directly and indirectly. Whether based on historical reality or faulty perception, holding the Western powers responsible made special sense against the backdrop of a powerful West and a powerless Middle East. From the days of the European colonial powers in the 19th century to the more recent interventions of the superpowers, there has been a pattern of diplomatic, military and economic presence tying the fate of the Middle East and its resources to the West. Whether motivated by oil, grand strategy or support for Israel, the

Western powers were either involved in, or perceived to be behind, most of the region's political crises.

As a result, for new generations of Middle Easterners perceptions of the West, and particularly of the U.S., dramatically changed for the worse. Long gone were the images of well-wishing Yankees who established schools, universities and hospitals, distributed food, and supported nationalist endeavors. Instead, fascination with a luster of American popular culture was only heightened thanks to Hollywood and American high tech—computers, video games, and satellite dishes. Yet in a paradoxical turn, as the lines of visa-seekers in front of U.S. consulates grew longer, a cloud of mistrust and resentment against the U.S. also settled over the region. The people in the Middle East began to view American society through the lenses of sitcoms and softwares. To many unaccustomed eyes, the U.S. seemed like the center of a greedy, materialistic and uncaring world obsessed with violence and promiscuity. The U.S.'s unreserved support for Israel, its backing of unpopular regimes, and its fighter jets over Middle Eastern skies only added to anti-American feelings.

2.

Mistrust toward the West deepened as a result of the problematic way the Middle East improvised its own version of modernity. Since the beginning of the 20th century, Westernization has transformed lifestyles and expectations. Yet, despite an undeniable measure of growth and material improvement, today's Middle East by most economic indicators is still one of the least developed regions in the world. It is grappling endlessly with failed centralized planning, high birthrates, lopsided distribution of wealth, high unemployment, widespread corruption, inefficient bureaucracies, and environmental and health problems. The frustration endemic among the young urban classes— often the children of rural migrants who came to the cities in search of a better life and a

higher income—is a response to these conundrums.

For the population of the Middle East, progressively younger because of high birthrates, uprooted from their traditional setting, and deprived of illusive privileges that they can see around them and on television screens but cannot have, the familiar and comforting space of Islam offers a welcoming alternative. Daily prayers, Friday sermons, Koranic study groups, Islamic charities—these are all part of that space. But so are the street demonstrations and the clandestine pamphlets, with their fiery anti-establishment, anti-secular, and anti-Zionist message.

In dealing with these restive multitudes, the governments of the Middle East and their associated ruling elites have little to offer. They are themselves part of the problem as they contribute to the public perception of powerlessness. In the period right after World War II, nationalist ideologies were highly effective in mobilizing the public against the European colonial presence. But over time they often hindered the growth of democratic institutions and the emergence of an enduring civil society. The army officers who came to power in Egypt, Syria, Iraq, and elsewhere through military coups, and prolonged their leadership through repressive means, invested heavily in anti-Western rhetoric. Yet facing the erosion of their own legitimacy, they learned to pay a lip service to the rising Islamic sentiments in their societies, exploiting them as a cushion between the elite and the masses and to suppress individual freedoms.

The predictable victims of this appeasement were the modernizing urban middle classes of the Middle East. Though small and vulnerable, these middle classes were crucial conduits for modernizing even as they preserved a sense of national culture. Egypt, Iraq, Syria, Turkey, and Iran, in their rush for an illusive economic growth, and greater equity, purposely undermined the economic bases of their middle classes. They did so through heavy-handed state planning and the mindless nationalization programs. The middle classes in the Middle East today, besieged and intimidated, are no longer willing or able to take up the cause of democratic reforms. They have instead given rise to a spoiled crust of the politically silenced and submissive class whose voice of protest is heard, increasingly, through extremist causes.

Out of this milieu came Mohamed Atta [who crashed one of the hijacked planes into the World Trade Center], a failed son of an affluent Egyptian lawyer. Another example is bin Laden's chief lieutenant, Ayman al-Zawahiri, a physician from a celebrated Egyptian family.

This staggering reorientation toward radical Islam needs to be understood in light of a deeper crisis of identity in the Arab world. In the post-colonial period, most nation-states in that region had to improvise their own ideologies of territorial nationalism in order to hold together what were often disjointed local and ethnic identities. At the same time they had to remain loyal to the ideology of pan-Arabism— the notion, or dream, that all Arab peoples make up one supernation—a project that was destined to fail dismally. Egypt came out of the colonial experience with what might have been the basis for its own Egyptian nationalism, but under Gamal Abdel Nasser, it traded that away for leadership of the pan-Arab cause. Yet the experiences of secular pan-Arabism, whether that of the Nasser era in the 1950s and 60s or the Ba'thist regimes of Iraq and Syria in the 1960s and 1970s, proved illusory to the intellectuals who championed it. It was even more unrewarding to the Arab masses who for decades were exposed to the state-run propaganda machines and to the often demagogic street politics. The harsh realities of the military and paramilitary regimes of the Arab world sobered even the most ardent supporters of Arab nationalism.

It was in this environment of despair that the disempowered Arab masses came to share the common cause of confronting Zionism. Resistance to the establishment of the Jewish homeland since the end of World War I and to the creation of the state of Israel in 1947 offered the Arab world a rallying point of great symbolic power. The subsequent experiences of

multiple defeats in wars against Israel revived in the Arab psyche memories of prolonged colonial domination. From the Arab nationalist perspective, Zionism was not merely another form of imagined nationalism rooted in the 19th century, but a project designed by the West to perpetuate its imperial presence and protect its vested interests in the region—the latest manifestation of centuries of enmity against the Muslim peoples. For many in the Arab world it was comforting to believe that the reason why hundreds of millions of Arabs could not defeat Israel was because Western powers were protecting it. And more often than not there was ample evidence to convince them of the validity of their claim.

3.

Not surprisingly, the sense of despair toward repressive regimes at home and helplessness against the consolidation of the neighboring Zionist state engendered a new spirit of Islamic solidarity. It was radical in its politics, monolithic in its approach, and defiant toward the West.

The decisive shift came not inside the Arab world but with the 1979 revolution in Iran. The establishment of an Islamic republic under the leadership of the uncompromising Ayatollah Khomeini evoked throughout the Muslim world the long-cherished desire for creating a genuine Islamic regime. Even though it was preached by a radical Shi'a clergy who committed enormous atrocities against his own people, the Iranian model of revolutionary Islam was viewed as pointing the way to an "authentic" and universalist Islam. Through cassette tapes and demonstrations, Iranian revolutionaries managed to topple the Shah and the mighty Pahlavi regime despite its vast military arsenal, secularizing program, and Western backing. Even more empowering was the revolution's anti-imperialist rhetoric.

After his followers besieged the American embassy and held its staff hostage in 1980–81, Khomeini labeled the U.S. as the Great Satan for backing the "Pharaonic" powers—a label for the shah and conservative rulers elsewhere in the region—and for repressing the "disinherited" of the earth.

The Iraq–Iran War of 1980–88 further established the appeal of the paradigm of martyrdom that had long been deeply rooted in Shi'a Islam. That conflict was portrayed as an apocalyptic jihad between the forces of truth and falsehood. In addition to defending their own nation, the Iranians believed they were exporting their revolution. As the slogan on the banners declared and as the battle cries of many teenage volunteers confirmed, the path of Islamic liberation stretched across the battlefields to the Shi'a holy cities of Karbala' and Najaf in Iraq all the way to Jerusalem.

Even if the Iranian revolution failed to take root elsewhere, the celebration of martyrdom found resonance far and wide. The revolutionary Shiites of Lebanon's Hezbollah, and later the young Palestinians who eagerly volunteered for suicide bombings on behalf of the Hamas and Islamic Jihad, saw martyrdom as a way of empowerment. It is not difficult to see the same traits among the hijackers of September 11.

The accelerated pace of Islamic radicalism in the early 1980s, whether inspired by the Iranian revolution or reacting to it, helped shape the outlook of a generation from which came the extremism of Osama bin Laden himself. In his twenties, he was a pious, though uninspiring, student in Jidda University in Saudi Arabia. He came from a superrich family with close connections to the Saudi royalty. In November 1979, he must have witnessed the siege of the Grand Mosque of Mecca and the revolt under the leadership of a messianic figure who claimed to have received direct authority from the Prophet to render justice. The quick suppression of this revolt by the Saudi authorities came only a month after the signing of the Camp David peace agreement between Israel and Egypt. The treaty was received by the Islamic activists throughout the Arab world as a betrayal to the Arab and Islamic causes. Only a year later, in October 1980, the Egyptian president, Anwar al-Sadat, was assassinated by a splinter group of the Muslim Brothers with which Ayman al-Zawahiri, bin Laden's future lieutenant, was associated.

The Mecca uprising and Sadat's assassination were both inspired by a tradition of religious radicalism going back to the Society of the Muslim Brothers in the 1920s and 30s and before that to the Wahhabi movement that began in the late 18th century. The central doctrine of Wahhabism was a return to the way of "virtuous ancestors," a highly regressive, monolithic interpretation of Islam known as Salafiyya, a doctrinal propensity that for centuries encouraged strict adherence to puritanical principles.

In the early 20th century, the Salafiyya played a central part in the shaping of Saudi Arabia as an Islamic state. It also served as the guiding doctrine for the Muslim Brothers' goal of moral and political reconstruction. Inspired by the ideas of Sayyid Qutb, a leader of the Muslim Brothers—who was executed in 1966 by the Nasser regime—this ideology received a new lease on life. A true believer was required to "renounce" the dark sacrilege of his secular surroundings. The primary targets were the regimes of the Arab world, whose secularism was labeled a return to the "paganism" of pre-Islamic times. . . .

The doctrine of Salafiyya and its articulation by Sayyid Qutb gained an overwhelming currency among Islamic radicals in the early 1980s. But the wilderness that might serve as a refuge for them could not be recreated in the oil-rich Saudi Arabia of bin Laden or in the tourist-infested Egypt of al-Zawahiri. Instead, Afghanistan beckoned. The burgeoning resistance movement against the occupying Soviet forces there was highly appealing to radical and moderate sentiments alike. It could unite activists of all Islamic persuasions for a common cause of fighting the spread of the godless communism.

Amanat then discusses how Osama bin Laden and other Arabs from Morocco to Yemen devoted to militant Wahhabism fought in Afghanistan, where they came to be known as Arab Afghans. In Afghanistan, bin Laden and his cohorts drew up plans for the creation of a world Islamic state governed by Islamic law, a revival of the medieval Caliphate. After the defeat of the Soviets, bin Laden returned to Saudi Arabia and then went to Sudan, now ruled by a militant Islamic regime. The Gulf War fueled his anti-Americanism, for he regarded as an affront to Wahhabi Islam the stationing of infidel American troops in Saudi Arabia, the home of Islam's holiest shrines.

4.

... Bin Laden's personal odyssey further affirmed his anti-American resolve. In 1994, under American pressure, the Saudi authorities revoked his passport and froze his assets. Two years later Washington succeeded in pressuring Sudan to deny him the safe haven he had enjoyed there. As a last resort he sought refuge with the Taliban, who had taken control of Kabul in 1996, in exchange for his financial and logistic support.

The Taliban was the other side of the al Qaeda coin. The Wahhabi propaganda campaign, which went on under Saudi auspices for at least two decades, was the chief factor behind the emergence of this militant student movement that eventually took over Afghanistan. In the 1980s and 90s through patronage and missionary work, financing the construction of new communal mosques from Indonesia and the Philippines to sub-Saharan Africa and Central Asia, training young students of many nationalities in pro-Wahhabi subsidized seminaries, making available to the public the Wahhabi literature, establishing interest-free charity and scholarships for the poor, facilitating the transfer of the Hajj pilgrims, and backing conservative clerical elements with Wahhabi proclivities, the Saudi establishment built a strong and growing network that is now changing the face of Islam throughout the towns and villages of the Muslim world. Inad-

vertently, this network proved to be a fertile ground for garnering support for bin Laden from Pakistan and southern Afghanistan to Central Asia, Africa and Southeast Asia.

The Taliban movement took root among the dislocated and deprived children of the Afghan refugees trained in the religious schools of Pakistan financed by private Saudi funding. Armed with Wahhabi fervor for jihad and little else, under the auspices of the Pakistani army intelligence these seminarians were organized into a fighting force. The political lacuna that came about as a result of the devastating Afghan civil war opened the way for the Taliban's gradual advance and eventual takeover. The regime they established embodied all the neo-Wahhabi zeal that was preached in the Peshawar schools. It revived and imposed a strict patriarchal order deeply hostile to women and their education and public presence. It allowed battering, even killing, of women by their male relatives, enforced facial veiling, and closed most girls schools. It displayed extraordinary intolerance toward Shiites and other minorities, obliterated even the most primitive symbols of a modern culture, and undermined all human and individual rights. In the name of purging Afghanistan of factionalism and ending the civil war, the Taliban turned it into a miserable fortress whose people suffered from starvation and isolation.

In the year that bin Laden arrived in Afghanistan, he issued a fatwa, or religious ruling, that called upon all Muslims to kill Americans as a religious duty. The 1998 bombing of the American embassies in Nairobi and Dar es Salaam was, as far as we know, his first attempt to put his own ruling into practice. This came at the time when al Qaeda's merger with Egyptian Islamic Jihad—led by Ayman al-Zawahiri, who had recently masterminded the killing of fifty-eight tourists in Luxor, Egypt—and other terrorist organizations drastically increased bin Laden's capacity to wreak havoc. The U.S. tried to punish him for the embassy bombings by firing missiles into his camps. His emerging unscathed gave him greater confidence and enhanced his reputation for invincibility in the eyes of his followers.

For bin Laden and his al Qaeda associates, the terrorist war against the U.S. was a struggle rooted in Islam's noble past and ensured of victory by God. In this context, the attack on giant structures representing American economic and military might was a largely symbolic act that would, they hoped, miraculously subdue their enemies, just as the infidels of early Islam eventually succumbed to the Prophet's attacks on their caravans. This theory of terror, violent and indiscriminate, though utterly against the mainstream interpretation of Islam, attracted a small but committed group of devotees who also saw self-sacrifice as a permissible avenue toward symbolic achievement of their goals.

In several respects, however, bin Laden's apocalyptic vision was grounded in reality and geared to the possible. He and his associates were men of worldly capabilities who could employ business administration models to generate revenue, invest capital in the market, create a disciplined leadership, recruit volunteers, incorporate other extremist groups, organize and maintain new cells, issue orders and communicate through a franchised network of semi-autonomous units on a global scale. This mix of the messianic and the pragmatic allowed al Qaeda to tailor its rhetoric to the grievances of its growing audience and to carry out recruitment and indoctrination on a wider scale.

The vast majority of Muslims do not approve of bin Laden's terrorism, nor do they share his ambition to build a monolithic community based on a pan-Islamic order. Yet there is an undeniable sympathy for the way he has manipulated grievances and symbols. The contrasting images of the "pagan" America and the "authentic" Islam find currency in wide and diverse quarters. One example is the young boys among Afghan and Pakistani refugees who were brainwashed in the Saudi-funded Wahhabi seminaries of Peshawar—and from whose ranks rose the Taliban (the word itself means "students"). Another is the new generation of Western-educated Arab middle classes who were recruited to al Qaeda's suicide cells in Europe.

We can read in the testament of Mohamed Atta, the Egyptian ringleader of the September 11 attacks, the typical obsessive enthusiasm of a born-again Muslim. As a reward for his resort to massive terror and destruction, which he carried out with resolve and precision, Atta seeks the Koranic promise of heavenly recompense especially reserved for martyrs. His literal reading of the sacred text is imbued with sexual references. "Know," he promises his accomplices, "that the gardens of paradise are waiting for you in all their beauty. And the women of paradise are waiting, calling out, 'Come hither, friends of God.' They are dressed in their most beautiful clothing." This is all the more glaring, and perversely pathetic, when contrasted with Atta's final encounters in a Florida strip club. One can only imagine that he was gazing at the barely-clad strippers of this world in anticipation of the houris—beautiful maidens awaiting the brave and virtuous—in paradise. This was the reward he expected for his martyrdom in the "battle for the sake of God," which he was waging, as he himself reminded us, in the "way of the pious forefathers." This surreal mix of the pious and the profane, backed by a litany of Koranic verses, reveals a discomfiting pseudomodern crust over the hard core of extremism.

As for bin Laden himself, he came into the spotlight after September 11 having shrouded himself and his cause in an apocalyptic aura. His October 7 statement broadcast on television, both in tone and content, alluded to a seminal narrative of Islam. Above all, he said, he placed his total trust in God as he waged the struggle of true believers against infidels, confident of the ultimate reward of martyrdom. His references to the impending fall of the "hypocrites"—those Muslim individuals and governments who were not supportive of his cause—and to the sure victory of the righteous on horseback and armed with swords—presumably in contrast to the sophisticated weaponry of his enemies—all have resonance in the encoded story of early Islam. In a statement at the same time, bin Laden's chief lieutenant, al-Zawahiri, referred to the catastrophic loss of Muslim Spain at the end of the 15th century. This, too, was meant to remind Muslims of the greater days of Islam before its defeat by Christianity, hence complementing bin Laden's vision of the glorious past.

5.

That al-Qaeda effectively communicates to a wide audience far beyond its own extremist circle there can be no doubt. In doing so, it has found abundant opportunities, thanks to the global media, and thanks to complacency and ignorance of Western intelligence services and law enforcement agencies. The dilemmas and inconsistencies of U.S. foreign policy in the region also provided al Qaeda with its weapons of choice to appeal to the frustration and anger of the mainstream Muslims worldwide.

At the core of the resentment so widespread in the Arab and Islamic world is Israel and its treatment of the Palestinians in the occupied territories. Hundreds of millions of Arabs, and increasingly other Muslims as well, are now more than ever informed through media about the Palestinians' unending confrontations with the Israeli security forces. . . .

Broadcast through the Arab networks, and more recently on the global al-Jazeerah television network based in Qatar—the outlet of choice for bin Laden himself—these tragic depictions are increasingly intermingled with symbols of Islamic defiance: the suicidal missions of Hamas and Islamic Jihad against Israeli targets, the fiery anti-American and anti-Israeli slogans and sermons in Friday congregations. Added to this is the enormous level of Islamic radical pamphleteering with anti-American and anti-Zionist content, not infrequently laced in the Arabic textbooks with flagrant anti-Jewish racial references.

The politically repressive regimes of most Arab countries permit anti-Zionist (and even anti-Jewish) expressions as a safety valve. This further adds to the symbolic value of the Palestinian cause as a powerful expression of Arab unity with growing Islamic coloring. Since the Intifada of 1986 and the 1993 Oslo Peace Accord, the thrust of Arab public opinion has been directed toward the fate of the Palestinians in the occupied territories rather than against the very existence of Israel. Yet the oppressive Arab regimes still use the hypocritical rhetoric of national security as an impediment to the growth of democracy in their own countries. In such a repressive environment the mosque often functions as a political forum. There the differentiation between Israeli conduct and American foreign policy fades. Arab public opinion widely believes that the Jewish lobby in the U.S. is the sole determinant of American policy in the region and therefore makes little distinction between U.S. foreign policy and Israeli abuse of the Palestinians.

Proponents of Muslim piety also hold American "corrupting influences" responsible for the erosion of the assumed "authentic" mores of Islamic austerity and devotion. These influences are widely associated with the worst clichés of American popular culture and lifestyle. In this world of misperceptions, the globally permeating images of promiscuity, ostentatious wealth, organized crime, random violence, drug use, gluttony and wastefulness contrast sharply with the idealized Islamic virtues of moral outrage, self-sacrifice, other-worldliness, brotherhood, and piety. The extremists eagerly and skillfully sell these contrasts to the ill-informed Muslim masses, who more than ever now rely on visual images thanks to the power of the electronic media.

To Muslim viewers around the world these exaggerated contrasts offer an elusive comfort, since they seem to explain the root cause of the perceived malfunction of their own government and societies. They are all the more suggestive because they are shrewdly tied up with the story of sufferings of the Palestinian people at the hands of the Israelis and those of the Iraqi people under U.S.-upheld sanctions. On top of that, they are constantly reminded of the "defiling" of the Islamic holy lands by the presence of American troops in Saudi Arabia.

Bin Laden is a master at exploiting these symbolic references. The U.S. and its Western allies have tried to convince the world, and especially the Muslim world, that the campaign against bin Laden and al Qaeda is not directed at Islam but at terrorism. However, that differentiation won't carry much weight in the minds of many Muslims so long as bin Laden, "dead or alive," has at his disposal such potent propaganda weapons. The issue is not only the danger that he or people like him will turn their extremist dream into a religious war between Islam and the West. Equally important is that they will provoke an escalating conflict between militant neo-Wahhabi Islam and the retreating forces and quavering voices of moderation and tolerance in the Muslim world. Bin Laden presents to much of his audience the image of a messianic prophet. Even if he is killed for his cause, he will, in their eyes, have died a martyr's death.

The Economist
"MARTYRDOM AND MURDER"

The following article in the British weekly *The Economist* analyzes a distinguishing feature of Islamic terrorism: the suicide or homicide bomber.

"I have always dreamed," says an anarchist in Joseph Conrad's novel "The Secret Agent," "of a band of men absolute in their resolve to discard all scruples. . . . No pity for anything on earth, including themselves, and death enlisted for good and all in the service of humanity." But, Conrad's anarchist complains, "I could never get as many as three such men together." These days, there seems to be a superabundance of people willing to die in order to commit murder: in Turkey, Saudi Arabia, Chechnya and Russia, Pakistan, Israel, Iraq, Afghanistan and elsewhere. Is this phenomenon new? If so, what explains it? And what can be done about it?

Suicide terrorism, like the slippery concept of terrorism in general, is harder to define than it may appear. For instance, are the suicide bombings in Israel really so different from previous incidents in which Palestinian gunmen and knifemen (and the occasional Israeli) launched assaults that they had little hope of surviving? They were scarcely the first to sacrifice their own lives in order to take others. In the first century AD, the Zealots and Sicarii, two Jewish sects, attacked the Roman occupiers of Judaea and their allies in public places.

The Assassins, a cult active in modern Iran and Syria from the 11th to the 13th centuries, killed their targets (mainly Muslim rulers whom they considered apostates) at close range and with no escape routes. Their name comes from the Arabic *hashishiyya;* the drug's powers were thought to explain the Assassins' oblivious bravery.

From the mid-18th century, other groups launched suicidal attacks against colonial rulers in India, Indonesia and the Philippines. Then there are the countless individuals who have died for a cause without taking others with them: think of Irish and Kurdish hunger-strikers, or of the human minesweepers despatched by Iran during its war with Iraq.

Yet for all these partial precedents, there is something novel about the type of terrorism in which the terrorist's death is a necessary and essential part of his act, not just an incidental cost. This type arrived in Lebanon in the early 1980s. Before then, modern groups such as the IRA and ETA, the Basque separatist movement, planned to escape after (or before) their bombings, mortar attacks and so on. Hizbullah's campaign of suicidal car and truck explosions— one of which killed 241 Americans in Beirut in

October 1983; 58 people died in a strike on a French barracks on the same day—changed the face of terror.

The fact that Hizbullah started the trend, and that its spread has coincided with the rise of other Islamic groups—Hamas, Palestinian Islamic Jihad (PIJ), al Qaeda and others—has led some to surmise that Islamic fundamentalism somehow explains it. Proponents of this theory can cite the lengths to which some terrorists go to justify their attacks in Islamic terms, manipulating the precedents set by the Prophet and his companions and finessing the meanings of three key concepts: suicide, martyrdom and *jihad.*

UNHOLY WARRIORS

The Koran is unequivocal about suicide: as a mark of despair in Allah, it earns eternal damnation. On the other hand, martyrdom— death in *jihad,* incurred in Allah's name—earns eternal bliss: "Think not of those who are slain in Allah's way as dead. Nay, they live, finding their sustenance in the presence of the Lord." The Koranic outline of the martyr's rewards in paradise is elaborated in the *hadith* (prophetic sayings and anecdotes) and has been embellished by generations of scholars. Islamic suicide bombers go to their deaths variously expecting to meet the Prophet and to see the face of Allah. Their sins will be forgiven, and they can intercede for their relatives on the day of resurrection. They will live amid rivers of wine and honey, and be married to 72 black-eyed virgins.

But should their bombings count as sinful suicide or glorious martyrdom? That partly depends on how the volatile concept of *jihad* is defined. For many Muslims, *jihad* is principally an internal struggle. But, especially since the advent of Wahhabism, a branch of Sunni Islam that evolved in the 18th century, the notion of *jihad* as external warfare has been revived. Despite Koranic injunctions to the contrary, some radical Islamic thinkers have justified the killing of civilians, and of other Muslims, in the name of *jihad.*

Likewise, suicide bombings—or "martyrdom operations," as some of their exponents prefer—have been rationalised as a praiseworthy embrace of death at the hands of the enemy, and as a legitimate tactic *in extemis.* Among other sophistic arguments, some terrorists say that Allah, and not the bomber, decides whether the latter will die, and whether women and children will perish with the *shaheed* (martyr). Some scholars believe that a newly strident view of martyrdom, adopted by many Shia Muslims after the Iranian revolution of 1979, informed the new species of terrorism that Hizbullah, a Shia group, developed not long afterwards.

A firm belief in paradise is clearly an asset for anyone strapping on a bomb. But all these theological somersaults suggest that religion may be as much a hurdle, which the perpetrators of "martyrdom operations" need to overcome, as a motive for their violence. Hizbullah's clerics, for example, have always been squeamish about suicidal missions. And, quite apart from these qualms, there is another compelling reason to doubt that Islamic fundamentalism accounts for the rise of suicide bombing: non-Muslims are among its most devoted practitioners.

HUMAN CRUISE MISSILES

The single most prolifically suicidal terrorist group is the LTTE, or Tamil Tigers. In the course of their attritional struggle for an independent Tamil state in northern Sri Lanka, the LTTE has, among scores of other attacks, bombed the World Trade Centre in Colombo in 1997 and assassinated two heads of state. LTTE suicide missions, which began in 1987, are inspired more by cultish devotion to Velupillai Prabhakaran, the group's leader, than by religion. The Kurdish PKK [in Turkey], which has deployed suicide bombers in its quests for Kurdish autonomy and for the release of its captured leader, Abdullah Ocalan, is influenced less by Islam than by Marxist-Leninism. So too is the Popular Front for the Liberation of Palestine, which perpetrated the first suicide strike in Israel for more than two months on Christmas Day [2003].

Another sort of explanation for suicide terrorism focuses on its practitioners' travails and poverty in this world, rather than their imagined delights in the next. It used to be the case that a Palestinian bomber conformed to a recognisable type: he was young, male, single, religious and unemployed. He often had a personal grudge against Israel—for instance, a relative who had been arrested or injured by the Israeli army. He may have hoped to secure earthly as well as heavenly rewards for his relatives, in the form of financial donations after his death, and the new house that his parents might be given after the Israelis demolished their old one as punishment for his crime.

But the affluence of many of the September 11th hijackers cast doubt on the notion that poverty was a necessary, let alone sufficient, condition for suicidal terrorism. And since the start of the second *intifada* in 2000, the profile of Palestinian bombers has changed: several have been well educated and less devout than those of the mid-1990s. The LTTE, and especially the PKK and Chechen terrorists, have preferred female bombers, because they attract, or used to attract, less suspicion. Some Palestinian groups (though not al-Qaeda) have also used women, conjuring up fresh religious sophistries to justify female martyrdom. Globally, says Yoram Schweitzer, an expert in suicide terrorism at the Jaffee Centre for Strategic Studies in Tel Aviv, the bomber has no clear profile.

A better way to understand the popularity of suicide attacks may be to focus on their advantages for the groups who commission them. Such operations are rarely, if ever, the work of lone lunatics. Hamas, PIJ and the other Palestinian groups who practise suicide terrorism recruit, indoctrinate and train their bombers. They write the texts for the video testaments filmed shortly before each self-immolation (making them unreliable records of the true motives of the "martyr"), which the bombers themselves watch to redouble their resolve.

They take the photographs that will later appear on propaganda posters. Then they deliver their foot-soldiers to pre-identified targets. Al-Qaeda is remarkable for the expertise and independence of its agents, but they too are trained and primed for their missions.

Suicide bombing is a corporate effort: in this respect, the closest historical analogy may be the *kamikaze* pilots who trained as a cadre to terrorise the American fleet in the Pacific in 1944–45. And suicide appeals to these groups principally because it is a good way to kill large numbers of people. Robert Pape, of the University of Chicago, calculates that between 1980 and 2001 13 people died on average in every suicide attack, whereas just one was killed in other terrorist incidents—excluding September 11th, which would make the death ratio much starker. For those whose aim is maximum destruction, not just maximum publicity, it is the natural choice.

This special deadliness is partly the result of the suicide bomber's ability to adapt the place and time of his detonation to the last minute. As Bruce Hoffman of Rand, a think-tank, puts it, the suicide bomber is "the ultimate smart bomb, or human cruise missile." If the bomber is spotted, he can detonate instantly. Fathi Shiqaqi, a founder of PIJ, used these unique advantages to jusify "martyrdom operations." The Palestinian groups regard suicide attacks as a way to counteract Israel's conventional military superiority.

DEPENDING ON DEATH

Suicide is also a flexible technology. Where Hizbullah used cars and trucks to attack well defended installations, Hamas, PIJ and some Chechen bombers mingle among civilians, their concealed belts or vests loaded with explosives and shrapnel. The LTTE, which turned to suicide because other methods were having frustratingly little impact, has despatched suicide bombers in boats, and to conduct assassinations: much easier if the assassin has no intention of escaping. Whoever sent the two suicide bombers who narrowly failed to kill General Pervez Musharraf, Pakistan's president, also on Christmas Day, understood that advantage.

Counter-intuitive though it may seem, terrorists also regard suicide attacks as low-risk, given the scale of devastation they can inflict. As Ayman al-Zawahiri, Osama bin Laden's right-hand man, has put it, "the method of martyrdom operations [is] the most successful way of inflicting damage against the opponent and least costly to the *mujahideen* in terms of casualties." No accomplices are needed for rescues or getaways. Nor is there much danger of bombers betraying their comrades: if LTTE emissaries survive the explosion, they bite a poison capsule.

As well as these tactical benefits, suicide terrorism offers a strategic one. After the debacle in Somalia in 1993, Mr. bin Laden concluded that sensitivity to casualties was the heel of the American Achilles; Palestinian terrorists think something similar about Israel. Suicide bombings juxtapose these groups' disdain for life with their victims' supposed love of it. This helps to create the impression of an undeterrable enemy, one freed by his self-disregard to strike anywhere: "I depend on death," says a would-be suicide bomber in "The Secret Agent," "which knows no restraint and cannot be attacked."

Simultaneous bombings magnify this sense of vulnerability; so do sequences of attacks. As Mr. Pape observes, almost all suicide missions occur as part of campaigns, often, as with the regular attacks on the Americans and their allies in Iraq, designed to liberate territory occupied by democracies. (Democratic governments, it is presumed, are more likely to be swayed by their citizens' deaths than others.) The cumulative effect of such campaigns was aptly described by Josephus, a classical historian who chronicled the anti-Roman insurgency in Judaea: "The panic created was more alarming than the calamity itself; everyone, as on the battlefield, hourly expected death. Men kept watch at a distance on their enemies and would not trust even their friends. . . ." Everyday activities become perilous; ordinary life begins to seem untenable.

Terrorists have some reasons to believe that such onslaughts work. Chief among those is the withdrawal of French and American forces from Lebanon after Hizbullah's atrocities. "We couldn't stay there and run the risk of another suicide attack on the marines," wrote Ronald Reagan, then America's president, in his memoirs. Other apparent concessions to suicide campaigns, such as temporary Israeli withdrawals from Palestinian territory in the mid–1990s, have been more ambiguous, but terrorists tend to interpret history in a way that burnishes their own efforts. For their part, the *kamikaze* pilots helped to convince America that Japan would fight to the last soldier. This conviction was partly why atomic bombs were dropped on Hiroshima and Nagasaki.

Finally, like other forms of terrorism, suicide attacks are designed to impress the terrorist's own constituency, as well as to coerce their opponents—and "martyrs" have a particular propaganda value. Some groups have embraced suicide to keep pace with rival outfits, with whom they are competing for recruits and support. This was the case in Lebanon, where other organisations, including some secular ones, imitated Hizbullah's new technique. Likewise, various offshoots of Yasser Arafat's Fatah movement, which once preferred ambushes and guerrilla attacks, took up "martyrdom operations" after the suicidal "successes" of PIJ and Hamas.

WILL THE BOMBER ALWAYS GET THROUGH?

The prevalence of suicide in contemporary terrorism has helped to persuade some observers that outrages from Rabat to Riyadh to Grozny are all the handiwork of al-Qaeda—just as, in the 1980s, conspiracy theorists believed that terrorism across the globe was being orchestrated by the Soviet Union. This sort of talk suits Mr. bin Laden; and the idea of a single, coherent enemy also has some appeal for westerners. In reality, suicide has spread not because of central co-ordination, but because it works. The term "suicide bombing," with its connotations of unhinged despondency, obscures the essential rationality of the method. Some in

Israel and America, arguing that it also obscures the victims, prefer "homicide bombings."

How can the targets of such attacks protect themselves? By picking on democracies, the terrorists can be reasonably sure that their adversaries will stop short of "the Mongol method" (i.e., wholesale slaughter of the population from which the bombers derive). Even so, suicide campaigns are often designed to madden their victims into inflicting collective punishment, thus further radicalising the terrorists' actual or potential supporters, who might otherwise be repulsed by the carnage that such extreme violence causes.

But there are subtler methods. Because they are corporate enterprises, disrupting or preventing attacks is not just a question of catching the bomber: there are also recruiters, trainers, reconnaissance agents, bomb-makers and safe houses. Israel prevents many attacks by penetrating these networks—though as Shlomo Gazit, a former head of military intelligence, points out, Israel knows roughly where its enemies can be found,

and so can monitor their movements and cultivate informers. Police in, say, London or New York do not enjoy that luxury.

Israel's checkpoints and cordons (also unlikely to be emulated elsewhere) intercept some killers; they also reassure the public that something is being done, thus countering the terrorists psychologically as well as militarily. Even when the bomber gets through, vigilant security guards who manage to keep pedestrian attackers out of restaurants or discotheques can massively reduce the number of casualties. Other sensible defensive measures include the rapid dispersal of crowds at the scene of an explosion, to protect them from follow-up strikes.

Such vigilance can make life grindingly tense. If possible, the best answer must be to choke the supply of the terrorists' prize asset—the bombers—through political compromise. Yet against the ultra-extremists of al-Qaeda, intelligence, disruption and vigilance may be the only ways.

---

4 Enlargement of the European Union

Although Europeans share a common cultural heritage, in the past the diversity of their history and national temperaments burdened them with bloody wars. After two ruinous world wars and the extension of Soviet power, many people recognized the need for some form of European unity. In 1951 France, West Germany, the Netherlands, Belgium, Luxembourg, and Italy formed the European Coal and Steel Community (ECSC) to promote economic cooperation. It soon expanded into the European Economic Community (EEC), or Common Market, a customs union that created a free market among member states. In the 1970s and 1980s Great Britain, Ireland, and Denmark, and in the 1980s Greece, Spain, and Portugal, joined the European Community (EC), which constituted the world's largest trading bloc. In 1991, in the Dutch city of Maastricht, the twelve members of the European Community negotiated the Maastricht Treaty, designed to shape Europe into a unified political and economic union. By 1993 the member states had ratified the Treaty, and in recognition of its aims, the European Community transformed itself into the European Union (EU). The EU membership grew to fifteen, with the addition of Austria, Finland, and Sweden in 1995. Some Europeans, particularly in smaller nations, are worried about their country's future in an increasingly integrated Europe: are they surrendering their national identity, along with their sovereignty, to the EU?

Bertie Ahern
"ENLARGEMENT IS ABOUT OPENING MINDS AS WELL AS BORDERS"

In 2004 ten states—Malta, Cyprus, the Czech Republic, Estonia, Latvia, Lithuania, Hungary, Poland, Slovakia, and Slovenia—were added to the European Union, bringing the total of member countries to twenty-five. And four other countries—Romania, Bulgaria, Croatia, and Turkey—will soon request entry. This enlarged membership of predominantly Central European countries represents the reunification of a continent long divided by the iron curtain of communism. The majority of new members are considerably poorer than the West European members; entry into the EU does not in itself bring wealth, and the economic demands of membership are rigorous. Since EU demands that new members be democracies, its enlargement has contributed to the spread of democracy in former communist lands. Vaclav Havel, former president of the Czech Republic, sees the essence of enlargment as

> a broadening of the area of commonly shared values. The basic contours of European values—shaped by the troubled intellectual and political history of Europe, and adopted, in part, elsewhere in the world—are, I believe, clear; respect for the individual, his freedom, rights and dignity; . . . the rule of law and equality before the law; protection of minorities; democratic institutions; separation of the powers of the legislative, executive and judiciary; plurality of the political system; inviolability of private ownership; private enterprise and the market economy; and the development of civil society.

In April 2004 Bertie Ahern, prime minister of Ireland and president of the Council of the European Union, delivered a keynote speech in Prague just prior to the enlargement of the European Union. Following are excerpts from Ahern's speech, in which he views the EU as a positive force for Europe's future, for it "is about opening minds as well as borders."

The ten new accession states bring with them new languages and new cultures. They bring with them also a new consciousness of, and fresh approach to, the European Union. Enlargement is about opening minds as well as borders. The new member states will bring a new vision to the European Union. This vision was shaped and determined by unique experience. The contribution that the new member states will bring can only help to make the European Union stronger and broaden its perspective on the world. . . .

The European Union that the Czech Republic and nine other states are about to enter, is a unique endeavour in world history. It was conceived at a time of war and strife. Neighbouring countries in Europe had fought each other to the death over land and resources. The very idea of these countries coming together to work for common goals was inconceivable to many.

And yet a small number of people nurtured a big dream. This dream involved pooling resources and sovereignty in certain areas to try to find a way that was better than war, rivalry and hatred. The result is the European Union that we know today. . . .

The European Union has delivered. It has achieved peace by providing a framework within which war between its members is unthinkable. Over the past fifty years, it has delivered prosperity, enabling economies to grow and people to thrive. It has been a force for democracy and equality, helping members to tackle poverty and exclusion. The old norms of war, invasion, exclusion, discrimination and chauvinism are history. This perhaps is the European Union's greatest achievement.

Proof of the European Union's success is most clearly demonstrated by the voluntary accession of new member states. On the first of May, the Union will have more than four times the number of member states it had at the beginning. The original six member states took a real and considerable risk when they established the European Union. They deserve our gratitude for paving the way and for adopting an inclusive approach to further membership.

In the 1950s, there was a significant group of people who firmly held the view that membership of the European Union represented a "surrender," an "abandonment" or a "dilution" of national sovereignty. Indeed, there are those who hold that view today.

I reject this idea completely. In an age of globalised trade and media, sharing sovereignty in agreed areas does not represent a loss. In fact, it is quite the opposite. It represents a real and tangible gain for states by giving them an influence for which they otherwise could not hope. . . .

Membership of the European Union has in fact enabled Ireland to achieve full sovereignty. Our people are no longer compelled to emigrate to find employment. Our membership of the European Union has enabled us to bring out the full potential of our greatest asset—our people. They are a successful, self-confident and outward-looking people. For me this is a real and concrete expression of increased sovereignty. Our success within the framework provided by the European Union enabled us to do this.

Before we joined the European Union, we were an isolated people on the periphery of Europe. We were in the shadow of our big neighbour, the United Kingdom. But arguing our case at the Council table proved we could punch above our weight. We could hold our own with the most powerful. We learned, in a very real sense, how to stand on our own two feet. We learned that our partners respected us when we made well-founded arguments seeking to protect our interests. We learned what solidarity meant and we came of age as a truly independent state.

As Irish society changed rapidly from being predominantly rural to more urbanised, our people grew in self-confidence. Opportunities were opened up for Irish women whose dignity was copper-fastened by the Union's insistence on equal pay and equal opportunity. Our workers learned the importance of health and safety legislation. Our young people travelled and learned to hold their own amongst their European counterparts.

We have witnessed both our own distinctive language and culture flourish in the context of a wider Europe. Far from being overwhelmed, support for the Irish language has grown considerably. A significant part of our first level education system is now conducted exclusively through the Irish language. The initiative for this came from Irish people who understood the importance of maintaining an indigenous culture within the wider European one. They realise that the European Union is no threat to that cultural identity.

I need hardly remind you of the extent to which our Irish music has touched the hearts of so many European citizens. Before we joined the Union, it was hardly known beyond our island.

So, for Ireland our sense of ourselves as independent and equal has grown within the Union. We do not feel threatened by any notion of big versus small. Our relationship with the United Kingdom has changed beyond recognition. It is now one of genuine partnership in our mutual search for reconciliation on the island of Ireland. I am convinced that the space the European Union provided was critical in allowing that mature relationship to develop.

This is where the real strength of the European Union lies. The spirit of tolerance, the respect for difference, the knowledge that we are all working as equals for all our people is what drives us on. The absolute commitment to finding compromise and providing a sense of ownership for all our people is fundamental to our actions. The idea of winners and losers is not what the Union is about.

As I look back at what thirty-one years of membership has meant for my country, it strikes me that we must never be complacent. Collectively and individually we must stay focused on what needs to be done to ensure that the European Union continues to succeed.

We find ourselves in a new set of circumstances. Twenty years ago, the greatest threat to our national security came from the possibility of a nuclear superpower conflict. Who thought then that the countries behind the iron curtain would shortly begin the process of joining the European Union and rejoining the family of European democracies? Who would have thought then that one of the major security threats facing our people today would be the threat of terrorism from non-state actors?

The European Union must continue to adapt, change and react in a creative way to the new circumstances in which it finds itself. We will have to continue to work for a system of governance appropriate to a complex and changing world. A system that is responsive to the realities which we face. This involves both the adoption of new and effective responses at the

European level and the fine-tuning of the European Union itself. . . .

The campaign to elect members to the European Parliament will provide the next opportunity for us to debate European Union issues. The campaign will allow us to articulate the practical advantages of working together within the European Union. These practical advantages range from making our Union safer by sharing information about terrorist threats, to enabling our citizens to travel more freely by providing them, for example, with an EU-wide health card.

The elections to the European Parliament are also a useful and timely reminder of the European Union's democratic foundations.

Democracy is the bedrock on which the European Union is founded and maintained. Membership is itself based on each of the member states being democratic and meeting and maintaining rigid democratic criteria. We cannot be complacent in the face of threats to our democratic systems. We have had a stark reminder of what it means to live without democracy in the Balkans through the 1990s and even up to recent times. The horrendous bombings in Madrid last month brought home to us the devastation possible from a group dedicated to the use of undemocratic means and ends.

Seeking to reengage people with the vital processes that affect their lives will be a key task in the coming years. As politicians, we will have to use every opportunity to reverse the trend towards disengagement from the democratic process.

Chapter 2

Section 1 p. 26: From *Discoveries and Opinions of Galileo Galilei* by Galileo Galilei, pp. 28–31, 51–53, 57. Copyright ©1957 by Stillman Drake. Used by permission of Doubleday, a division of Bantam Doubleday Dell Publishing Group, Inc. p. 28: From Galileo Galilei, *Dialogue Concerning the Two Chief World Systems,* translated by Stillman Drake (University of California Press, 1962). Reprinted with permission of University of California Press. *Section 2* p. 32: From René Descartes, *Philosophical Writings,* translated by Norman Kemp Smith. Reprinted by permission of Macmillan Press Ltd. *Section 3* p. 35: From Sir Isaac Newton, *The Mathematical Principles of Natural Philosophy, Book III,* trans. Andrew Mote (London: H. D. Symonds, 1803), II, 160–162, 310–314. *Section 4* p. 38: From John Locke, *Two Treatises on Civil Government* (London: 1688, 7th reprinting by J. Whiston et al., 1772), pp. 292, 315–316, 354–355, 358–359, 361–362. p. 41: First printing of the Declaration of Independence, July 4, 1776, Papers of the Continental Congress No. 1, Rough Journal of Congress, III. *Section 5* p. 42: From *Candide and Other Writings* by Voltaire, edited by Haskell M. Block, Copyright © 1956 and renewed 1984 by Random House, Inc. *Section 6* p. 47: From Denis Diderot, *The Encyclopedia Selections,* ed. and trans. Stephen J. Gendzier, pp. 92–93, 104, 124–125, 134, 136, 153, 156, 183–187, 199, 229–230. Reprinted by permission of Stephen J. Gendzier. *Section 7* p. 50: Extracts reprinted with permission of Macmillan Publishing Company from Cesare Beccaria, *On Crimes and Punishments,* translated by Henry Paolucci, copyright © 1963 by Macmillan Publishing Company. p. 51: From Denis Diderot, *The Encyclopedia Selections,* ed. and trans. Stephen J. Gendzier, pp. 229–230. *Section 8* p. 54: Reprinted with the permission of Pocket Books, an imprint of Simon & Schuster from Voltaire, *Candide,* from *Candide & Zadig* translated by Tobias George Smollett. Edited by Lester G. Crocker. Copyright © 1962 by Washington Square Press. Copyright renewed 1990 by Lester G. Crocker. p. 56: From Denis Diderot, *Rameau's Nephew and Other Works,* translated by Jacques Barzun and Ralph H. Bowen. Copyright © 1956 by Jacques Barzun and Ralph H. Bowen; copyright renewed 1984; pp. 188–190, 194–195, 197–199, 213.

Chapter 3

Section 1 p. 64: Selections reprinted with permission of Macmillan Publishing Company from John Hall Stewart, *A Documentary Survey of the French Revolution,* pp. 76–82. Copyright © 1951 by Macmillan Publishing Company, renewed 1979 by John Hall Stewart. p. 66: From *What Is the Third Estate?* by Emmanuel Sieyes, translated by M. Blondel. Copyright © 1964. Reproduced with permission of Greenwood Publishing Group, Inc., Westport, CT. *Section 2* p. 68: From Thomas Paine, *Rights of Man,* New York: Peter Eckler, 1892, pp. 94–96. *Section 3* p. 70: From Mary Wollstonecraft, *Vindication of the Rights of Woman,*

together with excerpts from John Stuart Mill, *Subjection of Women* (London: J. M. Dent & Sons, 1929), pp. 3–6, 10–12, 15, 60–61, 64, 73, 82, 161–164, 214–215. p. 73 Copyright © 1996 by Bedford/St. Martin's. From *The French Revolution and Human Rights* edited and translated by Lynn Hunt. Reprinted with permission of Bedford/St. Martin's. p. 75: From Lynn Hunt, ed. and trans., *The French Revolution and Human Rights: A Brief Documentary History.* Copyright © 1996 by Bedford/St. Martin's, Inc. Reprinted with permission of Bedford/St. Martin's, Inc. *Section 4* p. 77: *Republic of Virtue* by Maximilien Robespierre from *The French Revolution,* edited by Paul H. Beik. Copyright © 1971 by Paul H. Beik. Reprinted by permission of HarperCollins Publishers, Inc. p. 80: From *La Vendee et les Vendeens,* translated and edited by Claude Petitfrer. Copyright © Editions Gallimard, Paris, 1982. Reprinted with permission. *Section 5* p. 81: Diary passages from *The Corsican: A Diary of Napoleon's Life in His Own Words,* ed. R. M. Johnston (Boston & New York: Houghton Mifflin, The Riverside Press, Cambridge, 1910), pp. 140, 143–145, 166, 189, 322.

Chapter 4

Section 1 p. 88: From Edward Baines, *The History of the Cotton Manufacture in Great Britain* (London: Fisher, Fisher and Jackson, 1835), pp. 84–89. *Section 2* p. 92: From Adam Smith, *An Inquiry into the Nature and Causes of the Wealth of Nations;* reprint of the edition of 1813, ed. J. R. McCulloch (London: Ward Lock, n.d.), pp. 352, 354, 544–545. p. 93: From Thomas Robert Malthus, *First Essay on Population,* 1798, reprinted for the Royal Economic Society (London: Macmillan & Co. Ltd., 1926), pp. 7. 11–14, 16–17. *Section 3* p. 96: From Samuel Smiles, *Self-Help: With Illustrations of Conduct and Perseverance* (London: John Murray, 1897), pp. 1–3. p. 98: From Report from the Committee on the Bill to Regulate the Labour of Children in the Mills and Factories of the United Kingdom, *British Sessional Papers, 1831–1832,* House of Commons, XV, pp. 5–6, 95–96, 99–100. *Section 5* p. From A. Schroter and Walter Becker, *Die deutsche Maschinenbau industrie in der industriellen Revolution* in S. Pollard and C. Holmes, *Documents of European Economic History,* pp. 534–536. Reprinted by permission of S. Pollard and Colin Holmes.

Chapter 5

Section 1 p. 106: William Wordsworth, "Tables Turned," *The Poetical Works of William Wordsworth* (London: Edward Moxon, Son and Co., 1869), p. 361. p. 106: From William Blake, *Milton: A Poem in Two Books* (London: Printed by William Blake, 1804), pp. 42–44. *Section 2* p. 108: From Edmund Burke, *Reflections on the Revolution in France* (London: Printed for J. Dodsley, 1791), pp. 51–55, 90–91, 116–117, 127–129. p. 110: From *The Odious Ideas of the Philosophes.* p. 111: From John Stuart Mill, *On Liberty* (Boston: Ticknor and Fields, 1863), pp. 22–23, 27–29, 35–36. *Section 4* p. 113: From Ernst Moritz Arndt, *The War of Liberation,* copyright © 1913. *Section 5* p. 117: From *The Recollections of Alexis de Tocqueville,* trans. A. T.

De Mattos (New York: Macmillan, 1896), pp. 14, 187–189, 197–200.

Chapter 6

Section 1 p. 122: Charles Dickens, *Hard Times,* pp. 22, 63, 265. Copyright © 1854. *Section 2* p. 124: From Charles Darwin, *His Life Told in an Autobiographical Chapter and in a Selected Series of His Published Letters,* edited by his son Francis Darwin (New York: D. Appleton, 1872), I, pp. 77, 79, 98, 133–134. p. 126; Charles Darwin, *The Origin of Species* (New York: D. Appleton, 1872), pp. 1, 77, 79, 98, 133–134. p. 127: Charles Darwin, *The Descent of Man* (New York: D. Appleton, 1876), pp. 606–607, 619. *Secion 3* p. 129: From *Manifesto of the Communist Party,* Authorized English Translation, ed. and annotated by Frederick Engels, pp. 8–11, 16–20, 21–25, 28–29, 31–34, 48. Reprinted by permission of the Charles B. Kerr Company. *Section 4* p. 136: From William Booth, *In Darkest England* and *The Way Out* (London: International Headquarters of the Salvation Army, 1890), pp. 9, 11–16, 18–20. *Section 5* p. 139: From John Stuart Mill, *The Subjection of Women* (London: Longmans, Green, 1869), pp. 1, 8, 24–28, 91–92, 95–97, 185–186. p. 142: From *Pages from the Goncourt Journal,* edited and translated by Robert Baldick, pp. 18, 27. Copyright © 1984. Reprinted by permission of Oxford University Press, England. p. 143: From Almroth E. Wright, *The Unexpurgated Case Against Woman Suffrage* (London: Constable, 1913). *Section 6* p. 146: Speech by Herman Ahlwardt on "The Semitic Versus the Teutonic Race" (p. 147) from *Rehearsal for Destruction: A Study of Political Anti-Semitism in Imperial Germany* by Paul W. Massing. Copyright © 1949 by The American Jewish Committee. Copyright renewed 1977 by The American Jewish Committee. Reprinted by permission of HarperCollins Publishers, Inc. p. 149: From Theodor Herzl, *The Jewish State: An Attempt at a Modern Solution of the Jewish Question* (New York: American Zionist Emergency Council, 1946), pp. 76–77, 85–86, 91–93, 96. Reprinted by permission of the American Zionist Federation. *Section 7* p. 152: From *Cecil Rhodes* by John E. Flint. Copyright © 1974 by John Flint. By permission of Little, Brown and Company, Inc. p. 154: From Joseph Chamberlain, *Foreign and Colonial Speeches* (London: G. Routledge and Sons, 1897), pp. 102, 131–133, 202, 244–246. p. 156: From Karl Pearson, *National Life from the Standpoint of Science* (London: Adam and Charles Black, 1905), pp. 21, 23–27, 36–37, 44, 46–47, 60–61, 64. *Section 8* p. 159: From *The Will to Power* by Friedrich Nietzsche, translated by Walter Kaufmann and R. J. Hollingdale. Copyright © 1967 by Walter Kaufmann. Reprinted by permission of Random House, Inc. p. 161: From *The Antichrist from Twilight of the Idols/The Anti-Christ* by Friedrich Nietzsche, translated by R. J. Hollingdale (Penguin Classics, 1968), copyright © R. J. Hollingdale, 1968, pp. 115–118, 125, 128, 131, 156–157. Reproduced by permission of Penguin Books Ltd. *Section 9* p. 164: From *The Collected Papers, Volume 4* by Sigmund Freud. Authorized translation under the supervision of Joan Riviere. Published by Basic Books, Inc. by arrangement with The Hogarth Press, Ltd. and The Insitute of Psycho-Analysis, London. Reprinted by permission of Basic Books, a member of Perseus Books, L.L.C.

Chapter 7

Section 1 p. 169: Reprinted from Heinrich von Treitschke, *Die Politik,* excerpted in *Germany's War Mania* (New York: Dodd Mead, 1915), pp. 221–223. p. 171: Friedrich von Bernhardi, *Germany and the Next War,* Allen H. Fowles, trans. (New York: Longmans, Green, and Company, 1914), pp. 18, 21–24. *Section 2* p. 172: *The Black Hand,* trans. Marvin Perry from M. Boghitchevitch, *Le Proces de Salonique, Juin 1917,* ed. Andre Delpeuch (Paris, 1927), pp. 41–42, 45–48. *Section 3* p. 174: Roland Doregeles, "After Fifty Years," and "That Fabulous Day" in George A. Panichas, ed., *Promise of Greatness* (New York: John Day, 1968), pp. 13–15. *Section 4* p. 177: *All Quiet on the Western Front* by Erich Maria Remarque. *Im Westen Nichts Neues,* copyright © 1928 by Ullstein A. G.; copyright renewed © 1956 by Erich Maria Remarque. *All Quiet on the Western Front* copyright © 1929, 1930 by Little, Brown and Company; copyright renewed © 1957, 1958 by Erich Maria Remarque. All rights reserved. *Section 5* p. 181: From Georges Clemenceau, *The Grandeur and Misery of Victory,* pp. 105, 107–108, 115–117, 271–281. Reprinted by permission of Georges P. Clemenceau. *Section 6* p. 184: From *The Russian Revolution, 1917,* by N. N. Sukanov, edited and translated by Joel Carmichael, pp. 584–585. Copyright © 1955. Reprinted by permission of Oxford University Press. p. 185: From *Collected Works of V. I. Lenin,* Vol. 26, pp. 234–235. Copyright © 1964. p. 186: Excerpts from *Variety* by Paul Valéry, translated by Malcolm Cowley, copyright © 1927 by Harcourt, Inc. and renewed 1954 by Malcolm Cowley. Reprinted by permission of the publisher. p. 187: *All Quiet on the Western Front* by Erich Maria Remarque. *Im Westen Nichts Neues,* copyright © 1928 by Ullstein A. G.; copyright renewed © 1956 by Erich Maria Remarque. *All Quiet on the Western Front* copyright © 1929, 1930 by Little, Brown and Company; copyright renewed © 1957, 1958 by Erich Maria Remarque. All rights reserved.

Chapter 8

Section 1 p. 192: From Joseph Stalin, *Leninism: Selected Writings,* pp. 199–200. Reprinted by permission of International Publishers. *Section 2* p. 194: From *The Education of A True Believer* by Lev Kopelev, pp. 226, 234–235, 248–251, and translated by Gary Kern. English translation copyright © 1980 by Harper & Row, Publishers, Inc. Reprinted by permission of HarperCollins Publishers Inc. *Section 3* p. 197: Reprinted with the permission of Simon & Schuster Adult Publishing Group, from *Stalin: Great Lives Observed,* edited by T. H. Rigby. Copyright © 1966 by Prentice-Hall, Inc.; copyright renewed © 1994 by T. H. Rigby. p. 198: From *A Precocious Autobiography* by Yevgeny Yevtushenko, translated by Andrew R. MacAndrew, copyright © 1963 by Yevgeny Yevtushenko, renewed 1991 by Yevgeny Yevtushenko. Translation copyright © 1963 by E. P. Dutton, renewed 1991 by Penguin USA. Used by